Low Speed Automobile Accidents

Accident Reconstruction and Occupant Kinematics, Dynamics and Biomechanics

By

Alan J. Watts, Ph.D.
Dale R. Atkinson, B.S.
Corey J. Hennessy, M.A.

Legal Case and Commentary by Randall H. Kehl, J.D.

Accompanying Videotape by Samantha N. Lapin, M.S.

Lawyers & Judges Publishing Company, Inc.

Lawyers & Judges Publishing Company, Inc.

P.O. Box 30040
Tucson, AZ 85751-0040
(520) 323-1500
(602) 323-1500
FAX (520) 323-0055

Watts, Alan J.
Low speed automobile accidents : accident reconstruction and occupant kinematics, dynamics, and biomechanics / by Alan J. Watts, Dale R. Atkinson, Corey J. Hennessy : legal case and commentary by Randall H. Kehl accompanying videotape by Samantha N. Lapin.
p. cm.
Includes bibliographical references and index.
ISBN 0-913875-23-6 (hardcover)
1. Traffic accident investigation—United States. 2. Traffic accidents—United States. 3. Liability for traffic accidents—United States. 4. Evidence, Expert—United States. I. Atkinson, Dale R. II. Hennessy, Corey J. III. Title.
HV8079.55.W37 1996
363.1'2565—dc20

96-23978
CIP

ISBN 0-913875-23-6
Printed in the United States of America
10 9 8 7 6 5 4 3 2

Table of Contents

Part II: Occupant Kinematics and Dynamics

Appendix

Foreword

This book was started partly out of frustration with the lack of solid physics-based information on vehicle dynamics and occupant kinematics, particularly for low speed accidents. This is our attempt to fill that void.

The reader may wonder why we are involved in reconstruction in the first place. The history is that one of our Associates (Mr. Kehl, a lawyer) suggested that our company get involved in the business of accident analysis. We are a company of scientists and engineers with many years experience working on Government projects, frequently in the realm of rapid stress and strain effects in materials, whether due to impacts, rapid energy loadings (due to X-rays, charged-particle beams or high-power laser beams) or due to the use of explosives. Thus, we "plunged in" to the litigation game commonly known as being an "expert witness." To date, two of us (AJW and CJH) have actually given depositions and appeared in Court, with the majority being done by AJW. The other authors have aided in various aspects of computations, cross-checking of logic and results, and production of requested computer animations. We have analyzed cases involving product liability (breaking ladders, rupturing exercise balls), low-speed non-vehicle problems (falling doors in crates on a loading dock, supermarket trolley impacts into pedestrians, people falling out of chairs or falling on a hard floor), but mostly vehicle-related accidents.

We rapidly discovered that a surprisingly large number of vehicle cases involved "low-speed" accidents (usually less than 20 mph differential speed). An interesting logic applies for these cases. For a high-speed crash there is little argument over whether injury could be caused: instead the arguments center around who was at fault. However, for low-speed crashes the opposite frequently occurs. Often, the defense admits to causing the accident: the argument now centers around whether injury really resulted. This is hardly surprising: many low-speed accidents have the ability to involve some form of fraud. This fraud can range from a simple case of claiming *all* the observed vehicle damage was due to *this* accident, to claiming *all* the personal injuries are due to *this* accident. Sometimes, the vehicle was already damaged due to a previous crash; likewise a person may have already been suffering some disability from previous accidents or problems. In both cases, there can be an attempt to "recoup" such previous damage/injury costs by blaming *this* accident. Clearly, only some cases involve fraud, many are perfectly genuine. To decide which, some scientific understanding of the processes involved in low-speed accidents is needed.

We rapidly found that few people taught the vehicle aspects of low-speed impacts, and those few have only recently begun to teach this subject. Likewise, little of the biomechanical data could be readily applied for low-speed accidents. Well known "Reconstruction Schools" (Northwestern University Traffic Institute and the Institute for Police and Technology Management), and books on reconstruction (such as by Limpert) concentrate mostly on higher speed crashes. Despite voluminous reports published by SAE (Society of Automotive Engineers) there is no single paper which adequately deals with the low-speed problem. The biomechanical data is frequently based on laboratory experimental data. Much "interpretation" is required in order to relate this data to many low-speed accidents. As a simple example, consider the use of the Head Impact Criterion (HIC). This is evaluated by an integral of acceleration seen by a head versus time. Unfortunately, it involves a "loaded" (non-linear) integration. This is fine for the purposes of using instrumented dummies in staged car crashes. But how do you use this data to assess the likelihood of an individual suffering injury when the only factors you can determine with any reliability are the impact speed and the possible compliance of the impacted surface? Real car occupants are not instrumented with accelerometers!

We found that the most commonly used model (or algorithm) for performing energy-of-crush analysis (CRASH3) was not based on true scientific or engineering principles, but was instead based essentially only on limited empirical car crash data. This model does not correctly solve for low speeds since it ignores the realities of bumper behavior, neither does it account for vehicle bounce, both of which are important for low-speed collisions. Of course, it should be appreciated that CRASH3 was not originally developed for the purpose of solving specific crashes especially for those at low speed.

Accordingly, we decided to "start from scratch" and utilize our experience to study the problem from the perspective of known materials behavior and the application of physics and mechanical engineering . The result is a model that looks remarkably like CRASH3, and gives the same results as the latter at medium to high speeds. Indeed, it should be quite simple for users of CRASH3 to update the latter since the new model has essentially the same "form." The important distinctions, however, are that the new model logically incorporates bumper response and the coefficient of restitution (bounce), thereby allowing meaningful analysis of low-speed impacts.

In a similar vein, we have used our scientific backgrounds to "interpret" aspects of the biomechanical database and convert it from somewhat "arcane" data into something usable for low-speed car accidents. This can be done by employing well known scientific techniques such as "Dimensional Analysis." In this respect, we are merely following in the footsteps of Damask who has also "applied physics" to show how physics can "explain" the various injury mechanisms.

It may not be obvious why people who have studied such things as the effects of charged-particle beams in materials can reconstruct accidents. The answer is simple: whenever charged particles (electrons and protons) flow though a material they undergo scattering and energy loss. This energy loss heats up the material and generates stresses which then give elastic and/or plastic or elastoviscous material behavior. The "scattering" is simply multiple "bounces" with atoms. The bounces can be both elastic and inelastic. When inelastic the energy loss is mostly due to "ionization" or atom displacement. The rules for studying these effects are the *same rules* for conservation of momentum and energy as apply to car crashes, while the resulting elastic and/or plastic or elastoviscous material responses are again the *same* as those applying to the various structures of either a vehicle or human. *Physics is physics.*

It is our hope that this book will prove useful to many people, ranging from the lawyer dealing with a low-speed personal injury case, to other accident reconstructionists, engineers, police, insurance adjusters and, perhaps, even medics, all of whom have the need to understand the "low-speed" accident. If readers think we did a reasonable job, perhaps we can expand on this subject in the future.

Low Speed Automobile Accidents

Accident Reconstruction and Occupant Kinematics, Dynamics and Biomechanics

By

Alan J. Watts, Ph.D.
Dale R. Atkinson, B.S.
Corey J. Hennessy, M.A.

Legal Case and Commentary by Randall H. Kehl, J.D.
Accompanying Videotape by Samantha N. Lapin, M.S.

Chapter 1

Introduction

The Importance of Accurate Reconstruction

Over the past forty years there have been many studies of the effects of vehicle collisions and the consequential occupant kinematics. However, most of these studies have concentrated on the effects for the higher collisional speeds, generally above 30 mph. Little systematic study has been done for the much lower speed impact cases, such as those that induce either zero or small (a few inches) crush damage to the vehicles. Yet these lower speed cases are those frequently encountered in cases involving personal injury such as the well-known "whiplash" phenomenon, where one vehicle rearends another at *differential* speeds usually below 20 mph. According to General Motors, in 1986, more than one third of all injuries occurred in low speed crashes, below 20 mph.

The various car manufacturers, insurance groups (*e.g.*, IIHS, the Insurance Institute for Highway Safety) and US government (*e.g.*, NHTSA, the National Highway Traffic Safety Administration, part of DOT, the Department of Transportation) individually perform specific controlled car crashes to find the crashworthiness of the vehicles and the effects on drivers and passengers. These tests are usually done at speeds of either 30 or 35 mph into high mass immovable concrete barriers (the so-called rigid barrier), and mostly involve front-end impacts, although some investigate rearend, side and oblique impacts. Such frontal tests simulate the equivalent of a symmetric head-on collision between two similar vehicles with identical speed. The primary purpose of such tests is to ensure that the vehicles crush in a well-controlled manner so as to limit the decelerations of the occupants. They simultaneously verify the operation of occupant restraints meant to limit occupant injury due to excessive seatbelt chest loadings, impacts with steering wheels, dashboards and windshields, and strong femur loadings due to impacts with dash structures.

The 30 mph crash tests are mandated by the government to certify that vehicles satisfy the various FMVSS (Federal Motor Vehicle Safety Standards), especially number 208 that relates to occupant injuries to the head, chest and femur. This standard dictates that the maximum measured loads (done on anthropomorphic test devices [ATDs, or "dummies"], such as the Hybrid II or III) must not exceed a HIC (head impact criterion) of 1000, a chest acceleration of

60 g, a chest compression of 3 inches, and a femur force of 2250 pounds. (The meaning of HIC is discussed later in this book). These tests are usually done by the manufacturers, who stipulate that their vehicles passed the various requirements. Failure to pass can result in recall action and a requirement to fix the problem. The specifics of the various FMVSS can be found in references 1 and 2. The 35 mph tests are performed by testing organizations for NHTSA as part of the latter's NCAP program (New Car Assessment Program). These tests are not presently obligatory for the motor industry, and are used primarily to allow "comparison shopping" concerning crashworthiness. Being at a higher speed, these NCAP crashes involve an energy increase of about 36% versus the standard tests, and are designed to show "potential weaknesses." The NCAP results are presently made public in the form of a "star" rating, with five stars indicating very good response (less than 10% probability of serious injury) and one star indicating poor response (greater than 45% probability of serious injury). However, there is controversy over the usefulness of this rating system (ref 3). Greater specific details of each test result are available from NHTSA for those who want to inspect the real experimental data (ref 4). Although the NCAP tests do not presently require a government "pass," the very fact that adverse publicity could damage sales has effectively forced the motor manufacturers to self-guarantee a good crash response. Thus NCAP is rapidly becoming the "de facto" test against which vehicles are judged for crashworthiness. The latter term refers to the combined performance of both the vehicle and its effects on occupants, and is also known as the "second collision" (since the vehicle first crashes, followed by a second internal impact of the occupant with portions of the vehicle).

However, these tests are very limited from the viewpoint of providing data necessary for accident analyses and reconstruction, especially low speed collisions. Being performed at essentially a fixed speed (30 or 35 mph) and with limited directions of impact, the tests do not yield sufficient data to adequately characterize the overall crush behavior of vehicles as a function of variable impact speeds and/or directions. Existing published, and readily available, test data that *do* characterize behavior over a wider speed range tend to be non-current, and even then rarely involve impact speeds below 20 mph. Consequently, there are several uncertainties regarding interpretation of crush damage, particularly for collisions involving the lower vehicle closing speeds (*i.e.*, differential speeds), or for side and oblique impacts.

There is a common myth that, since vehicles are tested at 30 or 35 mph and declared safe (*i.e.*, they meet the FMVSS, and do well in NCAP tests), these vehicles are safe at any speed and in any collision at less than 30 or 35 mph. Unfortunately, this is not true. In fact, there have been cases where improvements in high speed crashworthiness (such as stiffer vehicle structures) have increased the risk of occupant injuries at lower impact speeds. Indeed, some cars that perform well in full-frontal crashes do poorly in off-center impacts (which replicate the more common driver side-to-driver side type of accident). These offset crashes are not yet part of the standard government required tests, although they may become so in the near future (European manufacturers such as Mercedes have done such tests for several years). In addition, the introduction of innovations like antilock brakes (ABS) is removing, or at least diminishing, some of the more traditional sources of evidence, such as tire skid marks. This makes the accident reconstructionist's task even more challenging. Thus, the ability to adequately interpret crush damage on vehicles is rapidly becoming more important, and a combined momentum and energy analysis becomes the primary method of reconstructing low speed crashes.

Unfortunately, very little is taught concerning lower speed collisions and the consequential occupant propensity for injury. Most of the "Reconstruction Schools," such as Northwestern University Traffic Institute (NUTI), and the Institute for Police and Technology Management (IPTM), and many independent books on accident reconstruction, concentrate on the higher speed collisions where serious injuries frequently occur, and vehicle damage is significant. Additionally, the crush models taught (such as CRASH3) were simply not designed for the lower speeds. Accordingly, while these models are adequate for the higher speeds they rarely work properly at the lower speeds, except sometimes by coincidence. Lastly, most of the various books and papers concerning occupant injury and biomechanics tend not to be directly linked to analysis of low speed collisions. Rather, they tend to concentrate on "scientific" (*i.e.*, laboratory experiments) explanations of damage mechanisms, but without much immediately obvious connection to real car crashes. Additionally, while there is much biomechanical data relating to "serious" injury (broken bones, ruptured livers, ripped ligaments, fractured skulls and significant brain damage, etc.) much less data exists concerning the "soft tissue" injuries (strained ligaments and muscles, herniated vertebral discs, damaged bursa, exacerbations of "repetitive stress problems" such as carpal tunnel syndrome, etc.) associated with low speed collisions. The "Reconstruction Schools" are primarily intended to teach police officers, who, by virtue of training (and frequently necessity) are usually interested only in the more serious crashes. Put bluntly, most police are already overworked, and, therefore, cannot afford to devote too much time to the seemingly "minor" low speed cases.

Consequently, few accident reconstructionists can adequately analyze such collisions and few can relate the seemingly low severity of the impacts with the probability of any occupant injury. Yet although low speed collisions rarely involve the really serious types of personal injury, their sheer numbers cause such accidents to have a significant socioeconomic impact. For example, it is stated (ref 5) that about 20% of all accidents reported to the police involve rearenders, many at low speed. This impact includes lost work days during early medical treatment, lost productivity due to induced longer term disabilities (usually of the less major variety), and medical expenses. Further, a significant fraction of low speed accidents result in civil (and sometimes criminal) legal action. Precisely because the accidents are low speed with limited vehicle damage, it is common to disbelieve that personal injury can occur ("Oh, it's just a 'fender-bender,'" is a common retort). This places low speed accidents in the realm of potentially fraudulent injury claims. While some claims are fraudulent, others are not.

Although this book deals primarily with low speed accidents, it should be appreciated that "low speed" really means *any* accident that results in minimal vehicular damage. Thus a crash between two vehicles moving at 100 mph (bullet) and 90 mph (target), in the same direction, produces the same *initial* effects as one where the speeds are 40 mph and 30 mph, or 10 mph and zero, respectively. Thus low speed refers to differential motion, not absolute speeds. Of course, for the case of high absolute speeds the secondary behavior of the vehicles can also be very important, such as a second crash with a fixed object (tree, bridge embankment, etc.).

This book is intended to provide accident reconstructionists, engineers, police, insurance adjusters and attorneys with the necessary tools and understanding for correctly interpreting and reconstructing these accidents, and to more readily appreciate just when and how occupant injury can occur.

The Relationship Among Medicine, Biomechanics and Physics as They Apply to Trauma

Defining the relationships and dividing lines among medicine, biomechanics and physics is important.

(i) Medicine is the determination of the specific form of injury to the human body (*e.g.*, *diagnosis* of ligament sprain, skull fracture, etc.), the subsequent line of *treatment*, and the corresponding *prognosis* for the future. Except those rare individuals with both a medical degree and a mechanical (physics or engineering) degree, a medic does *not* compute the actual forces and accelerations to cause damage. However, a medic can *reference* published data on experiments to help appreciate how the damage occurred. The actual identification of the specific damage is done through diagnostic equipment such as X-rays, CT scans, MRI (nuclear magnetic resonance imaging) scans, PET (positron emission tomography) scans, and SPECT (single photon emission computer tomography), EMG (electromyelograms) and various nerve conduction studies, etc. It is interesting that many of these diagnostic techniques originate in the world of physics. As an example, one of the authors of this book (AJW) studied nuclear magnetic resonance as part of his Ph. D., years before the medical community learned to apply it to their own specialty. Likewise, the authors have much background in the study of X-rays and nuclear effects owing to their past work done on behalf of the US and UK governments (*e.g.*, the UK MOD [Ministry of Defence] and the US DOD [Department of Defense] and DOE [Department of Energy]).

Excellent descriptions of how medics diagnose accident-caused injuries is given in the three-series video tapes "Medical School for Lawyers: 'The Complete Orthopedic Examination,' 'Medical Evidence of Soft Tissue Injury' and 'The Complete Neurological Examination'" (ref 6).

(ii) Biomechanics has three major components. (a) One component applies physics to an understanding of the workings of the human body (*e.g.*, as in explaining the operation of muscles and the basics of elasto-viscous responses, the flow of red blood corpuscles, and why these corpuscles are shaped the way they are [answer: to allow shape changes at constant internal pressure, and maximize surface area]) (*e.g.*, see ref 7). This aspect of biomechanics is sometimes called biophysics. (b) Another component concerns the design and development of artificial joints (etc.), and the effects of material incompatibility (*e.g.*, the avoidance of tissue rejection) and the computation or measurement of forces within the body during its natural behavior. This aspect of biomechanics is sometimes called bioengineering. (c) Only the third component concerns the effects of rapid trauma to the body (as occurs for a vehicle accident) (*e.g.*, refs 8 to 14) and the computation or measurement of forces within the body, and motions by the body, during and in response to this rapid trauma.

(iii) For rapid trauma, Physics (mechanics) involves the calculation and/or experimental measurement of forces, accelerations, stresses, strains, and kinematic motion of the parts of the body, *as if the body was an inert entity*. This is applicable to the human body ***IF*** the rapidity of the response is such as to prevent the natural feedback between brain and body. The typical innervation time for the brain to instruct the body to react (*i.e.*, apply muscles, etc.) is about 0.1 to 0.2 seconds, depending on the portion of the body (in general, the more distant the body segment from the brain, the longer the innervation time). If the problem to the body occurs over a much longer time, the response is considered human or biological. However, if the time scale is very short (as in a car crash) the response is purely mechanical, and the analysis and behavior are *the same* as for the analysis and behavior of an *inert* system. Bones behave like pieces of wood or metal and ligaments behave like leather straps, etc. Thus for rapid events the description of behavior is given by a physical analysis only, and the real difference between the analysis of a biological entity (man and other animals) and an inorganic one (metals, plastics, etc.) lies primarily in the specific details of material response. Instead of using an engineering handbook to obtain data on a particular metal (such as yield strength or fracture strength) use is made of the published database on human response (fracture strength of the femur, etc.).

Note that this last description explains why cadavers (dead human bodies) can be used for vehicle accident studies. The major difference between a live human and a cadaver is that the latter have no active brain, and thus cannot provide the biological feedback to allow innervation of the muscles. However, for a fresh cadaver (but past rigor mortis), practically all other aspects of the body respond in the same manner as for the living body (*e.g.*, bones, ligaments and intervertebral discs, the spinal cord, etc.). Thus, provided there is no need to invoke the brain-body feedback, the cadaver response is essentially identical to that of the living body. The same logic explains the use of ATDs (or dummies). Provided the ATD is bio-fidelic (and the more recent Hybrid III is good at mimicking human response for most, but not all, loadings) it will behave like a cadaver. The ATD is reusable, whereas, a cadaver usually suffers damage and is thus a one-shot experiment. Use of ATDs reduces the need for voluntary donations of cadavers. Unfortunately, both Hybrid III and its side-impact brother, BioSid, are usually least bio-fidelic when simulating the effects of low speed trauma.

This also explains how damage levels to the body are determined. Collaboration occurs between engineers (applying physics) and medics. The engineers set up the crash experiments, measure the accelerations and forces and body motions. The medics then study the person or cadaver to learn if a medical problem has been induced. Thus the trauma levels that cause damage can be determined. For ethical reasons, live persons are used only for the lower levels of trauma, whereas cadavers are used for the dangerous higher levels. The major factor missing for the cadaver experiments is that of pretensed muscles, since the latter obviously requires the brain. Pretensing of muscles has little effect on severe trauma, although (as described later) muscle pretensing can be very important in low speed accident injuries. Further, it should be appreciated that the initial muscle status is one of a switch: either the muscles are not pretensed or they are, during a short-lived accident. There is no way the human can change this status *during* the short-lived accident. The other factor missing for a cadaver is that of internal pressurization (*e.g.*, blood pressure and lung pressure). For biomechanical experiments investigating trauma to the brain, to lungs and to some internal organs it is necessary to artificially repressurize the cadaver to produce realistic responses.

(iv) "Causation" of death. Related to these descriptions is the legal definition of *causation* of death. Generally, it the job of the medical examiner to determine "causation" of a death when performing an autopsy. However, this is a *medical* determination, *not* a mechanical one. The distinction being made is that the determination of *how* a neck fracture occurred is a *mechanical* one within the realm of biomechanics without regard to the consequences, whereas the determination of the *consequences* (death) is a *medical* one. Few if any autopsies ever quote the *mechanical forces* involved.

To illustrate, consider a person who was accidentally hung and suffered the "hangman's fracture" of the axis vertebra. This fracture breaks the bone and severs the spinal cord, thereby paralyzing the person below the neck. As a result, the person can neither breathe nor keep the heart beating. The brain is starved of oxygen, and rapidly suffers shock (the rapid drop in blood pressure), and therefore dies.

Such a hangman's fracture requires significant force on the neck. This is achieved by dropping the body several feet and then violently decelerating the body as the rope suddenly tightens. With the majority of the person's weight acting below the neck this produces very high forces on the neck. Indeed, for a very thin wire such a drop can result in the "chopping" of the neck rather than simple vertebra/cord rupture. This is totally different from the case of a person merely being supported with a rope around the neck. For the latter case, the force is much lower and the person chokes (inability to breathe) or strangles (cutoff of the blood supply through the carotid arteries), which is the principle behind the garrote.

Organization of This Book

This book has four major parts, and an associated video. The first part discusses the mechanics of the vehicle behavior, and shows how the application of physical and engineering models leads to an updated version of the CRASH3 algorithm, but with subtle differences. These differences include the ability to incorporate the vehicle bumper responses and ability to account for coefficients of restitution (or vehicle bounce), both of which are important at low speeds. Other issues covered include vehicle rotational effects, sideswipe collisions, the time-scale of collisions, and the effects of payloads.

The second part discusses the dynamics of occupant motions. The issue of seat-bounce is included, and it is shown how the possibility for personal injury is very strongly dependent on the details of the vehicle behavior and the corresponding occupant motions. It will be shown how apparently similar accidents can give different probabilities for injuries. We will attempt to show that *"the devil is in the details"* and that blanket statements about injury causation are simply not tenable for low speed accidents. Injuries discussed include the so-called 'whiplash,' head impact, rib/chest problems, leg fracture, pelvic damage due to side impacts and the possibilities for induced carpal tunnel problems (CTS) and temporomandibular joint problems (TMJ).

The third part discusses aspects of legal issues, including witness testimony, qualifications of experts, admissibility conditions, cross-examination of expert witnesses, and the use of demonstrative evidence including animations.

Part four gives specific examples, many of which are not standard fare for reconstructionists. We give depersonalized examples of actual reports, covering cases where injury was expected to those where injury is not expected. We also give a "suspicious" case, where some degree of fraud may be involved.

The accompanying VHS videotape is intended for use with the examples given in Part Four of the book. This videotape contains animations that are directly associated with the book's examples. These animations should help illustrate the key points made in the text.

An appendix is included giving the derivation of several of the equations used in the text, and giving a summary of definitions.

Part I

Vehicle Dynamics

Chapter 2

General Material Loading Responses

In order to understand the response of vehicles during a collision it is necessary to first understand the generic behavior of materials to the application of loads. Whenever two bodies collide, forces will be generated between them which cause a deceleration of one body and an acceleration of the other. Newton's laws state that, at any instant, the forces must be identical at either side of the impacting interface. A force is a vector quantity, having both magnitude and direction. Thus, although the forces may vary with time and direction throughout the impact condition while the bodies remain in contact, they must also be equal in magnitude and opposite in direction at all time. This condition immediately satisfies the requirement of conservation of momentum, since the reduction in one body's momentum is replaced by an identical increase in momentum of the other body. The overall *averaged* direction of the force acting on each of the two bodies defines the principal directions of force. Except for *very* low speeds, the interaction of the vehicles with a third body (*e.g.*, a road surface) is negligible during the impact.

The energy of the interaction must also be conserved. Initially, the moving body(s) have motion and mass, and thus kinetic energy. After the impact, at least one body may still have motion and thus kinetic energy. This energy may involve both linear and rotational components. Except for the idealized case of a perfectly elastic collision, the total motional kinetic energy of both bodies after the impact will be less than that before the impact. Thus, some energy will have been consumed. Since total energy must be conserved, this merely means that the lost energy has been transformed into some other form. The major consumer of this energy is irreversible geometry changes in the bodies, which is the crush damage. Other minor absorbers of energy include the generation of heat, sound and light.

A body can suffer from two types of force application, purely external and internal. Consider two *equal* forces acting on opposite sides of a body and in opposite directions. The *net* external force is zero and so the net acceleration of the body is also zero. However, the body is either subject to compression or tension. If the two forces are *not* equal then the situation can be treated as if that due to two forces which do balance and the remaining force is unbalanced. For example, if 1000 pounds force pushes on the left of the body while only 800 pounds force pushes back on the right of the body, this is equivalent to a compression of 800 pounds and an acceleration force of 200 pounds to the right. This is illustrated in figure 1. Since a moving body has inertia, when it collides with something a force is immediately produced on the impacted surface which starts to slow the body. The other side of the body sees zero force. Thus there is a net force acting on the body which produces the deceleration. However, stress waves travel through the body and cause portions of the latter to be subject to local stresses and forces, which cause localized compressions and/or tensions. The body suffers a force gradient, with the highest force at the contact area for the impact, and zero at the other end.

For low forces the response of the body is elastic. Sudden impact at one end of the body causes elastic stress waves to travel along the body. These waves move very fast, having a speed (commonly called the speed of sound in the material) determined by the square-root of the ratio of the elastic (Young's) modulus to the material density. Typical wave speeds for car materials are about 3×10^5 cm/s to 5×10^5 cm/sec, or about 9,843 ft/s to 16,404 ft/s. Note that these speeds are about *ten times* the sound speed in normal atmospheric air (about 1050 ft/s)! For a typical car length of about 15 feet, the elastic wave takes only about 1.5 ms to travel the entire length of the car. Since a typical car crash lasts about 0.1 to 0.2 seconds, this means that the elastic wave travels at least 67 times the

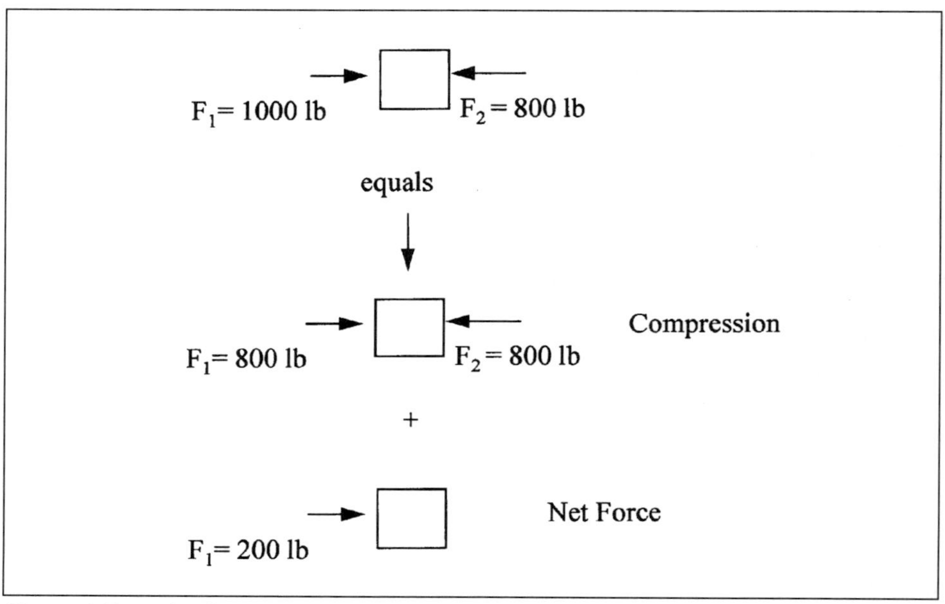

Figure 1 *Force Logic.*

length of the car (about 33 reverberations) during the time of first contact to the time of final disengagement.

For higher forces plastic flow starts. Now the effective modulus becomes much smaller. Consequently, the associated wave motion (the plastic wave) travels much slower, and is moving only a little faster than the actual collapsing impact surface of the vehicle relative to the remainder of the car. This difference in speeds versus time defines the actual thickness of the plastically crushed region. Thus a two-wave structure develops, namely a small amplitude elastic wave and a larger amplitude plastic wave. The small amplitude elastic wave slows down the uncrushed part of the vehicle, while the larger amplitude plastic wave is responsible for the permanent crush next to the impacted portion of the vehicle. This two-wave effect is shown in figure 2.

This *dynamic* behavior produces results which differ from normal static behavior. For static loading, it is always the weakest portion of the vehicle which first starts to collapse. This is because, under static loading, the entire structure is subject to the same load. However, under dynamic loading, the result of the traveling waves invariably causes crush damage next to the impacted region, even if the weakest part of the vehicle is farther back.

Indeed, in the world of the hydrodynamicist there is a test called the Taylor Rod Test. A uniform right-cylindrical rod of material is impacted against a rigid wall with the axis of the rod perpendicular to the plane surface of the wall. For

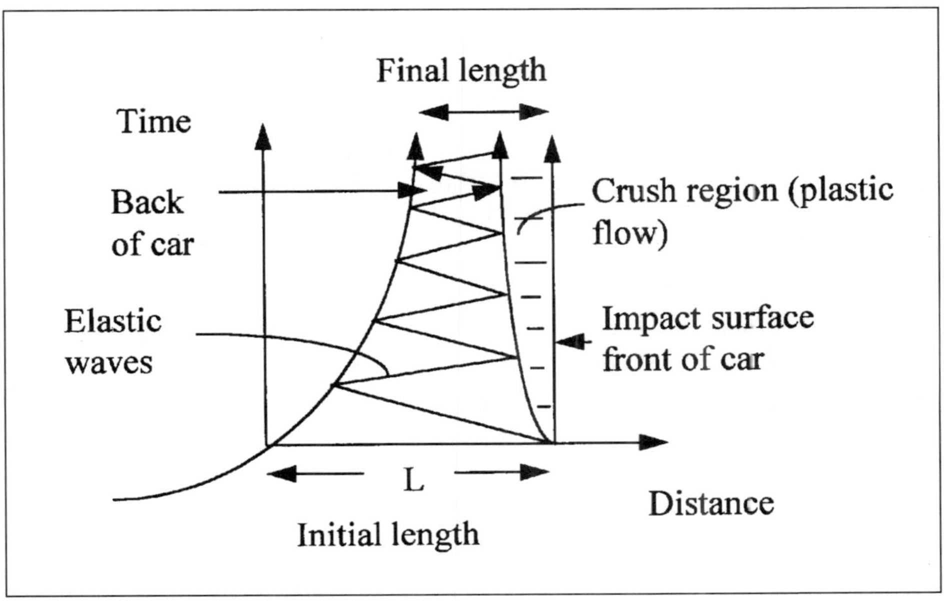

Figure 2 *Rigid Barrier Impact.*

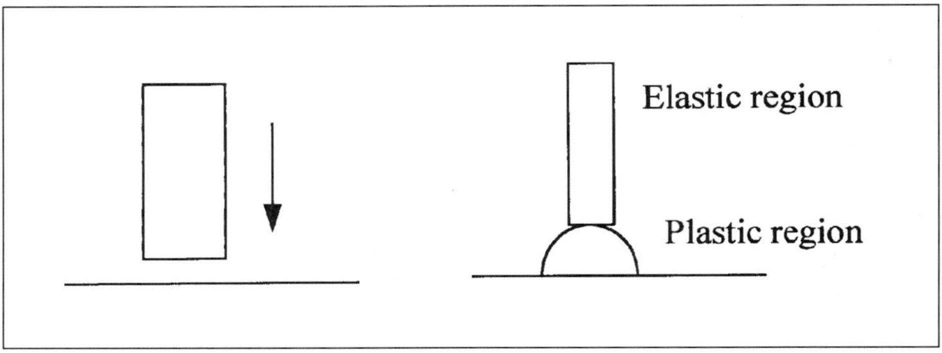

Figure 3 *Taylor Rod Test.*

sufficient impact speed the impacted end of the rod is observed to develop a mushroom shape, with the end splayed outward and shortened. This well-understood phenomenon is a classic test for any newly written hydrodynamics computer code, since failure of the code to properly predict the rod behavior is a sure sign of coding error. Figure 3 shows the Taylor test.

There are four basic response modes for a body when subjected to external force: (i) elastic, (ii) plastic, (iii) viscoelastic, and (iv) brittle, and combinations thereof.

Elastic Response. A body is said to behave elastically if the deformation induced during the application of a force is completely recovered when the load is removed, *and* the energy absorbed (more properly, stored) by the body during deformation is also recovered. Many materials display a linear response of force versus deflection in the elastic regime, and the slope of this line define the elastic modulus. However, it is not necessary for the response to be linear in order to be elastic. The simplest example of the elastic body is a perfect spring. The loading and unloading paths are identical on a force-deformation plot.

Plastic Response If a body deforms under load and *does not* recover its initial geometry upon release of the load, it is said to have undergone plastic flow. This results in a loading path different from the unloading path, and a force-deformation plot indicates a parallelogram type of loop. Because energy absorbed is the product of a force times the motion in the direction of the force, it follows that the body must have permanently stored (*i.e.*, absorbed) some of the applied energy in the form of plastic deformation. A body undergoing perfect plastic flow is one where the force to initiate plastic flow is a fixed limit, such that once exceeded the body continues to plastically deform until the load is removed. In reality, very few materials display this phenomenon (except very pure metals), instead they display the phenomenon of strain-hardening. Here, the force required to continue plastic flow continues to increase with increase in deformation. To a first approximation this increase in force is roughly linear versus the deformation. Thus, unless the applied force increases the degree of deformation limits. Ultimately, for a sufficiently large force the body will rupture. Until that point is reached, the body will absorb energy and fail to recover its initial geometry.

Note that so-called plastic materials (*e.g.*, bakelite, polythene, thermoplastics and thermosets; generically known as polymers) rarely behave in a plastic manner, and most tend to be brittle. Their name comes from the fact that most such materials are frequently extruded into their final form when hot and uncured, and this extrusion represents a plastic flow. To help avoid the confusion between plastic behavior and plastic material, this book will adopt the convention of using the word Plastic (capital P) to describe a plastic *material.*

Viscoelastic Response. If a body deforms under load such that it recovers its geometry upon release of the load, but does so by following a different unloading path, then it displays the phenomenon of viscoelastic response. Here, the initial geometry is recovered, but the body permanently absorbs some of the applied energy. This energy frequently appears in the form of heat, although the associated temperature rise for a one-shot compression is usually quite low. Examples of this behavior include many elastomers, and the spring/shock absorber system on vehicles, and several bumper systems, and, of course, the tires. The condition of having a return path different from the loading path again creates a loop in the force-deformation plot, and this loop represents the absorbed energy. As with plastic flow, this looping behavior constitutes the condition of hysteresis. Vehicle tires heat up with use due to the continual cyclic flexing that occurs as the contact point with the road causes flattening and rebound. Each cycle dissipates a small amount of energy within the rubber due to the viscous behavior. Thus the tire slowly heats up until the heat losses balance the energy dissipation. Since underinflated tires flex more than properly inflated ones they heat up faster, and the rubber then degrades faster.

Brittle Response. A material is said to behave in a brittle manner if it ruptures with negligible plastic flow, such as when glass breaks. Thus up to the point of rupture the response is almost purely elastic, but beyond this condition the material suddenly breaks. Clearly, such response indicates a go/no-go situation for interpretation of energy absorption. If the body in question does not break then an *upper* limit on absorbed energy is implied, whereas, if failure does occur a *lower* limit on energy absorption is implied.

Real materials frequently display combinations of all four responses, but to varying degrees. Most steels used for vehicle construction display primarily elastic and plastic responses. Viscous behavior reveals itself only for conditions of very high rates of deformation (known as strain-rate hardening, which is

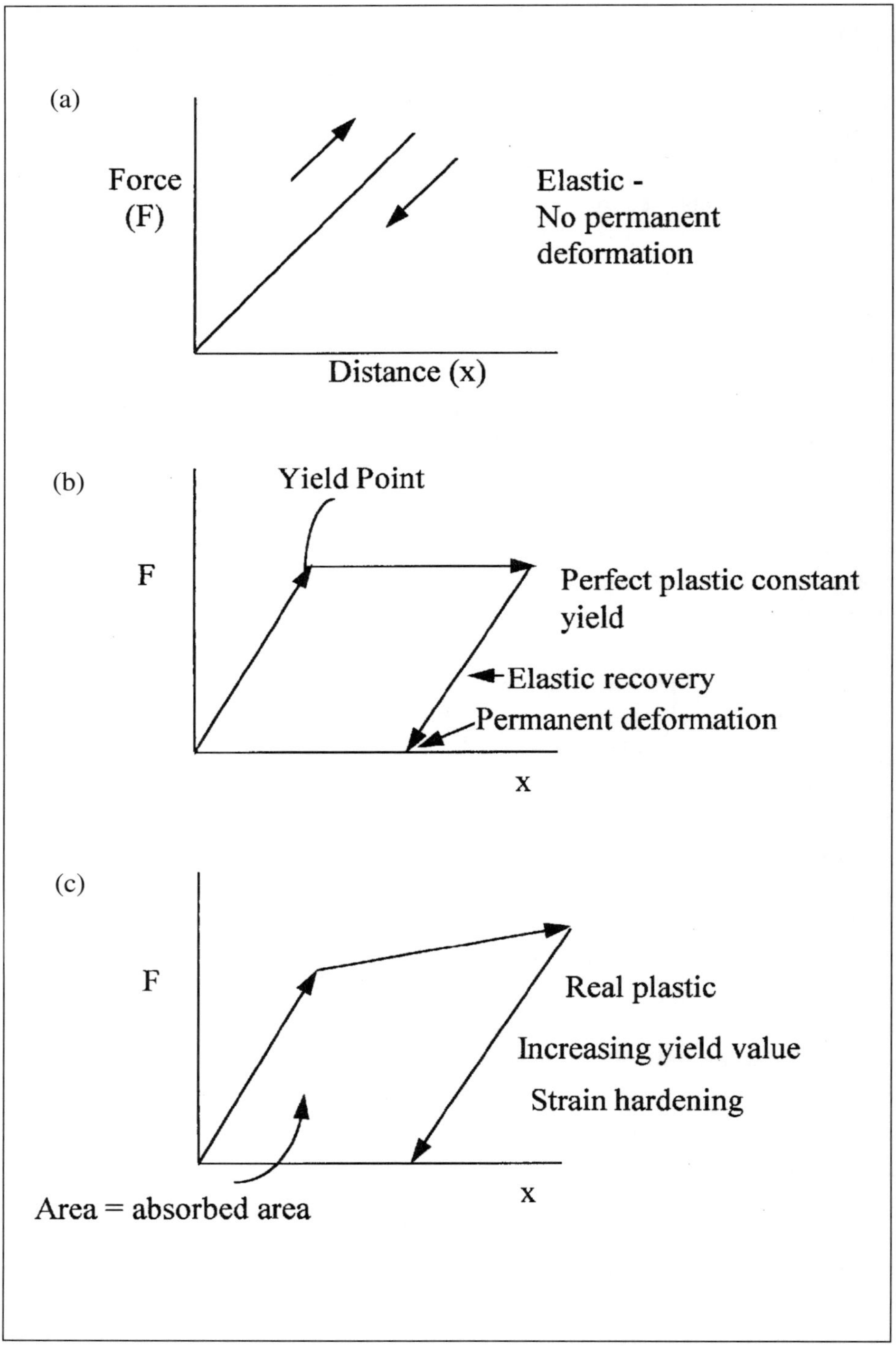

Figure 4a–4c *Material Modes of Response.*

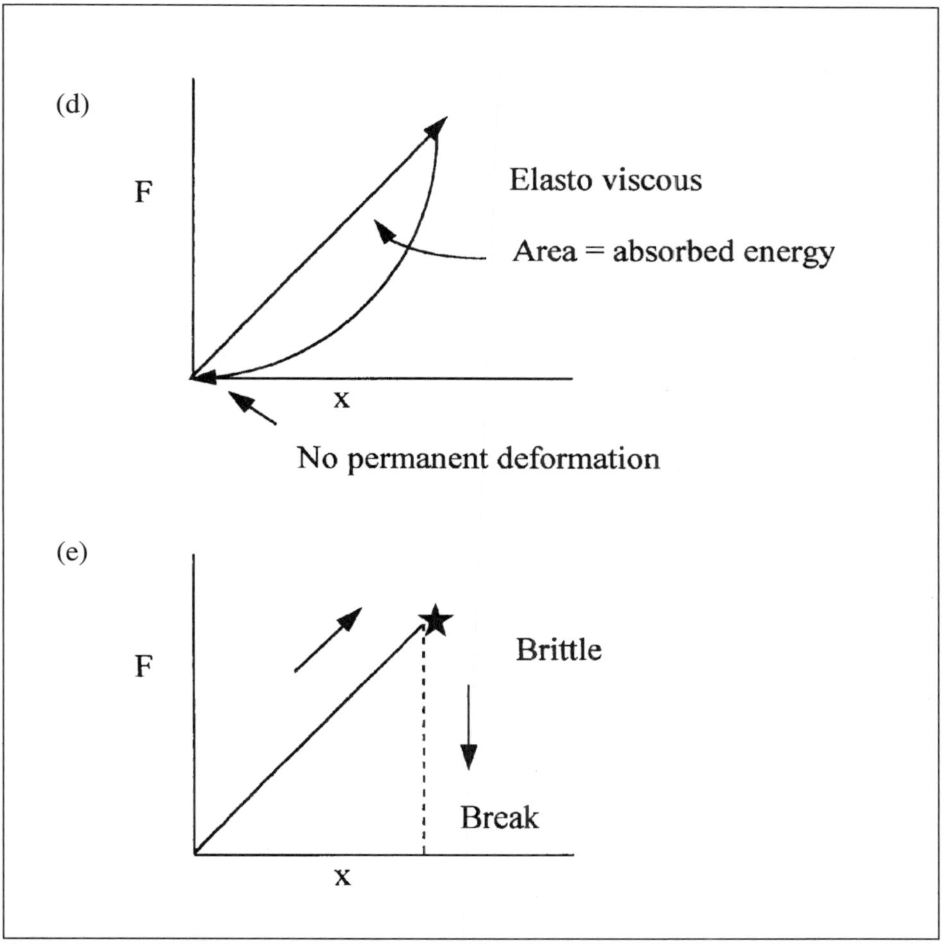

Figure 4d, 4e *Material Modes of Response.*

important for strong shock waves) or for hot metal approaching the melting point (not usually relevant for vehicle collisions). Figure 4 indicates the four major modes of response. We see that typical vehicle steel is initially elastic until the force exceeds the yield point. Thereafter, plastic flow occurs and continued deformation requires an increase in force. Upon release of the force, there is an elastic recovery, but also a permanent geometry change resulting in a plastic offset. This offset constitutes the vehicle crush observed after the impact. Materials such as fiberglass and ordinary or toughened window glasses usually display brittle responses, whereas laminated windshields display a mixture of brittle and plastic response.

Stress If the net applied force is divided by the perpendicular cross sectional area that the force acts upon, the resulting quantity is called the *normal* stress. If the force acts in the plane of the area, it is called the *shear* stress. Figure 5 illustrates the meanings of stress.

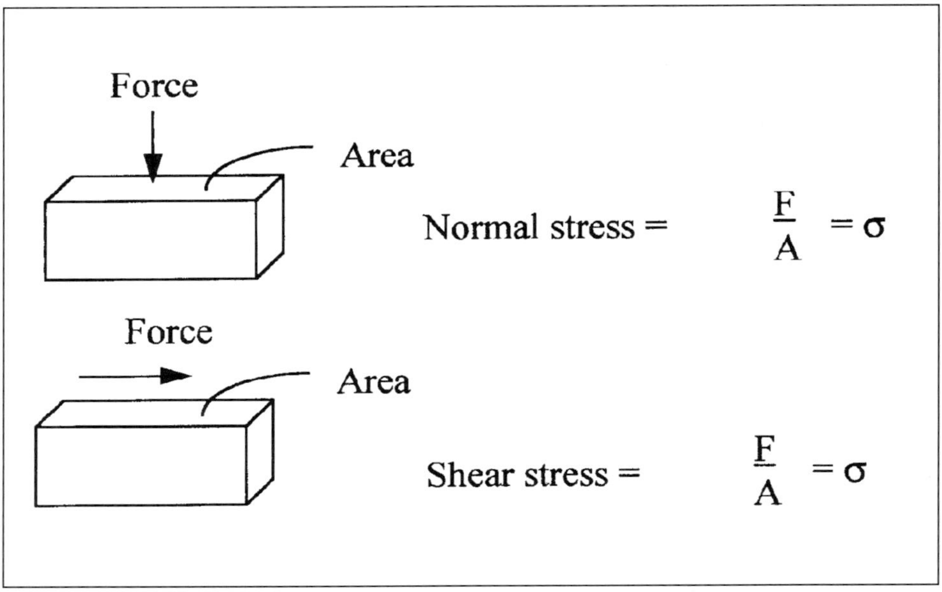

Figure 5 *Stress Definitions.*

Strain When a body deforms it develops strain. The strain is defined as the fractional change in geometry per initial geometry, and is thus dimensionless. Thus *linear* strain is the fractional decrease (or increase) in length per initial length. The integral of the stress versus strain gives a measure of the energy absorbed by the body. Specifically, this quantity is the energy per unit volume. If the cross sectional area is known, and the initial geometry length is known, then since stress x area = force, and strain x length = deformation, the area under the force versus deformation plot gives the total absorbed energy. If a *shear* motion is induced the strain is a *shear* one and is a measure of the twisting angle, and is also dimensionless.

Modulus is simply the ratio of the *stress* to the *strain*, and thus has units of stress. For a solid able to accept long-lived shears, the stress can be different in three mutually perpendicular directions. However, for a fluid, such shears cannot be maintained, and only short-lived viscous shears can exist during material flow. Consequently, the stress is normally forced to be the same in all directions. For this case, the stress is known as the *pressure*.

Note that the modulus must always be a positive quantity (an increase in strain must be accompanied by an increase in stress), since otherwise material instability occurs, as shown in figure 6. Thus, for a negative modulus the material would "run away," since increasing strain would require a lower balancing stress. For a fixed applied stress the material would simply continue straining until rupture occurred. Also, since sound speed is proportional to the square root of the modulus a negative modulus would imply an imaginary wave speed.

These remarks in the preceding paragraph refer to *true stress* and *true strain* (as used by physicists) rather than *engineering* stress and strain. For small

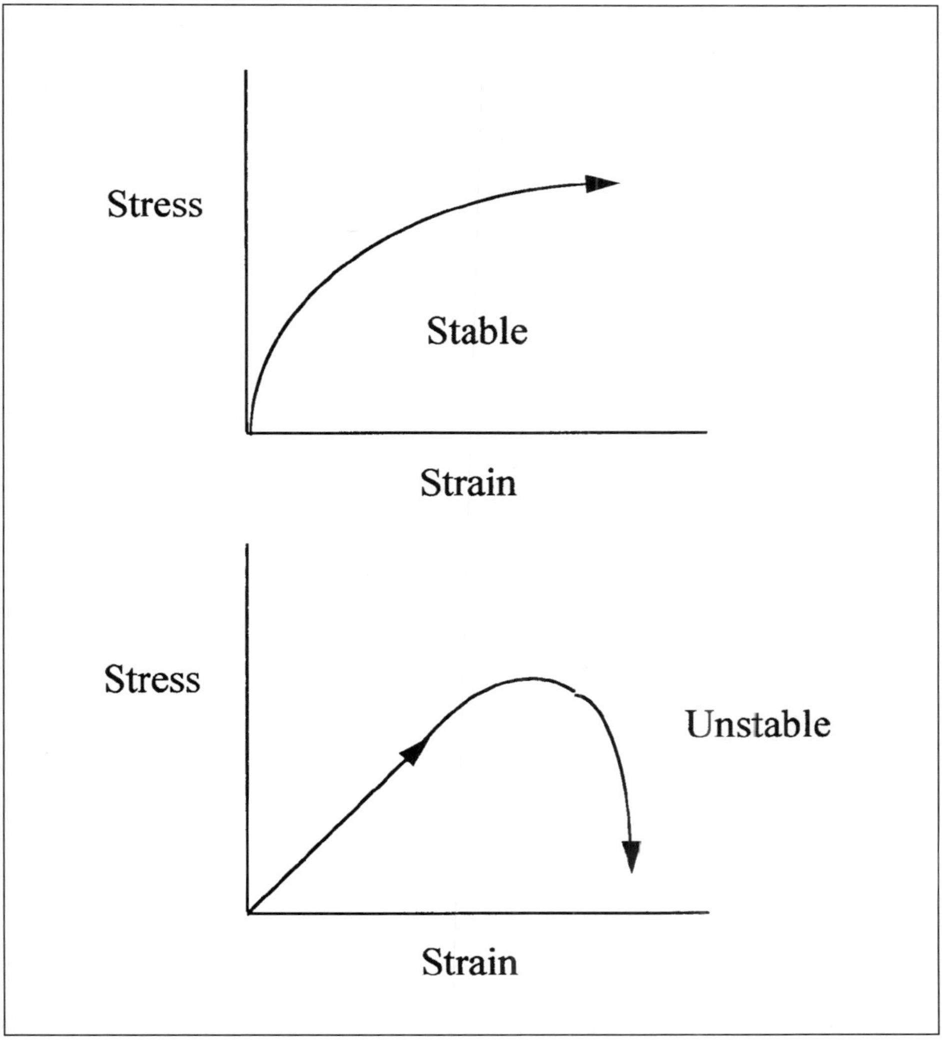

Figure 6 *Stress Versus Strain Options.*

values, there is no distinction, but for large strains and stress the two definitions differ. The engineering definitions of stress and strain both refer to the *original* cross-sectional area and length, respectively. True stress and strain refer to the *locally changing* values of area and length. These distinctions are introduced to help explain an apparent anomaly, namely the stretching of a thin wire or rod. Here, it is well known that runaway stretching does occur once a certain load is exceeded. However, this happens because of the "necking" that occurs, which actually reduces the local cross-sectional area, as seen in figure 7. Thus, the modulus appears to have become negative. In reality, the actual true stress at the necking region is still increasing, so the real modulus is positive. The necking behavior is really a structural effect rather than a material effect.

Sign convention For those who read physics and engineering text books, it should also be noted that the two professions disagree on sign convention. For the engineer, a compression is considered *negative* while a tension is considered *positive*. This occurs because an engineer considers it natural to first pull (or stretch) a material. However, the same engineers consider a gas pressure (such as steam pressure) to be *positive*. This switch can cause numerical confusion if a material changes state, and goes from being a solid to a gas. This is, however, a

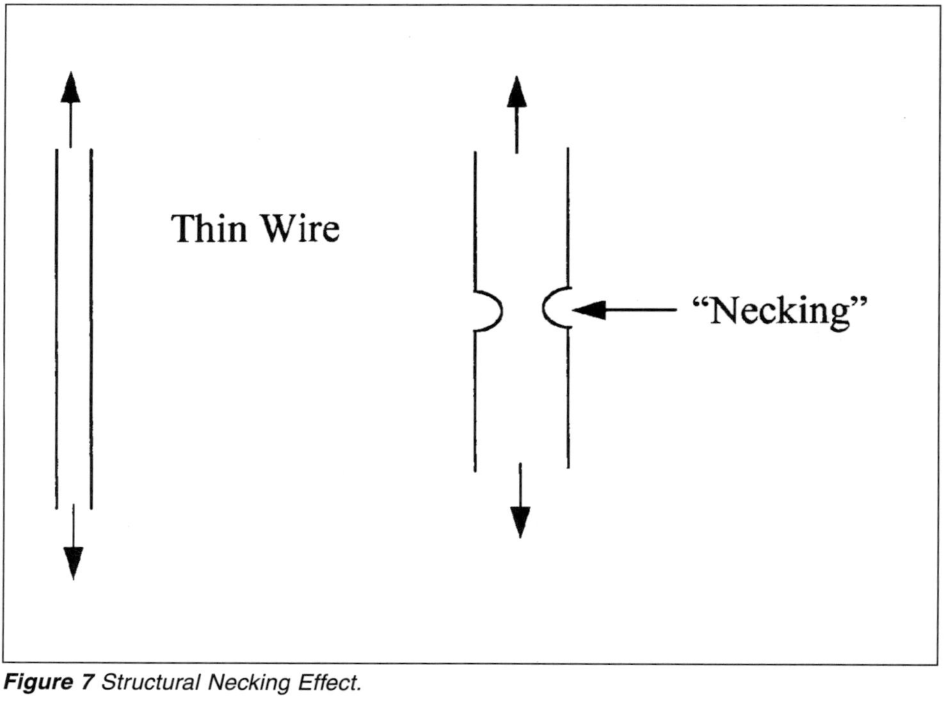

Figure 7 *Structural Necking Effect.*

rare consideration for most engineering (not many engineering conditions involve this effect). Physicists, however, are used to dealing with a more generic class of problems, where state changes are common. Consequently, physicists define pressure and compression both as *positive*, while tension is considered *negative*. This automatically avoids the problem of sign switching during phase changes. The only difference is in the sign used to describe the properties. This explanation is given merely to help those readers of standard texts who may become thoroughly confused by the difference between engineering's definitions and physics' ones.

Chapter 3

Vehicle Crush Response for Low Speed Impacts Into Rigid Barriers

The Bumper Response

Bumpers were first applied to railroad cars, mostly to protect the cargo rather than the car. Later, they were applied to road vehicles mostly to protect the vehicle rather than the passengers. This inversion of logic arose because railroad cars are inherently strong, while most road vehicles are generally weak since the weight must be kept low to allow for acceptable performance with limited engine sizes. The railroad bumpers were not intended to handle high speed collisions (such as train-into-train) but were intended to handle the lower speed differential motions between the cars, caused by the loose coupling systems used. Thus damage to the cars was not the concern; maintaining low induced accelerations to the cargo was the issue. Such bumper systems work very well at low speeds. Unfortunately, the automobile manufacturers seem to have lost this piece of insight. In their quest to minimize bumper performance (mostly to save weight) they seem to have forgotten that at low speeds bumpers actually protect the "cargo" of the cars: namely the passengers. Instead, car manufacturers concentrate on designing the vehicle itself to collapse somewhat like a bumper, which is necessary for higher speed collisions. However, this results in unnecessary repair expense even for low speed collisions.

It is important to realize that a bumper works by virtue of energy considerations, rather than simple consideration of forces or momentum. A given vehicle design will start to suffer permanent damage if the applied force exceeds a certain value, F_0. Thus a bumper must be capable of containing the energy of a moving vehicle while simultaneously keeping the peak force below the value F_0. To avoid structural damage a bumper must be capable of either storing or absorbing energy. The only real difference between these two approaches is that the storage method involves a significant bounce after initial compression, while the absorbing method minimizes the bounce. Note that a plastically responding bumper cannot recover. Consequently, such a bumper is a one-shot device of limited use, and is thus not used in practice, except for cheap pickup bumpers. The latter are usually connected directly to the frame horns. While the latter allow for some limited elastic response, most of the energy is consumed by actual permanent plastic bending of the bumper.

The simplest version of a bumper is a spring. Upon impact the spring will start to compress and the force will increase. Since the force acts in the direction of compression energy is stored in the spring. For a perfect, linear spring, this energy is simply E = 1/2 x F x d, where F is the built-up force and d is the compression motion amplitude. With F in pounds and d in feet, the energy is in pounds-foot.

If a vehicle has no bumper, the elastic range of response will be very limited. Although a real vehicle is not a simple solid chunk of material, its behavior will still mimic a solid, albeit a porous one. The amplitude of elastic deformation for the underframe of the vehicle is only about 0.07 to 0.12 inches for a solid car. This can be readily explained. Modern cars are designed to have controlled collapsible front and rear ends, which protects the passenger compartment by absorbing energy prior to large loads reaching this compartment. Note that the concept that the passenger compartment is “strong” is actually wrong, rather it is the protective energy-absorbing nature of the front or back of the vehicle which makes the compartment appear strong; for side impacts directly into the passenger compartment its weakness becomes apparent. This allows a gentle crush of the front and/or rear of the vehicle which limits the accelerations or decelerations experienced by the passengers. The collapsible front part of the vehicle is typically about 36 to 60 inches long. Automobile steel reaches its elastic limit for about 0.2% strain. Thus the motion is about 0.07 to 0.12 inches. Even if the total 15-foot length of a typical car were involved, the decrease in length for 0.2% strain is only 0.36 inches. These values would apply exactly if the vehicle were a simple solid piece of steel. In reality, since the vehicle is a structure which can buckle as well as suffer linear compression, the true linear motion is larger, but still quite limited, being about 0.5 inches. This limited deformation results also in limited energy absorption. Thus the elastic region of response is easily exceeded, and initiation of permanent frame damage can occur for very low impact speeds (about 1 mph for an impact into a rigid barrier). For the soft side and upper panels, damage can initiate even more easily.

These very low speeds can be understood by equating the vehicle kinetic energy with the stored elastic energy. Thus,

$$(w/2g)v^2 = (1/2)F_0D \text{ or } v^2 = (F_0/w)gD = 12R_0gD \text{ (D in feet)} = R_0g\,D \text{ (D in inches)}$$

where $12R_0$ is the strength-per-weight, g is 32.2 ft/s^2 and D is the amplitude of motion. For D = 0.07 inches, and $R_0 = 0.6$, v = 0.79 mph. Even for D = 0.36 inches, v = 1.8 mph.

Older cars (and most existing pickups, vans and trucks) were built with an independent chassis, with the remainder of the car panels, engine and transmission attached to it. Such a chassis gives a rigid frame, but also adds weight to the vehicle. Most modern cars no longer use independent chassis construction. Instead, most cars use the unibody or monocoque construction. Here the frame is an integral part of the overall bodywork, consisting of strengthened regions made by forming box sections, etc. This includes the sills under the doors. Some cars also employ subframes which are small remnants of the old chassis logic used for specific sections of the vehicle (*e.g*,.engine attachment). These newer techniques are more expensive, and thus only suitable for mass production work. However, they allow for lighter vehicles, and thus improved performance and fuel consumption.

In addition to the underframe vehicles also employ vertical frames called the "A," "B," and "C" frames. The A frame is the section containing the front door hinges, windshield and firewall. The B frame is the one that contains the front door latches, and the C frame contains the rear window and back door locks. Some vehicles (such as station wagons) have a D frame containing the rear end of the vehicle.

These various frames give the vehicles their rigidity and strength. It takes high forces to cause damage. However, because of the limited elastic strain capacity of structural steels, the frames do not allow for much energy absorption prior to plastic deformation. This is the purpose of the bumper.

The bumper is intended to allow a vehicle to impact another body and minimize any permanent structural plastic damage. For example, most good cars are fitted with 5 mph bumpers, although many trucks and pickups come only with cheaper 2.5 mph bumpers. The meaning of a 5 mph bumper is that a collision at no greater than about 5 mph into a rigid barrier will not cause any permanent body damage, in particular, to the lights, etc. Instead, only superficial scrapes and/or dents on the bumper should occur (note that the speed capability of bumpers is not a precise quantity). This means that the bumper assembly must be capable of absorbing the kinetic energy of the car. Since the force, F_0 , at which permanent damage initiates is fixed for a given vehicle, the only method available for increasing energy absorption is to allow for a significant bumper deformation amplitude. Further, since the energy increases with the square of the vehicle speed, the necessary bumper amplitude also increases with the square of the speed. Thus a 5 mph bumper requires four times the amplitude of a 2.5 mph one. These points are shown in figure 8. This effect explains the outcry from the car manufacturers when bumper limits were legislated, since a large bumper costs more to implement and is heavier (which counters attempts to improve fuel economy, a further government requirement). Note that the bumper response also allows a go/no-go analysis, since if there is no permanent damage to a vehicle then the energy involved must be less than the corresponding damage limit, and vice versa.

With a fixed maximum allowed force for a given vehicle design, the necessity to increase the bumper amplitude to increase the speed capability also means that the corresponding spring constant reduces, and the spring becomes softer.

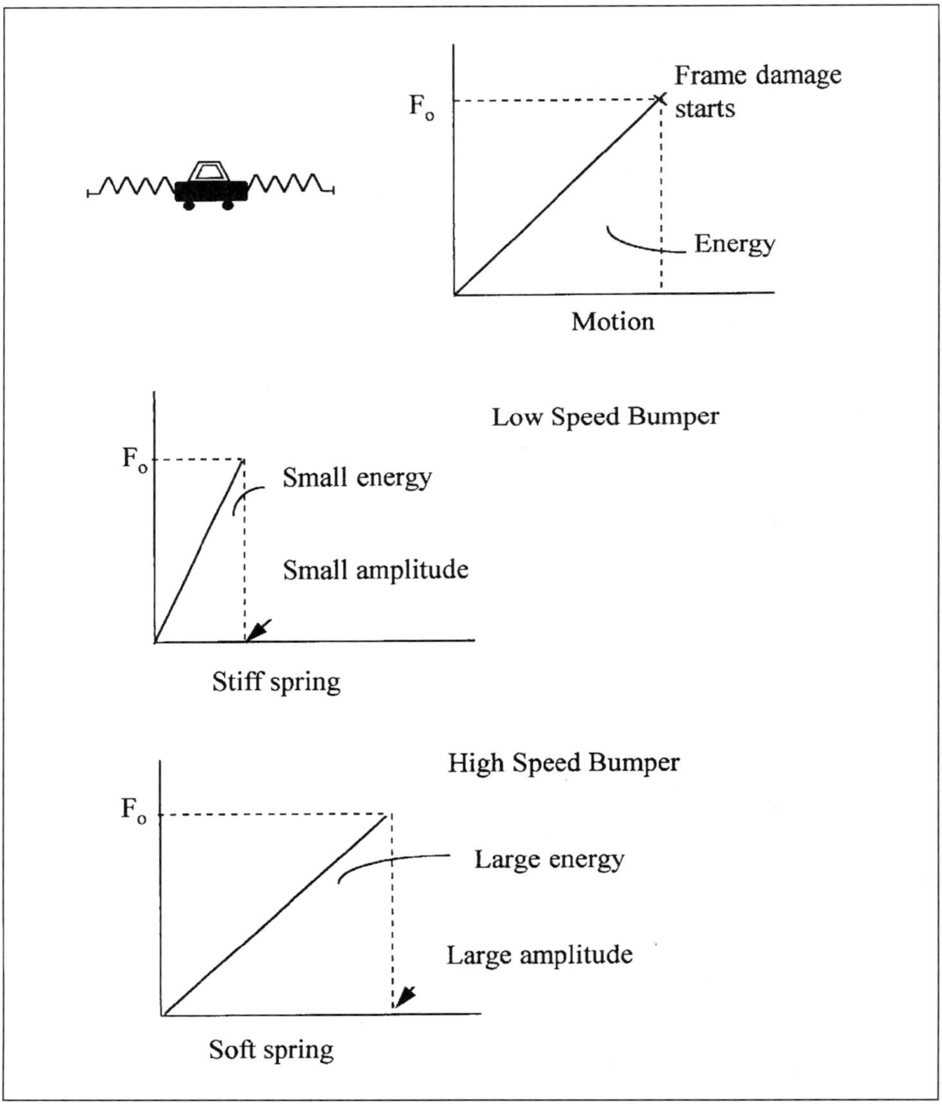

Figure 8 *Bumper Logic.*

This then reduces the acceleration imposed on the vehicle, and thus on the passengers. Thus, provided the upper limit of the bumper is not reached, the passengers suffer a smaller jolt. Put another way, for a fixed impact speed into a rigid barrier, the higher the bumper limit the better it is for the passengers. A softer spring also implies a lower oscillation frequency, and therefore a longer period for the compression/rebound. This increase in time allows a passenger more time to react by applying his muscles, which again usually makes the situation better and helps avoid injury.

Why not use high speed bumpers? The answer is that such a bumper would protrude significantly beyond the car proper (making it ugly, and thus unwanted by the customer), would weigh far more (worsening fuel economy and compromising CAFE requirements), and would cost far more (raising the price of the vehicle). Conversely, by using cheaper bumpers the cost of low speed repairs increases and the passengers are less well protected.

Note that bumpers are frequently tested using a swinging log-like pendulum, in addition to driving the vehicle at a rigid barrier. Likewise, rearend damage is frequently tested by impacting a stationary vehicle with a moving concrete "car" (see section 4.a (iii)).

Modern real bumpers do not act as simple springs. Instead, they employ some form of internal damping mechanism. There are two major types of bumpers; the "isolated" version and the "Plastic" version. The first type uses rigid metal bumpers that are attached to the vehicle frame via isolators. These isolators are small piston-in-cylinder devices. Figure 9 shows a typical isolator. The outer portion, nearest the bumper, is a cylinder containing high pressure nitrogen gas. This acts as a spring. The inner portion is a cylinder containing oil. Between these sections are two pistons. One is a floating piston, which separates the gas from the oil and acts as a movable barrier. The other is a piston with a small hole and a metering pin and is within the section containing the oil. As the bumper compresses, the piston with the metering hole is driven back into the oil, which in turn flows through the hole toward the floating piston. Simultaneously, the volume containing the gas is compressed. The oil flow develops a viscous force which adds to the gas force during the compression. When the bumper relaxes, the gas pressure forces the bumper back to its original position. Now the oil flows in the opposite direction through the hole. Consequently, the gas force and the oil force now compete with each other to give a smaller net force, so the bumper moves out more slowly than it compressed. The two-way flow of the oil causes fluid damping and permanent energy absorption (which heats the oil slightly). Thus, the bumper rebounds with less violence than a perfect spring.

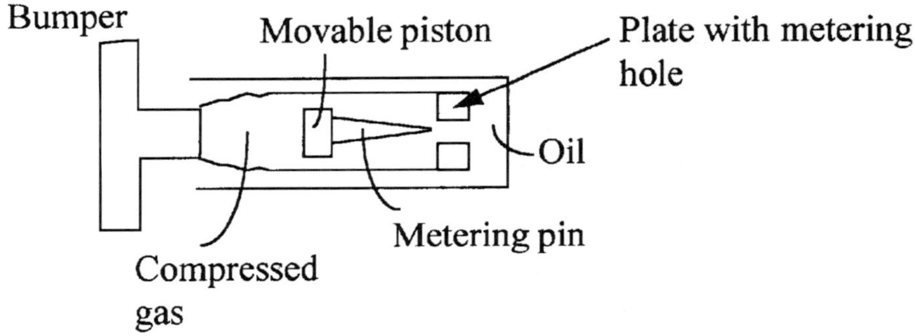

Figure 9 *Typical Isolation.*

The "Plastic" bumper is usually made of high density foamed polyurethane or polystyrene and attached to a rigid plate next to the vehicle frame. An alternative version uses Plastic in the form of an open-cell honeycomb structure. Both versions have similar mechanical response. These Plastic bumpers should not be confused with the rubberized-Plastic covering which many new cars use to hide metal bumpers. The latter system is mostly cosmetic. Here, we are discussing bumpers which are truly made of a Plastic material. The polyurethane has a natural elastoviscous response and small plastic response, which acts like a spring coupled with a fluid damper. Thus, once again the bumper relaxes back outwards slower than it initially compressed, and again absorbs some energy by slightly heating the Plastic. Be careful with the confusion between the bumper being made of a plastic material (Plastic), while its mechanical response is mostly elastoviscous and not plastic.

Regardless of type, all bumpers must store/absorb the initial vehicle kinetic energy while slowing the vehicle down. Upon subsequent relaxation, the degree of bounce simply depends on the degree of energy absorption during the complete cycle. Both types of bumpers should return to their initial positions provided the speed limit capability is not exceeded. However, for high impact speeds the isolators frequently need replacing even if the bumper itself is mostly undamaged. This is because the viscous force due to the oil flow increases with impact speed. Ultimately this force can become large enough to cause permanent frame damage since the isolator no longer isolates, but instead acts as a rigid rod transferring load to the frame. To avoid this, at high forces the metering pin is designed to "punch out" a larger hole in the piston. This allows easier oil flow and reduces the force. However, since this constitutes internal damage the isolator must be replaced.

The isolators sometimes leave telltale scrapes when compressed. These can sometimes allow for an estimate of degree of compression. However, this can be unreliable for several reasons. The production of a scrape is really a result of poor precision of the piston in the cylinder and poor lubrication. If the isolator were better made and lubricated it would behave like the piston/cylinder in the car engine. There would be negligible scraping or scoring. Thus the scrape marks are due to frictional drag acting on paint, or dirty or rusted metal. However, the scrapes are also only capable of giving information concerning the minimum motion of the bumper. This is because a loose fit of the piston in the cylinder readily allows canting when the piston is mostly out of the cylinder. But as the piston moves into the cylinder the degree of canting decreases, the piston more accurately aligns with the cylinder, and the propensity of the scrapes to occur decreases. If a piston seizes then the scrape is minimized, and the isolator does not isolate. Hence such scrapes invariably give only minimum motion data.

Experiments have been done (ref 15) to calibrate isolator piston motions versus impact speeds. To guarantee an observable scrape the pistons were spray painted with a white paint. Unfortunately, this information is of limited use to an investigator in the field, since real cars do not have this paint and some isolators leave no scrape marks at all (hence the need for the paint). Further, it was noticed that the observable length of the piston in the out position did not always indicate the true maximum possible piston motion before bottoming occurred. Many isolators bottomed with smaller net motions. The fractional bottoming varies from about 50% to 90%, dependent on design. Most such isolators (ref 15) have maximum possible amplitudes in the range of 40 mm (1.57 inches) to 80 mm (3.15 inches), with many about 57 mm (2.24 inches). The bottom line is that even impact speeds near the limit of the bumper capability can leave either no scrapes or apparently small scrapes, fooling the investigator into believing the impact was at lower speed than reality.

If the scrapes *do* indicate the true isolator motion then the maximum effective barrier impact speed is given by v_{max} = (observed scrape amplitude/maximum possible piston motion) x $v_{bumper\ limit}$, for a pseudo-linear springlike bumper response. Of course, to perform this calculation the maximum possible piston motion must also be known for the isolator in question.

Note that isolators behave differently when loaded in a static manner. At very low speeds of compression the oil flows readily without much force. Hence, the isolator response is due only to the gas compression. For a rapid dynamic collision, however, the oil force increases significantly and the isolator is much stiffer, presupposing dynamic impacts.

Similarly, many of the Plastic bumpers can completely compress and rebound without showing any obvious signs of motion afterwards. Indeed, the only indication of the bumper being overdriven is actual frame damage! The exception is for strong local loadings, where some small degree of imprint is seen. Such localized loadings include impacts with license plate holders, overriders, edges of other bumpers and, of course, collisions with narrow objects such as poles. These imprints occur because the polyurethane has a weak plastic response in addition to its elastoviscous response.

Vehicle Crush Characteristics

Consider the effect of a sudden application of force to a vehicle via the bumper, due to impact. We will consider here the case of a full frontal impact, such that the entire bumper is uniformly loaded. The case of incomplete impact will be addressed below. Initially, the bumper begins to move back in the direction of the vehicle, increasing its force with amplitude of motion. This increase is linear for a simple spring response, and pseudo-linear for most real bumpers. Eventually, the bumper bottoms out, and any increase in force is transmitted to the vehicle frame behind as a load capable of initiating permanent deformation. This deformation initially consists of localized plastic yielding where the bumper joins the frame. With a further increase in load, buckling of the main body parts constituting the frame occurs, and portions of this frame start to develop plastic hinges, where concentrated stresses cause strong localized plastic flow. The frame begins to collapse on itself like a bellows. As the frame collapses, other parts are driven into plastic flow. These parts include non-frame body panels which proceed to bend and buckle by virtue of being attached to the frame sections. Thus the vehicle progressively collapses and absorbs part of the impact energy by plastic flow. Eventually, the force peaks, and thereafter decreases back to zero. This peak force occurs at the time of maximum engagement of the vehicle and the second body. This means that it occurs when the deformation amplitude becomes a maximum for both bodies. This condition is the one where the maximum loss in kinetic energy occurs. As the force decreases, part of the contained energy is released in the form of recovered elastic energy. Most of this recovery is due to the spring-back of the bumper, but a small portion is also due to the natural elastic rebound of the vehicle structure. Finally, the force returns to zero and the vehicle is left with a permanent deformation but also suffers a bounce away from the other body.

These effects can be illustrated by figure 10, which shows a force-deformation plot of typical behavior. The initial steep linear portion, OA, is the elastic bumper response. At the point A the bumper motion limits (amplitude x_0) and the main body frame proceeds to collapse, following the path AB. At B the collapse stops (maximum deformation x_{max}) and the recovery is elastic along path

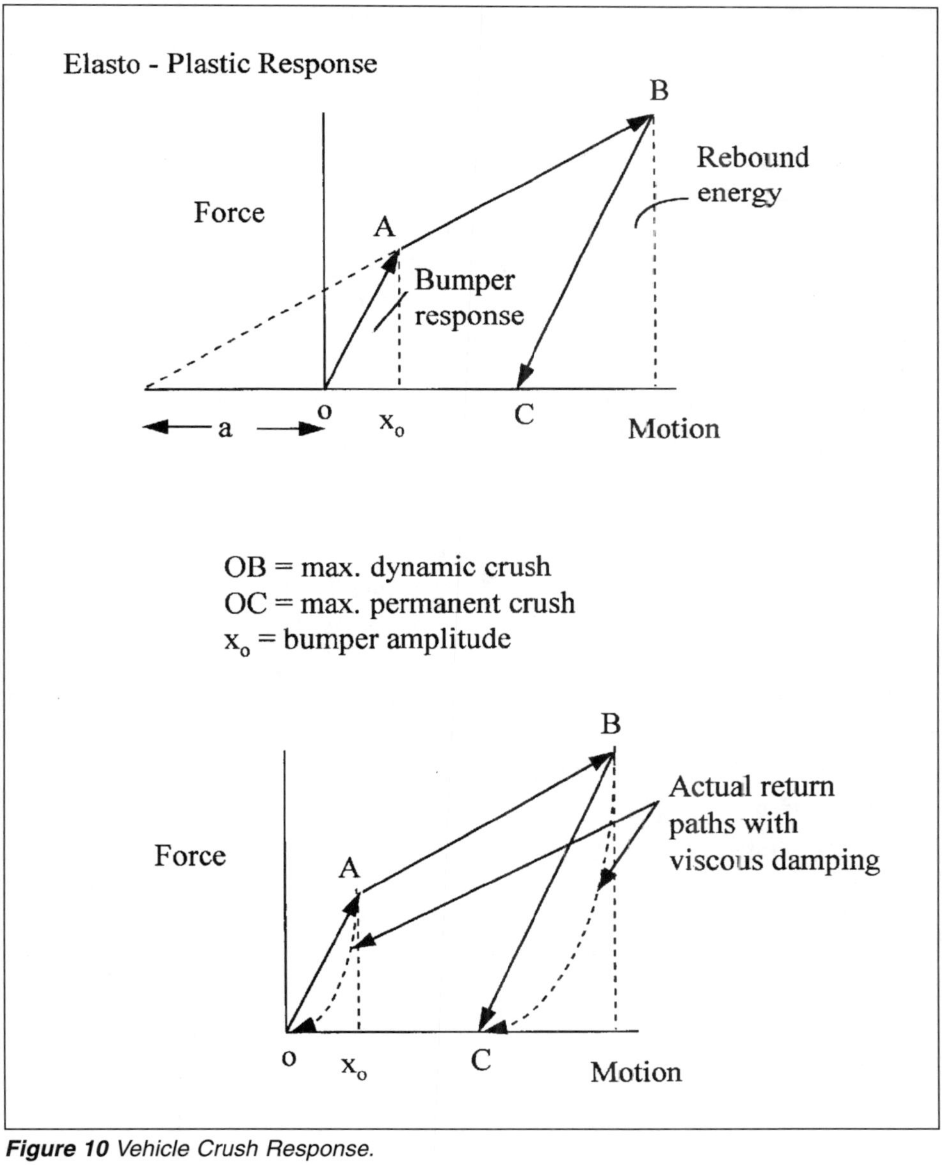

Figure 10 *Vehicle Crush Response.*

BC. Thus there is a permanent deformation of OC (deformation x_{final}), but a maximum deformation of OB. This is the basis of the POD model.

As frame collapse proceeds the absorbed energy increases with deformation amplitude. Let us define a dimensionless quantity, R, as the ratio of energy (foot-pounds) per incremental crush of deformation (inches) per weight of vehicle (pounds). Thus, R is a *specific rigidity* (rigidity per weight). If the vehicle collapse was simple plastic beyond the point A, then the value of R would be a constant. However, because of the strain hardening behavior, giving the slope AB, the value of R increases with deformation amplitude such that $R = R_0(1 + x/a)$, where R_0 is the initial value for incipient crush, x is the local crush and the quantity 'a' describes the slope of the strain hardening section, as indicated in figure 10. In reality, the section AB is not truly linear. Indeed, a detailed study would show that the required crush force oscillates with the degree of crush due to variations in local strength, but on average gradually increases with continued crush. However, within the uncertainties and limited experimental data for vehicle crushing, a presumption of simple linearity is reasonable, at least for small degrees of crush which do not cause an incursion into the passenger compartment.

From the definition of R, the force required to initiate body crush is just $F_0=12R_0w$, where w is the vehicle weight, and the factor of 12 arises because the energy is measured in foot-pounds while the deformation is measured in inches. Since force divided by mass is acceleration, we immediately derive that acceleration is equal to $12R_0$ in units of g, where g is the acceleration due to gravity (32.2 ft/s^2). Typically, many vehicles have values for R_0 (for structural frame damage) in the range 0.5 to 1.0. For example, for a 3000 pound car with R_0 = 0.6, the force to initiate crush would be about 21,600 pounds. At the bumper limit where permanent crush starts, the acceleration experienced by the rigid passenger compartment is in the range of 6 g to 12 g. Before the bumper limit is reached, the acceleration is roughly linearly proportional to the bumper amplitude, for a simple springlike response. Thus, during the impact the acceleration climbs very quickly from zero to the value $12R_0$ as the bumper motion limits. Thereafter, further deformation causes a slower increase in acceleration versus crush. However, for a high speed collision, the total deformation can become quite large (about 25 inches for an impact at about 35 mph into a rigid barrier). For example, if the value of the quantity 'a' is about 10 inches, then the peak acceleration becomes $12R_0(1 + 25/10)$, which is $42R_0$ (42 g for R_0=1.0, or 21 g for R_0 = 0.5). Clearly, the peak acceleration increases linearly with the crush amplitude, for a linear strain hardening material response.

Note that these impact forces and accelerations are *much higher* than the normal force between the vehicle and the road (the vehicle weight) and the frictional force on the road (Fw, where F is the drag factor, usually less than 1.0). Consequently, during the impact the connection to the road can usually be ignored, and the vehicle responses are as if they were floating in space. However, after the impact the effects of tire/road friction come back into play. This produces variable effects. For example, consider a car traveling south which is impacted sideways at the rear in the westward direction. The result is to give the

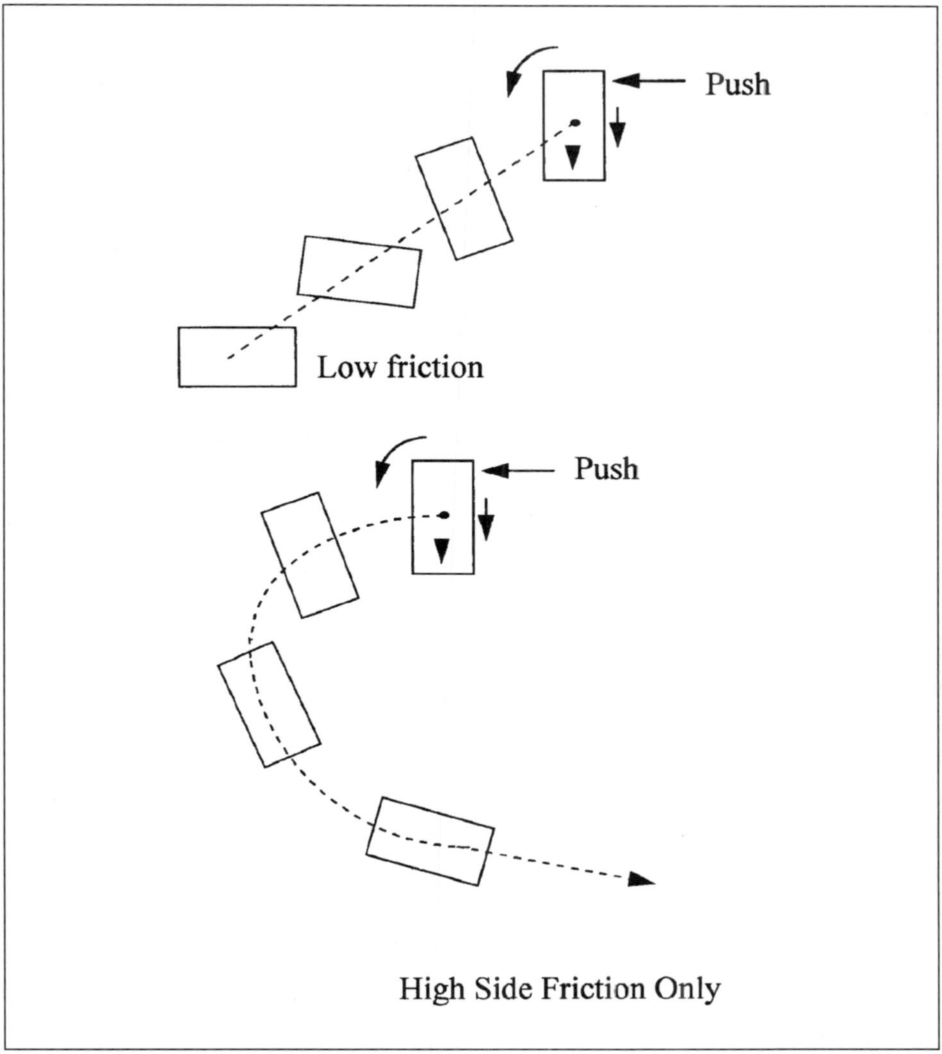

Figure 11 *Time/Road Effects.*

car center-of-mass a new heading which is southwest, while counterclockwise rotation is also induced. If the tire/road friction is very small, as on ice, these motions continue. However, if the wheels are not locked, so that friction applies only sideways to the wheels, then both the lateral motion and the rotation will rapidly cease, and the car can now continue on a new heading, which may be southeast. This is indicated in figure 11.

The issue of road friction becomes progressively more important as the impact reduces in severity. To illustrate, note that the typical tire/road friction is rarely much above 0.8 (except for special soft-rubber racing tires), so the maximum frictional force on the vehicle is about 0.8w. However, at the bumper limit the force acting on a vehicle is $12R_0w$. Even for a low R_0 value of about 0.5, this represents about 6 g acceleration. For a linear bumper force-deflection response, this means that the peak bumper force is proportional to the change in speed of the vehicle (delta-v). These two forces become equal when

(1)

$$delta - v = \Delta v = \left(\frac{0.8w}{12R_0w}\right)v_L$$

where v_L is the bumper limit speed. Thus, for $R_0 = 0.5$, and $v_L = 5$ mph, we equate the forces for a delta-v of about 0.67 mph. For lower bumper speed limits and/or higher R_0 values, the corresponding delta-v is even smaller. These low speeds represent the case where, for a stationary target vehicle, the impact is just at the limit where the car will start to be pushed against its own brakes. For lower impact speeds the car will simply rock on its suspension without net motion. Such small changes in speed are not normally associated with passenger injury. Thus, at speeds of interest it is usually true that the effect of tire/road friction can be mostly ignored for responses during the impact, especially for through-the-bumper collisions. For a soft-body impact (to a fender or middle of an unstrengthened door) the effective value of v_L is quite low, about 1 mph. Now the delta-v can be even lower, implying tire/road friction can be important for incipient damage to such soft parts. However, passenger injury is very improbable at these very low speeds.

If the vehicle impacts a rigid barrier, then:

(2)

$$E_{in} = 6R_0w\left(\frac{x_0 + a}{a}\right)\left[\frac{x_{final}^2}{a} + 2x_{final} + \left(\frac{a}{x_0 + a}\right)x_0\right] = \frac{wv_{in}^2}{2g}$$

with w in pounds; x_{final}, x_0 and a in feet; E_{in} in foot-pounds, and v_{in} in feet per second. This represents the area under the plot of figure 10, and is thus the initial vehicle energy measured up to the maximum deflection.

If a » x_0, we have $(x_0+a)/a \rightarrow 1.0$, and thus equation (2) approximates to

(3)

$$E_{in} = 6R_0 w\left[\frac{x_{final}^2}{a} + 2x_{final} + \frac{v_L^2}{12R_0 g}\right] \text{ with } \frac{v_L^2}{12R_0 g} = x_0 \quad \text{(see below)}$$

and thus, converting units, we can rewrite equation (3) as

(4)

$$v_{in}^2 = R_0 g\left[\frac{x_{final}^2}{a} + 2x_{final} + \frac{v_L^2}{R_0 g}\right]$$

with v_{in} and v_L in feet per second, and x_{final} and a in inches.

Here v_L is the so-called bumper limit speed. The quantity $v_L^2/12R_0g$ gives the maximum bumper amplitude (x_0, feet) before permanent crushing commences (*i.e.*, we equate $wv_L^2/2g$ with the triangular area OAx_0). For R_0=1.0, and v_L=7.335 ft/s (5 mph), this amplitude is about 0.139 ft or 1.67 inches, whereas, for R_0 = 0.5, the amplitude is about 3.34 inches. Thus the bumper amplitude is small, and the condition a » x_0 is easily satisfied, since 'a' is usually greater than 10 inches. Note that as $x_{final} \rightarrow 0.0$, so $v_{in} \rightarrow v_L$, as expected. The terms E_{in} and v_{in} represent the input energy and velocity, respectively. The necessary distinction between input energy and absorbed energy will be discussed below.

We see that the equations involve three terms, namely a constant one, a term linear in crush amplitude and a term dependent on the square of the crush amplitude. For x_{final} «2a and $2x_{final}$ » x_0 equation (4) approximates to

(5)

$$v_{in}^2 = 2R_0 g x_{final} \text{ or } v_{in} = (2R_0 g)^{\frac{1}{2}} x_{final}^{\frac{1}{2}}$$

(v in ft/s and x_{final} in inches) which implies a square-root response for velocity versus crush, and a linear relationship of energy versus crush. Note the correspondence between equation (5) and the well-known one for skid distances, namely

(6)

$$v_{in}^2 = 2Fgs$$

where F is the coefficient of friction (or drag factor) and s is the skid distance (ft).

When $2a < x_{final}$ the result approximates to

(7)
$$v_{in}^2 = \frac{R_0 g x_{final}^2}{a} \text{ or } v_{in} = \left(\frac{R_0 g}{a}\right)^{\frac{1}{2}} x_{final}$$

which implies a linear response of velocity versus crush depth and a square-law relationship of energy versus crush.

Figure 12 illustrates the behavior of equation (4), giving the collision velocity versus permanent crush for an impact into a rigid barrier. We see that there is: (i) a lower velocity limit necessary to induce permanent damage; (ii) an initial square-root behavior for velocity versus crush at the lower speeds; and (iii) a trend toward a linear plot at the higher speeds. It should be emphasized, however, that these equations are only good approximations up to a certain upper impact speed. The reason is that ultimately the vehicle crush will be sufficient for various hard or soft points to be involved.

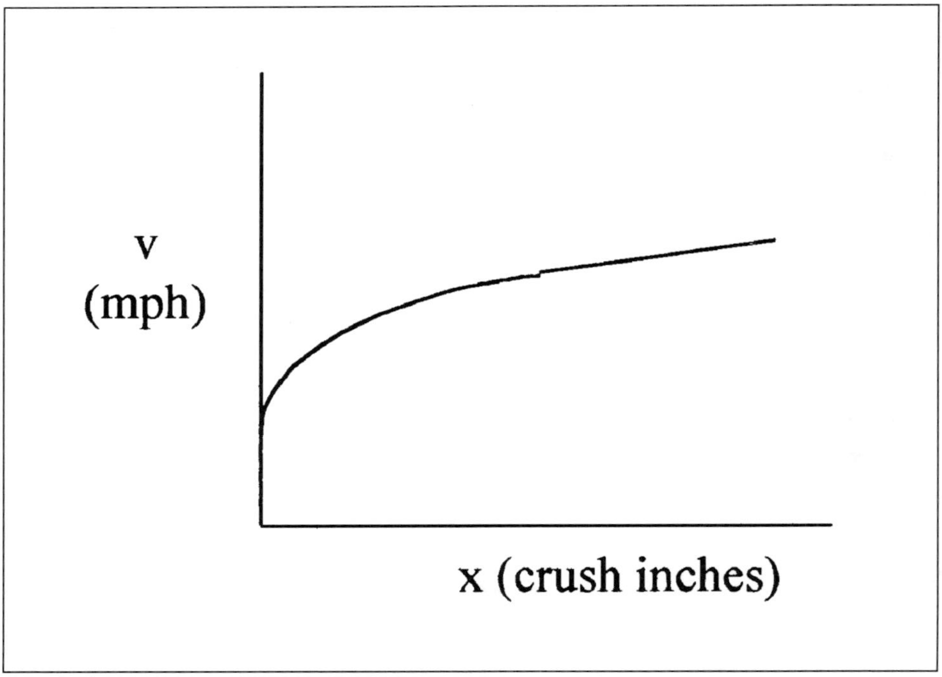

Figure 12 *Rigid Barrier Impact.*

For example, for excessive frontal crush eventually the collapse will involve pushing the engine and transmission assembly back and distortion of the A frame. Thus beyond this point the vehicle changes its rigidity (this is equivalent to suddenly changing the value of 'a'), and equation (4) will thereafter incorrectly predict the impact velocity. Specifically, the so-called "rigid" passenger compartment is frequently actually softer than the front of the vehicle. In particular, experiments indicate (ref 16) that the compartment behaves almost as a material with constant yield strength (no strain hardening). This results in a trend toward *more* crush versus increase in impact speed, or conversely, a lower implied speed for a given observed crush, at the higher impact speeds. The result is that a further kink occurs on the velocity-crush plot at the about 30 to 35 mph barrier impact speed, and the plot once again tends toward a square-root behavior. This point is discussed in reference 16.

Modern cars are designed to allow the engine/transmission assembly to shear off the vehicle frame and submarine under the passenger compartment. This minimizes the transferred force and consequential passenger compartment acceleration, and prevents them from being propelled through the firewall. This

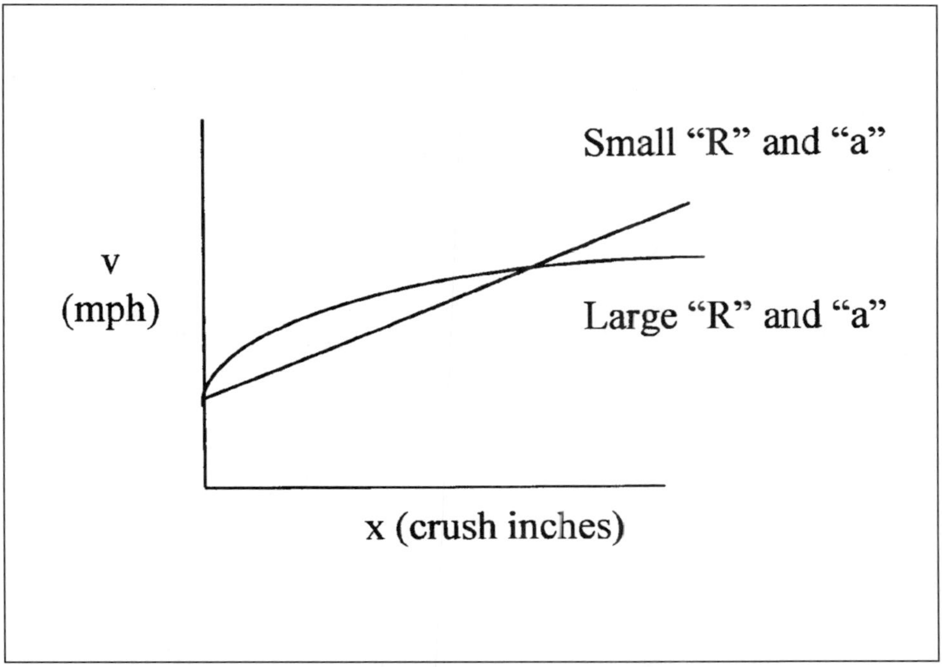

Figure 13 *Crush Characteristics for Variable R and a Parameters.*

makes it safer, especially for a front wheel drive vehicle. However, for a front engine/rear wheel drive vehicle this behavior can ultimately introduce another problem, that of the propeller shaft digging into the road and causing the vehicle to pole-vault over the contact point on the road.

Figure 13 indicates the effects of varying the R_0 and 'a' parameters. To ensure that a given observed crush occurs for a given impact speed (*i.e.,* the curve passes through a known point) these two parameters must be adjusted together, and a decrease in one implies a decrease in the other. It can be seen that for low values of both parameters the curve rapidly approximates to a straight line, whereas for larger values the curve approximates to the square-root law.

While the above discusses the response for a full-frontal impact that involves the complete width of a bumper, it should be noted that equation (2) actually applies to any component of a vehicle, provided that the appropriate values of R_0, 'a' and v_L are known. In this way, the total absorbed energy of a damaged vehicle can, in principle, be deduced from a summation of all the various components. However, this is rarely done and to do so would require detailed analysis of the response of each component, which is possible, but very time-consuming.

The Difference Between Input and Absorbed Energy

Equation (2) above references the input energy of the vehicle, which is directly given by its impact speed. If we assume that the force relief follows an elastic path parallel to the initial bumper/frame loading, the recovered energy is given by

(8)

$$E_{rec} = \left(\frac{wv_L^2}{2g}\right)\left(1 + \frac{x_{final}}{a}\right) = E_{bumper}\left(1 + \frac{x_{final}}{a}\right)$$

where E_{bumper} is the energy (foot-pounds) to initially bottom out the bumper.

Thus, the actual absorbed energy is approximately given by

(9)

$$E_{ab} = 6R_0w\left[\frac{x_{final}^2}{a} + 2x_{final} + \frac{v_L^2}{12R_0g}\right] - E_{rec}$$

or

(10)

$$E_{ab} = 6R_0w\left\{\frac{x_{final}^2}{a} + 2x_{final} + \left[\frac{v_L^2}{12R_0g}\right]\left[1 - \left(1 - \frac{x_{final}}{a}\right)^2\right]\right\}$$

or

(11)
$$E_{ab} = 6R_0 w\left[\left(\frac{x_{final}^2}{a}\right)\left(1-\frac{v_L^2}{12R_0 ga}\right)+2x_{final}\left(1+\frac{v_L^2}{12R_0 ga}\right)\right]$$

with x_{final} and 'a' in feet. This distinction in energies becomes progressively more important as the impact severity decreases, and can frequently be ignored for high impact speeds.

However, since most real bumper systems involve some degree of viscous damping, the actual recovered energy is usually only a fraction, f, of the perfect-spring value given above. This effect is discussed later. Thus equation (11) is really a lower limit for absorbed energy.

Note that because equations (2) and (11) contain both a quadratic term and a linear term for crush then a plot of $E^{1/2}$ versus crush will not be a straight line unless the square term dominates the linear term. Thus, straight-line behavior is not appropriate at low speeds.

Chapter 4

Crush Responses in Two-Vehicle Low Speed Collisions

In-Line Collisions

In general, collisions occur between two finite mass vehicles each with finite crush capabilities. For the rigid barrier interaction no significant energy is absorbed by the barrier, either in the form of crush damage or in the form of induced motion. For the two-vehicle impact, however, energy is transferred from the bullet vehicle to the target vehicle, both in the form of damage and motion. It can then be shown that the closing speed, v_c, of the vehicles is given by

(12)
$$v_c^2 = 2E_D g \frac{(w_1 + w_2)}{[w_1 w_2 (1 - e^2)]}$$

where the w's are the two vehicle weights and E_D is the total absorbed energy for damage to both vehicles. The quantity 'e' is the coefficient of restitution, which is the ratio of the difference in vehicle speeds after impact to the difference in speeds before the impact. It is a measure of how elastic the collision is, and is dimensionless.

Thus,

(13)
$$e = \frac{\left(v_2' - v_1'\right)}{(v_1 - v_2)} = -\frac{\left(v_1' - v_2'\right)}{(v_1 - v_2)}$$

where unprimed quantities are before the impact, and primed quantities are after the impact. Note the inversion in the order of speeds (1 versus 2). This occurs because the bounce associated with recovered energy is in the opposite direction to its initial motion. Mathematically, a ratio should always be defined with the numerator and denominator listed in the same order. Thus 'e' is usually a *negative* number, as stated in the second part of equation (13). However, many texts automatically invert the order to give a positive quantity, leading to unnecessary confusion, applying 'e' in equations as if it were a positive quantity. The only solution to this problem is to be very careful to make sure that any use of 'e' is done in a consistent manner. Throughout this book we use the *mathematical* version of 'e,' which is usually negative. Of course, for equation (12) the use of the square of 'e' means that the sign of 'e' is immaterial. However, the equations for post-impact speeds, given below, need the proper signs.

For a very elastic collision (no permanently absorbed energy) the value of 'e' becomes -1.0, whereas, for a very plastic collision (the maximum possible energy is absorbed) the value becomes 0.0. Thus all "normal" vehicle collisions must have values in the range 0.0 > e > -1.0.

Note that equation (12) is usually applied for the case of a collinear impact between vehicles, one that does not also induce rotations of either vehicle. If rotations are induced then the rotational kinetic energy must be accounted for. For this case the solution must include all forms of energy and the initial vehicle speeds are then deduced independently by noting the maximum loss in initial kinetic energies. However, it can be shown that this is merely the same as using equation (12) but with *effective weights*. These effective weights are discussed in section 4(d), which addresses vehicle rotations.

For standard rigid barrier crash tests the norm is to evaluate the final crush versus the known vehicle input kinetic energy, rather than the actual absorbed energy. High speed films of such impacts clearly show the recovered energy in the form of a bounce, and the vehicle is always found away from the barrier. However, this bounce is usually ignored in the definition of the energy associated with the corresponding degree of permanent crush. This is not an issue until one attempts to use equation (12) which requires the absorbed energy. Thus, the *input* energy should be associated with the maximum dynamic crush (which is temporary, and only measurable with devices such as high speed films) while the *absorbed* energy should be associated with the permanent crush.

An interesting example of double dipping can arise if these distinctions are not appreciated. Consider the following test case: a vehicle impacts a rigid wall and then bounces back with the brakes fully locked, thus leaving skid marks. The vehicle crush is noted. To deduce the initial vehicle speed at impact one has two choices. Either the standard permanent crush versus *input* energy can be used by itself, *OR* the energy deduced from the bounce skid marks is added to the actual absorbed energy for the crush. What is *NOT* allowed is to add the skid energy *and* the input crash energy, since the latter already includes the bounce energy!

Note that these arguments presuppose that vehicle damage is due to a bumper-to-bumper impact, where the major thrust is through the bumper and thus into the strong underframe of the vehicle. However, sometimes a non-bumper collisions occur. An example is when a car runs into the rear of a high four-wheeler with a bumper higher than that of the car. An alternative example is when a car is rapidly braking and adopts the nose-down, tail-up attitude. If two cars are braking the nose of the second car can easily submarine under the tail of the first one.

Whenever the impact is a non-bumper one large amounts of upper body damage can be caused, but this involves remarkably little energy, since the upper body panels are quite weak, and the crash does not involve the major vehicle frame. Thus the damage is really cosmetic, and often costs a lot to repair, but involves very little energy absorption compared to a through-bumper thrust. Similar upper body damage can be produced by a person wielding a hammer or baseball bat. For these reasons the standard energy approach cannot be used unless the real strength of the panels is known, and attention should be concentrated on any observed bumper/frame damage. As a general rule, the effective value of R for soft panel hits and for vehicle side hits is about one-half, or less, the value for direct bumper/frame impacts.

That vehicles really do bounce is demonstrated by inspection of the individual NHTSA reports, such as the NCAP ones (New Car Assessment Program). For example, the test of the 1994 Ford Probe 2-door model (ref 4) involves a standard frontal impact at 35 mph. The vehicle was found 2 feet (distance, s) away from the barrier posttest. The front section of the car deformed back enough to grab the two front wheels, and thus prevent rotation and act as if the front brakes were being strongly applied. Assuming a friction coefficient (F) of about 0.7 acting on the frontal weight fraction (f_w) of about 0.6 (no back wheel braking), this implies a bounce at a speed of

$$v_{bounce} = (2\ F\ f_w\ g\ s)^{1/2} = (2 \times 0.7 \times 0.6 \times 32.2 \times 2.0)^{1/2} = 7.36 \text{ ft/s} = 5.0 \text{ mph}.$$

The car impacted on a barrier which contained 36 load cells that give the force versus time history of the crash. The integral of this force-time data gives the net change in the vehicle momentum. This value was observed to be about 5730 lb-s. However, the vehicle weight was 3178 lbs, and at 35 mph (51.3 ft/s) this represents an input momentum of 5068 lb-s. Thus, the net change was about 5730/5068 = 1.13 times larger than the input momentum. This implies a reverse bounce of about 4.6 mph, consistent with the estimate above. Thus e = -5/35 = -0.14 for this high speed case. The same data is also obtained directly by integrating the deceleration versus time recording of the accelerometers attached to the rear seat x-members, which gives the velocity versus time. Practically all of the various cars tested (at the standard NCAP speed of 35 mph) indicate an initial rebound in the speed range of 5 to 7 mph.

Post-Impact Speeds

Consider vehicle 1 impacting vehicle 2 at speed v_0, with vehicle 2 initially stationary. The two speeds after impact are

(14)
$$v_2' = \left[\frac{w_1}{w_1 + w_2}\right](1 - e)v_0$$

and

(15)
$$v_1' = \left[\frac{(w_1 + ew_2)}{(w_1 + w_2)}\right]v_0$$

Thus the final speeds depend on both the weights and the value of 'e' (remember; 'e' is really negative for typical vehicle crashes). For a perfectly elastic collision e = -1.0. We obtain

(16)
$$v_2' = \left[\frac{2w_1}{(w_1 + w_2)}\right]v_0$$

and

(17)
$$v_1' = \left[\frac{(w_1 - w_2)}{(w_1 + w_2)}\right]v_0$$

If $w_1 < w_2$ this states that the bullet vehicle bounces in the reverse direction (*i.e.*, v'_1 becomes negative), since the numerator is clearly negative. For a plastic collision (e = 0.0) both v'_1 and v'_2 become equal (the vehicles stick together) at

(18)
$$v_1' = v_2' = \left[\frac{w_1}{(w_1 + w_2)}\right]v_0$$

Real collisions lie somewhere between these extremes.

In terms of the individual delta-Vs seen by the bullet and the target, equation (12) becomes

(19)
$$(delta - v_1)^2 = \Delta v_1^2 = \frac{2E_D g w_2(1 - e)^2}{[w_1(w_1 + w_2)(1 - e^2)]}$$

(20)
$$(delta - v_2)^2 = \Delta v_2^2 = \frac{2E_D g w_1(1 - e)^2}{[w_2(w_1 + w_2)(1 - e^2)]}$$

Note that (delta-v_1)/(delta-v_2) = w_2/w_1, as required by the law of conservation of linear momentum. Note that these delta-Vs are the important ones for consideration of personal injury.

Although the above example applied for a stationary target, the various delta-Vs apply for any initial target speed. Thus equation (12) is the differential closing speed between the two vehicles, and equations (14) through (20) give the differential speeds after the collision, all relative to the true initial target speed. Thus the entire process of vehicle speed changes can be adjusted up or down linearly with the initial target speed, since this is merely a consequence of conservation of momentum. Note that this is one of the few cases where velocities can be directly added, since most other cases involve additions of energy (*e.g.*, when adding the effects of both crush and skid effects).

Coefficient of Restitution

We see that to use equations (12), (14), (15), (19) and (20) we always require the value of 'e.' However, this value is rarely quoted. Instead, many reconstructionists use rules such as "…'e' is large for low impact speeds and small for high impact speeds." While this statement is generally true, it is useless for numerical purposes. Thus, a more rigorous method is needed to define the value. Although empirical equations exist for predicting values of 'e,' these are usually little more than curve fits to data, and rarely have much theoretical (and, hence, physical) basis. Such curve fits can be misleading, since they rarely apply over the entire speed range with any reliability. These fits frequently lead to asymptotes, such as the bumper speed limit, which fail to agree with known experimental facts. One such fit for 'e' is given by Wood (ref 17). However, he cautions that it only applies for differential impact speeds above about 5 mph. Since the latter is comparable with the bumper response limit, his equation is clearly of limited use for low speed collisions.

Indeed, the usual attempt to reduce all vehicular impact responses to simple curve fits invariably results in doubtful results for interpretation of low speed collisions. Such curve fits are couched in terms of regression coefficients with quotes of standard deviations. However, when these standard deviations are several mph (which they usually are) the fits become meaningless for analysis of low speed collisions, although they are usable for higher speeds. This is because for high speeds interpolation is used within the database, whereas for low speeds extrapolation is required. The latter is always a dangerous exercise if the data are not based on a good theoretical understanding of the physical behavior. Only those enamored with statistical analysis are content with such approaches, since these approaches have little to do with physics, engineering or reality!

A classic example of this problem is the use of an equation such as the following: v (mph) = 1.3 x_{max} (inches)-6, which is quoted in the *Accident Reconstruction Journal* (example, see page 8 of the July/August, 1995 edition). When x_{max} drops to zero this equation states that the vehicle is moving away from the barrier at 6 mph! Although such fits are reasonable for significant crush damage, they clearly fail to work at low speeds. The above equation does not apply for a crush below 6/1.3 = 4.6 inches. Of course, ARJ are aware of this issue, and do not claim that such equations are meaningful for low speeds.

Since e = (delta-bounce velocity)/(delta-input velocity) then e^2 = (bounce energy)/(input energy). Thus, the effective value of 'e' can be deduced by considering the recovered energy versus the initial input energy. The recovered energy of each vehicle is given by equation (8), for a simple-spring bumper response. Thus by summing the total recovered energies and dividing by the total input energy, the value of 'e' is determined. As a simple example, for a rigid barrier impact, and a perfect-spring response, we have

(21)
$$e^2 = \frac{\left\{\left(\frac{wv_L^2}{2g}\right)\left[1+\frac{x_{final}}{a}\right]\right\}}{\left(\frac{wv_{in}^2}{2g}\right)} = \left(\frac{v_L^2}{v_{in}^2}\right)\left(1+\frac{x_{final}}{a}\right)$$

thus,

(22)
$$e = \left(\frac{v_L}{v_{in}}\right)\left[1+\frac{x_{final}}{a}\right]^{\frac{1}{2}} \quad \text{(absolute value)}$$

Thus the value of 'e' gradually increases slightly with increasing vehicle damage, but decreases even faster with increasing impact speed. Also, note that the speed differential after impact is given by

(23)
$$(v_2' - v_1') = -(v_1' - v_2') = -ev_{in} = -v_L\left[1+\frac{x_{final}}{a}\right]^{\frac{1}{2}}$$

Since the quantity $[1+x_{final}/a]^{1/2}$ changes only relatively slowly with impact speed, the post-impact differential speed also changes only slowly with the impact speed, and is almost a constant value. This effect has been observed for many vehicle collisions (ref 2). Equation (23) explains the observed bounces off the rigid barrier for the NCAP tests.

Clearly, equation (12) is insensitive to the exact value of 'e,' provided the latter is small. Thus the solution is quite accurate for higher speed impacts, and an assumption of e -> 0.0 will yield reasonable results, and equation (18) will roughly apply. However, equation (12) is *very* sensitive to the value of 'e' when the latter approaches the value -1.0, as are equations (14) and (15). This applies for the case of a low speed impact. It should be noted that, while reconstruction schools like Northwestern University Traffic Institute (NUTI) do explain the meaning of restitution, they never actually use it in any equation. This is because such schools really teach only the effects of the higher speed impacts. Indeed, NUTI states "*...in very low-velocity impacts, however, restitution may have to be considered.*"

However, as mentioned earlier, most modern bumpers involve some degree of internal energy absorption owing to the use of viscous responses. This means that a download factor of 'f' is appropriate. Thus, e → fe, where f is less than 1.0. The previous description assumed that 'e' = -1.0 provided the bumper limit speed was not exceeded. Experimental data show that 'e' is generally somewhat less than -1.0 when the bumper limit is reached. Since viscous response usually gives forces proportional to speed, the simplest modification is of the form

(24)

$$f = \left(1 - \frac{pv}{v_L}\right)$$

where v is the impact speed (less than the bumper limit) and v_L is the bumper limit speed, and 'p' is a simple number less than 1.0. Experiments suggest that 'p' is about 0.3 - 0.5. Thus, at the bumper limit, e = 0.7 - 0.5 for many cars. For higher impact speeds the plastic deformation effects give the rapid drop in 'e' mentioned before. So for impacts exceeding the bumper limits the value of 'e' given by equation (22) should be multiplied by about 0.7 - 0.5.

It should be noted that even the rigid barriers generally use a facing sheet of 0.75 inches of plywood. Unfortunately, it is well known that wood itself displays significant plastic and viscous response (if you hammer on wood it will dent and only slowly recover). Further, this thickness of wood is not negligible compared to the amplitude of bumper motion, although it is small compared to the total crush for a 35 mph impact. Consequently, the observed bounce from the barrier is frequently a measure of both the bumper response and of the properties of the wood, rather than simply of the bumper assembly itself, and so misleading apparent low values of 'e' can be inferred for low speed impacts. Unfortunately, very few low speed barrier tests have been done without the plywood.

The reason for using the 0.75 inch sheet of plywood is to protect the rigid barrier. Although the barrier is made with a front surface of steel, after sufficient impacts the steel will suffer damage. Since the barrier is large and heavy, repair would be expensive. Hence the plywood is used as a sacrificial bumper, which is inexpensive to replace. The fact that the plywood needs to be replaced is proof that it suffers permanent damage, due to plastic and viscous deformation.

Another reason for confusion with regard to low speed values of 'e' concerns failure to conserve momentum in experimental car-to-car tests. Equation (21) applies only to a single vehicle/rigid barrier. For two vehicles impacting above the critical speeds defined below, we must add the two elastic energies for both vehicles. For example, Szabo and Welcher (ref 18) performed impacts using Ford Escorts for both bullets and targets. Tests were done with initial bullet speeds of 5 mph (2.23 m/s), 10 mph (4.47 m/s) and 15 mph (6.71 m/s) into stationary targets. Yet their own data indicated that at the common velocity the total momentum was only about 85% of the initial, and no discussion of the missing 15% is given. No braking was employed. Further, the measurements indicated that about 65% of the initial kinetic energy was absorbed for the two higher speeds.

For a totally plastic collinear collision of two identical bodies the maximum possible energy loss can only be 50%. To lose more implies an imaginary value of 'e.' Some other mechanism is clearly removing both linear momentum and energy. This makes the true value of 'e' difficult to determine. Lastly, Szabo and Welcher's measurements of vehicle accelerations frequently displayed double humps. These accelerometers were mounted at the vehicle centers of mass. This two-peak behavior was almost certainly a consequence of beating between the pseudo-spring response of car-on-bumper and the natural oscillation behavior of the car structure. Such beating can easily give erroneous response, because the measured result will vary from position to position in the car. The only way to avoid it is to use many differently located accelerometers and to average their responses. Better still, if the intent is to measure bumper response then the bumpers should be mounted on a very rigid body so that only the bumper behavior is measured rather than the combined bumper/car response.

Finally, it should be noted that very few so-called in line collisions are truly so. Many of the NCAP crashes indicate some form of yawing and pitching. High speed video frequently shows that the rear wheels lift up off the ground during the impact. This implies that the bumper thrust must be acting somewhat below the vehicle center of mass (CM). The resulting pitching rotation implies some of the initial vehicle energy has been converted into rotational energy. The same applies to any yawing. However, the pitching effect is small since the car only rises a few inches, whereas the 35 mph initial speed is the equivalent of a 41-foot drop under gravity.

It is sometimes mistakenly thought that conservation of momentum can be demonstrated by good repeatability of experiments. However, this merely demonstrates *precision*, not *accuracy*. The latter term relates to the correct answer, whereas the former only relates to repeatability, even if the answer is wrong each time. For example, a well-machined ruler may always give a length of 12.001 inches, or 11.999 inches, when measuring one foot, due to a systematic error caused by temperature effects (the ruler shrank or elongated).

The only real way to prove conservation of momentum between impacting vehicles is to perform an inverted test. Consider an impact between vehicles A and B. There is a decrease in velocity for A (-delta-v_A) and an increase in velocity for B (+delta-v_B) which are related purely by the weight ratio. Now reverse the experiment, and impact A with B. This will again give two delta-v' values, but now the ratio is inverted. If the product of the two sets of delta-vs equals unity, momentum is being conserved. Thus

$$\text{-delta-}v_A / \text{delta-}v_B = w_B / w_A \text{ and } \text{-delta-}v_B' / \text{delta-}v_A' = w_A / w_B$$

and thus

$$(\text{-delta-}v_A / \text{delta-}v_B)(\text{-delta-}v_B' / \text{delta-}v_A') = (w_B/w_A)(w_A/w_B) = 1.0$$

There have been several reports of simulated low speed car crashes where the data clearly implies that momentum is not being conserved since there have been cases that actually involved these inverted crashes. Unfortunately, the authors of these papers failed to note their problem! This makes the experimental data somewhat suspect, particularly where quotes of coefficient of restitution are being given. The values of ‘e’ for such tests vary wildly for many of these low speed crashes, and have even been known to locally *increase* with increasing speed. This is *normally* physically impossible unless the cars have some form of hidden internal energy source! While systems *can* be designed to cause increases in ‘e’ (such as the military’s reactive armor), there would be no useful purpose in so doing in civilian automotive applications. The coefficient of restitution can *only* decrease as impact speeds increase. This is due to either greater viscous damping or greater plastic flow. Thus, great care must be taken with regard to some of the published data.

The failure to conserve momentum sometimes has an obvious cause, such as cars applying brakes during impact. In these cases momentum is being transferred to the road. This effect is greatest when very low speeds (below about 3 mph) are involved. However, many of the tests do not involve braking. For these cases the missing momentum is less easy to explain. Part of the problem may relate to the time over which the data is measured. There is always some rocking motion of a car on its suspension when impacted, and this motion involves a natural oscillation period. Unless the data is recorded over a time equal to several such oscillations (which damp out), it is possible to catch the data during an oscillation and record an unexpected answer. Unfortunately, few authors give enough experimental data to allow for a simple evaluation of such effects.

Similar oddities have been noticed in the detailed NCAP reports. For example, the load cells on the rigid barrier occasionally read tensions. Since nothing can pull on these cells, this is not possible. The errant tensile readings are probably due to induced oscillations in the barrier and the cells themselves (dynamic overshoot). However, oscillations in the rigid barrier prove that it is not really rigid.

Critical Damage Speed

Since different vehicles have different crush characteristics, it is necessary to include these facts in order to determine the minimum critical impact energy that barely causes vehicle damage for a two-vehicle collision. One vehicle will be weaker than the other, and thus the general rule is that one vehicle will start to suffer damage at a first critical limit while the other is still within the bumper limit. Note that here the "bumper limit" may not actually involve a bumper; instead any threshold limit that describes the onset of permanent damage can be construed to represent a bumper. However, above a second critical limit, both vehicles will suffer damage. Thus, there is a window of limits. Consider a moving bullet vehicle impacting a stationary target vehicle. It can then be shown that the first limit is given by

$$v_{crit,1}^2 = \left[\frac{(w_1 + w_2)}{w_1}\right] v_{L2}^2 \left[1 + \left(\frac{w_2}{w_1}\right)\left(\frac{R_2}{R_1}\right)^2 \left(\frac{v_{L1}}{v_{L2}}\right)^2\right] \tag{25}$$

where the v_L values apply to each bumper limit, and R values apply to each vehicle. There are several options. In all cases vehicle 1 is the heavier and stronger one.

(i) For the rigid barrier case we set w_1 and R_1 to very large values (*i.e.,* the barrier is both massive and strong). The solution is simply $v_{crit,1} = v_{L2}$, as expected from the definition of the barrier bumper speed.

(ii) For $w_1 = w_2$, but a large value of R_1, we obtain $v_{crit,1}^2 = 2v_{L2}^2$. Thus, the critical speed is 1.414 x the bumper limit speed. This situation represents a collision with a similar weight body which is very strong and cannot crush (*e.g.,* a concrete "car" on wheels), and/or has no bumper. Note that this condition applies to some of the NHTSA and IIHS tests, where such a concrete "car" is indeed used to test for rearend and side collision damage (the vehicle is actually a very rigid-frame of steel on wheels).

(iii) For two identical vehicles, we obtain $v_{crit,1}^2 = 4v_{L2}^2 = 4v_{L1}^2$. Thus, the critical speed is twice the bumper limit speed.

Note that for a very rigid second body but with a weight different from the tested car, the critical speed for bumper damage depends only on weights and the car bumper limit. This is merely a variant on case (ii), and essentially removes the square-bracket portion of equation (25). This is the situation that applies to the pendulum test that is frequently used to test bumper responses, and regularly used by organizations such as Consumers Union to check for car response. For instance, by knowing the ratio of weights for the vehicle and pendulum, the drop height can be adjusted to give the necessary impact speed that corresponds to a rigid barrier crash at 5 mph. Consumers Union regularly does this test to simulate a 5-mph barrier impact, and then note the degree of induced damage. Those vehicles with 5 mph bumpers display zero damage, whereas those with weaker bumpers indicate damage. Although the amount of damage may be quite small, the cost of repair can easily reach $1000.

Equation (25) is based on the logic that vehicle 2 (the weaker one) has just absorbed enough energy to exceed its bumper limit, and has thus just reached its damage force ($F_{0,2}$), while vehicle 1 is only absorbing a fraction of its bumper limit energy and has not yet reached its own damage force limit. The force is equal in magnitude for both vehicles.

Equation (25) has "symmetry" built-in. To appreciate this, consider two vehicles which are identical *except* for their bumper speed limits. Let $v_{L,1} = 5$ mph and $v_{L,2} = 2.5$ mph. We also have $(w_1 + w_2)/w_1 = 2.0$, $(w_2/w_1) = 1.0$ and $(R_2/R_1) = 1.0$. Substitution into equation (25) then gives $v_{crit,1} = 7.91$ mph as the first critical speed for damage to either car. However, if we switch cars and invert the bumper limits, we obtain the same answer. This is to be expected since the critical closing speed must be independent of which vehicle has what properties, since it is a mutual answer.

The second critical limit is given by

(26)

$$v_{crit,2}^2 = \left[\frac{(w_1+w_2)}{w_1}\right]\left\{v_{L1}^2 + \left(\frac{w_2}{w_1}\right)v_{L2}^2 + \frac{\left(12ga_2[R_{0,1}w_1 - R_{0,2}w_2]^2\right)}{(R_{0,2}w_1w_2)} + \left(\frac{24ga_2}{w_1}\right)[R_{0,1}w_1 - R_{0,2}w_2]\right\}$$

This limit is seen to depend on the 'a' value of the weaker vehicle. This is because when the stronger vehicle just reaches its damage force value the weaker vehicle is already partway along its crush curve. As with equation (25), if the two vehicles are identical, $v_{crit,2} = 2v_{L1} = 2v_{L2,}$ etc.

When these facts are combined with equation (12) it is possible to derive the following equation giving the differential closing speed for a two-vehicle collision that involves damage to only one vehicle:

(27)

$$v_{close}^2 = \left[\frac{(w_1 + w_2)}{w_1}\right]v_{L2}^2\left[1 + \left(\frac{w_2}{w_1}\right)\left(\frac{R_2}{R_1}\right)^2\left(\frac{v_{L1}}{V_{L2}}\right)^2\right] + \frac{2gE_D(w_1 + w_2)}{(w_1w_2)}$$

Note that for high speed collisions the second term in equation (27) is much larger than the first term because of the large value of E_D. For these cases the first term can be ignored. This reduces equation (27) to the same as equation (12), but with e = 0.0.

In view of all the above, it should be obvious that it is *not* possible to deduce the vehicle impact speeds merely by looking at the vehicle damage. The degree of damage merely allows one to calculate the absorbed energies, then it is necessary to use equation (27) with the vehicle weights, R values and bumper limit speeds, in order to compute a speed. Finally, this speed is not absolute, but is instead the differential speed between the two vehicles. To establish absolute speeds other information is required, such as knowledge of the post-impact skid mark lengths.

To prove this latter point, consider a simple case of the bullet vehicle moving at 20 mph striking a target at zero mph. Are these the two speeds? Answer: NO! An equally good answer is that the two speeds are 920 mph and 900 mph! Why? Because the vehicles are on a rotating Earth and are moving around the latter's North-South axis at about 900 mph!. This simple, if perhaps, nonsensical, example illustrates very clearly that the only velocity derived from an energy-of-crush analysis is the *differential* speed.

Examples of the above logic for solution to the two-vehicle bumper-to-bumper impact are given in figure 14a, b and c. The independent variable is the total absorbed crush energy. Figure 14a gives the differential closing speed of the bullet vehicle versus the target as the crush energy increases, with the speed increasing from the lower critical speed at crush energy of zero. Figure 14b shows the corresponding behavior for the coefficient of restitution. As the crush energy increases, the value of 'e' rapidly decreases. Finally, figure 14c shows the post-impact vehicle speeds. Note how the difference in these latter speeds is almost constant.

All of the above logic presupposes that both vehicles have spring-like bumpers which return to their initial state after impact. This ensures that e = -(1-p) at the bumper limits. For real bumpers the effective value of 'e' is lower than -1.0 as the bumper limit speed is approached. However, this does not influence the definition of the critical speeds; it merely alters the post-impact speeds of the vehicles, causing the differential to be somewhat smaller.

Numerical Values of R and 'a'

There are several sources of data which characterize the actual crush response of many cars. These include data from the National Highway Traffic and Safety Administration (NHTSA, as quoted by Expert Autostats™, ref 19), from Limpert (ref 2), from Noon (ref 20), from the Northwestern University Traffic Institute

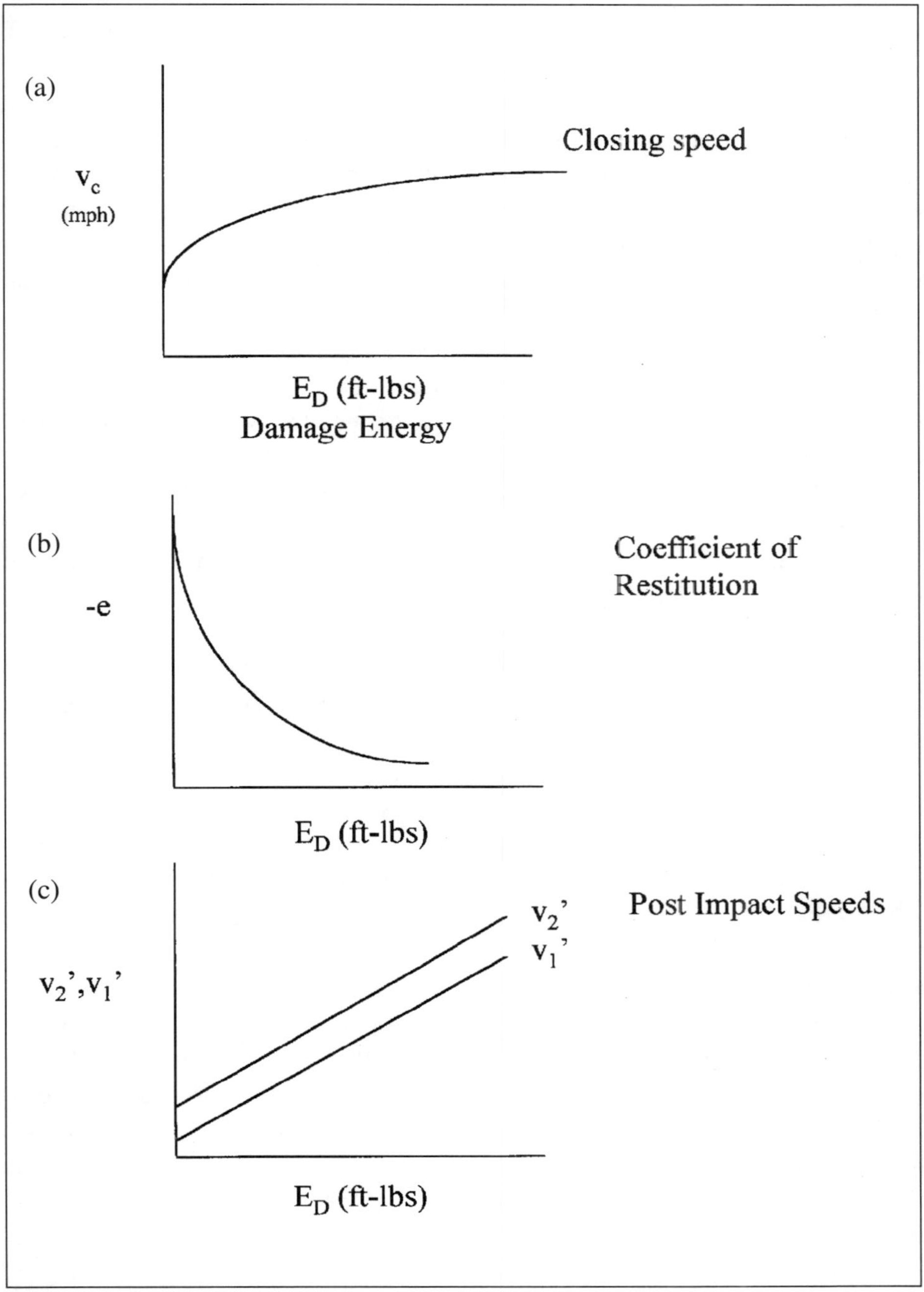

Figure 14 *Two-Vehicle Responses.*

(data from Severy, ref 21, and the CRASH3 model, ref 22), from Severy (ref 23), and from Lundstrom (ref 24). Other sources are also available (ref 25). Unfortunately, not all of these data are consistent.

Older data (Severy, Lundstrom) indicated that the crush depth versus impact speed was roughly linear for rigid barrier collisions. Also, data from Severy indicated that the under-seat peak deceleration was roughly a linear function of impact speed. However, scrutiny of these data show that these conclusions are not particularly convincing. For example, most of the impact speeds are clustered about 25 - 40 mph, with only a few data points at higher speeds and practically no data at lower speeds. Consequently, almost *any* line can be made to pass through the points. This linear approach is the one adopted by NUTI (using the CRASH3 model). This approach implies low values for both the R and 'a' terms. This then implies low initial vehicle accelerations at incipient crush but with very rapid increases in acceleration as crush depth increases (see also chapter 5(b)).

However, data from Expert Autostats™ and Noon imply an almost constant crush strength versus crush depth. Wood (ref 17) also assumes a step function of constant crush strength regions per step versus crush. This implies a multi-part square-root dependence of velocity versus crush depth, and thus large values of R and 'a.' Finally, Limpert gives empirical fits to data which again imply a rough square-root behavior.

It should be noted that all these various fits pass close to each other for impact speeds near 30 - 35 mph. This is hardly surprising, however, since this is where the majority of the data exist. However, only NUTI gives results which imply the existence of bumpers, with most other data asymptoting to zero speed at zero crush. This is clearly wrong. Unfortunately, the CRASH3 data frequently predict zero crush at speeds *greater* than 5 mph, which is also incorrect (unless it is proven that a specific vehicle has unusually good bumpers).

The data from both Noon and Limpert support a well-known fact, namely that for impacts into rigid barriers, larger cars suffer greater crush depths. Wood also notes a similar effect. The reason is simple: larger cars have longer hoods and can therefore be designed to have greater crush depths for a given impact speed. This accords with simple physics. Consequently, larger cars give lower decelerations to the occupants, and are therefore safer for the passengers. This effect gives R values which decrease as the vehicle weights increase. However, the crush force (*i.e.,* F=12Rw) increases with vehicle weight. Thus, larger cars are stronger than small cars. This results in a second effect: in a collision between a large car and a small one, the larger car always "wins" in that the crush depth is smaller for the large car than for the small car. Further, owing to the weight ratio, the large car suffers a smaller deceleration than does the small car. Again, larger cars are safer. Figure 15 illustrates the data from Noon. Wood states that the crush strength tends to scale with the vehicle mass to the 2/3rd power, while the crush depth itself scales with the 1/3rd power of the vehicle mass. This essentially agrees with the Noon and Limpert data. Note that, when normalized versus vehicle mass, a force proportional to the 2/3rd power of mass implies a power law for force-per-weight (R) which is the inverse of the 1/3rd power of mass. Thus Wood's data again indicates that as the vehicle weight increases so the value of R decreases (with roughly a $1/w^{1/3}$ law). Thus for an increase in weight of a factor of 2.0, the value of R decreases by about 1.26, while the actual crush force increases by about 1.59. Likewise, for a given speed, the crush depth increases by about 1.26 for a rigid barrier impact.

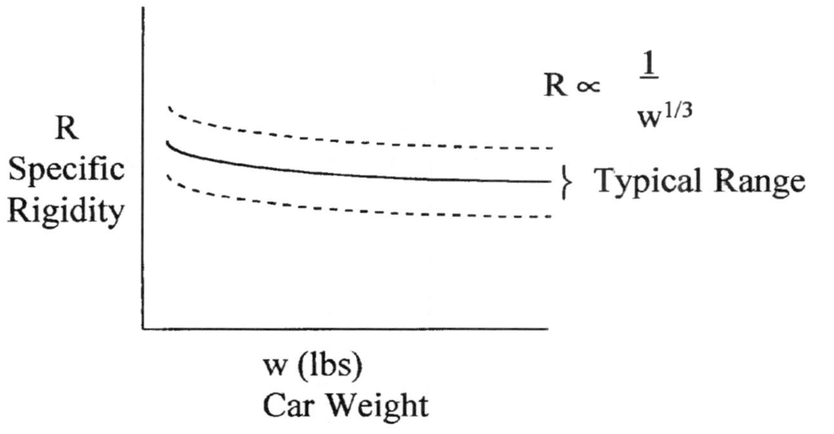

Figure 15 *Rigidity Versus Weight.*

Using these approximations we can rewrite equation (25) by noting that the ratio $(R_2/R_1)^2 = (w_1/w_2)^{2/3}$. Thus the product $(w_2/w_1)(R_2/R_1)^2 = (w_2/w_1)^{1/3}$. Hence, we obtain

(28)
$$v_{crit,1}^2 = \left[\frac{(w_1 + w_2)}{w_1}\right] v_{L2}^2 \left[1 + \left(\frac{w_2}{w_1}\right)^{\frac{1}{3}} \left(\frac{v_{L1}}{v_{L2}}\right)^2\right]$$

This effect of large car versus small car explains part of the dilemma with the NCAP car crash results. A simple study of the raw NCAP data implies that small cars can be just as good as large ones. However, the data only applies to the fixed speed rigid barrier tests, which are the equivalent of a mirror image crash between two identical cars with identical speeds. Real life frequently involves impacts between cars of different size, and thus *only then* does the advantage of larger cars become apparent. The problem relates to the fact that real traffic involves a spread in vehicle weights. If all vehicles were of the same weight then the NCAP results would directly relate to real accident crashworthiness.

This large versus small behavior is at the root of NHTSA's dilemma with regard to how to "explain" the meaning of its NCAP test results. Frequently, a "one-star" large car can actually be safer than a "five-star" small car, for the average mixed-weight crash. However, to state this in plain English NHTSA would encourage car buyers to always purchase large cars. Since large (heavy) cars consume more fuel, this would worsen the overall fuel consumption for the US as a whole. The predicament for NHTSA would then be that this response would fly in the face of another government ruling, the CAFE (Corporate Average Fuel Efficiency), which forces the automobile manufacturers to ensure that their average fleet of vehicles (by sales volume) maintains a certain overall fuel economy. We have previously pointed out that using different materials can improve the strength-to-weight ratios, thereby allowing lighter strong cars. Unfortunately, these "aerospace" techniques, such as using high-strength aluminum alloys (such as 7075) are much more expensive. Thus the consumer would balk at the resulting cost.

The Noon data really give the average values for R over speed ranges of 20 - 40 mph. Thus, we must reinterpret in order to obtain R_0 and 'a.' Figure 16 illustrates how this can be done. The correspondence is simply $R_{ave} = R_0(1 + x/2a)$. By comparing the options versus the data from Limpert and others the effective values can be deduced.

Contact Time

A vehicle crash occurs in a very short time. Treating the system as a mass-on-spring, the contact time is one-half the natural period of oscillation. This oscillation frequency is given by

(29)

$$\varpi^2 = \frac{K}{m} = \frac{Kg}{w} = (2\pi)^2 f^2 = \frac{(2\pi)^2}{T^2}$$

where w is the angular frequency (radians/s), K is the spring rate (force per unit motion, lbs per foot), m is the mass, w is the weight, f is the frequency (Hz, or cycles per sec), p = 3.1416, and T is the period. In the elastic regime the value of

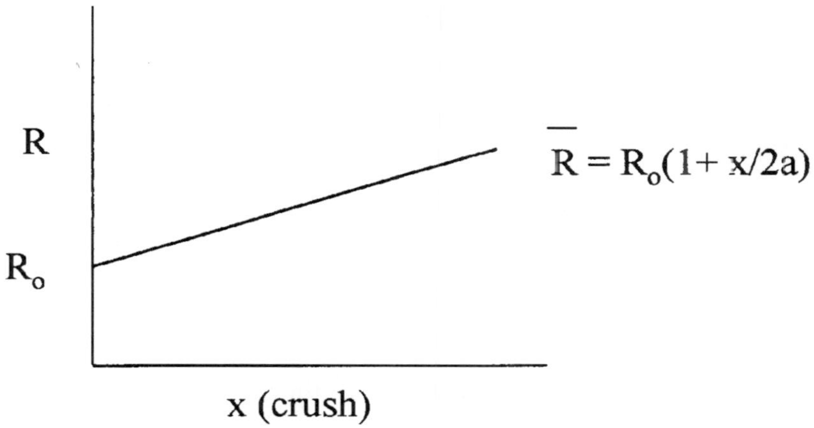

Figure 16 *Vehicle Rigidity Versus Crush.*

K is given by the incipient crush force ($12R_0w$) divided by the bumper amplitude ($x_0 = v_L^2/12R_0g$, see chapter 3(a)). Thus, we obtain

(30)

$$\varpi = 2\pi f = \frac{2\pi}{T} = \frac{12R_o g}{v_L}$$

Thus,

(31)

$$T = \frac{2\pi v_L}{12R_0 g}$$

For the rigid barrier case, an elastic collision involves a contact time given by one half of the period

(32)

$$t_{contact} = \frac{\pi v_L}{12R_0 g}$$

For $v_L = 7.335$ ft/s, and $R_0 = 1.0$, this is about 0.06 sec (!), and even for a low R_0 value of 0.5 the time is only 0.12 sec.

The rigid barrier case assumes that the second body is infinitely massive. For a two-vehicle collision, the contact time is one-half the period for the coupled pair. To compute this we use the reduced effective spring rate and reduced weight for the pair. The reduced spring rate and weight are given by

(33)

$$K_{red} = \frac{K_1 K_2}{(K_1 + K_2)} \quad \text{and} \quad w_{red} = \frac{w_1 w_2}{(w_1 + w_2)}, \text{ respectively}$$

Note that reduced values involve the ratio of product over sum. This is similar to the rule for parallel resistances in electrical circuits. This gives

(34)

$$t_{contact} = \left(\frac{\pi}{12 R_{01} R_{02} g}\right)\left[\frac{(R_{01}^2 w_1 v_{L2}^2 + R_{02}^2 w_2 v_{L1}^2)}{(w_1 + w_2)}\right]^{\frac{1}{2}}$$

When the two vehicles are identical, this gives the same answer as for the rigid barrier case.

For a plastic deformation the total contact time increases, but is still rarely much more than 0.1- 0.2 sec for most cases. These very short contact times are faster than a human response time necessary to innervate the muscles (typically 0.1 - 0.2 sec), which explains the inability of the occupants to immediately fight the induced motions by application of their muscles. Thus their body parts tend to flop around as for a rag doll. These effects are important for considerations of occupant kinematics. The exact contact time for the plastic case is given by using the effective spring constants for the plastic flow region of figure 10, line AB. This slope is simply $K = 12R_0w/a$ for each vehicle. Then we obtain

(35)

$$t_{contact} = \left(\frac{\pi}{2}\right)\left\{\frac{[R_{01} w_1 a_2 + R_{02} w_2 a_1]}{[12 g R_{01} R_{02} (w_1 + w_2)]}\right\}^{\frac{1}{2}}$$

If the two vehicles are identical we obtain $t_{contact} = (\pi/2)\ \{a/12R_0g\}^{1/2}$, which is also the answer for the rigid barrier impact. For equation (35) the value of 'a' is in units of feet. Note the leading factor of 1/2 in equation (35). This arises because the plastic contact time represents only one quarter (1/4) of a period, since it only applies during the loading part of the motion. This assumes moderate plastic deformation where the initial elastic response is overshadowed by the plastic response (otherwise during the loading phase we have a mixture of elastic and plastic response). For the unloading response we again have pseudo-elastic behavior, but also only for 1/4 period. Thus equation (35) really describes the stopping time before any bounce. Note that a measurement of this time gives the ratio (a/R_0) for the rigid barrier impact, which can be compared with the values deduced from the velocity-crush data. The total contact time for a crash is simply the sum of the plastic quarter-period (if crush damage occurs) and the elastic quarter-period. Setting a = 10 inches = 0.833 ft, and using $R_0 = 0.5$, the rigid barrier stopping time becomes 0.103 seconds, while for $R_0 = 1.0$ the time is 0.073 seconds.

Inspection of the detailed NCAP reports indicate that many vehicles stop in about 0.08 seconds, and disengage from the rigid barrier after about 0.14 seconds, in approximate agreement with these predictions. Plots of the speed versus time for these crashes also demonstrate that the responses are very similar to a damped half-cycle harmonic motion. Figure 17 illustrates typical speed versus time behavior for both low speeds and high speeds.

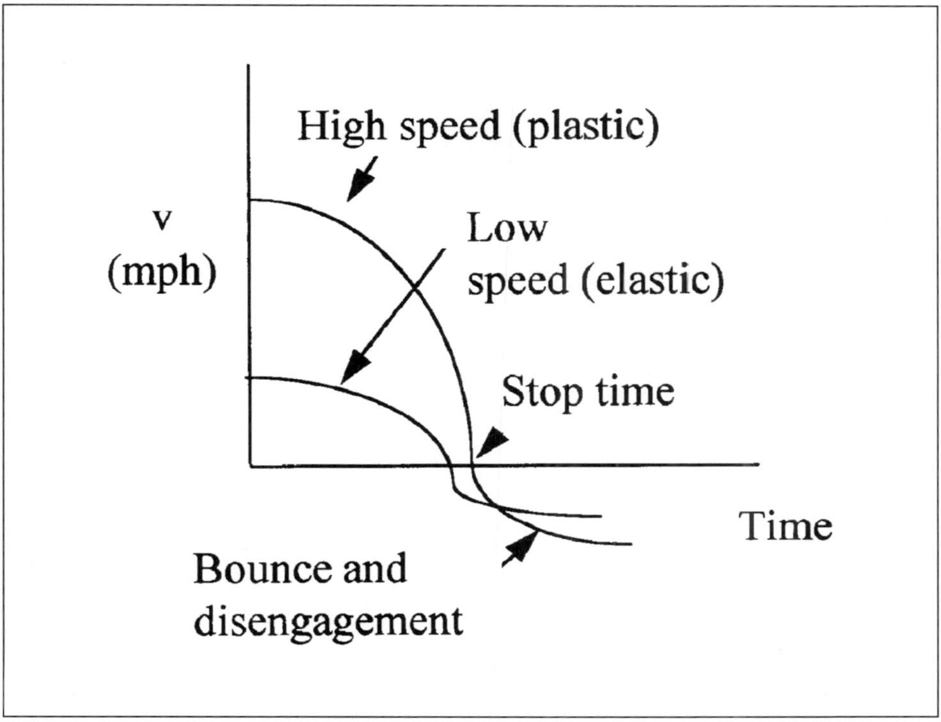

Figure 17 *Rigid Barrier Speed vs. Time.*

Distance moved during impact

It is important to realize that a stationary target moves very little during a low speed impact. For an impact which just reaches the target bumper limit the distance moved by the target while the bullet and target reach their common speed is only $(\pi/2 - 1)\ x_0 = 0.57\ x_0$, where x_0 is the bumper amplitude. The total distance moved by the target until vehicle separation is $\pi x_0 = 3.14\ x_0$. The value of $x_0 = v_L^2 / (R_0\ g)$ in inches with the speed in ft/s. For $v_L = 5$ mph = 7.335 ft/s and $R_0 = 0.5$ the bumper amplitude is only 3.34 inches. Thus as the vehicles approach their common speed the target only moves about 1.9 inches, and when the vehicles finally disengage the target motion would be 10.5 inches. The above analysis assumes the bumper assembly acts in a pseudo-elastic fashion, and ignores any target vehicle braking. With significant rebound damping the time to disengage increases, but the final bounce speed is also less, so the target motion usually slightly decreases during the rebound stage. For a target which is moving at initial speed v_0 the quantity $v_0 t_{contact}$ must be added to these motions. Figure 18 illustrates these effects.

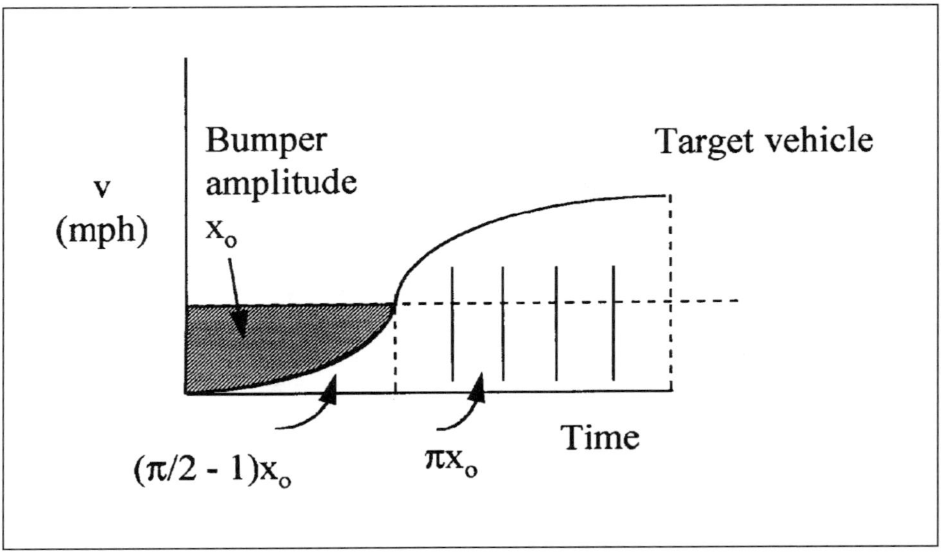

Figure 18 *Motion of Target.*

Braking during Impact

Because an impact takes a finite time and involves a finite motion, the application of braking involves a finite loss of energy and momentum to the road during the collision. While this effect is negligible at the higher speeds, it may produce significant effects at very low speeds. This may be partly the reason for some of the experimental problems mentioned before. Although most of the staged car-to-car crashes have not used braking, some degree of friction is always present.

A simplification can be employed to determine the effect of pre-applied braking for the target. Suppose the target has a bumper limit of 5 mph (v_L). If the vehicle is impacted from rest up to its bumper limit it will then bounce away to finally achieve the speed of $(1 \text{ -}e)v_L$. Thus for a perfectly elastic case the final speed is 10 mph, which is also the delta-v seen by the target. However, to reach the time of disengagement takes a one-half period (T/2), as given in equation

(32). If during this time the brakes apply a drag factor of f, then the vehicle speed will be reduced by approximately delta-v = fgT/2. This is only approximate since it ignores the fact that the target does not start moving until after the bumper force exceed the frictional force, as described in section 4i. Thus, this correction is an overestimation. Substituting for T/2 we obtain delta-v = $(\pi v_L/12R_0)$f. For v_L = 5 mph and R_0 = 0.5, delta-v = 2.68 f mph. Thus with hard braking (f = 0.75), delta-v = 1.96 mph. Hence the true peak speed reached by the target is now only 10 - 1.96 = 8.04 mph. This is the equivalent of having a value of 'e' of -0.607. If, instead, f = 0.4, the peak speed is about 10 - 1.04 = 8.95 mph, implying an effective 'e' of -0.79. Even for f = 0.1, the effective value of 'e' becomes -0.946. This effect helps explain why measured values for 'e' are always below -1.0, even for a highly elastic inherent bumper response.

Note that since delta-v is mostly determined by the half-period (T/2), which is not dependent on amplitude for an elastic system, the degradation in apparent 'e' becomes greater as the speeds decrease. Thus, for a push to 3 mph (the common speed of both vehicles) and elastic bounce to 6 mph, the delta-v of 2.68 f mph now reduces the peak speed to only 3.99 mph, for f = 0.75, and the effective value of 'e' is -0.33, even for a truly elastic bumper response. This simple logic states that the car hardly moves if the initial induced common speed is below about 2.68x0.75 = 2 mph, for hard braking. This is again a low value similar to that quoted in section 4i.

Note that when the target has its brakes applied it effectively increases its apparent weight at low speeds. This causes the bullet to slow more than it otherwise would. Thus, the target sees a reduced overall delta-v while the bullet sees an increased delta-v. However, these effects are occurring at such low speeds that personal injury is unlikely, unless the person has a predisposition to injury.

The above assumed that the frictional drag was f. However, this is the effective value since we are dealing with a two-vehicle impact. The effective value of drag is only equal to that of the target if both bullet and target have the same friction. Hence the proper value to use is given by $f_{average} = (f_{bullet}\, w_{bullet} + f_{target}\, w_{target})/(w_{bullet} + w_{target})$. Thus if the bullet is heavy and does not apply its brakes, the effective value of f is small, even for strong braking of the target.

The Engineer's Box

While figure 15 shows the gradual decrease in R with increase in vehicle weight, it also indicates a remarkably small spread in R values for a given weight. This can be explained by considering the "engineer's box." The engineer invariably finds himself struggling to satisfy several conflicting requirements. As a result, he finds he is in a box that limits his options. For example, he must: (i) minimize the weight to give good fuel mileage; (ii) ensure sufficient body rigidity to prevent body flex on rough roads; (iii) design the crush characteristics consistent with the vehicle not crushing too much or too little; and (iv) do this at a reasonable cost.

The net result is that two different engineers will tend to produce very similar designs in terms of crush characteristics for a given vehicle weight. This explains the observations of Wood, that most vehicles have remarkably similar strength/crush properties when normalized to the weights, regardless of maker or designer. However, a superior strength-to-weight car can be designed by using specialty metals, such as titanium and special aluminum alloy (as do very specialized car makers such as Bugatti), but the cost of the car then becomes prohibitive. The sheet metal panels can be replaced by fiberglass, but the latter is brittle and absorbs less energy than structural steel. Thus, this effect must be offset by redesigning the remainder of the vehicle. Note that this brittle response for fiberglass (and many other Plastics) explains why the frame of a car is not made with such materials. The car would crack in half rather than provide the gentle ride down associated with plastic deformation in metals.

The small observed spread in R values implies that exact numbers for a given vehicle are usually not necessary, unless high accuracy is intended in a given analysis. The uncertainties associated with using average behavior can generally be held to less than ±10% for speed predictions. Indeed, larger uncertainties can be attributed to unknowns in the exact conditions of an incomplete impact. Lastly, the actual measurement and determination of the crush depth itself is often ambiguous, since it is rare for the observed surfaces to move in a clean linear manner. Instead, the once-simple surface is frequently corrugated and folded in odd ways. In this respect, low speed impacts are actually simpler, since the small degree of damage usually involves a pushed-in bumper which is still basically straight.

Note that for litigation purposes it is rarely necessary to require very high accuracy in the computations. This is because court battles are usually of the form "was the speed greater than that necessary to…(exceed the speed limit, cause the injury, etc.)," and determining who was at fault. This rarely requires estimates with several significant figures, and such estimates would be meaningless for many cases owing to uncertainties elsewhere (*exact* drag factor on the road, weight of vehicle plus payload, bone breaking strength, etc.).

Rule of Thumb: The "one mph per inch crush" rule

An *approximate* rule frequently quoted is that each incremental inch of crush represents about one mph of equivalent barrier speed, for a full-frontal collision. Can this be explained? The answer is yes. Consider that when a car crashes the velocity-time history is essentially a damped sinusoid, and the time to stop (t_{stop}) is effectively a quarter period, where T is the period. Then it can be shown that the initial velocity (v) and the amplitude of motion (x, the crush) are related by v = ωx, where $\omega = 2\pi f = 2\pi/T = \pi/2t_{stop}$, where f is the frequency (Hz) and ω is the angular rate (radians/s). Since a typical crash causes the vehicle to stop in about 0.08 secs (ignoring any bounce), we obtain ω = 19.6 radians/s. Thus we get v (ft/s) = 19.6 x (ft), or v (mph) = 19.6/(12 x 1.467) x (inches) = 1.12 x (inches). Thus the numerical multiplier is a direct inverse function of the stopping time, and is close to the value of 1.0. This rule is only appropriate for the higher speeds, where bumper response can be ignored.

Incomplete and Side Impacts

If an impact does not involve the full width of a bumper, we have an incomplete impact. Clearly, this will give an asymmetric crush damage profile. For the same mean depth of crush, the volume of metal involved in the crush is necessarily less than that for the full bumper case, and the energy absorbed is also less. The issue is how to correctly interpret this effect. The CRASH3 model assumes that the damage energy should be apportioned in a linear manner as a function of damage width, and thus volume. This logic assumes that the vehicle is comprised of totally independent small parts, such that each part crushes independently of its neighbor. Clearly, this is not strictly correct since these parts have cross-connections. A simple example is the bending of a cantilever beam. When a load is applied to the free end of the beam, maximum amplitude of motion occurs at that end. But there is a stress distribution along the entire beam, and the maximum stresses occur at the clamped end. Indeed, the maximum absorbed energy occurs at the clamped end. Thus when plastic flow occurs it is at the clamped end, although the maximum observed permanent shift is at the free end. In a similar manner, crushing the right of a vehicle necessarily applies loads to the left side.

The concept that energy is proportional to the volume of damage would be correct for an isotropic homogeneous body such as a simple block of steel, where the strength and moduli are the same in all directions. However, a real car does not behave this way. Consequently, for an oblique or incomplete impact, it is necessary to resolve the forces and deformations into orthogonal ones along the longitudinal vehicle axis and perpendicular to this axis, and to sum the independent energies. Nevertheless, the use of the volume concept is reasonable for first-order analysis. Thus if the damage profile extends only across the fraction, f, of the car width, the corresponding energy and force terms are also a fraction f of the values for a full-width deformation, at least to first order. However, Wood has pointed out that for typical car structures, there is a tendency for the internal stresses to average out regardless of the exact details of initial loading. This fact is the simplest explanation for why the "f value" logic works.

A classic application of this logic is for a car impact in which only one half of the bumper is contacted. For full compression of this one half, this implies only one half of the stored energy compared to a full bumper impact. Since kinetic energy is proportional to the square of speed, this implies that the effective bumper speed limit is only $(1/2)^{1/2} = 0.717$ the normal value. Thus a 5 mph bumper acts as if it were a 3.54 mph one. This then is the value to set v_L to for use in equations (25), (27) and (28).

The offset crash is receiving special attention these days since it is a very common type of crash, and is not presently part of the government testing requirements. The IIHS in particular has been studying this problem since this type of crash frequently involves significant injuries to the legs of the driver, even though the deceleration seen by the driver is actually less than for a full-bumper impact at the same speed. To understand the issue, consider the case of a half impact, where the crash involves only one half of the bumper width. At a given speed the fixed energy is absorbed by approximately only one half the car width, thereby making the absorption of energy twice the full-bumper value in terms of energy-per-volume. This is the equivalent to increasing the effective crash speed (*i.e.*, equivalent barrier speed) by a factor $2^{1/2} = 1.414$ as far as depth of crush is concerned for the impacted half. This produces a crush significantly larger than for the full-bumper case on the impacted half, thereby explaining the leg injuries.

For example, at 30 to 35 mph with a springlike crush response (*i.e.*, the strain-hardening response given by equation 2), a full-bumper crush of 24 inches may become about 34 inches on the impacted half. This will convert a crush that does not reach the occupant compartment into one that encroaches into the passenger compartment and causes leg injuries, especially for the driver's side where the foot pedals are. However, the net retarding force is lower, thus giving a lower net deceleration of the vehicle. This is because although the greater crush implies a larger force-per-width, the peak crushing force only increases by about $2^{1/2} = 1.414$, while the width is only 1/2 the full vehicle width. Thus, the actual total force is only $2^{1/2}/2 = 0.717$ the value for the full-bumper case. This argument ignores the fact that an offset collision also induces rotations of the vehicle, which actually reduces the net energy loss. Some of the lost energy is converted into rotational energy instead of crush energy. Thus, the deceleration experienced by the driver is actually less than the factor given above, and the degree of crush is also less. Nevertheless, the amount of crush is larger than for the full-bumper case, and can lead to significant leg injury.

For a side impact on a vehicle there can be considerable uncertainty in the crush response. A major reason is that, unlike a full-front or full-rear impact, the strength of the side of most vehicles varies significantly from point to point. Whereas the side frames (A, B and C) and wheel/axle assemblies are hard points, the sides of fenders and the middle of doors tend to be much softer. Thus the effective strength depends on where and how the vehicle is impacted, which depends on such factors as whether the bumper of the bullet vehicle straddled the vertical frames of the target one. On average, the R value for such soft structure response is usually in the range of about 0.2 - 0.5, versus the range 0.5 - 1.0 for bumper/frame response.

However, although these effects make accuracy of interpretation of a side impact worse than for a frontal or rear one, Newton's third law can be usefully employed. Suppose the bullet vehicle itself has a full-frontal impact with the front side portion of another vehicle. Since the frontal collision can be reasonably interpreted, the absorbed energy and maximum force can be deduced for the bullet vehicle. Then, Newton's law states that the maximum force acting on the target is also that for the bullet. Since the two vehicles' crush depths can be measured, an estimate of the absorbed energy for the target can be made. From this, the total absorbed energy is derived, and although the value for the target is less certain than for the bullet, the total has an intermediate accuracy which can still yield useful interpretation. In essence, this approach is one where a calibrated vehicle is used to calibrate the other vehicle. This logic has been invoked by Hull (ref 26), and Wood.

Partial or Sideswipe Impacts

Many vehicle collisions involve sideswipes, where one vehicle effectively runs along the side of the other. This type of collision is peculiar in that it involves a *positive* coefficient of restitution. For a normal impact the difference in speeds first decreases to zero (at which point both vehicles have the same speed) and then increases again by an amount that depends on the degree of elastic bounce. Since this process reverses the order of speeds (*i.e.*, the target is now faster than the bullet) we are dealing with a *negative* coefficient of restitution, as explained in section 4(a)(ii). However, for the sideswipe, the CMs of the two vehicles generally do not reach a common speed, and the impact finishes with the bullet still moving faster than the target. Thus, the ratio of speed difference post-impact to that pre-impact is positive.

Note that this type of impact involves far less vehicle damage than for the normal type. Also, it generally induces significant rotations of the vehicles. If one vehicle (target) approaches slowly from the side and impacts the side door of a faster moving vehicle (bullet) at a high angle (*e.g.*, near 90 degrees between vehicles) the result is to induce a rapid rotation of the target but a slower rotation of the bullet. A similar effect occurs if the bullet vehicle perpendicularly strikes the far end of the target. See figure 19. Further, the transferred linear momentum to the target is also quite low, as is the corresponding speed change, while the angular momentum and energy are significant. These effects occur because for the high speed bullet, the impact force is directed almost through the bullet vehicle CM inducing little rotation. For the target, the impact was effectively along the front surface, and thus the force is directed almost perpendicular to the vehicle axis. Hence, the torque arm is a maximum and can cause very rapid rotation.

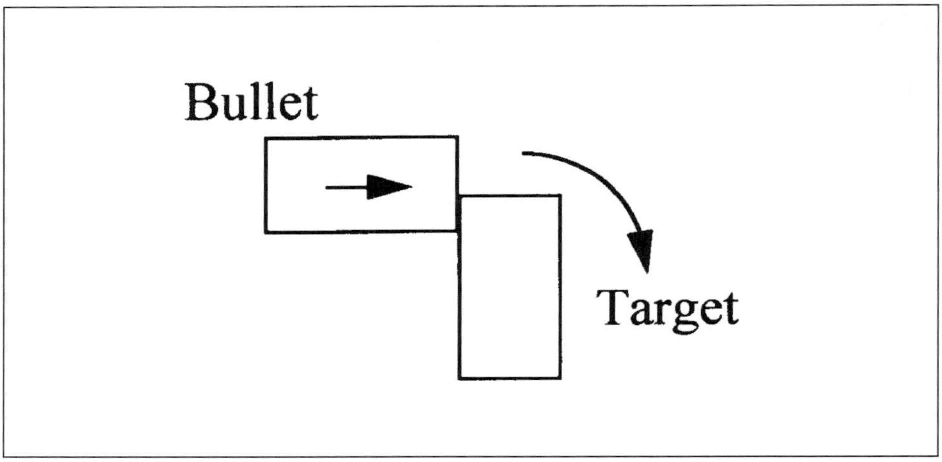

Figure 19 *"End Hit" on Target – Rapid Target Rotation.*

Note also that this same effect frequently occurs for an impact between a car and a pedestrian. Here, a low frontal hood and bumper can cause the pedestrian's body to be both accelerated forward and to suffer a rotation (feet upward). The result can be that the pedestrian is thrown onto the car hood. However, while the result is accurate, the mechanism is wrong. In reality, the pedestrian's body (center of mass) achieves a speed less than that of the car, and thus we have a positive coefficient of restitution. The car actually drives under the rotating pedestrian's body, causing the latter to go onto the hood. For high speeds the pedestrian can actually go completely over the car, since the car is able to completely drive under the body. The differential speed of the car versus the pedestrian implies a kinetic energy for the pedestrian, as if the pedestrian were moving rapidly at a stationary vehicle. Likewise, the rotation also implies energy. When the sum of these energies is large enough, the pedestrian can climb against gravity and go completely over the vehicle, including cartwheeling. For an excellent description of the myriad ways in which pedestrians can interact with vehicles see the book and video by Eubanks (ref 27).

Induced Rotations

If a vehicle impact does not involve a force which passes directly through its center of mass (CM) (a non-centered impact), then rotations are induced. The angular rotational rate is given by

(36)
$$\varpi \text{ (radians/s)} = \frac{Ftr}{I}$$

where F is the applied force, t is the time of application, and 'r' is the effective torque-arm , and I is the moment of inertia about the vehicle CM, or about a fixed axis. Note that one radian is 180/p = 57.3 degrees. Since P = Ft is the induced momentum change, and v_{CM} (change) = P/m = Pg/w, and v_{rot} = rw, the rotation has velocities superimposed on the linear motion changes. Here, v_{rot} is the induced rotational velocity of the pushed part relative to the CM axis of rotation. The moment of inertia of the body can be written as $I = mk^2 = (w/g)k^2$, where 'k' is known as the radius of gyration. For a car rotating about its own CM, the value of k is approximately given by $k^2 = L^2/12$, where L is the car length (obviously the true value can be obtained for a given vehicle, such as the quotes from Expert Autostats [ref 19]). It can then be shown that the net speed of the car CM motion is given by

(37)
$$v_{CM} = \frac{v_{hit}}{\left(1 + \left(\frac{r}{k}\right)^2\right)} \quad \text{or} \quad v_{hit} - v_{CM} = v_{CM}\left(\frac{r}{k}\right)^2$$

where v_{hit} is the local common induced hit speed at the distance r from the vehicle CM. The hit speed is the common speed for both vehicles that occurs at the point of contact. The act of imparting rotation as well as linear motion of the CM means that the vehicle has two forms of kinetic energy, namely linear and rotational. The linear part is simply

(38)
$$E_{lin} = \left(\frac{w}{2g}\right)v_{CM}^2$$

while the rotational energy is

(39)
$$E_{rot} = \frac{I\varpi^2}{2} = \left(\frac{w}{2g}\right)k^2\varpi^2 = \left(\frac{w}{2g}\right)\left(\frac{k}{r}\right)^2 v_{rot}^2$$

Thus the total energy is

(40)
$$E_{tot} = \left(\frac{w}{2g}\right)[v_{CM}^2 + k^2\varpi^2] = \left(\frac{w_{eff}}{2g}\right)v_{CM}^2$$

or

(41)
$$E_{tot} = \left(\frac{w}{2g}\right)\frac{v_{hit}^2}{\left(1+\left(\frac{r}{k}\right)^2\right)} = \left(\frac{w_{eff}}{2g}\right)v_{hit}^2$$

where w_{eff} is the effective weight of the vehicle which gives the same total kinetic energy. Thus a rotating body acts as if its weight is changed, such that

(42)
$$w_{eff} = w\left[1+\left(\frac{k}{r}\right)^2\left(\frac{v_{rot}}{v_{CM}}\right)^2\right] = w\left[1+\left(\frac{r}{k}\right)^2\right]$$

if we reference to the CM velocity, and

(43)
$$w_{eff} = \frac{w}{\left[1+\left(\frac{r}{k}\right)^2\right]}$$

if we reference to the HIT velocity. Equation (43) is the more useful version.

Thus, when r = 0.0 (*i.e.*, we have a centered hit with the thrust passing through the vehicle CM) the effective weight is just the true value, whereas, for a significant value of torque-arm, r, *the effective weight of the target decreases significantly as seen by the bullet vehicle*. This means that the common value v_{hit} is higher than otherwise expected, as if the struck vehicle were lighter. However, the corresponding value of the target vehicle center of mass velocity, v_{CM}, is lower by the factor $(1 + (r/k)^2)$. Thus, the struck vehicle can develop significant rotation but have a relatively small induced change in its CM motion.

As an example, suppose the bullet (1) has an initial speed v_1 and impacts the target (2) on the latter's front at 90 degrees to the latter's longitudinal axis. Let the initial speed of the target be zero. Assume the bullet sees a thrust through its CM and so does not spin. For the target, however, $k^2 = L^2/12$ (roughly), and $r = L/2$ or $r^2 = L^2/4$, assuming the target CM is at the midpoint of its long axis. Thus the factor $(1 + (r/k)^2) = (1 + 3) = 4$. Then the common hit speed is given by

(44)
$$v_{hit} = \frac{w_1}{\left(w_1 + \frac{w_2}{4}\right)}v_1$$

while the actual target CM speed is given by

(45)
$$v_{CM,2} = \frac{v_{hit}}{4} = \left(\frac{1}{4}\right)\left|\frac{w_1}{\left(w_1 + \frac{w_2}{4}\right)}\right|v_1$$

and the rotation speed is

(46)
$$v_{rot,2} = v_{CM,2}\left(\frac{r}{k}\right)^2 = 3v_{CM,2} = \left(\frac{3}{4}\right)\left|\frac{w_1}{\left(w_1 + \frac{w_2}{4}\right)}\right|v_1$$

The rotation rate is

(47)
$$\varpi = \frac{v_{rot}}{r} = \frac{2v_{rot}}{L} = \left(\frac{3}{2L}\right)\left[w_1 + \frac{w_2}{4}\right]v_1 \quad \text{radians/sec}$$

These quotes ignore any vehicle bounce. This is usually reasonably valid since most such collisions involve the soft non-bumper impacts where the coefficient of restitution is usually small.

As an example, if w_1 = 3000 lbs and w_2 = 4000 lbs, and L_2 = 14 feet, we obtain

v_{hit} = 0.75 v_1, $v_{CM,2}$ = 0.1875 v_1, and $v_{rot,2}$ = 0.5625 v_1 and ω_2 = 0.08 v_1

Compare these values with the normal central-impact common speed of v_{hit} = 0.42857 v_1 and zero rotation. If v_1 = 44 ft/s (30 mph) we obtain

v_{hit} = 22.5 mph, $v_{CM,2}$ = 5.625 mph, $v_{rot,2}$ = 16.88 mph, and ω_2 = 3.54 rad/s = 202 deg/s

For a simple centered impact, we would have $v_{hit} = v_{common} = v_{CM,2}$ = 12.86 mph, and zero rotation. If both vehicles have non-centered impacts, the same treatment is applied to each vehicle. Thus, we establish the values of r and k per vehicle. Figures 19 and 20 illustrate the overall logic.

The true definition of moment of inertia for a rectangular prismatic body about any axis perpendicular to one of the body's plane surfaces is

(48)
$$I = m\left(\frac{L^2 + W^2}{12}\right) + mQ^2$$

where L is the length, W is the width, and Q is any offset between the CM of the vehicle and the axis about which the vehicle is rotating, with the latter perpendicular to both L and W for a yaw spin. Q = 0.0 if the vehicle spins about its own CM. This equation assumes that the vehicle acts as if of uniform density.

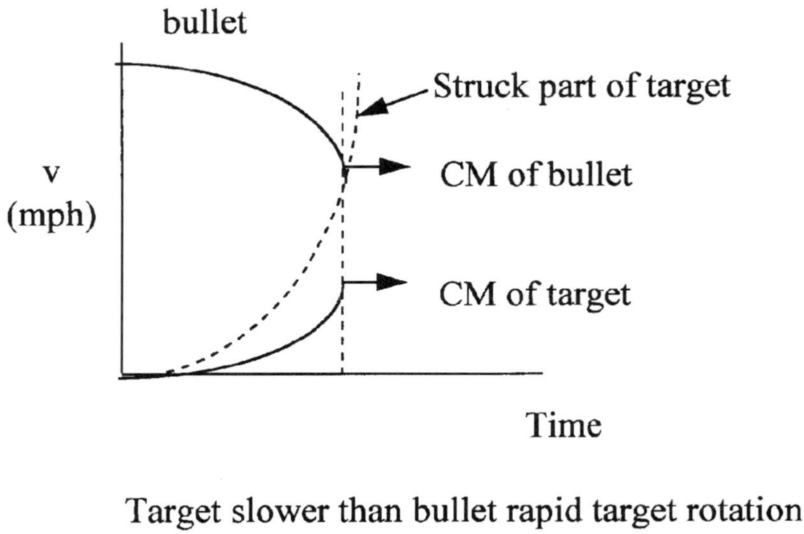

Figure 20 *Velocity-Time for "End Hit."*

Because a real car is not uniformly dense, and tends to have its mass closer to the center, the effective value of ($L^2 + W^2$) is actually quite close, numerically, to the value L^2. Hence, by pure coincidence, the previous approximation. Note that Limpert also gives an approximation, namely $k^2 = (L \times WB)/7.76$, where WB is the wheelbase. Numerically this is similar to $L^2/12$ for many cars. However, this approximation is only good for vehicles (such as a car) which are not designed to carry a significant payload. With pickups and vans the approximation is much worse due to the larger difference between an empty and loaded vehicle. When empty, the mass is closer to the vehicle front and the value of the radius of gyration (k^2) is usually less than $L^2/12$, whereas for a heavily loaded vehicle with weight toward the back the value of k^2 can be larger than $L^2/12$. For such cases it is advisable to obtain a proper quote of the moment of inertia in order to obtain k^2.

The combination of linear CM motion and rotation causes a point away from the impact region to achieve an instantaneous speed of zero. This point is known as the center of percussion (COP), illustrated in figure 21. It lies on the side of the vehicle CM opposite the strike point on the longitudinal axis at the distance $q = k^2/r$, from the CM. Thus for the previous example, $k^2 = L^2/12$ and $r = L/2$, hence $q = L/6$ from the CM away from the impact point. Thus the total distance

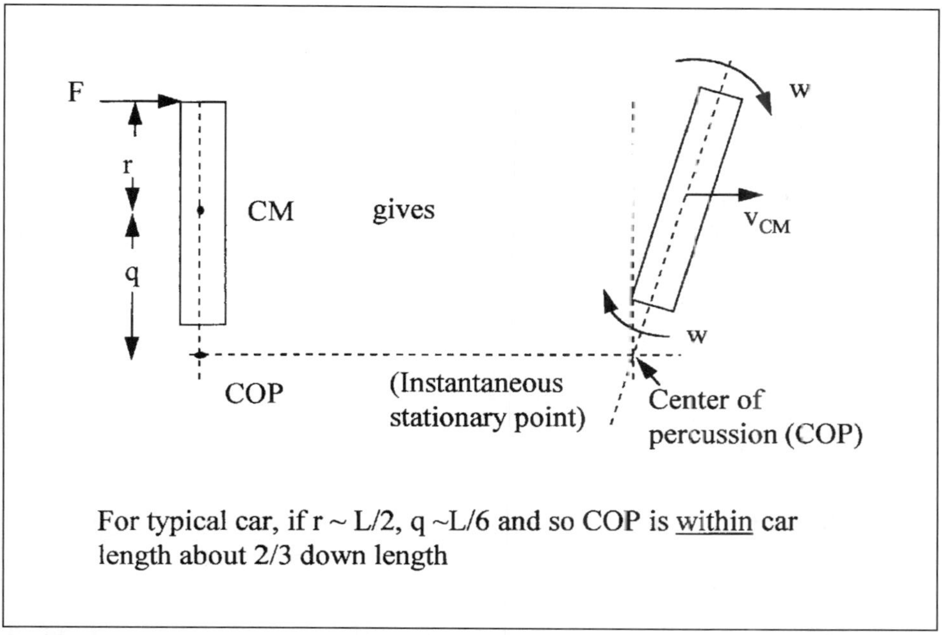

Figure 21 *Rotation About the Center of Percussion.*

from the impact point is (L/2 + L/6) = (2/3)L. For many cars this is roughly the position of the rear axle. Due to the action of the differential this is a preferred rotation point, since it minimizes any tendency for side motion tire scuffing. Hence, many cars apparently rotate about their rear axle when hit sideways at the front. Note that as $r \to 0.0$ so $q \to \infty$. Thus, the COP moves a large distance away from the vehicle. A central hit can be viewed as one with very slow rotation occurring about an axis at infinity.

Such rotational effects are also important for the study of vehicle occupant motions. Note that these rotational effects also apply for the case of the side-swipe. In particular, note that the rotation rate is a function of the imparted momentum change, the moment of inertia and the torque arm, whereas, the linear induced change in speed is a function of only the momentum change and the weight. Thus a knowledge of the rotation rate gives data on the corresponding linear motion, since the two are directly related. If the principal direction of force and torque-arm are known there is a fixed relationship between the induced rotation rate and the induced change in linear momentum (CM speed).

The off-center side hit is easily recognized. It produces minimal net target motion but with large rotation, and small apparent crush damage.

Movie Theatrics

It is unfortunate, but many movies demonstrate both *real* physics and *false* physics; which is shown seems to depend on what particular aspect the producer wishes to illustrate. Movies are intended to be spectacular. Thus, a producer frequently EMBELLISHES FACTS IN ORDER TO MAKE THE MOVIE MORE INTERESTING. This is distressing, since many court jurors watch these movies and may not appreciate the difference between reality and special effects. This then behooves the expert witness to adequately explain the difference and convince the triers of fact of the physical realities.

Examples of false behavior include:

(1) the vehicle nearly always burns or explodes in a crash. This is nonsense. Government regulations apply to the issue of fuel leakage and spark-ignition of fuel, and vehicle manufacturers must design their products to minimize such burns and explosions. Indeed, despite the notoriety of side impacts on some side-tanked GMC trucks and the rearend impacts on the Ford Pintos, the reality is that very few actual explosions occurred. Indeed, one TV company wishing to illustrate the problem with the GMC trucks got itself into legal trouble when it was disclosed that it had used small explosives in order to guarantee a fuel-tank impact explosion!

(2) in a rearend impact with a parked, stationary target car, the bullet vehicle can jump up over the target, usually with an induced roll, so as to land on its roof. This is also nonsense. The trick to making this happen is to use asymmetric ramps hidden behind the target car. No normal crash involves this absurd behavior.

(3) a vehicle can successfully jump across a missing piece of road (bridge, etc.). A classic example of this nonsense is seen in the movie *Speed*, where a city bus apparently jumps a gap in an almost-finished piece of new interstate highway. Not only is the road height the same at both sides of the gap, but the bus mysteriously adopts a nose-up position while landing on the far side of the gap. This effect was again produced only with the use of special ramps (carefully hidden from the camera!) on the approach side of the gap. Under real conditions the front of a vehicle will immediately start to rotate with a downward acceleration as soon as the front wheels leave the road and the back wheels are still on the road. Once the back wheels leave the road the rotational acceleration stops, and the vehicle now moves downward under gravity but with a fixed forward rotation. Thus only if the second side of the road is sufficiently lower than the first can

the vehicle avoid plowing front-first into the wall on the second side. The vehicle can never adopt the nose-up attitude without special ramps, or an inclined approach side to the gap. See figure 22.

(4) a high speed crash can nearly always be suffered without bodily injury even for occupants who do not wear seatbelts and/or have vehicles without airbags. This is most unlikely in real life, yet many movies imply that the occupants can invariably walk away from serious crashes (including rollovers) without a scratch!

On the other hand, many movies also show real physics. In particular, *Speed* demonstrated very nicely the effect of the frontal sideswipe. Here, the same city bus was shown impacting sideways the front of various stationary cars, including police cars. The movie realistically illustrated how these police cars moved very little (CM motion), but suffered rapid rotations so as to rapidly swing out of the way of the bus, with the latter barely slowing in the process (due to the huge ratio of bus weight to the effective "reduced" car weight).

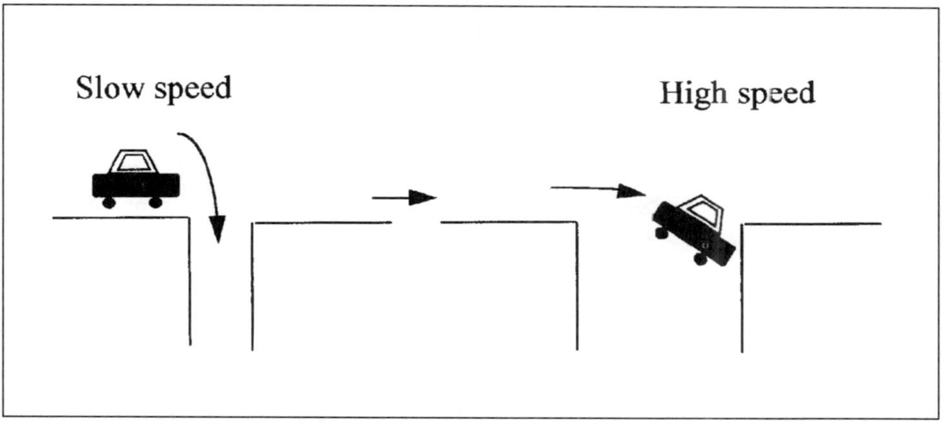

Figure 22 *Real Behavior on Jumping a Gap.*

Payload Considerations

Payload is any weight in excess of the curb weight of the vehicle. It includes occupants, shopping bags, tools, and camper shells. How should payload be treated with regard to momentum and energy calculations? Provided the payload remains attached to the vehicle, and can undergo only limited differential motion versus the vehicle, it should always be included as part of the total weight for momentum calculations. This is because the payload momentum has nowhere else to go. (However, see below.) Shifts in the payload will produce small shifts in the net CM but otherwise have negligible effect. However, for energy calculations the treatment depends on how rigidly the payload is attached to the vehicle.

For example, a camper shell is normally fastened in a rigid manner to the pickup truck. Consequently, its kinetic energy is directly transferred to the vehicle and thus helps contribute to any crush of the latter. This does not apply for any movable, or loosely-coupled, payload. Here, differential motions occur, and the kinetic energy of the payload is usually dissipated within the vehicle, and does not contribute significantly to the vehicle crush. As a simple example, consider a loose tool box in the trunk. With a violent sudden stop of the vehicle, the tool box will continue forward within the trunk. Its kinetic energy will be dissipated by some frictional drag on the trunk carpet, but most will go into the sudden thump into the structure at the back of the rear seats. Consequently, there will be some degree of damage within the trunk and little of the energy ends up causing additional vehicle crush.

The same effect occurs for the occupants. If an occupant were immobilized within a plaster cast which was rigidly fixed to the vehicle, two things apply. First, there would be no differential body segment motions and so no injury (ignoring internal organ movements, such as for the brain, heart, and liver). This explains why very securely fastened occupants tend not to suffer injury except at very high crash speeds, as was proven by Col. John Stapp (USAF), of the well-known rocket sled tests and resulting annual Stapp Car Crash Conferences sponsored by SAE (ref 28). Second, the energy of the occupant is transferred to the car to increase the latter's crush. However, in the absence of such a rigid cast the occupant will move relative to the vehicle, and there will be differential body segment motions. The occupant runs into either the steering wheel or dash, or is stopped by the seatbelts or an airbag. Thus we have an internal impact. However, here the occupant's initial kinetic energy is dissipated by stretching the belts, deforming the steering wheel or dash, or by producing personal injury. Indeed, it is precisely because the occupant's energy does not simply transfer to the vehicle that injury can occur, or there would be no source for the injury mechanism, all of which involve sudden energy absorption by the human body.

This internal impact is the meaning of the second collision with regard to the definition of crashworthiness. Since the vehicle is very heavy relative to an occupant (typically about 20 times the weight) the moving occupant's momentum is transferred to the vehicle but very little of the energy is transferred. In fact, equation (12) applies. For the human body the coefficient of restitution is small (a lot of the human body is elastoviscous). Rewriting equation (12) we obtain

(49)

$$E_D = \left[\frac{w_1 w_2}{(w_1 + w_2)}\right]\left[\frac{(1-e^2)}{2g}\right]v_c^2$$

where E_D is the absorbed energy, and v_c is the closing speed (person versus car). If '1' is the vehicle and '2' is the occupant, then since the vehicle is so heavy compared to the occupant, equation (49) approximates to

(50)

$$E_D = \left(\frac{w_2}{2g}\right)(1-e^2)v_c^2 = \left(\frac{w_2}{2g}\right)v_c^2$$

since 'e' is also small. Thus almost the entire initial kinetic energy of the occupant is dissipated within the crash between the occupant and the vehicle, and little is left over to contribute to the other impact between the vehicle and the original hard body (another car, etc.). For a 20-to-1 car-to-occupant weight ratio, and a value of 'e' of 0.2, about 0.91 (91%) of the occupant's energy does not get transferred to the overall vehicle to contribute to the latter's crush. Thus, in general the payload is not part of the weight of the vehicle for purposes of energy-of-crush calculations, unless the payload can be considered rigidly attached to the vehicle, and is unable to dissipate its kinetic energy within the vehicle.

However, an unrestrained payload can also sometimes cause problems even with conservation of momentum. For example, consider a pickup truck weighing 3000 lbs impacting an identical target truck. Let the bullet have a 1000 lb payload at the rear of the bed, and let this payload be on rollers (small friction). If the impact speed was 10 mph we would ordinarily compute the common speed as (3000 + 1000)/(3000 + 1000 + 3000) x 10 mph = 5.71 mph. But this applies only for a rigidly-mounted payload. For the unrestrained payload, the initial impact is as for two equal-mass vehicles, in which case the common speed is 5.0 mph. The vehicles will subsequently bounce apart and disengage. Let the coefficient of restitution be 0.6. Then the target will reach 8.0 mph, while the bullet will slow to 2.0 mph. The typical time to do this is about 0.14 seconds. During this time the bullet has an average speed of about (10 +2)/2 = 6 mph and moves about 1.23 feet. However, the payload continues at 10 mph and thus moves 2.05 feet. Thus the payload moves a differential distance down the truck bed of about 0.82 feet = 9.9 inches. Clearly, for a long truck bed this motion can be less than that needed to reach the truck cab region. Thus, the payload was not part of the momentum calculation for the initial truck-to-truck impact, and it behaved as a separate third body. Given sufficient time, the payload will eventually catch up to the cab. It is at this time that the momentum of the payload comes back into play. Now conservation of momentum requires the bullet vehicle and its payload to come to a new common speed. This will be given by $v_{average}$ = (1000 lb x 10 mph + 3000 lb x 2.0 mph)/(4000 lb) = 4.0 mph. Thus, the bullet suffers a sudden forward jolt. However, this occurs after the two trucks have disengaged, and thus does not contribute to the original truck-to-truck collision. See figure 23.

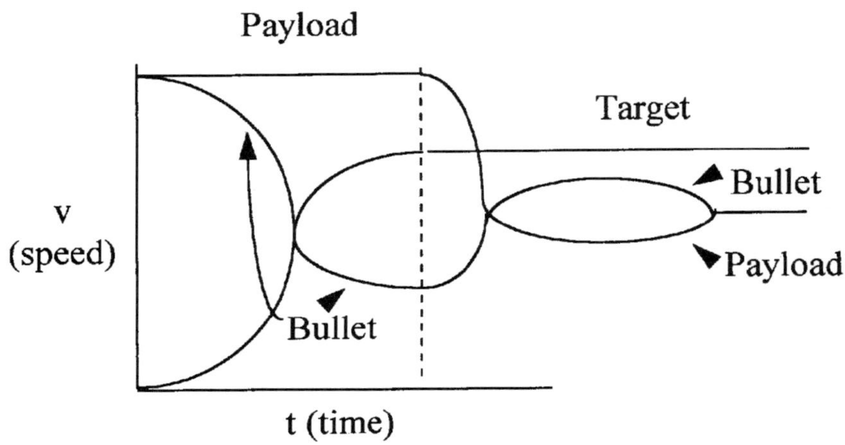

Figure 23 *"Loose" Payload Effects.*

Sensitivity Analysis

Thus far, all the equations give the implication that for known input parameter values precise calculations can be performed. In reality this is nonsense, because all the input values are rarely known accurately. Excepting constants like g (note that even g varies slightly from place to place on the Earth, but the change is small) all other parameters invariably have uncertainties associated with them. Simple examples include real drag coefficient of friction, true skid mark length, and true total vehicle weight. If a payload is added to a vehicle at its center of mass the total weight will increase, but there is negligible change in the radius of gyration. However, if the payload is not at the vehicle CM then there is an increase in both the weight and the radius of gyration. Such effects are rarely known accurately. Thus, all actual calculations must involve uncertainties.

A simple approach to this problem would be to merely rework the equation(s) using credible extremes in the individual parameter values. However, since it is unlikely that all uncertainties are high or low simultaneously, this approach usually gives too large a range in possibilities. In general, there is a tendency for the uncertainties to somewhat cancel each other. There are several mathematical techniques for handling this problem. We will limit our discussion here to a well-known one, namely the log-differential technique.

To apply this technique we perform the following maneuvers. First, write the equation. Then rewrite it in logarithmic form. Finally, differentiate the log version of the equation. Now insert the credible uncertainties to achieve a credible estimate of the overall fractional error.

First, a reminder of the rules for logarithms:

(51) $$\log(abc) = \log(a) + \log(b) + \log(c) \text{ and } \log\left(\frac{a}{b}\right) = \log(a) - \log(b) \text{ and } \log(a^n) = n\log(a)$$

The differential of a log is simply d(log(a))/da = Δa/a.

Take the simple equation for speed from skid, $v^2 = 2fgs$. In log form this becomes

(52) $$2\log(v) = \log(2) + \log(f) + \log(g) + \log(s)$$

Differentiating,

(53) $$\frac{2\Delta v}{v} = 0 + \frac{\Delta f}{f} + 0 + \frac{\Delta s}{s}$$

Note how the differential of the constants (2 and g) are both zero, since there is no uncertainty.

Rewriting,

(54) $$\frac{\Delta v}{v} = \left(\frac{1}{2}\right)\left[\frac{\Delta f}{f} + \frac{\Delta s}{s}\right]$$

As an example, suppose the value for friction is between 0.6 and 0.8, with a mean of 0.7. The fractional uncertainty is about ±0.1/0.7 = 0.143. Suppose the skid mark is between 38 feet and 42 feet, with a mean of 40 feet. The fractional uncertainty is about ±2/40 = 0.05. Then the overall fractional uncertainty in the velocity is ±(1/2)[0.143 + 0.05] = 0.096 (9.6 %). Then the average calculated speed of 42.5 ft/s = 28.9 mph has an uncertainty of ±2.79 mph. Thus the credible range of speed is between 26.1 and 31.7 mph. The same values are obtained by direct substitution of the extremes into the original skid equation.

Note how equation (54) states that the fractional error in v is only one-half that of the fractional error in either f or s. This is because the skid equation involves a square-root of speed versus skid. Thus any equation which involves a nth-root of a quantity has only a (1/n) fractional error versus the fractional error in the parameters within the equation.

Equation (54) involves two fractional errors. To account for the fact that such errors can compete with each other (move in opposite directions) we can apply the RMS (root-mean-square) logic for random errors to obtain an even more credible estimation of the final fractional error in speed. This simply states

(55)

$$\left(\frac{\Delta v}{v}\right)^2 = \left(\frac{1}{2}\right)^2\left[\left(\frac{\Delta f}{f}\right)^2 + \left(\frac{\Delta s}{s}\right)^2\right]$$

For the above example this gives $\Delta v/v = 0.076$ (7.6 %). If there is only one parameter with uncertainty (such as f) then the RMS value is identical to the log-differential value.

Chapter 5

Computer Modeling Methodologies

Introduction

Many low speed accidents, such as a simple rearender, involve inline collisions. For such collisions the standard momentum solution cannot give unique solutions. This is because when the momentum vectors (preimpact and postimpact) align with each other there is insufficient data for a solution, with more variables than equations to solve them. Hence the emphasis on energy-of-crush solutions. However, the standard versions of the latter also usually give errors at low speeds, mostly because they were not written for low speed applications.

The CRASH3 Program

Many accident reconstructionists do energy-of-crush analysis by using the CRASH3 program, which was developed by CALSPAN (ref 22), or variations of the same logic. This is the model used by NUTI and many others. Unfortunately, there are logical errors in this methodology, and thus in any computer program based on it. Since the following involves what might seem to be a somewhat harsh critique of CRASH3, a little history is needed.

It should be noted that CRASH3 was not initially written for the purpose of performing a specific crash reconstruction. Instead, it was written for NHTSA to allow interpretation of classes of accidents, and sometime later CRASH3 was released to the public domain. Unfortunately, it immediately began to be used to solve specific accidents, apparently without much understanding of its limitations.

The model assumes that vehicles crush as if behaving as a dissipative spring, with a linear increase in crush force versus the degree of crush. This linear part of the logic is reasonable, and agrees with the model given earlier. However, the reason given for it is incorrect; in reality it occurs because of the strain-hardening of metal, as mentioned before. Further, this plastic response occurs after the elastic behavior, which itself involves a much stiffer force-crush curve (see fig 10, line OA). Thus there should be an obvious kink in the force-deformation plot when the yield point is reached. The only time this kink will not appear is if the slope of the bumper compression response happens to be identical to the crush stiffness slope of the vehicle. However, this is unlikely, since it would require very soft bumpers.

The CRASH3 model assumes that the extension of the force-crush plot to the left of the zero crush point represents the elastic response of the vehicle (see fig 24). This is also incorrect; it merely represents the mathematical extension of the curve and has no physical meaning! The true elastic/plastic behavior is as given before in figure 10, which clearly shows the kink. The CRASH3 model uses only two measured parameters, namely A (pounds/inch) and B (pounds/inch^2), and a *derived* parameter, G (pounds). These are parameters per unit width (W, inches or feet) of the vehicle. Thus, each should be multiplied by the width in order to obtain the total vehicle values. The value of AW gives the incipient crush strength (force, pounds), the value BW gives the linear increase in strength versus crush (force per incremental crush, pounds/inch), and the value GW *supposedly* gives the elastic energy to initiate crush (lbs-ft). Note that $G = A^2/2B$.

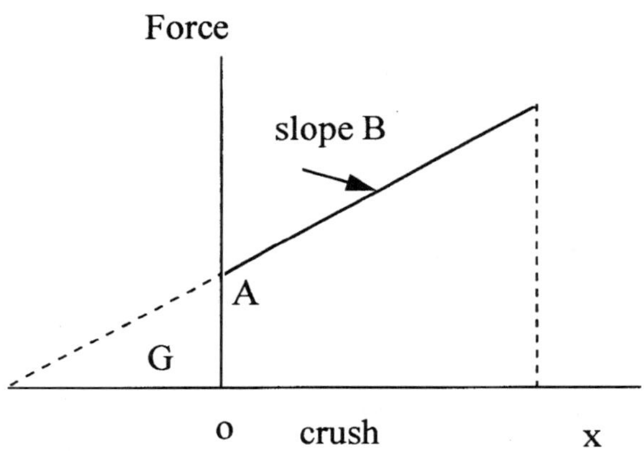

A = incipient crush force per width
B = incremental force per width
G = extension area per width

Figure 24 *CRASH 3 Force-Crush Logic.*

The implied elastic flexing of the vehicle before any permanent crush is simply A/B (inches). Likewise, the implied critical speed for collision into a fixed rigid barrier is given by

(56)

$$v_{crit}^2 = \frac{2gGW}{w} \quad (\text{ft/s})^2$$

where w is the vehicle weight (pounds), and W is the car width (feet).

A quick look at some of the numbers used in the CRASH3 model immediately reveals some irregularities, and even total absurdities. Consider a 1977 Ford Thunderbird. This vehicle has a length of 215.5 inches, a width of 78.5 inches, and a weight of 3907 lbs. Then, for the *rear* end of the Thunderbird (a class 4 stiffness category vehicle), the numbers imply a value of A/B = C of about 27 inches and a critical speed of about 15.7 mph! This critical speed is obviously considerably higher than any real bumper limit. Here, C is equivalent to our ‘a’ term. For the *front* of this vehicle we have a C value of 10.5 inches (not quite so absurd as the rearend value, but still well in excess of the true bumper amplitude), and the critical speed is about 9.7 mph. Similar oddities arise for practically every other listed vehicle and impacted vehicle surface. Even for frontal impacts into rigid barriers, the elastic flexing turns out to be no smaller than about 5.7 inches, and as large as 10.5 inches. Yet real bumpers have an amplitude of only about 3 inches since this is how far they extend beyond the bodywork. Of course, the A value merely gives the incipient force to cause damage, while the B value is merely a description of the strain hardening slope. The two have nothing to do with each other (because the yield strength and the strain hardening slope are not related), and hence nothing to do with G or the true bumper amplitude.

Using the above quotes for the Ford Thunderbird, we can also derive the effective R values. Thus, for the front, R_0 = AW/12w = 356 (lb/in) x 78.5 (in) / (12 x 3907 (lb.)) = 0.596. The rear value is almost identical. So, at the instant of incipient frame crush, the vehicle passenger compartment sees a peak deceleration of about 12 x 0.596 g = 7.15 g. For a total crush of about 20 inches, the R value becomes $R_0(1+ x_{crush}/C) = R_0(1+ x_{crush}(B/A))$ = 0.596 x (1+ 20/10.5) = 1.734, and the peak deceleration is now 20.81 g.

The problem with the CRASH3 model is that it was not based on known engineering concepts. Instead it was developed empirically on the basis that, experimentally, the impact velocity versus crush depth data implied a straight line. Close scrutiny of such data, however, reveals that this was more wishful thinking than anything else, and was forced by very few (and sometimes only *one*) data points for the higher speeds. (Note: standard accepted engineering and scientific practice demands that *multiple* data points must be obtained before any credence can be given to experimental data). Removal of the high speed points immediately allows for a nonlinear curve fit, as given empirically by Limpert and Noon. This behavior for the higher speeds is simply an example of the sudden changes in stiffness of the vehicle due to engagement with characteristic points such as the engine, A frame, or passenger compartment. If sufficient data points existed, it would be found that the velocity versus crush plot suddenly becomes steeper above a certain high speed where engine engagement occurs, and then less steep above another speed where the passenger compartment starts to collapse. However, with only widely-spaced data, the appearance can be of an intermediate, and steep, pseudo-straight line. To correctly handle these changes in higher-speed stiffness it is necessary to employ additional parameters in the equations.

By assuming the linear velocity-crush relationship and assuming that the G term represents the elastic energy, the logic of the CRASH3 model forces a constrained group of values of A, B and G which frequently give odd implied bumper behavior, and *always* yield straight line data for velocity versus crush, which is hardly surprising, since this was presumed going into the analysis!

Note, however, that the CRASH3 model involves the same three terms as does the modified model given before: a constant term, one dependent on a linear relationship versus crush, and one dependent on the square of the crush. Only the individual constants in the equation change. For this reason, the CRASH3 model does give good values for the intermediate equivalent barrier impact speeds (*e.g.*, about 20 to 50 mph), as seen in figure 25, where all the models are very close. However, at the low incipient crush speeds CRASH3 gives poorer predictions, and generally overestimates the impact speeds for a given level of crush. Compare this with the data of Noon and Limpert, however, whose curve fits ignore the existence of bumpers. However, neither Noon nor Limpert claim their approaches are suitable for low speeds, and Limpert specifically warns not to expect good data below about 15 to 20 mph equivalent barrier speeds using his empirical curve fits.

Comparing the CRASH3 model versus our model (POD's model), we find that the equivalents are $A = 12\ R_0\ w/W$ (W in inches), $B = 12\ R_0\ w/(aW)$ (both a and W in inches), and $G = (w/2gW)\ v_L^2$ (with W in feet), and 'a' = A/B = C. CRASH3 sets $G = A^2/2B$.

Note that the real difference is that for our model we do *not* equate $G = A^2/2B$. This is the key to avoiding the problem of locking the A, B, and G parameters together in a forced fashion. In order for CRASH3 to avoid unrealistically large values of G, the value of A must be kept small, while B is

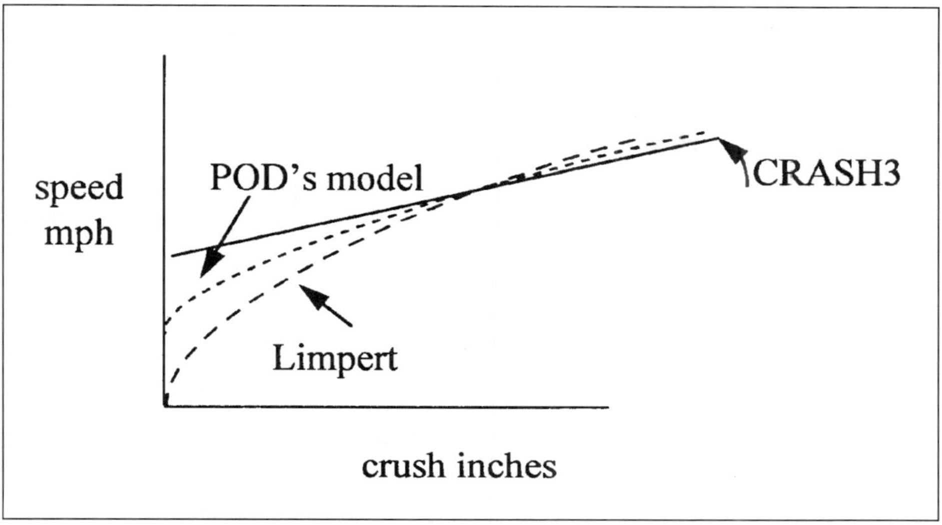

Figure 25 *Comparison of Speed Crash Models.*

large. However, this is equivalent to giving small R_0 and 'a' values. It was pointed out before that small values of these two parameters automatically lead to the straight line response for velocity versus crush. The problems occur because CRASH3 has only *two* parameters, which attempt to be compatible also with the bumper response. For our model, there are *three* free parameters, and the bumper response is set independently of the other two. A really true model would use at least four independent parameters, but the experimental data are usually too sparse to justify this for modeling purposes.

Note also that the CRASH3 model does not define any coefficient of restitution. In fact CRASH3 is unable to define such a quantity for the same reason that it wrongly predicts low-speed behavior; namely, the logic of the G parameter, and the "missing kink" in the force-crush plot. Since the model assumes that the elastic energy is the integral under the extension of the force-crush plot to the left of the zero crush point (without the kink), then any attempt to invoke elastic recovery would immediately force the model to retrace its crush path and end up with *zero crush*! What CRASH3 really does is to assume vertical jumps for the initial loading (zero force to incipient crush) and final unloading (maximum force back to zero). Since this implies no associated displacements, there are also no associated changes in energy. The elastic energy to reach crushing is then independently added to the model in an inconsistent manner. These problems vanish when using our more realistic model.

Where the CRASH3 model directly uses energy arguments to deduce collision conditions, there are also simplistic velocity-versus-crush models. The latter are only appropriate for full frontal or rear impacts, and cannot be used for partial and sideswipe impacts. One such model is that presented by Campbell (ref 29). Again, this model assumes a linear relationship of the form $v = b_0 + b_1 x$, with b_0 the incipient damage speed and b_1 the slope of the velocity-crush line, with x the inches of crush. This model strictly describes impacts into rigid barriers. The energy for a crush can be deduced by using the *E*quivalent *B*arrier *S*peed (EBS). Thus, we merely equate

(57)

$$E_D = \left(\frac{w}{2g}\right) v_{barrier}^2 = \left(\frac{w}{2g}\right)(EBS)^2 = \left(\frac{w}{2g}\right)[b_0^2 + 2b_0 b_1 x + b_1^2 x^2]$$

where the barrier speed is from Campbell's equation. However, note that, as with CRASH3, there is no restitution and no distinction between input energy and absorbed energy. Thus, both the CRASH3 and Campbell approach work well only for higher speeds.

To actually use CRASH3, the damage region is divided into several (usually five) equal sections. Thus, there are six measurements of crush; two end ones and four inner ones. Each section defines a mean crush depth, and the CRASH3 equation is applied to each section to obtain the section energy. Then all the energy terms are summed to obtain the total crush energy. This approach explains why the vehicle strength is given in terms of unit width of damage.

For an impact which is not perpendicular to a vehicle surface, a correction factor is employed. This factor is $(1 + \tan^2 q)$, where q is the off-normal angle of the thrust. This approach works reasonably well provided that the angle never exceeds 45 degrees. For higher angles the solution should be viewed as a collision on an orthogonal surface. Thus, a 70-degree impact on the front is really a 20-degree impact using "side impact" strength values. Note that, strictly speaking, the term $\tan^2 q$ should actually be tanq tana, where a is the approach angle for the effective closing velocity vector of the two vehicles, and q is the direction of the PDOF versus the vehicle longitudinal axis (see ref 17); however, the distinction is small and well within the other uncertainties. The logic of the correction factor is that for an angled thrust the true deformation motion is larger than the apparent value perpendicular to the surface by the factor 1/cosq. Since the force also increases with deformation for a springlike response, this also implies that the corresponding energy increases by $(1/\cos q)^2$ which is the same as $(1 + \tan^2 q)$.

Since CRASH3 has the same general terms as our derived crush equation (a constant, a term linear in crush and a term dependent on the square of the crush) then it also asymptotes to the simpler linear-only terms for very small crush, appropriate for low speed crashes. Indeed, the velocity-crush equation of Campbell also produces the familiar three terms if it is rewritten in terms of input energy versus crush, as given in equation (57).

To actually use CRASH3 the following equation is used for a 5-segment damage region,

(58)
$$E=\tfrac{W}{5}[5G+\tfrac{A}{2}(C_1+2C_2+2C_3+2C_4+2C_5+C_6)+ \tfrac{B}{6}(C_1^2+2C_2^2+2C_3^2+2C_4^2+2C_5^2+C_6^2+C_1C_2+ C_2C_3+C_3C_4+C_5C_6)](1+\tan^2\theta)$$

where the individual 'C' values are the x_{crush} values (inches), and W is the damage-zone width. This equation is merely a trapezius treatment for the five segments and six crush depths.

For a one-zone full-bumper determination of energy, CRASH3 gives the simple equation

(59)
$$E=W\left[\left(\frac{A^2}{2B}\right)+Ax_{crush}+\left(\frac{B}{2}\right)x_{crush}^2\right]$$

Multiple Hits on a Vehicle

Occasionally a given vehicle may suffer more than one impact on the same part, such as two sequential hits on its front bumper. If the first impact is totally elastic (within the bumper limit) there will be no effect on the response for any subsequent impact. However, if the first impact exceeds the bumper limit then the crush response is modified for any second impact. The result is determined by the force-crush plot shown in figure 26. Consider the crush path OABC. For a second impact, the new loop will be CBDE, where D is a new maximum deformation, and E is the new final crush. Thus, the major effect of a prior plastic crush is to increase the effective value of F_0 (*i.e.*, give the path CB instead of OA). There is no change in the slope of the strain hardening portion, namely AB (and, correspondingly, BD). In the language of CRASH3, this is the same as saying that the 'A' parameter increases, but the 'B' parameter stays constant.

The above logic merely states that the elastic paths are retraceable, and that multiple sequential impacts merely open up the plastic loop. Thus, the overall sum of crush damage is directly related to the *total* plastic absorbed energy for *all* the impacts. Indeed, this summed energy approach has been used as a way of increasing the database using a single vehicle and multiple impacts over a range of impact speeds (ref 16).

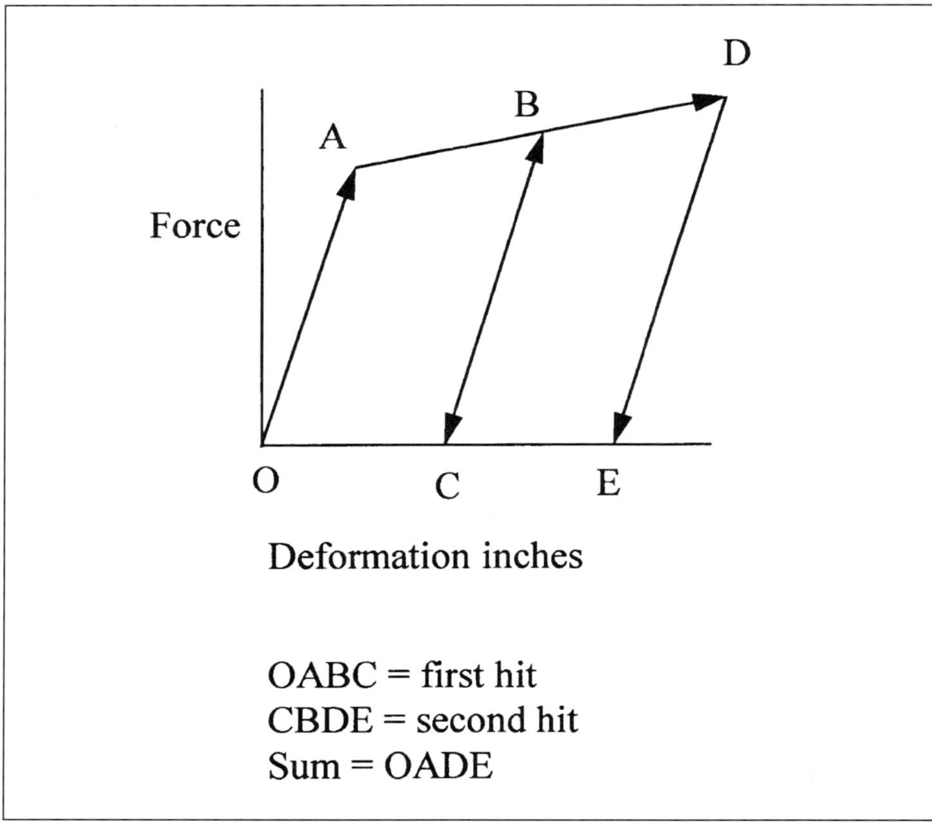

Figure 26 *Multiple Vehicle Hits.*

Issues to Watch Out For

Another code frequently used is SMAC, and its derivatives. SMAC is a forward simulation code, meaning that, given some initial conditions, SMAC predicts the resultant vehicle motions. It does this by computing the mutual forces between the vehicles and then tracking, as a function of time, the ensuing results. However, to compute these mutual vehicle collision forces SMAC uses an algorithm even less scientific than CRASH3, assuming a purely linear force-crush relationship without any initial force offset. In short, it completely ignores the existence of bumpers and ignores the concept of a required minimum force to initiate permanent crushing. Further, although SMAC tries to include restitution, it does so by applying a correction that has nothing to do with physics or engineering, and is simply a "mathematical fudge" (see figure 27). There have been papers describing methods for trying to make SMAC and CRASH3 agree with each other

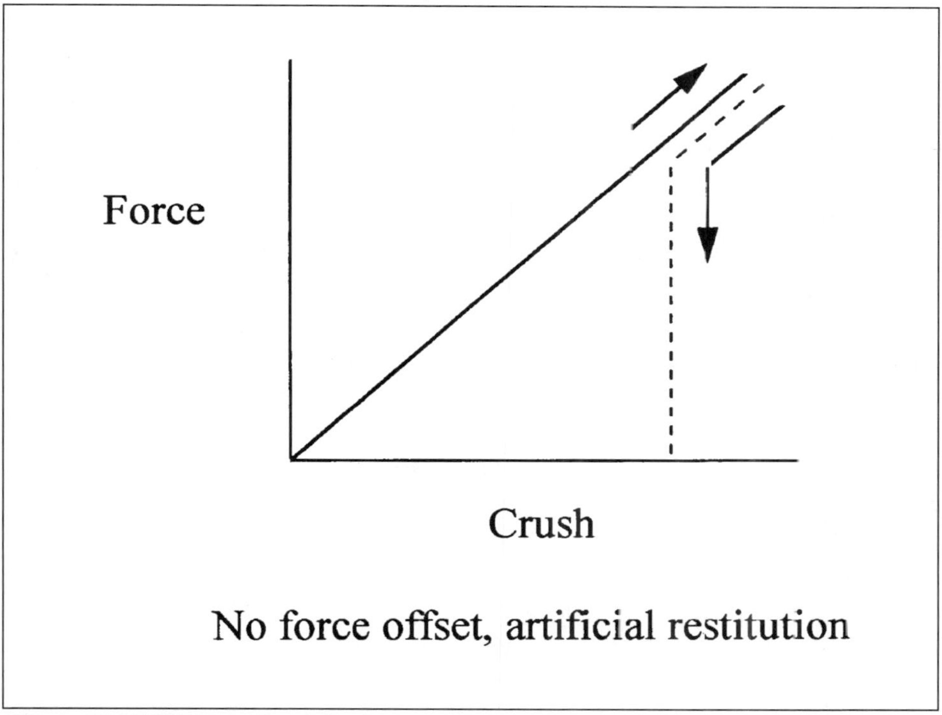

Figure 27 *SMAC Force-Crush Logic.*

(ref 30). However, since the two algorithms differ with respect to the initial force offset, there is no way such efforts can ever succeed except over small ranges of options. This is a simple mathematical consequence of the form of the two algorithms. To allow the two algorithms to agree, they must both have the same form. Despite our previous statements concerning CRASH3, the fact remains that its form is fundamentally correct (we merely disagree on the interpretation of certain parameters). As with CRASH3, the major errors in a SMAC analysis occur for low speed impacts. Both algorithms give respectable solutions for the higher speed collisions. Thus, to solve the discrepancies between the codes, it is SMAC that needs redefining to be more like CRASH3. Better still, *both* codes should be rewritten to agree with reality.

It must be appreciated that, although computer programs are wonderful labor saving devices, they are limited by what their authors are willing or able to program into them. It takes a lot of testing and debugging for a programmer to identify *all* the potential pitfalls in a program. Most commercial programmers do not have the luxury of spending a lot of time finding these pitfalls. Consequently, it is inevitable that the relatively inexpensive reconstruction codes that are available will have some inaccuracies. In general, such codes can be expected to perform 95% to 99% of all calculations without a problem. It is the remainder that give trouble. Only a user with considerable scientific/engineering expertise can be expected to immediately recognize the pitfalls one may encounter when using such codes. Thus, second looks are advisable to ensure the code output makes sense.

The authors of this book are well-seasoned scientists and engineers who have worked many years on behalf of various government (US and UK) scientific and engineering agencies. This includes developing and working with very powerful codes developed at the National Laboratories, such as Sandia National Laboratories/Albuquerque (SNLA). These codes are very good and exceedingly complex (many require workstations, such as the SUN, or even CRAY supercomputers, to run). Consequently, they usually include a few errors when first written. The authors of these codes are painfully aware of the possibility of such problems. Indeed, they usually invite users of these codes to inform them of such errors, to allow the programmers to correct them. Indeed, SNLA always puts a disclaimer on their reports and/or codes to the effect that they may not necessarily represent the final opinions of the Labs, and may contain errors.

THIS PROBLEM OF COMPLEX CODES HAVING ERRORS HAS LED TO A "STANDARD JOKE" IN THE PC WORLD. If a new version of a "working code" is released, "wait a few months for the bugs to be found and corrected before buying!"

Bottom line: always use physics and engineering to crosscheck any code before accepting its answer.

Part II

Occupant Kinematics and Dynamics

Chapter 6

Kinematics versus Dynamics and Biomechanics

Kinematics describes the induced body motions, including induced rotations, that can occur without considerations of the forces which are applied. Thus it refers to geometry changes. Dynamics refers to the corresponding forces and induced stress and strain states, and consequently the potential for damage. Thus a sudden application of a force to an arm subject to bending will cause a bend to develop over time and to achieve a given net motion. Simultaneously, the bending will cause the buildup of internal stresses and strains, which may eventually cause rupture.

An example of the relationship between kinematics and dynamics is the explanation of what happens in the hitting of a baseball. Kinematics describes the bat motion, and the consequential trajectory and spin of the ball, whereas dynamics describes the forces, the temporary flattening of the ball, its subsequent rebound, and the stress conditions within the ball and the bat. If these stresses become sufficiently large, either the ball may rupture or the bat may break.

The combination of kinematics and dynamics when applied to a biological entity is biomechanics. Biomechanics includes the mechanical explanation of how birds fly, how fish swim, and how snails crawl, and is used to explain why walking faster than a certain speed causes the person to change gaits into running (ref 31). The last explanation is simple: The act of walking involves a rotation of a straight leg pivoting on the floor. As a result, the hips are subjected to an upward centrifugal acceleration which depends on the speed and the leg length (acceleration = speed^2/length). When this acceleration exceeds 1.0 g, the body starts to lift off the ground and running becomes the more efficient mode of motion. [The exception to this is "speed walking," whose rules require that one foot must be in contact with the floor at all times. Here, the walker has to adopt an unusual hip action in order to continue walking without bouncing off the floor.] For the typical leg length of 3 feet, this condition occurs for a speed of about 9.83 ft/s = 6.7 mph. Small children, with their shorter legs, reach this limit even sooner (*e.g.*, at about 3.9 mph for legs only 1 foot long), explaining why they frequently break into a run when trying to keep up with adults.

Some Generalizations on the Human Body

The study of how the human body is put together is anatomy. This can be considered part biology, part medicine, and part general science. A description of induced pain, lack of normal mobility, method of treatment, etc., is *medicine*. Conversely, a description of the loadings (forces and stresses, etc.) and on the body, and its consequential responses, is *mechanics*. Despite being an animate object, the human body is subject to exactly the same laws of physics as any inanimate item.

Very little of the human body, with the exception of some small flow in bones and cartilage (non-ossified bone) and long-term creep in intervertebral discs, displays the phenomenon of plastic flow. Indeed, the closest equivalent to true plastic flow is the tearing of ligaments, tendons and muscle fibers, which involve a permanent set until healed, the gradual sagging of skin with old age, and the gradual compressive creep of discs under loads which last a very long time. Thus, most forms of insult to the human body are of the form damage/no damage, as with a brittle material, rather than of the permanent set, as with plastically deforming metals. Practically all soft tissue is elastoviscous, while bones are mostly elastobrittle, but with some viscous response.

These are important differences between the human body and the typical vehicle construction. One of the consequences of these differences is that humans rarely bounce much when impacted. Instead, the impact energy is converted into heat (an example of this effect is the act of shivering, where the viscous muscular energy is turned into internal heat) or bruising (ecchymosis) where the small blood vessels can locally rupture.

Another consequence is that the dynamic response of much soft tissue is different from its pseudostatic behavior. For example, under rapid loading the peak rupture stress increases above that for slow loading. Simultaneously, the maximum strain to rupture usually decreases. Thus, the tissue displays a stiffer response. However, the integral of stress-strain usually changes only by a small amount, and thus the absorbed energy changes very little up to the point of induced damage, although the return path even for no damage is usually significantly different from the loading path, giving the hysteresis effect. This fact frequently means that energy solutions to human body trauma response are often the most reliable and appropriate, with viscous solutions a strong second contender.

The vast majority of soft tissue has a density very close to that of water, and is composed mostly of collagen. Collagen is a fibrous gelatinous protein made of at least twelve different amino acids, and generally has a twisted rope geometry. Bones are a composite consisting of a collagen matrix containing small crystals of hydroxyapatite (a calcium-phosphorus hydroxide, specifically $Ca_3(PO_4)_2.Ca(OH)_2$). The crystals are very small, being about 200Å x 50Å x 50Å. (Note: 1A = 10^{-8} cm). This structure gives a material which is light (average density about 2g/cm^3, only twice that of water) and is both strong and able to limit crack propagation by the process known as crack blunting. The apatite crystals provide the rigidity, while the collagen fibers provide the flexibility. This composite is rather like reinforced concrete, with the crystals acting as the concrete and the collagen acting as the steel rebar.

Most bones have varying density and structure across their diameters. The structure of bone is somewhat similar to wood, having cells which form parallel lamellae in concentric sheets. The outer portion is compact and has the highest density, while the inner section, known as cancellous, is of lower density. This geometry provides for strength in bending while allowing for minimal overall weight. Since any object suffering simple bending has minimum stress down the center line (the null line), there is no need for great strength in the central section. Some long bones, like those in the legs, make use of this fact by having a central cavity (the medullary cavity) which is used for the production of bone marrow. Cracks in bones, the most common form of damage, can heal themselves if properly treated, since bone is a living item with its own blood supply. Bones can be strong and are able to accept compressive stresses of up to about 22,000 psi, although they are stronger in pure compression than in tension or shear. This is stronger than most forms of wood and Plastic, but weaker than most metals.

The bones of the skull are plate-like. The construction is as a sandwich, with two outer compact regions (the tables) surrounding a less dense region (the diploe). All bone has a dense fibrous coating, the periosteum, to which other tissue (tendons, ligaments, skin, etc.) is attached. The periosteum has an outer layer of connective tissue with fat cells, while the inner layer consists of fine stretchy fibers. It contains the nerves and blood vessels that supply the bones. In young life it is thick and rich in blood vessels, but it becomes thinner and loses blood vessels in later life. If the periosteum is lost due to trauma or disease, the bones can waste and die. The periosteum can become inflamed with tenderness and swelling due to injury or infection, causing pain, fever and chills. Sometimes, blood or a watery substance (an edema, or pooling of fluid) can form under the periosteum.

Bones are continually being remodeled by a process of absorption and regeneration. If the body requires calcium elsewhere the bones can provide it by partial absorption by the rest of the body (which thins the bone), whereas with an excess of calcium the bones retrieve it by rebuilding themselves. This process is the reason for osteoporosis problems, particularly in women beyond menopause who require extra calcium. Note that the anecdotal history of little old ladies falling and breaking their thighs or hips is usually wrong! In reality, the bone breaks first, due to ostoeporotic weakening, and thus causes the fall (ref 32). What is less obvious is that bone strength changes according to the loads applied. In the absence of applied loads the bones tend to be absorbed by the body and become weaker. This effect has been observed for astronauts who spend significant time in a "zero g" environment. Conversely, exercise increases the strength of bones, and not just muscles. In fact, bones actually remodel themselves so as to provide maximum strength in accordance with the applied loads, via a feedback mechanism. This occurs because bones are piezoelectric. Upon application of a load, the small geometry change, the compressive strain, induced in the bone causes an electric field to be produced. This electric field then guides the remodeling of the bone such that the strength is produced as required.

Muscles work in tension, and provide no useful effect in compression. The muscles used voluntarily for skeletal motion are striated (banded, due to the local sarcomere geometry, which are the basic units of the muscle containing the two fiber types of actin and myosin). Other (involuntary) muscles, including those used for moving food through the digestive tract and those of the heart, are smooth. They act as adjustable tension springs. Muscles are many individual and parallel fibers which coordinate to act as a single muscle. The various fibers are joined with connective tissue, and come in bundles which are themselves encased by connective tissue. The fibers in human muscle have a diameter of about 30 microns (1.0 micron = 10^{-4} cm, or 0.00004 inches). Muscles operate by contracting, which is controlled by various motor neurons, which cause fibers of actin and myosin to slide over each other. It is rare for more than about two thirds of the fibers to be actively shortening at any one time. The maximum strength of muscle is developed at about the halfway length between fully contracted and fully relaxed. At either extreme the force that can be generated decreases.

The human body has a fixed number of skeletal muscle fibers. Hence the technique of muscle building is one where the individual fibers grow in size, such that the total possible load bearing capability increases. With a very strong person it is sometimes possible for the muscles to actually be capable of breaking the person's own bones, although this usually only occurs for a demented person (such as one on PCP or "Angel Dust"), since normally the pain reaction would limit the application of the muscles. As an inert object (when minimally innervated) skeletal muscle behaves as an elasto-viscous material, and stiffens up with rapid stretching. However, under load the rate with which the muscles can contract is roughly inversely proportional to the load (references 7 and 31).

The muscles develop maximum strength when contracting at about 1/3 of their maximum possible rate. The maximum load capability is inversely proportional to the rate of stretching. This gives a response opposite to that of an elasto-viscous material (*i.e.*, a softening effect). The combination of these two effects frequently results in a pseudo-constant torque behavior if a pretensed muscle tries to control a rapidly moving part of the body.

Muscles can usually exert stresses of up to about 44 psi (ref 31). This is only about 3 atmospheres (one atmosphere = 14.7 psi). However, for a muscle with large cross-sectional area this can imply a large total force. For example, the hamstring muscle for healthy young men can be about 23.25 inch^2, or a cylinder of diameter 5.44 inches. Thus, the total force can be up to about 1023 pounds. For a typical male body weight of 170 pounds, this is about six times the body weight per leg! Even the small muscle of the thumb can exert about 30 pounds force. The human jaw can exert a force of about 55 pounds at the incisors, and about 200 pounds at the molars (this difference is due to the lever-arm effect of the position of the masseter muscles versus the hinge point for the jaw, and the position of the different teeth versus this hinge point). With an average muscle fiber diameter of about 30 microns, an individual fiber can exert a force of about 5×10^{-5} pounds.

Muscles act like a pseudo-fluid material: they have a Poisson's ratio (n) of about 0.5. Poisson's ratio is the ratio of lateral strain (fractional stretching) to longitudinal strain (fractional shortening). When the value is about 0.5, the total volume tries to remain constant (this happens with many elastomers and with fluids). Thus, as muscles shorten so they also thicken in the transverse direction (hence bulging biceps, etc.). If the muscles are prevented from thickening, as when put in a plaster cast, then they are unable to contract and do any work, and will start to atrophy. This explains many of the problems associated with the use of immobilized muscles, and indicates that plaster casts must be used for the shortest time possible. The pumping action of muscles helps the blood flow, and to remain healthy muscles must be continually used.

Muscles perform work when the force they develop moves through a distance in the direction of the force. However, it is well known that muscles become fatigued even if they do not produce a net motion (as in merely holding a heavy weight without either lifting it or dropping it). The simplest explanation for this is to consider muscle activation to be similar to the workings of an electromagnet. Application of the magnetic field allows the magnet to pick up ferromagnetic (iron-based) materials and thus do work. However, to produce the magnetic field in the first place requires an electrical current in the wiring. Since the wiring has finite resistance (ignoring theoretical superconductors) this means that energy, known as Joule heating, is always being consumed even if the magnet does not move the piece of iron. The equivalent for muscles is that chemical energy is always required to activate them even if they do not move anything. This produces the tiring effect.

Muscles always work in opposing pairs. Thus, to allow for body motions there are always two or more muscles that control opposing motions, because muscles can only apply tensions. Thus, to straighten the elbow, the triceps tighten and the biceps loosen. To bend the elbow, the reverse occurs. Standing straight involves continual balancing of the muscles to the front of the body and those to the back; likewise those on either side. This is normally done without conscious effort after years of practice. However, if one thinks about standing straight it is often observed that the body starts to wobble! Too much conscious effort can override the unconscious learned behavior!

Damage to muscle is usually in the form of a strain, which consists mostly of torn fibers, primarily those of collagen. Many times these can heal, but for serious rupture only partial healing (scarring) may occur. Since muscles have a parallel fiber geometry, the proper healing approach is for the fibers to reattach end-to-end and remain parallel. A scar occurs when this fails to happen, and, instead, the fibers repair by cross-linking. This latter effect leads to a region of muscle which is both less elastic (less compliant) and weaker. Also, by acting as a local stress riser within the remaining muscle bundle, it causes enhanced stress development around the scar, in a similar manner as a hole or crack does in metal or Plastic. This again enhances the probability of further damage, especially ripping around the scar. Note that similar cross-linking occurs in several Plastics which are sensitive to ultraviolet light. When this happens, the Plastic becomes considerably more brittle. Cyclic motions due to daily heating and cooling then allows cracks to occur (such as the behavior of a typical car Plastic dashboard when left out in bright sunlight!).

The standard method of coaxing the fibers to realign properly is the application of gentle motions. This is the basis of much physical therapy. The intensity of the therapy can increase as the damage progressively repairs itself. Failure to apply the gentle motions can readily promote scar growth. Hence total, or prolonged, immobility after muscle ripping can be very bad.

Skeletal muscles represent about 40 to 50 percent of a typical man's weight, and about 30 to 40 percent for a woman. These large fractions explain why pretensing of muscles is so important for mitigating many forms of injury, particularly at lower speeds.

Ligaments and tendons act as straps and can take both tension and shear, but are not useful in compression. They act much like dead, very stiff, muscles.

Ligaments join bones to other bones or cartilage, and are usually flat or sheet-like, while tendons join muscles to bones, and tend to be more cylindrical. Damage to tendons and ligaments is generally in the form of a sprain, which consists of tearing of the fibrous elements. If only partial healing occurs, scar tissue is again developed. The scar will also suffer tensile rupture at loads below those for the original healthy tissue, so the initial trauma-induced damage can recur. In some cases of high loads the ligaments can rip off parts of the bones, in a process is known as avulsion, to which they are attached instead of themselves ripping. Small avulsions promote re-growth of the bone and this is a common reason for the development of bony spurs or osteophytes.

Ligaments are intended to keep bones in correct alignment and are not intended to survive very large loads. Tendons move within lubricated sheaths known as bursa and act as springy extensions of the muscles joining bones, and are intended to be strong. Tendons can survive very large stresses, greater than 8000 psi. They act mostly in an elastic manner with a small degree of viscosity, with about 7% loss in energy per complete stretch-and-release cycle. While the degree of extension strain is small, usually less than 10%, this elastic behavior helps relieve the muscles of the need to stretch as much and provides for rebound energy that cannot be provided by the muscles. Such rebound is needed for cyclic activities such as walking and running.

Intervertebral discs act as shock absorbers, and are made of cartilage (this is the gristle in meat). They can support compressive, tensile and shear loads, but are strongest in compression and weakest in shear, especially torsion, which is a twist about the spinal axis. They are filled with a gel-like liquid (the nucleus pulposus, mostly water-based) which viscously moves within the disc. Being essentially hydrostatic, they support the same compressive stress in all directions, with only the outer fibrous skin (the annulus fibrosus) controlling shear and tensile behavior. This response allows for an even distribution of stress between the bones regardless of tilt and/or twists.

Most parts of the human body are capable of self-healing. However, the two notable exceptions are the brain and the intervertebral discs (the discs have little in the way of blood supply). Damage to the discs can be induced by excessive loadings, which cause a weakening in the skin of the disc, or a rupture at the disc-to-bone interface and sometimes with bone avulsion. The skin weakening can allow for protuberances or even rupture, such that a portion of the disc sticks out beyond the bone space. This is like the behavior of a car tire with a weak spot in the sidewall. Such a protuberance represents a bulging disc, while an actual leakage of the gel is a hernia (an HNP). Either mechanical distortion can sometimes impinge on the nerves (this is radiculopathy if it involves the nerve roots) and spinal cord which run down the spine. If this happens, it produces several neurological effects including localized pain and radiating pain and/or loss of sensation elsewhere in the body. Strongly loaded nerves can cease to send their appropriate signals to muscles, resulting in atrophy.

However, many bulges and herniations produce no symptoms, especially if they do not impinge on the spinal cord or nerves. Note that discs cannot easily bulge in the anterior direction, because of the existence of the anterior longitudinal ligament which runs down the frontal aspect of the spinal vertebrae. On the posterior part of the bone, but anterior to the spinal cord, there is the posterior longitudinal ligament between the bones. This likewise holds the disc in place, but does allow the bulging of a disc to the sides of this ligament, including back toward the spinal cord due to motion of the ligament, especially if the latter is lax with negligible tensile load. Other spinal ligaments are the ligamentum flavum which joins the vertebrae posterior to the spinal cord, the various intervertebral ligaments which individually join the spinous and lateral processes, and the supraspinous ligament which connects the most posterior tips of the spinous processes. All but the intravertebral ligaments are single ligaments which run the entire length of the spine. If serious ripping of the ligaments occurs, this can lead to instabilities in the spine, since they are no longer able to hold the vertebrae in their correct anatomical positions.

In a normal person the discs start to naturally degenerate beyond the age of about 25, largely due to a gradual dehydration of the nucleus pulposus. With the gradual dehydration of the discs there is a tendency for the discs to slowly flatten, allowing the vertebrae to move closer. This effect explains the old age shortening often observed in the elderly. Until this happens, the discs are very strong. They can actually accept spinal axial compressive loads greater than the strength of the bones to which they are attached. Some people degenerate faster than others due to illness and/or odd chemical reactions within the body. A degenerated disc ruptures more readily than a healthy one. Bones also lose strength with age (especially due to osteoporosis). Thus the issue of whether the bone or the disc breaks first depends on which degenerated fastest. However, to confuse the picture further, strong trauma loads to a disc can also enhance the degeneration, sometimes producing a "chicken and egg" problem when trying to determine whether an accident caused an injury, or it was merely an effect of aging.

The stress conditions in the discs need to be understood. Under pure axial compression down the spine, the nucleus pulposus is always under compression, and being a viscous fluid this is a uniform pressure, except during rapid stress changes when viscous shear stresses also develop. However, the annulus fibrosus bulges out into a barrel shape. This produces hoop tensions around the circumference with compressions down the disc. Whenever a body has different stresses in orthogonal directions there are also internal shears developed. If the spine is subjected to a net axial tension, the nucleus pulposus is still under pressure (although of lower value), but the annulus fibrosus now develops mostly tensions. If an external shear is applied to the spine, the disc will try to slide sideways. This superimposes shear stresses on those already existing. If the spine suffers from a bending moment the concave side of the disc will become axially compressed, while the convex side will be stretched. This produces complex stress distributions around the disc. Lastly, if the spine is twisted about its axis this subjects the discs to a torsion. The discs are usually most vulnerable to such torsion, especially when the torsion is combined with other loading such as axial compression.

Ordinarily, large torsion motions are prevented due to the design of the vertebrae, which normally do not allow for much vertebra-to-vertebra twist. However, abnormalities in the bones, including fractures, may allow larger twists which then allow damage to the discs. Note that the cartilaginous fibers in the annulus fibrosus are slanted like the fibers in a bias-ply car tire. When subjected to a prolonged load the discs are observed to exhibit the phenomenon of creep. This is a slow flow-like process whereby the discs slowly change their geometry. Normally, this effect is small since the average person continuously moves and prevents a long-lived stress state.

Cartilage is a non-ossified version of bone, and is found on the outside of bones, especially at the rubbing surfaces at joints. The cartilage contains nature's lubricant, synovial fluid. This fluid has remarkable properties, such as the lowest coefficient of friction known to man (far better than man-made silicones or Teflon®) and the ability to increase its viscosity under strong loading (a little like the behavior of multi-grade viscosity automobile oils). There are also local sacks that contain the synovial fluid at various joints, and around tendons. These are called bursa. If these sacks develop leakage, the joints start frictionally moving on each other, and the condition of bursitis occurs. A similar effect occurs with some types of infection within the bursa, which can cause localized inflammation and rubbing, and pain with joint movements.

Whenever damage occurs to the body there is always the possibility of the damaged item causing localized impingement or stretching of neighboring nerves. Thus many forms of hard (easily identifiable) damage, such as a significantly sprained ligament, can also involve associated nerve problems, which can reveal themselves by abnormal bodily response elsewhere (*e.g.*, damage in the neck can cause problems in the arms and hands, etc.) This is the source of the Brachial Plexus Syndrome, a.k.a. the Cervical Rib Syndrome, a.k.a. Thoracic Outlet

Syndrome. Since different nerves in the spine control different regions, or dermatomes, of the body, a physician can identify which regions of the spine have been affected by mapping out the affected parts of the body.

The spine consists of 7 cervical vertebrae, 12 thoracic vertebrae and 5 lumbar vertebrae. Below the bottom lumber vertebra, there are several bones which fuse to act as one, namely the sacral/tail (coccyx) bone. The spine is not straight, but has a natural curvature seen from the side. This curvature helps to provide resilience by causing a bending motion in addition to a simple squeezing motion of the discs when the spine is subjected to longitudinal compression and/or tension. This is somewhat similar to the behavior of a spiral spring. The cervical and lumbar regions are concave toward the back (posterior) while the thoracic region is concave toward the front (anterior). If the cervical and lumber curvatures become excessive, the condition of lordosis applies, while excessive curvature of the thorax gives the condition of kyphosis ("hump back").

As a result of neck trauma such as a whiplash, muscle spasms and/or displacement of cervical vertebrae (spondylolisthesis) can cause loss of lordosis (the neck straightens). This is frequently considered a poor indicator of future improvements. A spasm is the condition where a muscle locks into a rigid condition. A swelling of the vertebrae (spondylitis) usually involves stiffness and pain; if only a stiffening occurs this is called spondylosis; while a freezing of a joint is called ankylosis. The vertebrae are numbered from top (superior) to bottom (inferior), starting with the atlas (C1) directly under the skull and the axis (C2) below. The cervical vertebrae are thus C1 through C7, those of the thorax are T1 through T12, and the lumbar region is L1 through L5, with the sacral bone being S1. This terminology also describes the disc regions. Thus, a disc between bones L4 and L5 is described as the L4-5. Note that the top-to-bottom direction is also known as the cephalic-caudal (head-to-tail) direction.

All the vertebrae hinge with respect to each other at the facet joints (the jaw also has similar facet joints). These are small regions close to and just behind the central cord which allow for articulation over relatively small angles, bone-to-bone. It is because of the large number of vertebrae that large overall angular motions are possible. The facets have sliding surfaces (condyles) that point in different directions relative to the vertical as we move from C1 to L5. These sliding surfaces also cause coupling motions to occur. Thus a simple side rotation (motion about a vertical axis, as in twisting left or right) usually also induces a forward (flexion) or rearward (extension) motion, frequently inducing a left/right bending effect also. This coupling, and the preferred directions of motion vary down the spine. Toward the head, motions include flexion/extension, rotation, and left/right bending. In the lumbar region the motion is mostly limited to flexion/extension, with little rotation. The facet joints have their own little synovial sacks and ligaments, which can be damaged and which contain nerves causing pain when trauma or disease occur.

Most of the vertebrae are similar except for changes in size and orientation of the facets. However, the top two bones next to the head are unique. These are C1 (the atlas; next to the skull) and C2 (the axis). The atlas allows for the "yes" nodding action, while the axis allows for the "no" head rotation. The atlas vertebra is unusual in that it does not have a developed posterior protuberance (the spinous process). The C1 bone is also unique in that it does not have a body and thus also does not have a disc; it is mostly a ring structure. The axis vertebra is unique in that it has a bony protuberance which projects upward at the anterior surface. This piece looks like a tooth (hence the name "dens," or "odontoid"). Its purpose is to allow for the attachment of lateral ligaments that hold the C1/C2 complex together, and allow for the "no" head rotation.

The neck is the most articulated region of the spine. The thoracic region is relatively limited because of the attachment of the ribs, which cause this region to act as a somewhat rigid chamber. The lumbar region is quite supple in the flexion/extension directions, but has limited motion in the rotation or lateral bending modes. This is because the facets in the lumber region are mostly in the vertical plane (*i.e.*, the planes of the condyle surfaces lie in the sagittal plane, the one that cuts the body vertically into left and right). This causes the lumber region to be vulnerable to front-to-back, and *vice versa*, horizontal shears.

The vertebrae all have a central hole (or foramen) through which the spinal cord passes. This central hole is another example of the minimum-stress condition for bending. Thus, ordinarily the various bending and twisting motions of the spine apply very low loads to the cord. The vertebrae are usually considered to act in thirds. The anterior third is the region between the anterior ligament and about halfway to the posterior ligament which contains about half the body of the vertebrae and the discs. The second (central) third contains the second half of the body and discs and the posterior ligament. The third portion is between the posterior ligament and the posterior part of the spinous processes, and includes the ligamentum flavum, the intervertebral ligaments and the supraspinous ligament, and the articular facets and lamina (part of the lateral processes) and includes the spinal cord. The facets are barely behind the cord, and are part of the last third. This division into thirds allows for an appreciation of the kinematic motions. The central region usually involves the least motion, and acts as the pivot point, while the first and third regions have the maximum motions.

The vertebral spine must ordinarily support the person in the upright position. Consequently, the load bearing requirements increase with position down the spine. Whereas the neck region needs only to support the head, the lumbar region must support the entire upper body. Consequently, there is a gradual increase in size of both the bones and the discs in going from C1 to L5. This type of geometry is seen in many engineering settings, with the Eiffel tower being perhaps the best-known example. The average head weighs about 10 pounds, whereas the upper body above the hips weighs about 50% of the total body weight, or about 80 pounds for the average person weighing about 160 pounds. Also, the spine must be capable of supporting far more than the static weight of the upper body, as when a person bends over and lifts a heavy weight.

An analogy is with a construction crane. Consider a person bent at about 90 degrees, with their upper body roughly parallel to the ground. Their overall center of mass must be above the feet to prevent toppling. To achieve this, the legs must be bent at the hips and/or knees. Let the person weigh about 160 pounds, and also be holding a 50-pound weight. Suppose the distance from hips to arms is about 24 inches. The upper torso has its mass at about 12 inches from the hips. Then there is a downward moment of about (160/2 x 12) + (50 x 24) = 960 + 1200 = 2160 inch-pounds, applied at the hips. To balance this moment, the muscles along the back must provide the same counterbalancing moment. However, these muscles are only about 2 inches from the spine and hips. Hence, the muscle force must be about 2160/2 = 1080 pounds. This is a large force, about 13.5 times the upper body weight, or 6.75 times the total body weight.

To prevent this tensile muscle force from collapsing the spine, the spine must provide reaction (push back) with an equal compressive force. Since ligaments, tendons, and muscles cannot support significant compressions, this load must be provided by the vertebral bones and discs. Thus the intervertebral bones and discs must be able to withstand the 1080-pound load. The load varies along the spine, being largest at the hip region and smallest at the arm region. Further, with the upper body parallel to the ground, there is also a large vertical shear at the L5-S1 region (of 80 [upper body] + 50 [load] = 130 pounds), with smaller shears at the arm position (of about 10 [head] + 3 [neck] + 50 [load] = 63 pounds) and a progression along the spine. These large compression/shear forces at the lower back explain the common complaint of backache and "slipped disc" due to incorrectly lifting heavy weights. See figure 28.

The correct approach for the lifting heavy weights is to keep the weight close to the torso and lift with the knees rather than by trying to straighten the back. This greatly reduces the two torque-arms of 12 inches (upper body) and 24 inches (arm to hips). For example, if these two lengths can be reduced to 1 inch (spine almost vertical) and 9 inches (weight pressed against the chest), the corresponding bending couple becomes (80 x 1) + (50 x 9) = 80 + 450 = 530 inch-pounds,

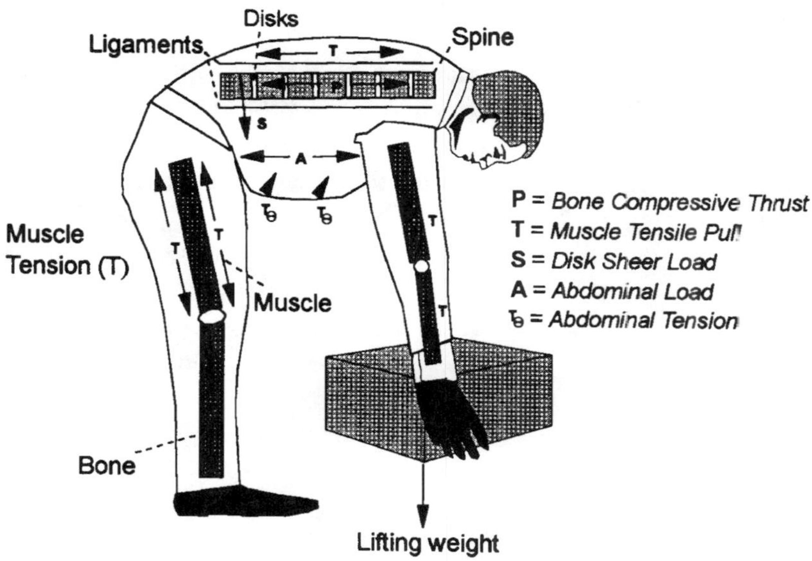

***Figure 28** Illustration of Body Forces When Bending and Lifting.*

and the muscle tension and spinal compression loads become 530/2 = 265 pounds. This is a factor of only 0.245 of the previous example. Simultaneously, the shear forces are also much smaller.

It is also necessary to realize that trauma injury does not always reveal itself immediately. A classic example is the herniated disc (HNP). Under very high loads the disc may rapidly, almost instantly, rupture. This may be associated with a burst of a vertebral bone, where the bone breaks into several segments that displace radially outward relative to the center of the "body" portion. Since the disc is attached to the bone, this can rupture the disc. However, for lower loads a degenerated disc may suffer an *initiation* of damage, but may take some time (days, weeks or months) to fully develop into an obvious hernia.

There are many examples of this situation in the world of physics. Perhaps the best-known is the cracking of a car windshield. If a full-size brick is thrown at a windshield, it is common to immediately fracture it. However, if a small stone hits the windshield, it is common to suffer only a small chip and a small amount of localized cracking. But, over time, the cracks gradually extend until eventually the entire windshield needs to be replaced. This behavior occurs due to small amplitude cyclic stresses, such as those due to the vibrations of driving or those due to daily heating and cooling. Either way, the cracks begin to grow, and as they do so the stresses needed to continue crack propagation decrease (long thin cracks require lower stresses to propagate than do short ones), thereby exacerbating the situation.

In the same way, sudden trauma may produce the equivalent of the small chip-and-crack in a weak disc. Thereafter, the cyclic stresses of daily activity may provide the mechanism to cause gradual extension of the small damage region until, eventually, a full-blown herniation occurs, seemingly due to a minor event such as turning over in bed.

It is also important to realize that with a multi-segmented structure, such as the spine, injury occurs whenever the local force (or stress) exceeds the local strength. This effect explains some apparent anomalies. For example, consider the case of a person landing vertically very hard on their tailbone, with their upper body almost vertical. Since the tailbone has little padding (unlike the "sides" of the buttocks, which provide significant padding due to the fat and muscles) such a landing can produce significant vertical deceleration of the upper body. This explains why a tailbone landing is so jarring.

Upon impact with a hard floor, the largest forces are at the base of the spine, and there is a gradual decrease in force up the spine, with the lowest force at the top of the neck. At first sight, this may appear to suggest that injury is most likely at the lower spine. For example, for a vertical deceleration of 20 g (comparable to what an Air Force pilot suffers during an emergency ejection) the force at the base of the spine may be about 1200 pounds, while the force at the base of the head is only about 200 pounds. This is because the upper body weight is mostly determined by all the mass above the hips less the mass of the articulating arms; such articulation effectively decouples the arms for short-lived actions. Then the effective upper body weight of our typical person is about 160/2 [upper body] - 20 [arms] = 60 pounds, and with a 20 g thrust this gives 20 x 60 = 1200 pounds force. The head, however, is about 10 pounds in weight, so the same 20 g thrust only produces a 200 pound force. However, since the spine is designed with progressive strength, with the lower portion stronger than the upper portion, the gradient of applied force is counterbalanced by the gradient in strength.

For an efficient structure (one where the gradient in strength exactly balances the gradient in applied force) this results in an counterintuitive prediction: either *all* of the structure is overloaded simultaneously, or *none* of it is. In reality, this never happens; instead, the structure fails at its weakest point. However, the meaning of the weakest point is that region where the ratio of local strength to local force is less than unity. This can occur anywhere up the spine, and may apply for a bone or a disc. Thus, for a degenerated disc in the neck the failure may occur in the neck, even though the forces are much lower in the neck than at the base of the spine. Such effects are frequently observed in real accidents. Figure 29 illustrates these effects.

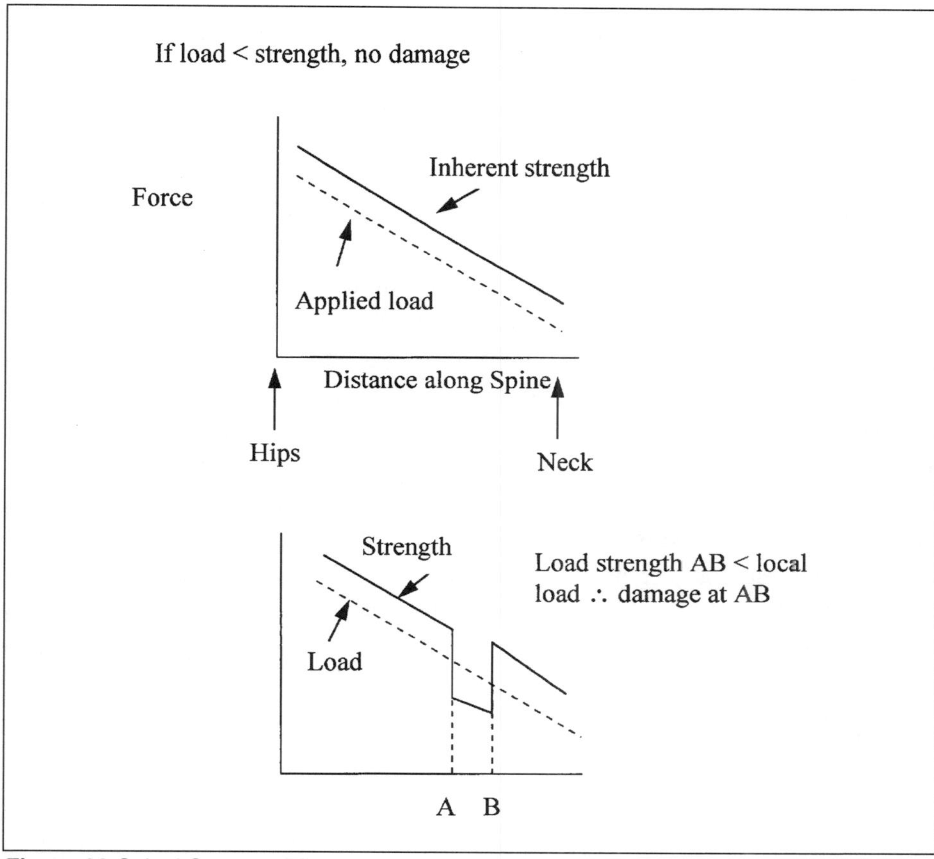

Figure 29 *Spinal Strength Effects.*

The brain and the spinal cord have three "coatings." The outermost layer is called the dura mater. Next to this, slightly inboard with only a small gap, is a very thin gossamer layer called the arachnoid. Further inboard and with a larger gap is the pia mater. The pia mater is directly adjacent to the brain/cord, while the dura mater is next to the skull/vertebrae. The cerebral/spinal fluid flows between the arachnoid and pia mater layers. With head injury internal bleeding can occur, leading to pooling of blood. Depending on which layer this occurs under or over, this gives different hematomas. Bleeding outside of the dura mater, just under the skull, gives an epidural hematoma; bleeding under the arachnoid gives a sub-arachnoid hematoma; while general bleeding above the brain is a subdural hematoma. Similar problems can occur with the spinal cord, which is effectively an extension of the brain.

While the CSF is a true viscous fluid, the brain actually has a small shear modulus and can withstand small permanent shearing motions. It behaves mostly as a viscous fluid and is usually considered incompressible for significant stresses. The small shear modulus gives the brain a Poisson's ratio slightly less than 0.5. Both the CSF and the brain have densities only slightly higher than water (1.0 g/cm^3).

Man-made materials are usually made to specifications governed by their intended application. Thus a given alloy of aluminum is made with tight tolerances with regard to composition and heat treatment. Consequently, a given alloy has well-defined properties, such as yield strength, rupture strength and modulus. However, people are not made according to specification. Accordingly, it is important to realize that different people have differing thresholds for injury. This can be a function of age, size, and sex (children are weak, as are old people, compared to the "healthy 25-year-old," and women tend to be weaker than men, all other things equal). Even for otherwise similar people, *without* medically determined signs of significant degeneration (which can only lower the possible thresholds for injury), observations indicate a possible three-to-one range in tolerance levels for injury. Throughout the remaining chapters reference is usually made to the average person, however, the possible range in individual thresholds must be considered.

Chapter 7

Neck Injury

Rearend Collisions

Consider the well-known "whiplash" problem that occurs when a car is rearended. First note that this moniker was not invented by a scientist, since it is a poor description (ref 33); the mechanism bears little resemblance to a true whiplash. True whiplash is a consequence of a traveling wave motion passing down a tapered whip. The result is that a relatively small amplitude motion at the handle end is converted into a much larger motion at the tip. The tip moves very fast, even achieving supersonic speed; hence the crack (which is really a miniature sonic boom). For a person's head/neck motion a better and more accurate description is "acceleration/deceleration motion," or "extension/flexion motion."

When a vehicle is suddenly accelerated forward, the body moves forward with the vehicle and the seat. However, the unsupported head moves forward slower, since forces must be applied via the neck. Thus, although *everything* (car, seat, torso, and head) is moving forward, the differential motion between the torso and the head appears to be a backward rotation of the head about a horizontal axis parallel to the seat back. In medical parlance such a neck motion is called extension, while the forward equivalent is called flexion. Rotation is used medically to describe motion about a vertical axis, as when turning the head left or right in the "no" motion. For typical head/neck geometry, the center-of-mass (CM) of the head moves at only about 0.56 times the speed of the torso and shoulders, causing the head to appear to move backward at about 0.44 times the speed of the torso/shoulders. See figure 30.

These differential motions can best be understood by considering the view seen by a camera positioned on the ground outside the vehicle and one attached to the vehicle. The external camera would show all items moving forward, whereas the internal camera would show only the relative rearward/forward motions of the head/neck versus the vehicle. This latter behavior, however, is the one experienced by the occupant.

The differential motion occurs because the head is not simply accelerated by a force acting directly through its CM; instead, the force acts through the neck, in an offset manner. This behavior can roughly be described by a simple

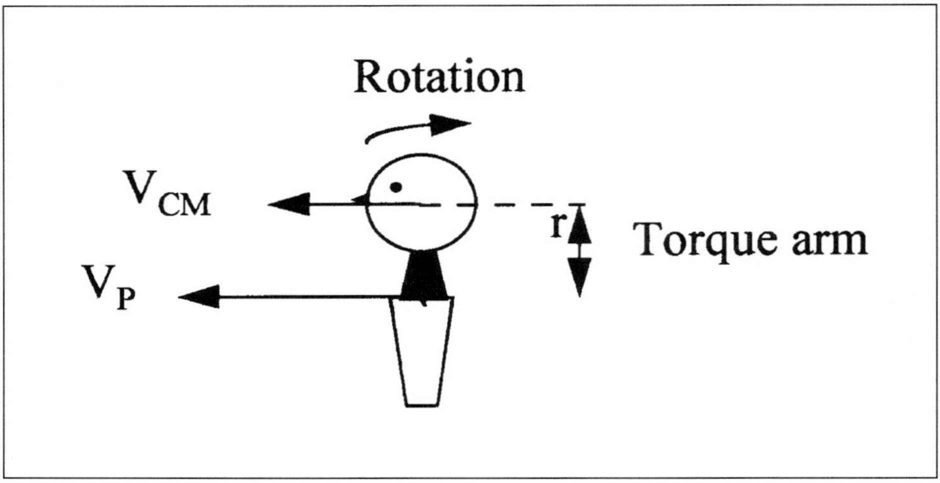

Figure 30 *Head Rotation as a Result of a Linear Thrust.*

head-on-a-stick model, where the motion is treated, to first order only, as rigid body rotation about an axis. Let the distance between the head CM and the point of force application be 'r,' which is the torque arm (distance from the head CM to the rotation point at the lower part of the neck). For a typical head/neck structure, this is about five to seven inches (references 34 and 35). The head has a moment of inertia, I, given by $I = m k^2$, where m is the mass and 'k' is the radius of gyration about the head CM about a horizontal axis through the head. For a typical head, $k^2 = 0.5 R^2$, where R is the average radius of the pseudo-spherical head, about 3.0 to 4.0 inches for small to large adults. For a uniform density sphere, $k^2 = (2/5) R^2 = 0.4 R^2$. However, the head is neither uniform nor truly spherical, but has a low density inner portion (the brain) and a higher density outer portion (the skull). Consequently, the value of the radius of gyration is slightly larger. Typical values are k = 2.12 to 2.83 inches. Since the rotation occurs about a horizontal axis in the lower neck, rather than about the head CM, the law of parallel axes must be applied to obtain the actual radius of gyration about the rotation point. Thus, $k'^2 = k^2 + r^2$. This ignores the smaller correction due to the mass of the neck itself (about 3 lbs.). It can now be shown that the induced velocity of the head CM is approximately given by

(60)

$$v_{CM} = \frac{v_p}{\left(1+\frac{r^2}{k'^2}\right)} = \frac{v_p}{\left(1+\frac{r^2}{(r^2+k^2)}\right)} = 0.56 v_p \quad \text{(absolute range of 0.5 to 0.63 } v_p\text{)}$$

where v_{CM} is the speed of the head and v_P is the push speed for the neck/shoulders. Thus the typical head starts moving at about 0.56 times the speed of the neck/shoulders. Because equation (60) involves the ratio of r and k, absolute values are not very important. Further, the numerical value of equation (60) changes only by relatively small amounts for even moderate changes in specific values of either r and/or k. Thus, one rarely needs to know the specific measurements of a given person.

To illustrate the insensitivity of equation (60) to changes in r and k, consider the two following extremes. The first extreme assumes the head shrinks to a point. In this case k becomes zero. Substitution into equation (60) gives the answer $v_{CM} = 0.5\ v_p$. The other extreme assumes the head grows until R = r (*i.e.*, the neck apparently shrinks to zero length). Further, we assume the head is a thin shell, with all the mass at the outer surface. For this thin shell, $k^2 = (2/3)R^2 = (2/3)\ r^2$. Substitution into equation (60) now gives $v_{CM} = 0.625\ v_p$. Thus, the range is very small, and the average is about $v_{CM} = 0.56\ v_p$ for realistic conditions.

We previously showed that the degree of crush damage to a vehicle depends on the differential impact speeds of the bullet and the target. In the same manner, it is the differential speed of the lower neck (near the shoulders, the C6/C7/T1 region) versus the head that determines the subsequential possible damage. This differential speed is known as delta-V, and applies provided the change is rapid. As an example, if the delta-V (v_p) of the torso was 11 mph, the head moves forward at only 6.16 mph, and thus rotates backward at 4.84 mph (7.1 ft/s). The typical length from the pivot on the neck to the CM of the head is about 7 inches (0.58 ft) for an adult. This implies a rotational rate of about 7.1(ft/s)/0.58(ft) = 12.2 radians per sec. One radian is 57.3 degrees of rotation; thus we have 700 degrees per second (this is equal to almost two complete revolutions per second — *very* fast). A normal head/neck can only typically extend about 60 degrees, although the maximum for some is nearly 90 degrees, before bottoming at its natural limit (references 8, 9, 34, and 35). Thus, it only takes about 60/700 = 0.086 sec to reach the limit.

This rotation rate is too fast for the muscles to be innervated, and the head flops like that of a rag doll. Experiments have shown (ref 36) that the average person *starts* to innervate their neck muscles within about 0.08 seconds, but does not develop full strength until about 0.14 seconds. Note that the typical eye blink takes about 0.1 seconds. These experiments have been done on volunteers and measured typical forces that can be applied to fight a rearward neck extension. For men these values were about 30 - 50 lbs. torque, with women achieving somewhat lower values, for "average" people (rather than for those who engage in serious weightlifting, etc.).

The above description of the head/neck motion is a simplification; the real motions are even more complex. Initially, as the base of the neck moves forward with the upper torso, the head remains stationary for a short time. Consequently, the neck undergoes a short-lived backward shear motion such that the neck axis leans back. Since the head has not yet moved, this gives the effect of an apparent small *forward* rotation of the head versus the neck, and, in the absence of any upward thrust on the body, will also cause the neck to stretch. Shortly thereafter, the head starts to rotate backward about an axis at the joint between the skull and the first vertebra (at the occipital condyles). Some rotation also occurs at the C1/C2 joint between the Atlas and Axis cervical vertebrae, especially rotation about the vertical axis, which is important for a turned head.

The first joint mentioned above is the one that allows the nodding ("yes") action of the head without a need to bend the neck, but the maximum possible angle is small, less than 20 degrees. The second joint mentioned (C1/C2) is the one mostly responsible for allowing the shaking ("no") motion of the head. Then the major bending and pivoting of the neck proceeds. The pivoting mostly occurs about the joint at the C6/C7 vertebrae near the base of the neck, while the rest of the neck mostly bends and also suffers a shear. Truly accurate modeling of these complex motions requires a computer code that solves the various coupled differential calculations. However, the simple head-on-a-stick model described before gives a reasonably good first approximation for estimating when damage may be induced, much as a car speed can be inferred from skid marks even though it is rare for the exact coefficient of friction to be known.

A simple way of viewing the system is to treat the neck (bones with discs between them) as a flexible stick that can rotate about a lower hinge. To the front and back are two leather straps (the ligaments), which are initially loose but which tighten for sufficient rotation (*i.e.*, the front strap tightens for a rearward motion, and the back strap tightens for a forward motion). Parallel to the straps are adjustable elastic bands (the muscles, especially the sternocleidomastoid, which joins the sternum to the skull behind the ears, and is responsible for moving the head forward), which can start with differing degrees of initial tautness. The primary muscles used to move the head backward and thus resist forward flexion are the semispinalis capitis (occiput to the C7 and T1 to T6 vertebrae), the splenius capitis (occiput and mastoid process of temporal bone to vertebral spines of C7 and T1 to T4) and the longissimus capitis (mastoid process of the temporal bone to the transverse processes of T1 to T5 vertebrae). These are aided by the trapezius (which is mostly used for shrugging the shoulders).

For lax muscles, the neck easily rotates until the ligaments tighten, and thereafter further rotation requires very rapid increases in force in order to stretch the ligaments. If the muscles were initially loose, the ligaments suffer first. However, if the muscles were very taut to start with, then they may be injured instead of or in addition to the ligaments, for sufficiently high loads.

With extreme stretching of ligaments and/or muscles, the discs become vulnerable to tensile and/or shear damage. With very high loadings, the bones themselves can be damaged, or can try to ride over each other causing subluxations (partial or temporary bone shifts) and/or dislocations (complete permanent bone shifts). Meantime, the spinal nervous system can become damaged either by transient impingement caused by relative motions of the ligaments, muscles, bones and discs, or by permanent effects such as herniation of the discs or parts of broken bones, or due to other effects such as localized induced tissue inflammations. If the vertebral bones have bone spurs (osteophytes), which can impinge on the disc and/or nerve during the violent movements, then the localized concentrated loadings that occur over the small size of the spur can cause damage at even lower levels than for normal structures.

In the absence of a well-positioned headrest, the only mechanism for stopping the head rotation is the application of forces within the neck itself. If the occupant does not already have their neck muscles tensed, then a typical head rotates over about 60 degrees with little restoring force. This is because the head weighs about 10 lbs., and in the normal, upright, almost-balanced position, only very small forces are needed to keep the head up. However, as the neck exceeds its maximum natural extension (the physiological limit), it enters the hyperextension region and stiffens up rapidly, such that further angular motion requires a rapid increase in force. For a sufficiently large force, damage to ligaments, muscles, discs, etc., can occur. Because the head starts moving slower than the torso, but must eventually catch up with it, the force must be capable of applying the increase in kinetic energy over a small rotation angle, and thus distance. Because the initial speed of the head is only about 0.56 times that of the torso, this gives an energy increase of

(61)

$$delta - E = \Delta E = \left(\frac{w}{2g}\right) v_p^2 (1 - 0.56^2) \ \text{ft-lbs} \ = 0.69 \left(\frac{w}{2g}\right) v_p^2 \ \text{ft-lbs}$$

where w is the head weight (typically about 9 to 10 lbs., references 8, 10, 34, and 35), v_p is the push speed on the car/seat/torso (equal to the example delta-V of 11 mph, given above), and g is the acceleration due to gravity (32.2 ft/s/s). Thus, delta-E = 27.8 ft-lbs, for w = 10 lbs., and delta-V = 11 mph.

The head can move over a maximum additional angle of about 20 degrees, and usually closer to only about 10 degrees, at or near its limit. With a torque arm length, neck to head, of 0.58 ft, this gives a possible maximum stopping distance of about

(62)

$$delta - X = \Delta X = 0.58 \text{ (ft) x } \frac{20 \ (degrees)}{57.3 \text{ (degrees per radian)}} = 0.202 \, ft \ = 2.43 \text{ inches}$$

The corresponding average force is given by F = (delta-E)/(delta-X) = 27.8/0.202 = 114 lbs. This is a torque force, acting perpendicular to the neck's local axis. The peak force can be even larger, twice this value, or 228 lbs., for a simple linear elastic behavior, but is of shorter duration.

Experiments show that for the whiplash motion it is not the neck tension or shear forces that cause the damage, but rather the torque about the occipital condyles. Reference 8 states that the safe envelope for the typical neck implies that the torque force should not be allowed to exceed the ligamentous damage limit, about 190 lbs.. Note that an allowed limit is really an estimate of a tolerance for the human body. This data is based on either healthy live males or male cadavers (women are rarely tested), with no preexisting neck damage. Women are usually more flexible than men, but they are also usually weaker due to less muscle, ligament, and bone mass. For this example, the average computed force is approaching the allowed, or danger, level, while the peak force has exceeded the limit. Of course, this example has also assumed no muscle action.

An alternative calculation can be done. At large neck rotations, greater than 60 degrees, the force necessary to accelerate the head to catch up with the rest of the body can be considered as a force acting mostly along the neck, rather than at 90 degrees to the neck. This force is a tensile one acting through the neck. For this situation the distance involved is now the actual maximum axial extension of the neck (*i.e.*, pulling the head upward away from the shoulders). This maximum extension is very small, being limited by the allowable stretch in the vertebral discs, surrounding ligaments, and the muscles. Consider the vulnerability of these items individually.

Suppose the extension was solely due to stretching the discs. There are six discs between the head and the shoulders, between the seven cervical vertebrae (references 9, 10, 34, and 35). Each disc is about 0.25 inches thick (ref 10). The maximum extension per cervical disc is about 80% stretch (ref 10). Thus, the maximum longitudinal stretch for a neck is about 6 x 0.25 x 0.8 = 1.2 inches = 0.1 feet. Thus for the same change in kinetic energy (27.8 ft-lbs) the corresponding force is about 278 lbs. The upper allowed direct tensile load on the average neck is about 250 lbs. (ref 8). Thus, for this example, the computed force is in the neighborhood of the danger level. This calculation has also presupposed that all six discs were uniformly stretching and sharing the load. If the load is non-uniform, the problem can be worse, since a single disc may be overloaded while the remainder are underloaded. As before, this is also the average force, and the peak can be larger.

The average area of a cervical disc that supports this load of 278 lbs. is about 0.46 in^2 (ref 10). This is the outer rim area of the disc which is fastened to the bones. Thus the corresponding stress through the discs is about 278 lbs/0.46 in^2 = 604 lb/in^2. Quotes for the maximum strength of cervical discs when in tension are about 500 lb/in^2 (ref 10). Thus, for a contact area of about 0.46 square inches the maximum allowed load is about 230 lbs, similar to the quote above.

However, because of the non-linearity of the stress-elongation response, an even better approach to the problem is to consider the maximum strain energy absorption of the cervical discs. This is done by calculating the integral of the stress-elongation data for cervical discs, and then multiplying this value by the cross-sectional area of the discs and the thickness of the discs. Damask (ref 10) gives the plot of stress versus elongation, from which the rupture integral is found to be equivalent to 256 lb/in^2 x 0.78 = 200 lb/in^2. For a cervical disc the cross sectional area is about 0.46 in^2 and the thickness is about 0.25 inches. We then find that the rupture energy is given by

$$E_{rup} = 256\ (\text{lb/in}^2)\text{x}\ 0.46\ (\text{in}^2)\text{x}\ 0.25\ (\text{in})\text{x}\ 0.78 = 23.0\ \text{in-lb} = 1.91\ \text{ft-lb}.$$

Thus each cervical disc ruptures at an energy loading of about 1.91 ft-lb. Note that this also implies a maximum axial tensile load of 117.5 lb, lower than the value of 278 lb computed above. Then for six cervical discs the total rupture energy is 6 x 1.91 ft-lbs = 11.43 ft-lbs. Since our previous calculation gave a total energy change of 27.8 ft-lbs we conclude that, for this example, the cervical discs would be strained beyond their rupture limits, *IF* the neck load were borne *only* by the discs. In reality, the load is also shared by the ligaments and/or the muscles.

The neck ligaments rupture for a peak stress of about 640 lb/in^2 and the cross sectional area is typically about 0.28 in^2 (ref 10). Thus, the rupture load is about 0.28 in^2 x 640 lb/in^2 = 178 lbs. Again, this value is close to the previous estimates of the neck loads. Thus *this* example (shoulder push speed = 11 mph) implies possible disc and/or ligament damage. Of course, these calculations treated the ligaments and discs individually. In practice, both discs and ligaments normally combine to support the total load. However, if one item first ruptures and the load remains, then the second item may become vulnerable.

When the neck stiffens it behaves roughly as a linear spring, with the increase in force proportional to the increase in angle. For a linear spring the absorbed energy is proportional to the peak force squared. But the available energy is also proportional to the push velocity squared (equation (61)). Thus the peak force is roughly proportional to the push speed, ignoring muscle action.

This overall behavior can be described to first order by assuming the model illustrated in figure 31. Here we plot the torque force on the neck versus the rotation angle. The neck will initially rotate freely up to its natural limit (I_{nat}). This is the natural extension. Then the neck enters the hyperextension region, and rapidly stiffens. Based on the data of Mertz and Patrick (ref 8), the spring rate in this stiff region can approach about 14 lbs. per degree of rotation. The arc motion is 'r' x I, with I in radians. For 'r' of about 7 inches, this makes the value of k = 1400 lbs/ft motion (or 117 lbs/inch). This model now allows for an understanding of the possible responses by invoking energy considerations. For example, let the initial applied neck torque, in the initial tensed state, force be F_{init}. Rotation through the natural angle dissipates the energy delta-$E_1 = F_{init}$ x 'r' x Inat, with I_{nat} measured in radians. Once the neck stiffens, the remaining energy dissipation is delta-$E_2 = F_{peak}^2 /2k$, with k the spring constant, assuming a pseudo-linear neck response.

Thus, the total dissipated energy is the sum of these two delta-E terms. This total is now equated to the delta-E given by equation (61). Thus

(63)

$$0.69\left(\frac{w}{2g}\right)v_p^2 = F_{init}rI_{nat} + \frac{F_{peak}^2}{2k}$$

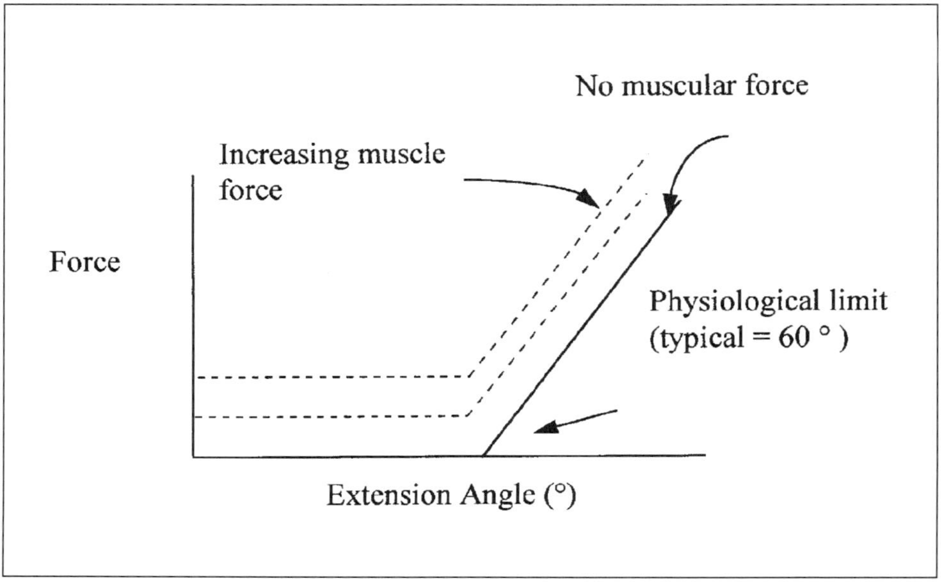

Figure 31 *Neck Torque Behavior.*

Rewriting, we obtain

(64)
$$F_{peak}^2 = 2k\left[0.69\left(\frac{w}{2g}\right)v_p^2 - F_{init} r I_{nat}\right]$$

We note that if the second term in equation (64) is small (*i.e.*, small initial tensing and/or small natural angle of rotation), we obtain F_{peak}^2 proportional to v_p^2, and thus the peak force is proportional to the push speed. However, as the second term becomes larger, so the value of F_{peak} decreases for a given value of v_p. If $F_{peak} < 0.0$, the solution implies that the natural angular limit, Inat, was not exceeded. Thus, all the energy was accommodated by the muscles, and the ligaments and/or the discs were not subjected to a significant load. See figure 32.

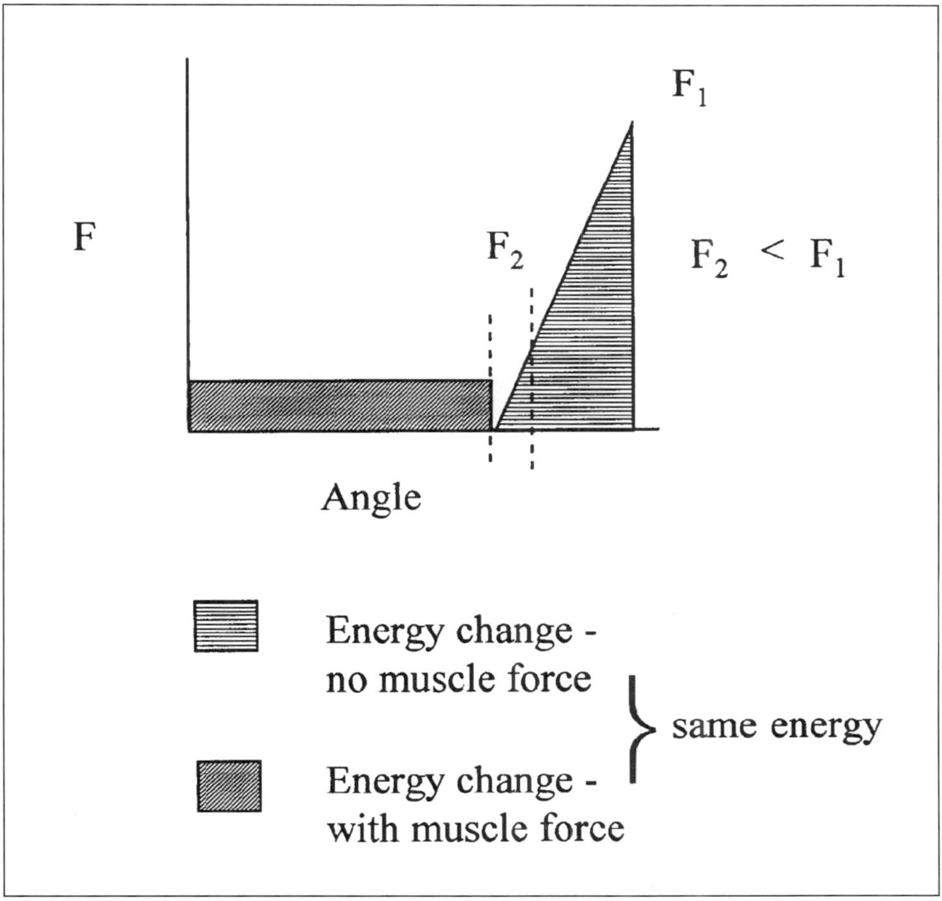

Figure 32 *Neck Energetics.*

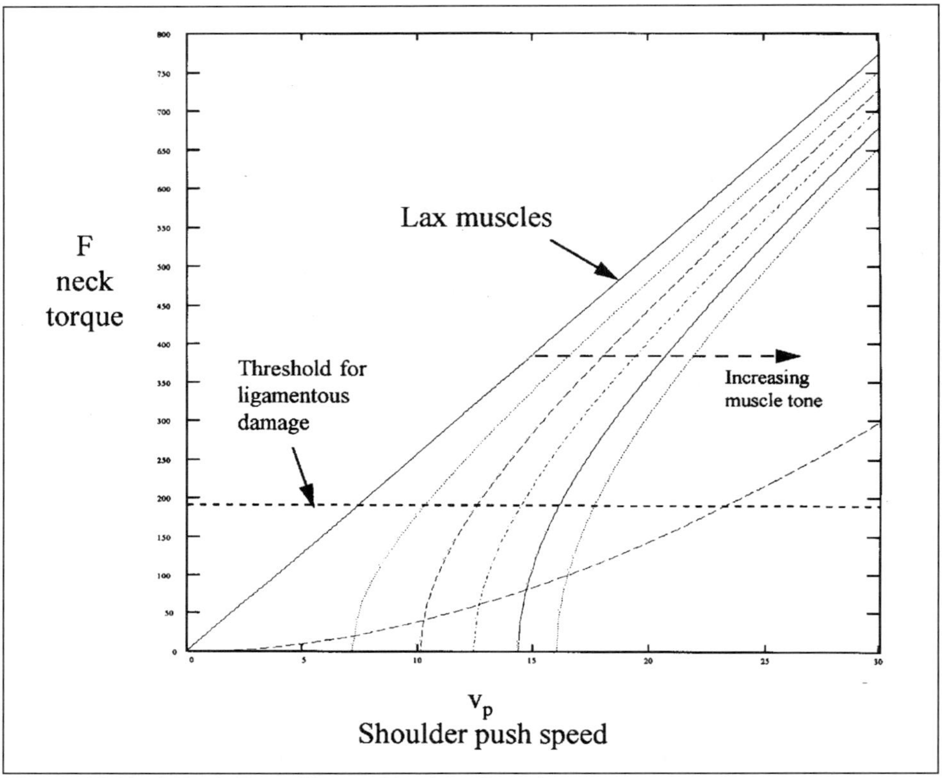

Figure 33 *Neck Peak Force Versus Shoulder Speed.*

Figure 33 demonstrates the results of equation (64). The linear rising line is the case of the product $F_{init} I_{nat}$ = zero, while the series of curved lines to the right indicate increasing values of this product, in increments of 20 lbs x 60 degrees = 120 lb-degrees. The heavy upward rising curve gives the locus where $F_{peak} = F_{init}$, and thus the region below this latter curve indicates where the neck's natural extension is only partly exceeded. For finite values of initial neck muscle tension, the curves become zero at finite values of push speed. The place where the curves assume zero value at finite push-speed values are called the zero-limit values. For each such push speed this indicates the upper speed at which hyperextension starts, and for lower push speeds there is *no* hyperextension as far as ligament stretching is concerned.

For example, since the energy of rotation is proportional to the square of the push speed, then if the actual push speed for a given impact is only a fraction, f, of the corresponding zero-limit value, and the implied head-neck rotation is only a fraction, f^2, of the physiological limit. Thus, if an initial neck muscle tension indicates a zero-limit push speed of, say, 10 mph, with a physiological angle of

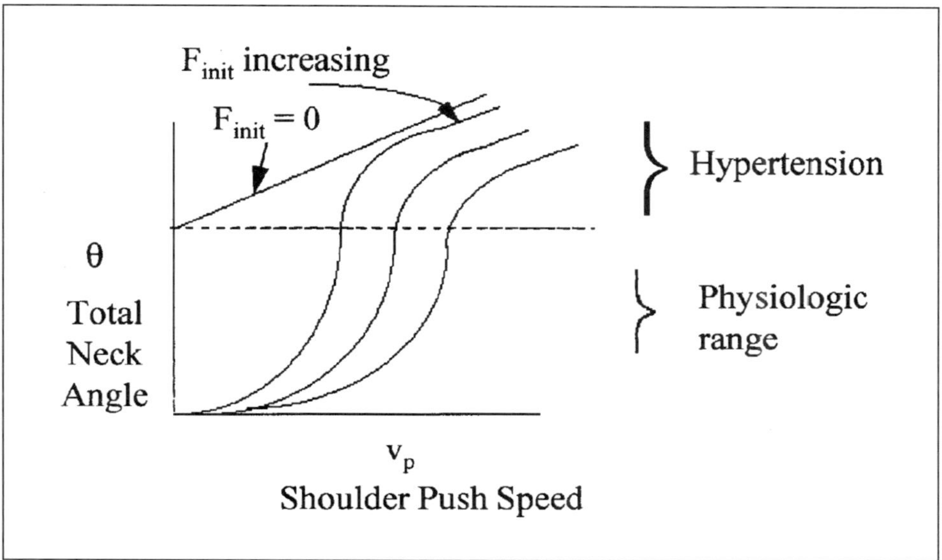

Figure 34 *Neck Angular Rotation Versus Shoulder Speed.*

60 degrees, then for a fixed muscle tension an actual push speed of 8 mph implies an actual neck extension of only (8 mph/10 mph)^2 x 60 degrees = 0.64 x 60 degrees = 38.4 degrees. See figure 34.

Figure 33 clearly illustrates the reasons for the complications in interpretation of whiplash damage, since it demonstrates the various significant parameters involved. For example, damage is not simply a function of rotation angle, nor is it a simple function of initial muscle tensing or natural extension angle. Likewise, the exact force to cause damage will vary between people. However, figure 33 allows rapid interpretation of the possibilities. If the damage force on a normal healthy individual, without prior neck damage and/or lesions, is about 190 lbs. equivalent torque, we see that for an untensed neck this level is reached for an induced push speed (of the shoulders) of about 7.5 mph, whereas for a strongly tensed neck (100 lbs. torque) with 60 degrees of natural rotation, the level is reached at a push speed of about 17 mph.

Note that the factor of 0.69 in equation (64) was related to the average behavior for a neck, as described in equation (60). This was given by (1 - 0.56^2) = 0.69, as seen in equation (61). For someone with a longer-than-average neck this factor increases. For example, the upper limit of this value is (1 - 0.5^2) = 0.75. This implies that a long neck will slightly worsen the situation, allowing the critical speed to drop slightly. This may explain why women tend to suffer whiplash more often than men, since, on average, women have longer necks than do men.

However, the effect is not large since equation (64) predicts that the peak force is proportional to the square-root of this factor.

For the case of someone with such prior damage or susceptibility, the danger levels can be significantly lower, since scar tissue and/or herniated discs are known to be much weaker than normal healthy tissue (ref 10). For these cases, the maximum rotation is usually limited, and the maximum allowed force is also limited; thus the energy absorbing capabilities can be seriously impaired. Unfortunately, there are no available reliable estimates of limits for pre-damaged tissues (presumably because weak or pre-injured individuals would not wish to volunteer for experimentation). For example, consider a person with a prior neck problem, such that their natural neck extension is limited to only 20 degrees, and their damage level is only 70 lbs., due to scar tissue. With only a small initial tensing of the neck muscles, this damage level will be reached at a push speed of about 2.5 - 3.0 mph! Note that the lower push speed range is similar to, or even lower than, the speeds typical for causing vehicle damage. Thus, human body damage *can* occur with either zero or very small amounts of vehicle damage, and it is not necessary to have copious vehicle damage in order to hurt the human body.

Thus, for the normal healthy average person, damage can be expected for push speeds in the range of about 7.5 - 17 mph, depending on individual strength, natural extension, and initial muscle tensing. However, for a person with a predisposition to damage and limited range of motion, the damage could occur at much lower push speeds.

Of course, in order to take into account any predisposition to injury there must be some evidence of its existence. This evidence is most commonly obtained from medical data. In an ideal world, everyone would be inspected before they were involved in an accident; unfortunately, it is not common practice for people to visit medics purely to have themselves checked out for non-troubling abnormalities. If everyone were so inspected, then an analyst would have pre-impact data concerning range of motions (ROM) and degeneration of discs and bone problems such as osteophytes. Armed with this knowledge, the analyst could compare pre- and post- values of ROM and/or have a firm basis on which to characterize a person as being unusually vulnerable. Such comparative data rarely exists for a person involved in their first accident. However, the data may exist for those who have several sequential accidents, since the clinical measurements from accident number one can provide the needed data for analysis of accident number two and so on.

If a headrest (or, more properly, head *restraint*) is properly positioned behind the head and not too far away, the large neck rotation/extension that causes injury is prevented, and the hyperextension region is not reached. Further, the force necessary to stop the head is now provided by the headrest, rather than by the neck itself. Thus, the neck is less likely to suffer, and the worst that usually happens is that the occupant suffers from a mild bruise on the back of the head. For a properly cocooned driver, with good initial support for both the torso and the head (usually implying that the headrest is actually initially touching the head, preventing relative motion), survival can occur to speeds above 40 mph and accelerations of above 40 g (references 9 and 23; these references contain much information obtained by the USAF, NASA, Wayne State University and various car manufacturers). Note that all of the above discussion has presupposed that the value of v_p is identical to the sudden delta-V of the car.

It is important to realize that even if the muscle innervation time is too long to adequately allow the muscles to prevent excessive neck angular extension, there is an automatic reflex action whereby the muscles will switch on anyway. Such a late such activation causes problems. For instance, the muscle tension may peak when the neck has already reached its peak extension and is in the process of rebounding into the flexion position. In this case the sudden application of strong muscles will now exacerbate the rebound motion. Further, whereas the backward extension of the head/neck implies an initial tension in the neck due to the lag in head motion and the effects of centrifugal force due to rotation rates, the application of muscle tension by the sternocleidomastoids implies a reactive compression in the neck and thus in the discs. Thus, the force history in the neck is very complex. Early in the collision, when muscle tone is negligible, the neck loads are primarily those of tension and shear, whereas at later times, with muscle activation, the loads become compressive and shear. It is not surprising that the modes of damage are complex, and not easily predictable.

The Seat Bounce

Car seats are typically built more for comfort than for support. There is a compromise between the comfort of a seat and its ability to cause seat bounce and worsen the whiplash effect. This bounce can occur because the typical car seat has a coefficient of restitution of about e = -0.3 to -0.7 (ref 10). This is a combination of both the behavior of the cushion and the seat back frame. For small seat compression it is mostly the cushion that provides the damped bounce (e = -0.3). However, for larger loads on the seat, the cushion bottoms out and now the motion is dominated by the mostly-elastic seat frame. Hence the value of 'e' increases, giving greater bounce.

Figure 35 illustrates the typical behavior of a seat back. The plot shows force versus deflection of the frame and cushion, with the force applied about halfway up the seat back. Note that for small compressions the spring rate (force per

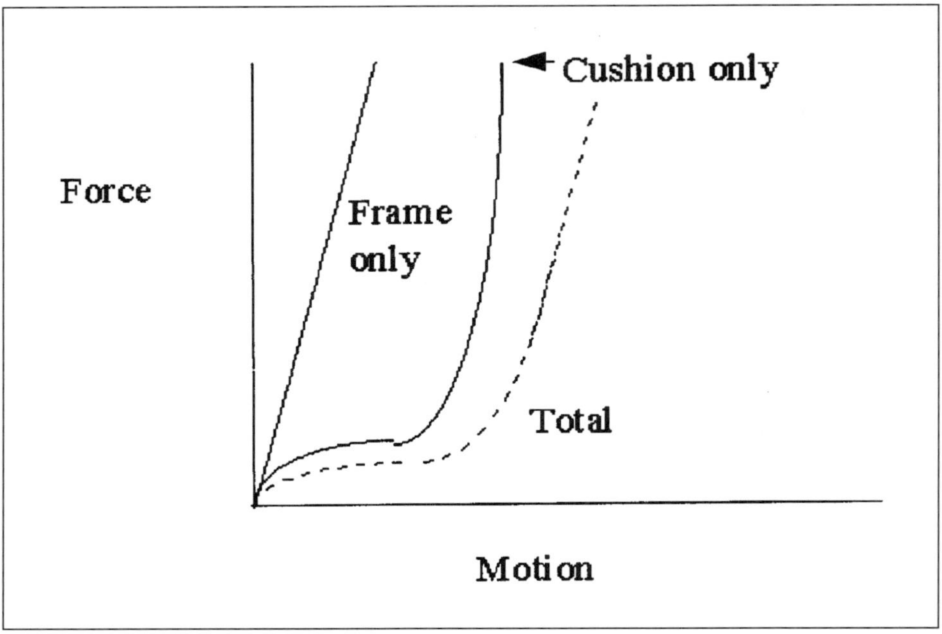

Figure 35 *Seat Back Behavior.*

deflection, k) is quite low, usually in the range of k = 20 - 50 lbs/inch compression, mostly in a horizontal direction. However, beyond a certain deformation the cushion bottoms out, and the spring rate becomes significantly larger, and can reach about k = 300 lbs/inch compression after passing through a transition region. Now the motion is mostly an angular rotation about the bottom of the seat back, with the torso rotating about the hips. Ultimately, for sufficiently high loads the seat frame itself suffers from plastic yielding and proceeds to rapidly collapse with increasing load, and finally breaks. These effects have important consequences.

Obviously, any seat design (even the sheet-steel seats found in fighter aircraft) always has *some* compliance, so it is necessary to understand why a highly-compliant seat produces problems. The explanation concerns the natural frequency of the torso-seat pair versus that for the vehicle-vehicle impact. An analogy is the difference between using your hand to bounce up and down a rigid rod with a weight on the end versus having the weight dangling on a very flexible spring. In the first case, the weight simply moves with your hand, *i.e.*, in phase with the hand motion, and with the same amplitude of motion; whereas in the second case, the motion of the weight displays an obvious lag, or phase shift, versus your hand, and the amplitude of motion may be smaller or larger than the hand motion, depending on the relative frequencies.

The worst possible condition happens when the two frequencies (car-to-car and torso-seat) are identical, causing resonance. Under resonant behavior, the peak amplitude and speed of the torso-seat pair can increase, effectively increasing the value of the coefficient of restitution. When a vehicle is suddenly pushed forward, it behaves as if undergoing a half-cycle oscillation superimposed on a mean speed. Thus the rigid rod analogy will give a seat/torso motion which is the same as the vehicle motion, whereas the soft spring analogy will cause a delay in seat/torso motion until after the vehicle has already reached its final speed.

For a rigid seat, the first frequency is sufficiently high that the torso-seat pair essentially follows the motion of the vehicle with negligible differential motion. In this case, the peak acceleration seen by the occupant equals that of the vehicle. This can reach 6 - 12 g when the bumper reaches its limit. For a stationary target, this corresponds to a sudden jump to the bumper limit speed at the point where the two vehicles reach their common speed, followed by a vehicle bounce to a higher speed. Thus, if the bumper limit speed is 5 mph this condition corresponds to a jump to the common speed of 5 mph and then a slower increase in speed to the final speed of about 8.5 mph.

However, for a soft seat, the frequency is sufficiently low that the vehicle acts as if it instantly reached its final speed, while the torso-seat pair is only just starting to move. Now the peak acceleration can reach the value v_{final}^2/a_{eff}, where 'a_{eff}' is the effective seat compression amplitude. This effective amplitude is the sum of the actual car motion during the impact plus the actual compression of the seat relative to the car. Unless 'a_{eff}' can be made very large, this can again result in similar torso accelerations as for the vehicle itself. For instance, for the same final speed of 8.5 mph and a car with a R_0 value of 1.0 and bumper limit of 5 mph, the motion of the car is only about 0.95 inches to reach 5 mph and about 5.0 inches to reach 8.5 mph (see chapter 4). If the corresponding seat amplitude is 4 inches, the effective seat amplitude is between 4.95 and 9.0 inches. This gives a peak acceleration of about 12.5^2 (ft/s)^2/0.75 (ft) = 208 ft/s^2 = 6.5 g, which is still comparable to the acceleration of the car.

Let the seat back have a weight w_s. Since the seat back acts as a series-spring, the effective weight is about $w_s/3$. For a spring constant of k, and an upper torso weight of about w/2 (where w is the person's total weight), the natural oscillation frequency of the torso/seat is given by f (Hertz) = $(1/2\pi)(kg/(w/2 + w_s/3))^{1/2}$, with k in lbs/ft motion, g in ft/s^2, and w and w_s in lbs. For k = 30 lbs/inch = 360 lb/ft, w = 160 lbs., and w_s = 30 lbs. this frequency is about 1.81 Hertz. The oscillation period is 0.55 seconds. Thus, the time to bottom in the seat is the quarter period or 0.14 seconds. Note that this is similar to the typical time for a two-car collision to reach disengagement. Thus, the torso reaches the final speed of the car just as bottoming of the cushion occurs, and will then bounce back out of the seat.

For a linear force-distance behavior, the maximum stored energy of the seat is given by $E = (1/2)ka^2$, where 'a' is the true seat amplitude relative to the car. Typically, the soft cushion response ceases for amplitudes greater than about 2.5 inches (0.21 ft), since most seats have only about that much padding. Then for k = 360 lb/ft, the maximum energy is about 7.8 ft-lbs. For a torso weight of 80 lbs. and effective seat back weight of 10 lbs., this corresponds to a speed of about 2.4 ft/s = 1.6 mph. The corresponding peak acceleration given to the torso and seat back is given by accel = $(2\pi f)^2$ a. For the above frequency and seat amplitude this is about 27 ft/s^2, or about 0.83 g. The corresponding peak force experienced by the torso is about 0.83 x 80 lbs. = 67 lbs. This is less than the compression force of 30 (lb/inch) x 2.5 (inch) = 75 lbs., because the compression force is accelerating both the torso and the seat back. This low force is unlikely to cause problems. However, this soft response is clearly limited to low speeds.

For a significantly higher speed the seat stiffens and now rotates. Suppose the total true seat amplitude became 8 inches. This represents 2.5 inches of cushion compression in a horizontal direction and a further 5.5 inches along an arc pivoting about the seat back bottom, and measured about halfway up the seat, about 12 inches up the seat back. This corresponds to an angular rotation of about 26.3 degrees in addition to the initial seat back angle. The initial 2.5 inches of motion store the previous 7.8 ft-lbs of energy. However, the remaining 5.5 inches store about (1/2)3600 (lbs/ft)0.67^2 (ft^2) = 808 ft-lbs; hence, the total stored energy is about 816 ft-lbs. Because of the rotation of both the torso and seat back about the hips/bottom of the seat, the effective weights of both the torso and seat back are about 4/3 their true values. Thus the torso apparently weighs about 4/3 x 80 = 106.6 lbs, and the effective weight of the seat back is about 4/3 x 1/3 x 30 = 13.3 lbs., for a total of about 120 lbs. This assumes a uniform weight per length for both the torso and seat back, and is a consequence of rotational inertia. This corresponds to a speed of about 20.9 ft/s = 14.3 mph. Further, when the hard portion of the seat response dominates, the oscillation frequency also increases to about 4.95 Hertz. The period now shortens to about 0.2 seconds, while the quarter period becomes 0.051 seconds. The latter is less than the time for a two-car collision, where the time to reach common speed is typically about 0.08 seconds. Thus, the actual response of the torso/seat oscillation asymptotes to the actual car acceleration. This is because, whenever the driving frequency, due to the car-car interaction, becomes significantly less than the response frequency of the seat-torso combination, the latter approaches the driving response, and the two motions become similar as described above.

In the absence of any significant vehicle motion, the peak acceleration seen by the torso would be about $(2\pi f)v_{final} = (2\pi 4.95)20.9$ ft/s^2 = 650 ft/s^2 = 20.2 g, giving a peak force on the torso of about 1615 lbs. However, in reality, for a sudden push to 14.3 mph the car motion itself is about 12 inches for the same characteristics of car bounce plus some crush. Then, using v_{final}^2(ft/s)^2/(8 + 12) (inches) = 262 ft/s^2 = 8.1 g, we see that accelerations in the range of 6 - 8 g are easily achieved for impacts that exceed the bumper limits of the vehicle, and the stiffening of the seat actually helps reduce the maximum possible values. However, the tradeoff is the greater bounce on the seat, because the oscillation is now dominated by the spring response of the seat frame itself rather than by the cushion. The seat frame response is quite elastic. Thus, for the higher jump speeds the effective coefficient of restitution increases to a larger value, such as - 0.7.

Unfortunately, the really stiff seat behavior only occurs for large seat compression amplitudes. In reality, there is a transition region as the response changes from cushion behavior to frame behavior. This means that the oscillation frequency slowly changes from the slower-than-car to the faster-than-car, and thus encompasses the resonant condition. Thus, for speeds in the 5 to 15 mph range the response can give significant accelerations to the torso.

Upon first being accelerated forward, the upper torso will sink back into the seat by a amount dependent on the spring rate of the seat, usually a maximum of a few inches. This has the effect of initially reducing the distance between the head and the headrest. However, this reduction in distance only applies to the cushion deflection, which dominates only for low speeds. Once the seat frame response dominates, the headrest moves back with the seat, and the head no longer catches up with the headrest. When the seat bottoms, the torso is moving at the same speed as the car. Thereafter, the torso now bounces forward, moving *faster* than the car. This excess forward speed is about v_{forw} = e delta-V. Thus for a vehicle delta-V of 11 mph, v_{forw} = 3.3 to 5.5 mph, since for this speed range the seat is in the transition region between the cushion-only response and the stiff-frame response.

Therefore, the true push speed for the shoulders is the sum of the vehicle delta-V and the excess bounce speed. Thus $v_{push} = v_{car} + v_{bounce}$, or $v_{push} = (1 - e)v_{car} = 1.3v_{car}$ to $1.5v_{car}$. Clearly, the corresponding vehicle delta-V to cause the same effect on the neck is lower than before by the factor 1/1.3 = 0.77 or 1/1.5 = 0.67. If the seat belt correctly locks up when the torso regains its initial position in the seat, the torso is rapidly stopped, and it merely oscillates between the belt and the seat. However, the neck still responds to the combined car and seat bounce. Thus, the previous shoulder push speed range of 7.5 - 17 mph for possible damage lowers to about 5.3 - 11 mph *for the vehicle,* if the seat is very compliant and

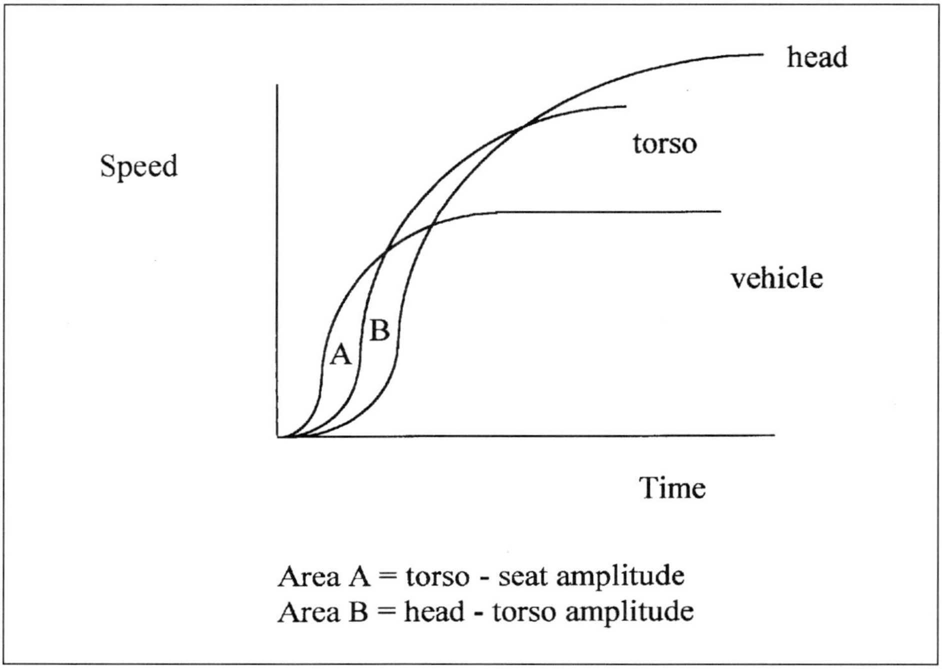

Figure 36 *Induced Differential Motions: Car/Torso/Head.*

the head did not contact the headrest during its rearward motion. Figure 36 indicates the possible motions.

Sometimes, the belt can actually retract as the body moves into the seat, and result in very tightly locking the body to the seat. For this case, there is little or no bounce, and the maximum push speed for the shoulders is the same as that of the vehicle. Other times, the belt fails to lock sufficiently fast, and the body can bounce and move all the way to the steering wheel or dashboard, causing an impact on the head and/or the chest. Note that during this unrestrained seat bounce the torso is again moving faster than the head, so a second rearward whip of the head can occur. If the head was stopped by the headrest during the first rearward motion, then this second whip will occur as for a lower speed rearender, and thus cause little damage. However, if the head was not stopped by the headrest during the first motion, then the bounced-induced second whip will add to the rearward neck rotation, as described above, and, since the body and head are moving away from the seat, the headrest can no longer help. Thus the problem can be worsened by having a very compliant (*i.e.*, comfortable) seat back!

The net result of all these motions explains many of the occupant's confusing and apparently contradictory post-accident statements. The occupant invariably claims to have been thrown forward, and/or to have had their head whip back, and/or have been thrown into the steering wheel, and/or have been trapped in their seat belts, *all* due to a rearend collision! All these possibilities exist. Being thrown forward does not necessarily imply a front-end collision. Figure 36 demonstrates the various possibilities for car motion, torso motion and head motion.

A large amount of test and human tolerance data are also to be found in references 1 and 9. In particular, reference 9 states that, for a rearend collision giving a vehicle delta-V of 10 mph, the probability of neck damage is 0.7, whereas for 15 mph it is about 1.0. In both cases no headrest was assumed, and the occupant was assumed to be expecting the impact with tensed muscles. Without tensed muscles, the claim is that the situation is worse, in agreement with the analyses given above.

Experiments have been performed by West (ref 17). These involved both moving bullet cars into stationary target cars and driving cars backwards at rigid barriers. The volunteers involved wore accelerometers, allowing the head accelerations to be measured. The results indicated that the resulting accelerations were roughly proportional to the sudden delta-v experienced by the cars. Most importantly, West's plot of acceleration versus speed can be converted into force versus speed by assuming an average head weighs about 10 lbs. We then find that his force-speed line lies just under our own calculations for maximum force-speed given in figure 33, and based on equation (64). West's data is the equivalent to the occupants having a small degree of initial muscle force prior to the impacts. Other experiments on human volunteers are well described in reference 28.

The ideal seat design is not practical. The ideal design would be as follows. First determine the actual profile of the spine for an individual. Now make a rigid skin for the outer surface of the seat that conforms to this individual. Then provide springing/damping behind this surface form. Such a seat will apply loads uniformly to the individual's spine, preventing hard point loadings. The latter occur with a real, typical, seat owing to the fact that a normal person has spinal curvature, resulting in maximum initial loads at the pelvis and mid-thorax. These hard point loadings cause sudden straightening of the spine, and associated vertical thrusts up the spine (see references 11 and 28). Note that this behavior even occurs for seats with built-in lumbar supports. This occurs because, even with the lumbar support, the local stiffness of the seat varies with thickness. Clearly, customizing seats on an individual basis would make seats very expensive, and thus it is not practical. The usual approach to making seats comfortable is to make them too soft. Simply making a seat with a generic semi-rigid surface merely makes the seat very uncomfortable for the average person (remember the desks you had in grade school?), since such seats rarely fit any specific individual. Also, even the ideal seat will only work if the seat back is kept vertical, in order to prevent ramping effects on a sloping seat back.

It should be noted that the hard point loading which induces rapid straightening of the spine is also responsible for rapid sudden loading of back muscles. Such loadings can induce muscle spasms. These spasms would not exist if the seat profile were a perfect fit to the occupant and the seat back was vertical. Such spasms are probably a consequence of the automatic reflex response of the muscles to sudden body motions. Due to the natural delay in muscle innervation, the muscles can switch on when the body motion is recovering from the vertical thrust, similar to the previously mentioned action of neck muscles. Thus, as the spine rebounds from its initial extension and the muscles simultaneously reach peak tension, the net axial compressions can peak such that the spine suffers larger thrusts than normal. Consequently, the average bad fit of a typical seat back can induce these muscle spasms. Such spasms can be induced if the reflex arc is partially unmediated due to problems with the central cord. Indeed, the use of lumbar supports in cars can sometimes be a liability. The reason is that, although such supports may make the seat more comfortable during low loadings such as those from merely sitting in the seat, the result of sudden acceleration may induce significant hard point loading and differential loading along the spine of the occupant. This is because any device that does not induce uniform loadings along the occupants' spine will result in the production of differential accelerations along the spine.

One last problem should be mentioned with regard to seat backs. While not common, some seats, especially older bench seats, have a metal bar running across the lower back. For a sufficiently hard rearend thrust, this bar can be forced into contact with the lower part of the occupant's spine after compression of the cushion. Such bars are usually less than one inch in diameter; however, they can apply loads of several hundred pounds in the process of suffering a permanent plastic bend. Because the local contact area is small and concentrated, this can sometimes apply loads that can cause bone fracture, usually in the L4 or lower regions, including the sacrum. In addition to causing bone fracture, this localized load can also induce local shear action which can cause problems for the intervertebral discs immediately above the load.

The Seat Back Angle

Few drivers have their seat backs truly vertical. Rather, it is usual for the seat back to lean at between about 10 and 25 degrees. However, the driver still keeps his head erect. The result is the driver is in an anatomic position of having an initial flexion to his neck equal to the seat back angle. This produces several effects. First, we note that the typical headrest is attached to the seat such that tilting the seat backward results in a larger initial gap between the driver's head and the headrest. Most headrests can only be adjusted in a plane parallel to the seat back. If the headrest is in the down position and too low to catch the occipital bone of the driver, the initial flexion of the neck merely increases the total angle of motion for the neck prior to the latter reaching its physiological limit in extension. This is useful in that it increases the time taken to reach this limit, thereby giving the driver slightly more time to react and apply his muscles, although this is useful only at the lowest speeds. For the lax-muscle state, this increase in backward angle motion has negligible effect on the peak loads placed on the ligaments. However, with pretensed muscles, the larger necessary angular motion is beneficial. Now the muscles can absorb more of the energy since the arc motion is larger prior to reaching the neck extension limit. This limits the peak ligament loads in the same way as increasing the initial muscle tone.

Figures 33 and 34 indicate the response of the neck as a function of the product of initial muscle tone and physiological angle. The initial flexion is the equivalent to increasing the physiological angle or increasing the initial muscle tone. Thus, having the neck in a forward flexion and having initial pretensed muscles helps to minimize the peak neck loads in a rearend collision. However, it reduces the forward flexion angular motion for a frontal collision. Note, however, a low headrest can also merely act as a fulcrum for the neck, such that the lower part of the neck contacts the headrest and then allows the head to hyperextend over the headrest.

Very Low Speeds

More recent data is available for studies at very low speeds (references 11 and 28). Here groups of two vehicles were allowed to impact with accelerations for the rearended targets in the range of +1.9 to +5.0 mph and decelerations for the bullets in the range of -2.0 to -5.7 mph. This study is important because it revealed the existence of unexpectedly large vertical accelerations and decelerations along the necks of the rearended occupants, in addition to the normally expected longitudinal ones. These additional motions were attributed to several factors. First it was observed that the wedge, or ramping, effect of the angled seat itself caused an initial upward thrust on the body. This ramping is relative to the seat back, which itself is actually dropping due to rotation, giving only a small absolute net head motion relative to the ground. However, this ramping motion also caused the occupant's head to rise higher versus the headrest. Thus, the experiments often demonstrated that the head rotated down onto the headrest unless the latter was very high to start with. Indeed, when the occupant's head hit downward onto the headrest it was observed that the force could be sufficient to actually push the headrest from its raised position down to the seat.

Secondly, the occupants' spines were observed to rapidly straighten during the early thrust. These two motions then reversed themselves at later times. However, only for times longer than about 0.2 to 0.25 secs were the subjects "obviously" (the paper author's expression) able to use their own muscles to help control the motions. It was observed that several of the subjects did suffer from transient discomforts lasting up to several hours, but no one suffered any permanent damage. However, the authors did conclude that for a delta-V of about 5 mph, the conditions were close to the threshold for *"...very mild, single event musculoskeletal cervical strain injury."* Compared to the previous example, for a delta-V of 11 mph, a 5-mph case will involve only $(5/11)^2 = 0.21$ times the corresponding delta-E, and thus much lower peak forces. For a pseudo-linear stiffening response of the neck, the peak force would be about $5/11 = 0.45$ times the value for the 11-mph case.

The existence of an early upward neck thrust produces a small initial forward flexion of the head. This occurs because the head CM is slightly to the anterior side of the occipital condyles. An upward thrust causes a torque-arm effect, which induces the motion. This explains an anomaly: in many previous studies using high-speed photography the head was observed to initially nod forward, although there was no obvious force to produce this motion. Consequently, many analysts considered this motion some form of an artifact. With the observation of the rapid spine-straightening, the dilemma can be explained.

One qualification should be stated concerning this recent study: their own data indicated that they were not conserving linear momentum (*i.e.*, + (w_1 delta-V_1) did not equal - (w_2 delta-V_2)) by up to about 30%. This may have been due to some early-time, unnoticed, vertical or side motions of the vehicles. However, practically all real-life collisions will suffer from this effect, since it is rare for the thrust between two cars to exactly be parallel to the road surface. The conclusion is that real collisions probably induce strong vertical thrusts along occupants' necks in addition to the previously calculated rotations and axial forces, since many collisions involve braking vehicles, which typically adopt the nose-down, tail-up attitude. A vehicle with this attitude will exaggerate the vertical motions on the neck.

Thus far, we have ignored the possibility that the vehicle has its brakes on during the impact. For high speeds this will have negligible effect. For very low impact speeds, though, braking can modify the head/neck response. This is because the braking provides a reverse acceleration to the head, and can thus slow down the rotation. At high speed, this effect is too weak to prevent the head rapidly reaching its natural limit. For these very low speed cases the impact will be elastic. The maximum rotation angle induced is given by

(65)

$$q=\frac{\left(\frac{r}{k^2+r^2}\right)\left(\frac{v_0^2}{2fg}\right)\left(\frac{2w_1}{w_1+w_2}\right)^2}{1+\left(\frac{r^2}{k^2+r^2}\right)}$$

where the angle, q, is measured in radians (one radian = 57.3 degrees). Note how the angle is proportional to the square of the initial impact speed, v_0, and to the inverse of the coefficient of friction, f, and also depends on the ratio of vehicle weights. If $w_1 = w_2$, r = 7 inches, k = 2.7 inches, and f = 0.7 (near-skid condition), we obtain

(66)

$$Angle = 1.01v_0^2\ (ft/s)^2\ \text{degrees, or } Angle = 2.18v_0^2\ (mph)^2\ \text{degrees}$$

Thus for v_0 = 5 mph, the angle is about 54.5 degrees, while a typical maximum possible rotation of 90 degrees occurs for v_0 = 6.4 mph. Such an impact speed is usually below that needed to induce vehicle damage. We see that for very low impact speeds the head rotation can become less than that to reach a typical headrest. If the latter requires about 45 degrees, then v_0 = 4.54 mph.

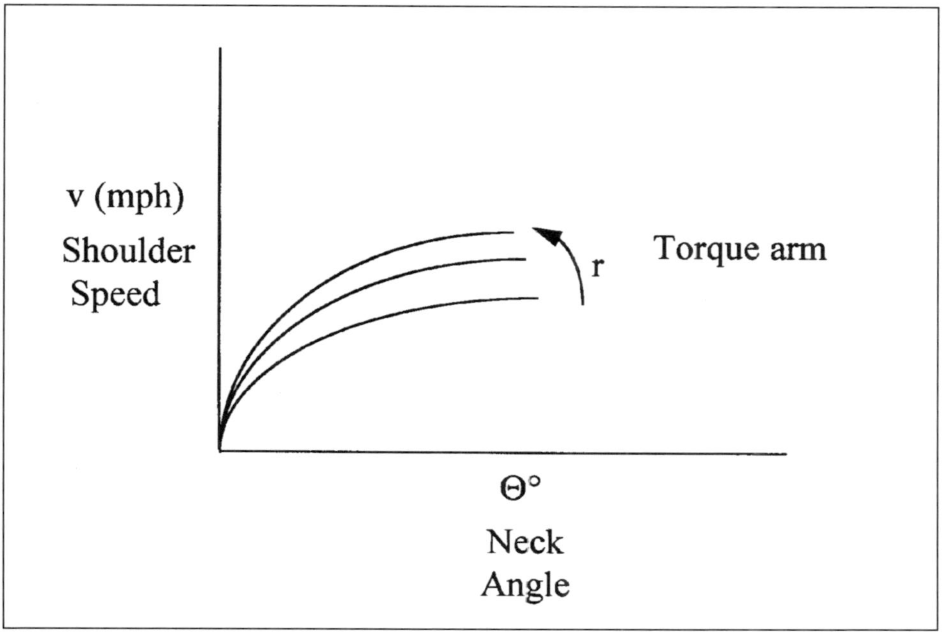

Figure 37 *Neck Rotation Effects.*

In reality, the above calculations are merely another example of the lightly tensed neck situation discussed in reference to figure 33, since a deceleration of 0.7 g is equivalent to a very low neck restraint due to muscles. For example, for a head weight of 10 lbs., and the factor of 0.56 for head versus neck (equation 60), the initial torque force is about 0.7 x 0.56 x 10 = 3.9 lbs. Figure 37 illustrates the results of equation (65) for a series of torque-arm lengths (neck to head CM), showing the relatively small sensitivity to exact values of the latter.

The Turned Head Condition

Another condition that can affect the seriousness of induced injuries is having one's head turned at the time of the accident, such as when an occupant is looking sideways when impacted. The typical maximum angle of side rotation about a vertical axis for a person is about 79 degrees (ref 35). The act of turning the head tightens the ligaments and muscles on the neck, leaving less further possible motion before the system bottoms out. This is the equivalent to reducing I_{nat} to a very small value. There is also a torsional shear on the intervertebral discs. Consequently, a sudden rearward rotation for a turned head will cause the neck ligaments and muscles to more rapidly stiffen up, than for a forward facing occupant, and induce a combined shear/tensile load on the discs.

Because the CM of the head is slightly forward of the spine and not directly above the cervical spine, an induced rotation about a horizontal axis also induces a rotation about a vertical axis, although of a smaller rate, thus further increasing the disc shear. The net result is that the occupant's head/neck can be driven to its natural limit very quickly, without a large angle of rotation. This can lead to damage even with a properly positioned headrest, since most vehicles only allow for vertical adjustment of the headrest and give no mechanism for altering the distance between the back of the head and the restraint; thus, if the gap is too large, neck damage can occur. For a 7-inch neck rotating 60 degrees, the backward motion parallel to the ground is 7 x sine 60 = 6.1 inches. Many headrests are positioned with gaps much larger than this, and a great deal depends on the inclination of the seat back. The greater the inclination of the seat back, the greater becomes the possible gap between the occiput bone on the head and the headrest.

It is of interest to note that many of the smaller cars (especially the foreign-made ones) tend to have the better headrest designs. Frequently the headrests are built with a forward tilt, such that even for a rear-tilted seat the headrest is still mostly vertical and reasonably close to the head. They also tend to be taller, often extending considerably above the horizontal line joining the eyes and the ears. It is mostly the larger US cars that have the poor designs, especially the older (pre-1990) models, which tend to have low headrests that are also a significant distance from the occiput bone.

A recent report published by the IIHS is rather disturbing (ref 37). This report states that only 3 of over 120 modern cars have headrest designs that the Institute considers "good," with another 8 considered "acceptable." A further 34 cars were rated "marginal." This implies about 91% are "marginal," "poor," or "bad." Small wonder whiplash continues to be a frequent problem! The IIHS report states that the proper headrest position is *"directly behind and very close to the backs of people's heads - the closer the better."*

Overall Experimental Conclusions

The results of the various human volunteer rearend experiments are as follows:

(a) For a normal person a sudden delta-v of about 5 - 6.8 mph can be tolerated, even without a properly positioned headrest, with only temporary (hours to days) claims of neck pain.

(b) With a well-positioned headrest the tolerance was up to 10-mph delta-v, again with only minor neck pain.

(c) For someone with mild preexisting neck problems, a delta-v of 5 mph could be tolerated without serious pain, for a properly positioned headrest.

All the above involved volunteers with negligible warning of the impending impact, and presumably with relatively lax neck muscles (they were all told to relax, but probably had some small degree of muscle tension since they knew an impact was imminent).

(d) For someone expecting the impact (Patrick, ref 38) and applying strong neck muscles, a delta-v of about 10 mph was tolerated, even though the headrest was missing.

All these experimental data are in basic agreement with the model given in equation (64) and illustrated in figure 33 (Table 1). What is important are the experiments that have not yet been done, as indicated in Table 2. In the absence of significant prior degeneration of discs, or the presence of scar tissue of ligaments, the injuries induced for loads lower than the ligamentous damage level are usually muscle strains and induced spasms. These problems are usually transient, and tend to heal over a time period of less than six months, and frequently much faster.

A useful discussion of whiplash studies is given in the Accident Reconstruction Journal (September/October 1995). This quotes several findings reported in the September 16, 1995, edition of the IIHS newsletter *Status Report*. Of interest

Table 1

Neck Injury Theoretical Predictions

	With Properly Positioned Headrest	Without Properly Positioned Headrest
Normal Healthy Person	Up to 13 mph push speed: Transient pain only (hours to days)	Up to 6.5 mph push speed: Transient pain only Above 6.5 mph push speed: *Injury Possible*
Person Predisposed to Injury	Up to 6.5 mph push speed: Transient pain only Above 6.5 mph push speed: *Injury Possible*	Above ~3 mph push speed: *Injury Possible*

Table 2

Human Volunteer Experimental Data

	With Properly Positioned Headrest	Without Properly Positioned Headrest
Normal Healthy Person	Up to 10 mph Δ Target Speed*: Transient pain only (hours to days)	Up to 5 mph Δ Target Speed*: Transient pain only Above 5 mph Δ Target Speed*: *No Data*
Person Mildly Predisposed to Injury	Up to 5 mph Δ Target Speed*: Transient pain only Above 5 mph Δ Target Speed*: *No Data*	*No Data*

*Torso push speed not measured

is the fact that Swedish studies have indicated that many whiplash problems occur for impacts below about 12 mph, and the IIHS also list only 5 out of 164 cars as having good headrests. This assessment is based on geometry, namely the height of the headrest versus the occupants head and the gap behind the head. "Good" means that the distance below the top of the occupant's head is less than 2.4 inches (6 cm) while the gap behind is less than 2.8 inches (7 cm). "Poor" means these values are greater than 3.9 inches (10 cm) and 4.3 inches (11 cm), respectively.

Frontal Collisions

In many cases of a lower speed collision, the rearended (target) occupant suffers neck/back problems, whereas the occupants of the other vehicle (bullet) do not. The major explanation for this is that the bullet vehicle suffers a sudden deceleration which causes a forward flexion of the head, known as an anteflex, provided the occupant is restrained by the seatbelt. The neck is much stronger in the anteflex mode. This occurs because the muscles and ligaments holding the head are further from the pivot point for the head at the back of the head than at the front (references 34, 38, 39, and 40). The rear part of the vertebrae have protruding pieces, known as the spinous process, to which the ligaments and muscles are attached. Consequently, the lever-arm principle allows for smaller forces for a forward motion. Reference 8 states that the corresponding maximum allowed torque force for this motion is about 450 lbs. to limit possible ligamentous damage. However, the corresponding large angular rotation is also limited by the chin impacting the chest, at which point part of the load is removed from the neck and transferred to the chest.

For a very severe forward motion, the impact of the chin on the chest could cause a new rotation about the chin contact point, and the neck load can again increase. Consequently, once this happens the neck load can increase to about 560 lbs. before ligamentous damage occurs. Figure 38 demonstrates the anteflex case. This solution is similar to that for figure 33 for rearward extension, except that the value of the spring constant factor 'k' is about 3 times as large for the anteflex case (k = 46 lb/degree = 4519 lb/ft). This causes the neck to more rapidly stiffen up in the forward direction, again due to the larger torque arm and greater ligament mass. It is readily seen that the lower damage limit of 450 lbs. is not reached until speeds above about 16 mph are reached for someone with lax muscles, while for a pretensed muscle tone of 20 lbs. this limit rises to about 22 mph, while for a strong person with a pre-tensed neck at 100 lb., the upper limit of 560 lbs. is reached at about 36 mph. Indeed, for muscles pretensed to 20

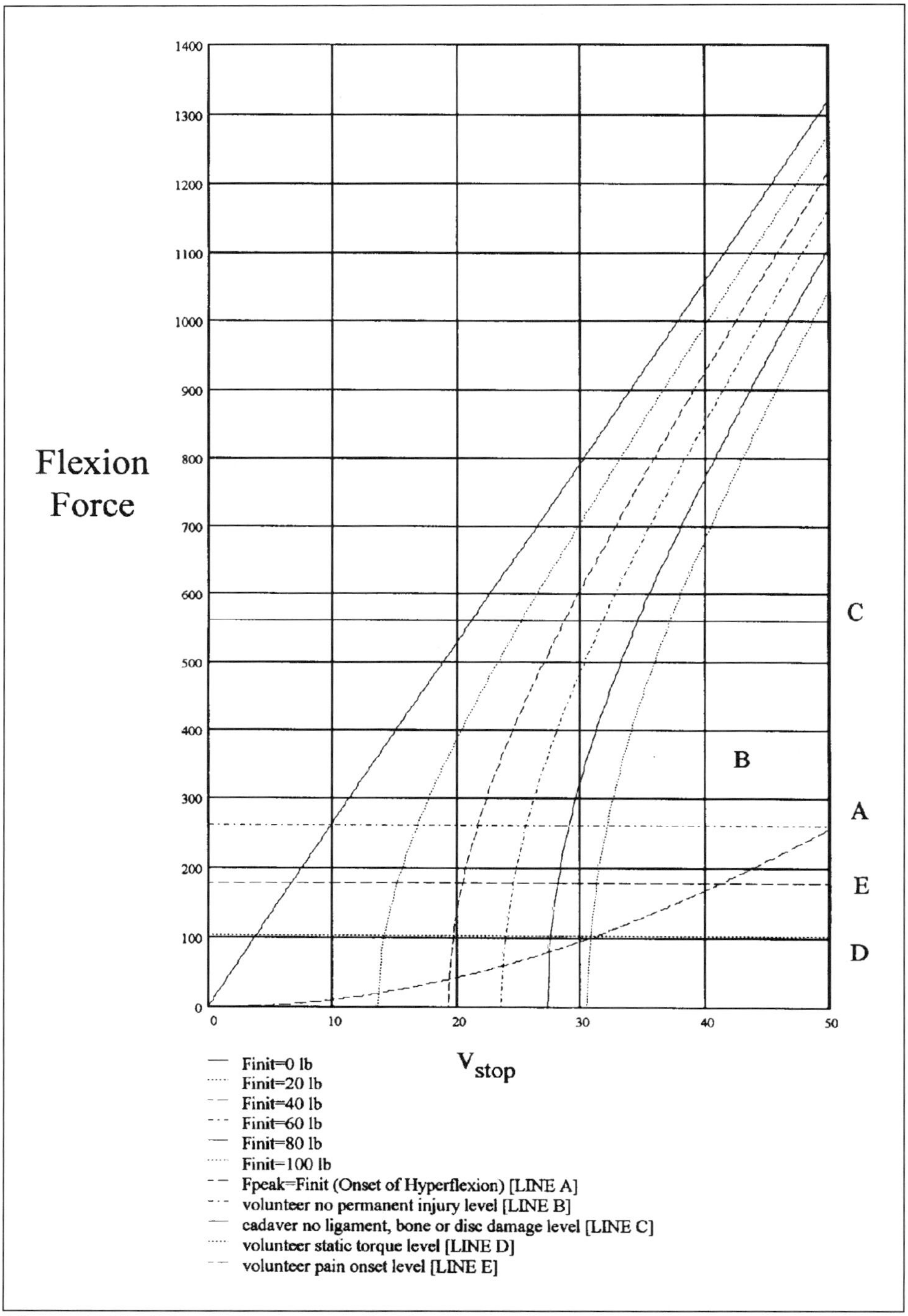

Figure 38 *Neck Peak Force versus Sudden Stop of Shoulders.*

lbs. the chin does not reach the chest unless the speed exceeds about 13 mph. For all these case, the speed is the sudden decreased speed rather than the push speed.

Practically all of these same points are also discussed in references 12 and 13. These two reports state that, for the normal healthy adult, no serious permanent damage is expected or observed for rearend collisions for push speeds below about 7 mph. However, they state that this situation does not necessarily hold for persons with prior dispositions to injury and/or weakness. Of interest is the fact that reference 12 gives a pseudo-linear plot of acceleration of the head versus the push speed. Converting from acceleration to force, *this line is almost identical to the straight line in figure 33.* Reference 12 indicates the maximum non-damaging acceleration at about 14 g (force = 140 lbs. for a 10 lb. head) based on the work of Mertz and Patrick (ref 8), while the ligamentous damage level of 190 lbs. (also ref 8) implies an acceleration of about 19 g. However, reference 12 is based totally on experimental data, while figure 33 is based on theory. In view of the various approximations, the agreement is considered quite good.

Analogues

A well-known analogue to the low speed rearend vehicle impact is the collision between two football players. Such players frequently collide at speeds of up to 18 mph, with one traveling much slower than the other. (For comparison, note that the 10 second, 100 yard dash represents a mean speed of about 20.5 mph with a peak of about 25 mph, while the four-minute mile represents an average speed of 15 mph.) The coefficient of restitution of the human body is very low. Thus, when two similar-weight players impact there is little bounce and they each have a post-impact speed of about one-half the original impact speed, and the slow target player can suffer a delta-V of about 9 to 10 mph. If the impact thrust is between his shoulder blades (on his back) he will suffer a similar whiplash motion as will a rearended car occupant. Several players have recently suffered neck problems arising from these motions, ranging from temporary discomfort to severe neck trauma, including several cases of paralysis (*e.g.*, Dennis Byrd and Mike Utley).

The only real differences between this situation and the rearended car occupant are that the football player wears a helmet, and is usually much fitter and stronger than the average person. The helmet increases the effective head weight and moment of inertia somewhat, making the player slightly *more* susceptible to the whiplash injury. However, under normal circumstances the player is expecting to be hit, and thus has his (very strong) muscles tensed. Under these conditions the muscular forces accommodate the required delta-E of the head over the full range of induced angular rotation. This prevents the sudden sharp increase in force as the neck motion limits, since most of the energy has already been accounted for (again, see figures 32 and 33). Thus, under most normal conditions, the player is not seriously hurt. However, if the player relaxes his guard and is then hit, serious damage can easily occur, in a manner similar to a vehicle rearender.

Predisposition versus Preexisting

Frequently, a court trial may involve the issue of whether the injured person had a *predisposition* to injury, or instead was suffering from a *preexisting* problem. The distinction is as follows. Suppose the person has an built-in susceptibility, which is not causing any problems prior to the accident. This susceptibility may include congenital effects, such as an unusually thin skull (the eggshell problem), or it may be degeneration with age, or the residual effect of past trauma. Provided the person has no impairment prior to the accident, this condition is considered a predisposition. The mere fact that a given individual is more vulnerable to injury than the average person does not normally remove the argument that the other person causing the accident was the proximate cause.

However, suppose a person suffers injury in one accident and has not fully recovered (medical parlance: resolved), when a second accident occurs. Now the increased susceptibility is usually considered to be due to the first injury. In this case, the second injury is frequently viewed as an exacerbation of an already existing problem. This condition is referred to as a preexisting problem. When this condition can be demonstrated, it is common for the defense in the second accident to try to minimize their liability by transferring significant blame to the first accident.

Clearly, these issues are those argued by the attorneys. However, the issue of the distinction between predisposition and preexisting conditions will frequently be raised either during a deposition or during a trial. In either case, the expert witness needs to understand the basis of the distinction, if he or she is to be of any help to the proceedings.

A simple way of illustrating the difference between predisposition and preexisting is to consider a plot of cumulative cost versus time. This is appropriate since all injuries involve money, both in the form of medical costs and lost earnings, and in the form of litigation to make the injured person "whole" again.

Immediately following an accident the costs rapidly increase, but then slow down with time. Ultimately, if the person recovers the costs reach a plateau. At this point the event is finished, and the person is supposedly back to normal. Thus, a plot of costs versus time will then show a flat horizontal line. If a second accident occurs this will be a distinct event, and the plot of costs will again increase, but only after the obvious plateau following the first accident. The existence of the plateau is what makes the two accidents distinct. However, recovery from the first accident may leave the person with an enhanced predisposition to injury. Although the person may be free of pain and obvious impairment when performing normal everyday activities, they may have residual weakness(es), such as scar tissue in a ligament. Thus the person may be more easily injured in a second accident. This could either increase the costs of a second similar accident, or could allow for injury at a lower level of trauma. Prior to the first accident the person may have an impact threshold of, say, 8 mph, whereas after this accident the threshold may drop to only, say, 4 mph. This is clearly an example of induced predisposition.

Suppose, however, the second accident occurs before recovery from the first is finished. We now have a case of a *preexisting* injury. The plot of costs will now show a kink with a second rise. This will occur before the plateau associated with the first injury. Can the costs be logically apportioned? Although there is no standard way of handling this problem, one approach is as follows. Imagine that the first injury is rapidly resolving, and that a medic can reasonably predict the future treatments and associated costs. Then these future costs are due to the first accident, since they would exist even without the second accident. Now subtract the sum of the previous costs and these future costs, both due to the first accident, from the overall sum of costs for both accidents. This leaves the true cost of the second accident. This approach is reasonably obvious if the

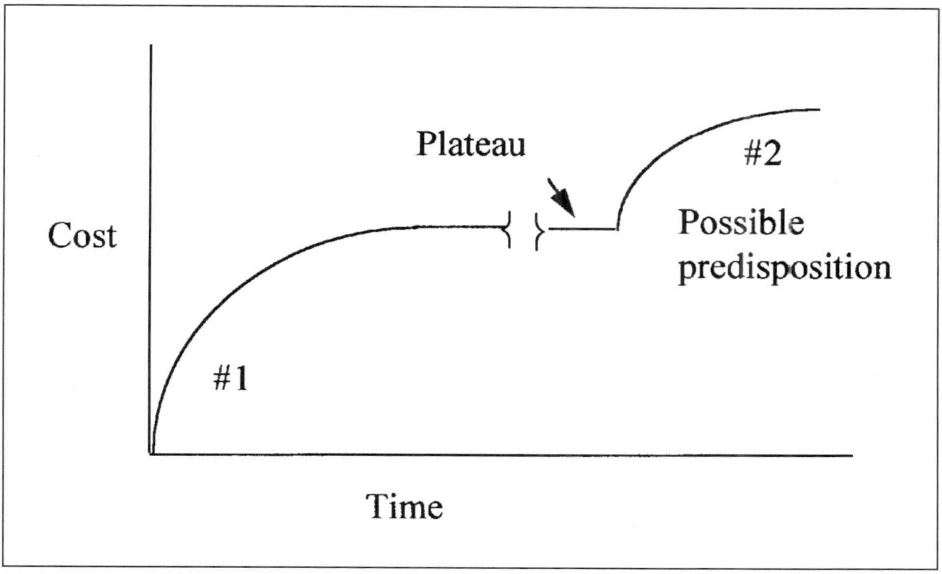

Figure 39 *Predisposition: Clearly Separate Accidents.*

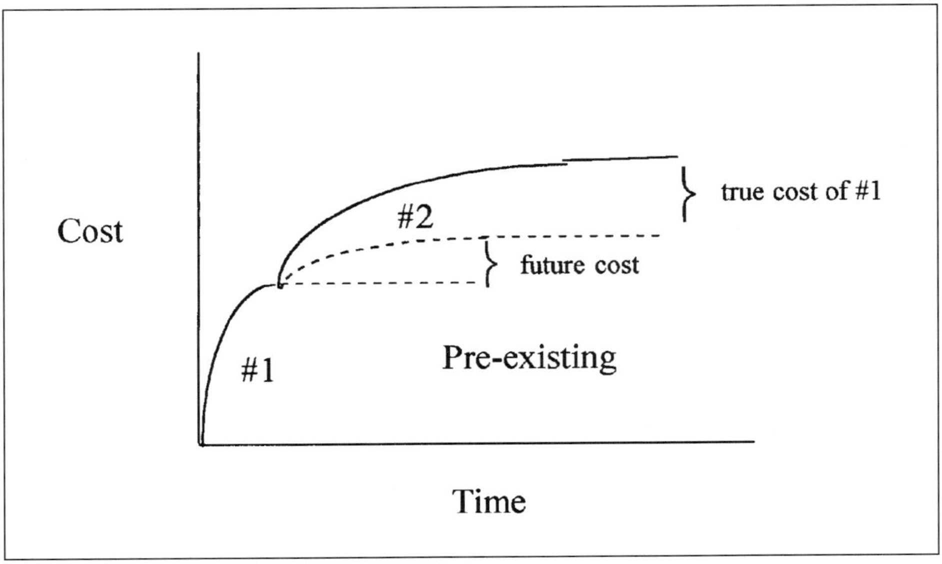

Figure 40 *Pre-existing: Overlapping Accidents.*

medic can indeed make a meaningful prediction of the future costs. This is relatively easy if the first accident is mostly resolved. However, the issue becomes very problematic if the second accident occurs soon after the first, since now the medic has only just started on treatment for the first accident, and may not be able to easily predict the future costs. Sometimes two accidents occur so close in time that treatment has not even started for the first accident. In this case the more usual approach is to simply share the overall combined costs of the two accidents (ref 41).

Of course, the above logic assumes that the defense buys the argument that either accident could cause injury. It is here that an expert who can both reconstruct the accidents, indicating severity, and perform a biomechanical assessment, indicating propensity for injury, can be of importance. Figures 39 and 40 illustrate the logic of cumulative costs versus time.

Chapter 8

Head Injury and Brain Damage

Rotational Accelerations and DAI

This section concentrates on potential damage to the head or brain, much as chapter 7 described mechanisms capable of damaging the neck structure. One mechanism known to cause damage to the brain is very rapid rotational acceleration of the head. Under these conditions the brain attempts to keep pace with the skull via internal shearing forces. The brain can only rotate and follow the motion of the skull by virtue of initial forces at the attachment area with the skull and then via the development of viscous shearing forces within the main body of the brain.

The skull is rigid, whereas the brain has the consistency of "viscous water." The brain mostly "floats" within the skull, suspended/surrounded by the cerebral-spinal fluid (CSF). It should be noted that the brain is only attached to the skull via arteries and veins, which can be ruptured relatively easily for excessive brain/skull differential motions. This can produce epidural, subarachnoid, and/or subdural hematomas. The brain connects to the spinal cord via the brain stem and the spinal cord is attached to the spine. Thus, there is a limit to the stretching of the brain/spinal cord versus the spine. This effect can put unusual strong loads on the basal (lower) part of the brain and such induced trauma is usually damaging, and therefore considered important.

Differential motion of the brain versus the skull causes local shearing which can create damage at the outer regions of the brain (the gray matter), particularly where the brain rubs past the inner skull projections on the lower half of the skull. The internal shearing motion causes damage deeper within the brain (the white matter). This involves injury to the axons and occurs over a wide region. This injury is known as diffuse axonal injury (DAI). Reference 14 gives data that indicate that the threshold for human brain DAI occurs for rotational accelerations of greater than about 1800 radians/sec^2. This is when concussion starts, even larger rates are needed for significant DAI damage. Note that this type of injury does *not* require actual impact contact of the head with another object.

The angular acceleration of the head is given by

(67)
$$\frac{I}{s^2} = \frac{Fr}{m(k^2 + r^2)} \; radians/s^2$$

where F is the torque force seen by the head CM, r is the torque arm between the neck rotation point and the head CM, and k is the radius of gyration of the head about its own CM. Substituting data from above, for response in the neck hyperextension region, this can be rewritten as

(68)
$$\frac{I}{s^2} = \left(\frac{F}{radian}\right)\frac{rgI}{w(r^2 + k^2)}$$

where F/radian is 14lb/degree = 802 lb/radian, r = 7 inches = 0.58 ft, w = 10 lbs, g = 32.2 ft/s^2 and k = 2.75 inches = 0.229 ft. Thus we obtain

I/s^2 = 3838 (radians/s^2) x radians motion = 67 (radians/s^2) x degrees motion.

Thus a peak angular acceleration of 1800 radians/s^2 is reached for an angular rotation in hyperextension of 1800/3838 = 0.47 radians = 26.9 degrees. However, at 14lb/degree this implies a torque force on the head of about 376 lbs. This is higher by about a factor of 2 than the value to start serious neck damage in the form of ligament rupture, as given before. Thus we conclude that the very rapid deceleration of the head in the hyperextension region can start to cause DAI brain damage, or at least cause concussion, at levels somewhat about twice those to initiate neck damage. Since individuals will have different thresholds, this implies that these two critical levels are moderately close, and that some may suffer neck damage only, while at even higher levels others may also suffer brain damage. Note that all of this occurs *without contact* with another item, and is entirely due to the neck entering the hyperextension region or being subject to rapid angular acceleration from other causes.

This logic also determines the correct design of a headrest. From the argument above, it is obvious that the correct positioning requires the headrest to be at a height to contact the rear of the occiput bone, and also be close enough to the head to prevent the latter from allowing the neck to enter the hyperextension region. However, while these two factors will prevent neck injury, they are insufficient to guarantee avoidance of brain injury, since the head deceleration due to the headrest itself may be too severe. Thus, the headrest must have sufficient compliance to ensure that its induced deceleration is lower than the critical value of about 1800 radians/s^2. For a neck length of 7 inches this implies the deceleration seen by the CM of the head must not exceed about 1050 ft/s^2, which is about

32.6 g. For example, consider a rearend push of about 15 mph, which gives a rearward head/neck rotation speed of about 6.6 mph = 9.68 ft/s (16.6 radians/s, or 951 degrees/s). Then, to avoid exceeding the above deceleration, the stopping distance needs to be at least 0.0446 ft = 0.54 inches (0.0765 radians, or 4.4 degrees). The minimum time to stop the head must be 0.0092 secs (about 10 ms). Thus, the head rest must stop the head in a *greater* distance than this, regardless of whether the neck enters the hyperextension range. Conversely, if the headrest is *too* compliant, the allowed rotation may become large enough to once again allow for the hyperextension of the neck.

Clearly, these considerations place a relatively tight tolerance on the correct placement and compliance of a headrest. For example, suppose we wish to ensure no entry into the hyperextension region at a total angle of 60 degrees. Then the head must first reach the headrest after a maximum rotation of less than 60 - 4.4 = 55.6 degrees. This corresponds to a horizontal head motion of about 5.8 inches. Many headrests have too large a gap. The only "correct" position for the headrest is next to the head.

Note that while in the pseudo-elastic hyperextension region, the head flexes on the neck as a mass-on-spring. It can then be shown that for a typical head the natural oscillation frequency is about 10.6 Hz (cycles per second), and the period is thus 0.095 sec. The stopping time for the head is one quarter period, of about 0.024 second. This time is very short compared to the time quoted before (about 0.13 sec) for the head to move through its physiological range.

Head Injury Criterion (HIC)

The HIC applies to the case of *direct contact* impact of the head, and essentially only considers linear decelerations. It defines the threshold where either skull fracture or brain damage initiates. This brain damage is not the DAI type, but instead involves such effects as contusions, internal bleeding, localized bruising, effects of bone penetration into the brain, and the effects of rapid stress wave propagation through the brain. Included is the *contre-coup* (counter-blow) phenomenon, whereby reflection of the stress wave at the side of the head away from the impact site (*i.e.*, at the opposite pole) leads to a sudden drop in internal pressure. The individual stress waves transverse the head in only about 1 ms. However, for a sustained deceleration of the head (several ms duration) a pressure gradient develops, with the highest pressure next to the impact point and the lowest pressure at the opposite side of the head. This sudden pressure drop is given by $\Delta P = \rho ra$, where r is the density of the brain (about 1.0 gm/cm^3), r is the radius of the inner skull (about 3 inches, or 7.62 cm), and 'a' is the acceleration. Thus, an acceleration of about 150 g (about 150 x 32.2 ft/s^2 = 4830 ft/s^2) causes a pressure drop of about 16.5 psi (1.16 atmospheres). Since one atmosphere is about 760 mm of mercury (Hg), this represents a drop in pressure of about 882 mm Hg. However, the brain normally operates at a blood pressure of at between 840 and 880 mm Hg, about one atmosphere plus 80 - 120 mm Hg (diastolic to systolic pressure). Thus our example lowers the net pressure to about zero, thus becoming a true vacuum. Since the brain vessels are designed to function within the environment of positive pressure, this is a sufficient drop in pressure to allow the blood vessels to overexpand and rupture. Experiments show that for an induced contact pressure rise of about 24 psi brain damage can initiate, and for a pressure rise of about 34 psi brain damage is severe. Data given by Damask (ref 10) relate these pressure changes to head accelerations. The 24 psi level occurs at about 132 g, whereas, the 34 psi condition occurs for about 187 g.

Recent three-dimensional modeling of the head using a finite element scheme (ref 45) has essentially confirmed these points. Subtle differences include the fact that the above-discussed pressure gradient is not centered in the middle of the head; instead, the gradient is biased away from the impacted side. Thus the pressure drop at the contrecoup position is a little less than for the above simplified calculation. Also, this modeling confirms the well-observed clinical fact that impacts on the rear of the head, on the occiput bone, are more likely to produce significant contre-coup effects than are frontal blows.

The concept of the HIC derives from early studies performed by Wayne State University. It is based purely on empirical data, and has not yet been satisfactorily explained by theory. The accepted definition involves an integral of head acceleration to the power of 2.5 versus time. Thus the HIC is given by (ref 1)

(69)

$$HIC = (t_2 - t_1)\left[\frac{1}{(t_2 - t_1)} \int acc\, dt\right]^{2.5}$$

where the times indicate a window and 'acc' is the local value of acceleration. For accelerations in units of g (32.2 ft/s^2), this integral must not exceed the value of 1000. This is based on FMVSS (Federal Motor Vehicle Safety Standards) regulations. The logic of the HIC only applies over short time windows, such as less than 0.035 sec. This is necessary, or else for a long enough time [1000 sec, or 16.6 mins] even a 1.0 g load would imply damage! Some analysts believe the time limit should be only 16 ms. For a time window of 0.035 sec, the corresponding acceleration is about 60 g. Thus, HIC only applies for accelerations above this. It should be noted that the threshold for skull fracture and brain damage are *totally independent*. The one can occur without the other. However, the data for skull fracture *overlap* the data for brain damage. Consequently, the *same* HIC of 1000 is used for either damage mode. For the case of a uniform acceleration over a time window (*i.e.*, a "square" pulse of acceleration), equation (69) can be rewritten as

(70)

$$v_c^4 = 3.6x10^6 s^{1.5} \quad or \quad v_c = 43.6 s^{0.375}$$

with v_c the closing impact speed in mph, and s the stopping distance in feet. It is known that skull fracture can occur for a sudden energy change of from about 33 - 75 ft-lbs, with an average of about 50 ft-lbs (ref 23), which is the equivalent of a 10 lb head dropping freely through 5 feet.

For example, a person who falls over sideways and hits their head on a flat, rigid, concrete floor can be at the damage threshold. A 5-ft vertical fall gives a terminal speed of about 17.9 ft/s = 12.2 mph. From equation (70) this yields a stopping distance of about 0.0336 ft = 0.40 inches. Since a rigid floor has negligible deflection, this implies that this distance is the natural amplitude of skull/brain motion, a mixture of bone deformation and/or brain motion within the skull, allowable before damage. This also implies that impact speeds below about 12 mph are unlikely to cause skull or brain damage, even for impacts on very rigid surfaces, provided the surface is flat and does not cause severe localized "point loading." Note that this example gives a head deceleration of about 148 g, and a stopping time of about 0.0038 seconds! Also, note that $148^{2.5}$ x 0.0038 = 1000, or the critical HIC level.

We conclude that at the level of a rearend vehicle impact which can cause neck damage the head does *not* reach the critical HIC, even if it hits a rigid headrest. For example, for the critical push speed of about 7.5 mph, the head's backward speed is only about 3.3 mph. The problem could occur for a *high speed* rearender. Suppose the headrest compliance amplitude is 2.0 inches. Adding the 0.4 inches of "natural" deflection gives a total stopping distance of 2.4 inches = 0.2 ft. Then equation (70) gives a critical speed of 23.8 mph. Since this is only 0.44 times the push speed, the push speed must be about 54 mph! Thus, the car must suffer a delta-V of 54 mph for a stiff seat, or at least 39 mph for a soft seat.

However, this same calculation indicates why seatbelts or airbags are necessary for *frontal* impacts. Here, it is rare for such items as steering wheels or dashboards to deflect as much as two inches, except for at high speeds. Thus a *forward* impact can exceed the HIC for differential speeds (head versus target) lower than 24 mph. Likewise, the behavior of airbags must be such that they do not produce too rapid a deceleration of the head. For example, the standard NCAP test involves a rigid barrier impact speed of 35 mph. To avoid exceeding the critical HIC, equation (70) states that the stopping distance needs to be about 0.56 feet = 6.7 inches. This explains why airbags are designed to immediately deflate after reaching full expansion. Unfortunately, if the occupant is sitting too close to the airbag when it inflates the bag may itself punch the head sufficiently hard to exceed the HIC.

One advantage of an airbag is that, being flexible, it is capable of conforming to the shape of the head. This immediately allows a good distribution of loads on the head, making the localized stresses less than for an impact with a hard flat object. Thus this property raises the threshold for skull damage. However, damage to the brain usually depends on the relative motions internal to the skull, and the conforming nature of the airbag will have less effect, except to prevent penetration problems associated with skull fracturing and bone segments being depressed back into the brain.

However, airbags do not normally activate for rearend collisions. Suppose the driver has on a loose belt (or none) and suffers the seat-bounce described in chapter 7. If the brakes are being applied, the car will decelerate but the upper torso and head will continue at the induced bounce speed. Suppose the delta-V for the car is 10 mph (v_1), and the seat coefficient of restitution is 'e' = 0.3, and the car decelerates at 'a' = 0.7 g (near skidding). Assume the head-to-steering wheel distance (s) is about 2.0 feet. The torso/head will move forward out of the seat at about 13 mph (v_2, 19.1 ft/s), while the car will slow from 10 mph (14.67 ft/s) to zero. We wish to find the impact speed of the head on the steering wheel. To compute this we solve

(71)
$$s = v_2 t - \left(v_1 t - \frac{at^2}{2} \right)$$

which gives the differential motion of head versus vehicle, with 't' the time to impact. Rewriting,

(72)
$$\frac{at^2}{2} + ev_1 t - s = 0$$

This is a quadratic with the solution

(73)
$$t = -\frac{ev_1}{a} + \frac{(e^2 v_1^2 + 2as)^{\frac{1}{2}}}{a}$$

Then, the speed of the car at the impact time is $v_1' = v_1 - a\,t$. Hence, the impact speed of the head on the steering wheel is given by

(74)
$$v_{impact} = v_2 - v_1' = v_2 - v_1 + at = ev_1 + at$$

Clearly, this equation only applies provided the vehicle has not stopped prior to the head impact, or else the impact speed equals the initial head speed.

Substituting, we obtain t = 0.269 secs, and v_{impact} = 10.46 ft/s = 7.13 mph. Even for a very rigid (non deflecting) steering wheel, this impact speed is below that to exceed the HIC of 1000. Indeed, from figure 41 we see that the HIC is below the value 200. Thus, such an impact may stun the driver, but is unlikely to cause permanent damage to the head and/or brain. Even if the initial vehicle delta-V increases to 20 mph (29.3 ft/s), the time to impact becomes t = 0.1839 secs, and the impact speed becomes v_{impact} = 12.95 ft/s = 8.83 mph. Thus the impact speed increases by less than a factor of two, and damage remains unlikely.

Although the HIC = 1000 appears to be a go/no-go threshold the actual probability of skull/brain damage is given by a logist curve (a sigmoid curve, ref 3) of the form

(75)
$$P_{injury} = \frac{1}{[1 + \exp(5.02 - 0.00351\ x\ HIC)]}$$

Figure 42 shows this probability as a function of the HIC. We see that for HIC = 1000, the probability of damage is about 18%, whereas for HIC = 500 the probability is only 3.7 %, for HIC = 1500 it is 56 %, and for HIC = 2000 it is 88%, etc. Clearly, the probability climbs rapidly once it is above the HIC = 1000 case. Figure 41 indicates the results of equation (70), giving the impact speed of the head versus the stopping distance for four values of HIC (200, 500, 1000 and 1500). Superimposed are three horizontal lines indicating drop impact speeds

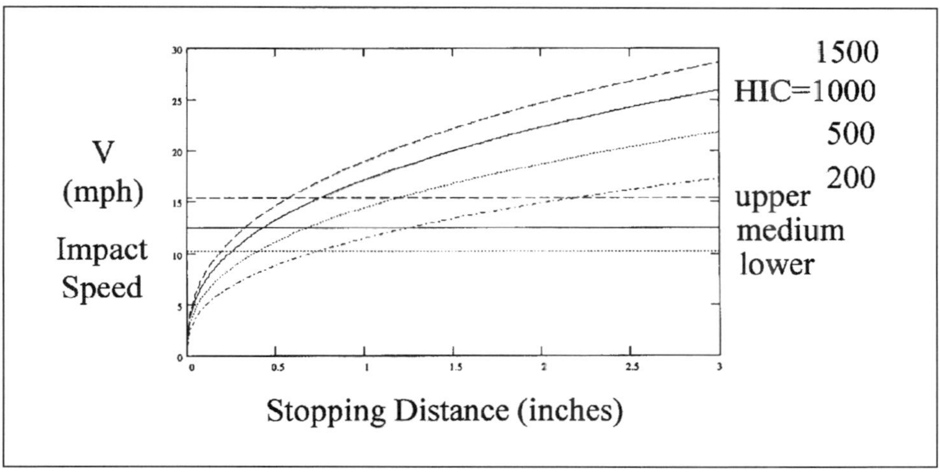

Figure 41 *HIC Logic: Velocity Versus Distance.*

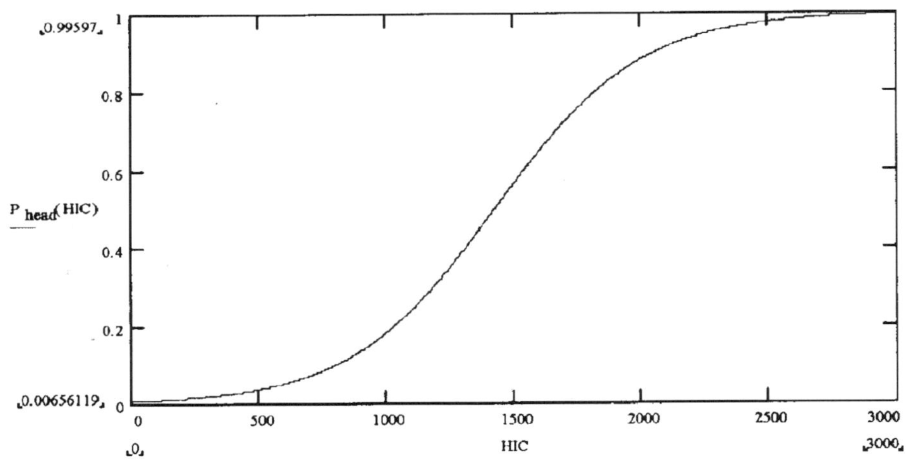

Figure 42 *Head Injury Probability Versus HIC.*

for impact energies of 33.3 ft-lbs (lowest limit equal to a fall of 3.3 ft onto hard concrete), 50 ft-lbs (average, a 5-ft fall) and 75 ft-lbs (maximum, a fall of 7.5 ft) (all ref 23). For any given HIC and fall-damage energy there is an intercept. An example is the intercept of the HIC = 1000 line and the 50 ft-lb line. This occurs at a speed of about 12.5 mph and a distance of about 0.4 inches.

To appreciate the effect of increasing the stopping distance at a given impact speed, we move to the right of the interception point by the amount of the distance. We see that this causes the fixed-speed line to intercept curves of ever-lower values of HIC. Thus for a total distance of 0.65 inches, an increase of about 0.25 inches, the result is HIC = 500, while for a total distance of about 1.25 inches, an increase of about 0.85 inches, we have HIC = 200. Clearly, adding padding can dramatically lower the head injury. This is the same logic used for helmets. The same figure shows that for an impact speed of about 20 mph the HIC would be considerably in excess of 1500 without protection (read vertically on the plot for the distance of about 0.4 inches). This would imply probable death. However, by adding about 1.0 inches of extra stopping capability, for a total distance 1.4 inches, the value can be reduced to HIC = 1000.

The effect of a compliant surface is shown in figure 43. This shows impact speed versus stopping distance, but has superimposed a sloped straight line, indicating a compliant surface with stiffness of about k = 1000 lb/inch. This line is obtained by equating the head kinetic energy with the stored elastic surface energy. Thus $(w/2g)v^2 = (k/2)x^2$, where w is the head weight (10 lbs), and x is the amplitude of deformation for the compliant surface. Thus, $v = (kg/w)^{0.5}x$, and a springlike surface gives a linear relationship between speed and motion. The amplitude of motion of the surface is added to the natural motion of the head: thus the straight line has its origin at the natural limit value (about 0.4 inch). A very rigid surface gives a vertical line: hence the HIC of 1000 is reached at about 12.5 mph. However, for the finite compliance, the same speed gives the lower HIC point about 150, whereas, the HIC of 1000 requires an increased speed of about 25 mph.

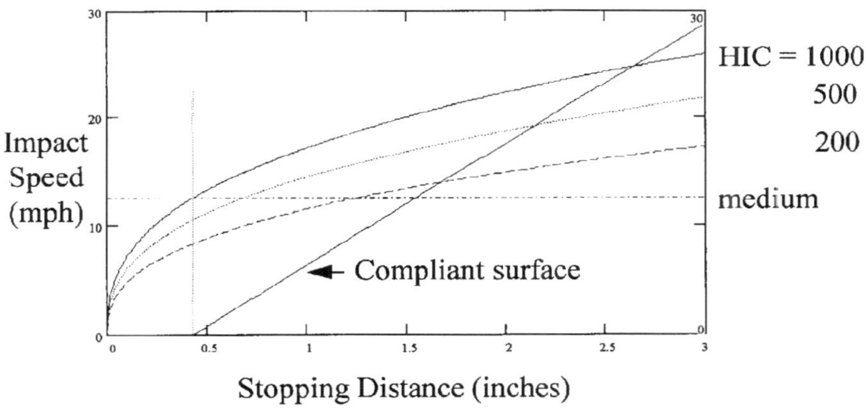

Figure 43 *Effect of Compliant Impact Surface.*

Chapter 9

Chest and Femur Loadings

The FMVSS regulations (ref 1) also specify the maximum allowed loads for the occupant's chest and femur in addition to their specifications regarding head injury previously discussed. These regulations do not assume that the occupants are properly belted with a combination lap/shoulder harness for the mandatory 30 mph test crashes, but *do* assume so for the NCAP tests at 35 mph. The chest load limit is 60 g, and should not last more than 3 ms (the so-called "3 ms clip"), while the femur limit is 2250 lbs thrust along the leg from the knee to the hips. The chest acceleration is primarily due to loads from the seatbelt and/or the airbag, or due to impacts with the steering wheel or dash, whereas the femur load is assumed to be due to impact with the car's lower dash structure.

An additional definition of chest damage is that the chest should not deflect inward by more than about 3 inches for an adult. Excess deflection will cause fracture of the ribs and possible puncturing of the lungs, while excess deceleration can cause rupture of internal organs (liver, spleen, heart, etc.). If the deceleration is solely due to the seatbelt, the loading will be localized to the contact area of the belt. This loading pattern is different for the driver than the passenger, since for the driver the shoulder belt runs from the left shoulder to the right hip, and *vice versa* for the passenger (at least in the US, where we drive on the right). Conversely, for an airbag the loading can be over a larger area. The latter condition can help reduce localized damage, but will have little effect on internal organ motion. These force calculations assume that the seat remains in place. Many two-door cars have folding front seats, which sometimes do not correctly lock into place. In the latter event the force on the chest increases, since now the additional weight of the freely moving seat back must be included. Fortunately, the seat back is quite light. An even worse condition occurs if the seat itself breaks off its attachment points, since now the entire seat weight must be included. Note that such breakages *have* been observed in some of the NCAP rigid barrier tests (see ref 4).

Many studies have shown (ref 43) that a good description of chest damage is given by assuming a viscous limit. This limit is given in terms of local speed of frontal chest versus the vehicle times the fractional compression of the chest. This limit is given in terms of $(VC)_{max}$, where V is the impact velocity and C is the compression. The reference to "max" means that the limit is determined by the local maximum in this quantity when calculated as a function of time history. The limit is about $(VC)_{max}$ = 1.3 m/s = 4.27 ft/s. However, the allowed 3 inches of chest compression represents about 30% fractional strain, since the average chest is about 10 inches deep front-to-back. Thus the limit is about (4.7/0.3) ft/s = 14.2 ft/s, or about 9.7 mph.

Observations of the chest's behavior show that under rapid loading, the chest first behaves almost elastically and develops a force of about 800 ±200 lbs with only a small deflection. Thereafter, the peak force limits and further chest compression continues with a pseudo-constant force (there is an initial peak followed by a shallow dip and then another peak). Upon release of the force, the chest re-expands and the force rapidly drops. In the absence of permanent injury, the chest recovers completely and the force returns to zero. This is an elasto-viscous response, and the force-deflection plot involves a loop that represents the absorbed viscous energy. The above numbers imply that a typical chest can tolerate an input of about 800 lb x 1/4 ft = 200 ft-lbs of energy, while the actual absorbed energy is somewhat less, about 140 ft-lbs, with about 60 ft-lbs being elastically recovered. The typical chest weighs about 40 lbs, so the corresponding impact speeds to give 200 ft-lbs or 140 ft-lbs are about 12.2 mph or 10.2 mph, respectively. These values are close to the previously quoted speed.

The human torso represents about one-half the total body weight (references 10, 34, and 35). Thus for a 150 lb individual, this is about 75 lbs. Thus an acceleration of 60 g implies a peak force of 60 x 75 = 4500 lbs. This is comparable to the required strength of seatbelts. Such a force can cause significant chest motion. However, this calculation is deceptive. Unlike a rigid item such as bone, the thorax region is compressible. Upon initial impact it is the frontal portion of the chest that first sees the large deceleration. This includes the sternum and the forward portions of the ribs. These represent only about one-third of the actual chest weight. For a 40-lb chest this is about 13.3 lbs. Hence the 60 g deceleration is really an initial force of about 13.3 x 60 = 800 lbs, in agreement with the previous quote of observed chest compression load. In reality, as the sternum rapidly decelerates so the back of the thorax (the spinal region) continues to move and decelerates at a slower rate. Thus the spine "overtakes" the sternum, causing chest compression. Ultimately, the sternum and spine decelerate at the same rate. This occurs when the chest compression "bottoms." Since the chest force is a pseudo-constant value of about 800 lbs, this means that the entire 40 lb chest now decelerates at about 20 g. Thus, the initial 60 g deceleration of the sternum is short-lived, and the later-time deceleration is closer to 20 g.

A typical femur represents about 0.1 of the total body weight. Thus, for a 150 lb individual, this is about 15 lbs. Hence the allowed peak force of 2250 lbs represents an acceleration of about 2250/15 = 150 g, on the assumption that *only* the femur weight is involved. If other portions of the body are accelerated simultaneously via a thrust through the knee, then the effective reaction mass is larger and the corresponding required acceleration is lower. When a force is applied through the knee cap, the femur will undergo compressive strain and thus shrink slightly. Additionally, the knee and hip joints will attempt to close up slightly, and the knee cap (patella) will flex and try to flatten. The total motion is small, less than about 0.3 inches.

If the leg impacts a rigid surface, only this 0.3-inch motion is available. The corresponding energy absorption is about 2250 (lbs) x 0.3 (inches)/12 (inches per foot) = 56.3 ft-lbs. For a 15 lb femur, this represents an impact speed of about 15.5 ft/s = 10.6 mph. Suppose, however, the dash structure deforms by about 1.0 inches. Now the total deformation is 1.3 inches, and the corresponding energy absorption is 244 ft-lbs, and the critical impact speed is now about 32.4 ft/s = 22.1 mph. Clearly, to avoid serious femur/knee damage, either the impact speed must be kept low, or the dash structure must be capable of significant deformation.

The proper use of a well-behaved seatbelt can prevent lower limb motion forward toward the dash. However, if the impact is severe enough to cause collapse of the A frame, the dash can be propelled back at the occupant, and thus again cause injury! This occurs in "offset" collisions at above about 30 mph. Naturally, if the occupant is not wearing a belt, or if it is very loose, then impact can more readily occur. Unfortunately, if the entire occupant body moves forward into the dash, the effective weight becomes more than just that of the femur. Thus it may transpire that the effective weight is about 50 lbs instead of 15 lbs (due to part of the torso weight being included, etc.). In this case, the critical impact speed with the dash deforming by one inch is about 17.7 ft/s = 12.1 mph. The general equation for computation of the femur damage is

(76)

$$v^2\ (ft/s) = \frac{2g\,2250s}{w} \quad or \quad v^2\ (mph) = \frac{2g\,2250s}{2.152w}$$

where s is the total stopping distance (feet), w is the weight (lbs), g is the acceleration due to gravity (32.2 ft/s^2) and the factor 2250 is the FMVSS threshold of allowed force (lbs).

It should be noted that the *unrestrained* occupant does not necessarily impact the interior portions of a vehicle at the initial vehicle speed. This is because the occupant can reach items such as the steering wheel before the vehicle has stopped. As a very simple example, suppose the vehicle decelerates at the rate 'a.' The distance moved by the vehicle in a time 't' is simply $x = v_1 t - 0.5at^2$, while the distanced moved by the occupant is $x = v_1 t$ (ignoring seat friction, etc.). Then, the differential motion of the occupant versus the car is $0.5at^2$. Thus, if this differential distance is 's,' we obtain $t = (2s/a)^{1/2}$, and the impact speed is thus $v_{impact} = at = (2sa)^{1/2}$. This is merely our old friend the "skid equation," but with very high deceleration. For example, suppose the value of v_1 = 30 mph = 44 ft/s, and the value of 'a' = 15 g = 483 ft/s^2, and 's' = 1.0 ft, then the impact speed is 31.1 ft/s = 21.2 mph. For a lower vehicle speed of 10 mph = 14.67 ft/s, the deceleration of the vehicle is lower, and may only be 10 g. Then the above logic gives an impact speed = 25.4 ft/s = 17.3 mph. This answer is clearly wrong, since it is now larger than the initial car speed. Thus, the impact speed on the steering wheel can be less than the initial vehicle speed for large speeds, but becomes equal to the car speed at the lower speeds. Similar arguments apply to the effective impact speed of the chest on a steering wheel.

For many chest impacts on hard items like steering wheels the ribs may be cracked. For cadavers of elderly people, ribs have been observed to fracture at loads of below 200 lbs, because bone strength decreases with age. Studies have indicated that women are more likely to suffer rib fracture then are men, for a given impact speed. In general, men fracture one rib for crash speeds of about 15 mph, while women do so for speeds of less than 10 mph, for belted occupants. To a first approximation, the number of rib fractures can be given by an equation of the form N = Av, where A is a constant and v is the impact speed. For men A = 0.06 ribs/mph, while for women, A = 0.26 ribs/mph (ref 44). Thus, for a sudden drop in speed of 10 mph relative to the vehicle, an average man is unlikely to suffer rib fracture, whereas a typical woman may suffer two or three rib fractures.

Chapter 10

Assorted Injury-Related Data and Vehicle Safety Considerations

The Drunken Driver/Occupant

Folklore and anecdotal evidence both suggest that a drunk is injured less than a sober person when involved in an accident. The argument is that drunks are flexible, and thus withstand impacts better. However, the previous arguments concerning whiplash pointed out that pre-tensing of muscles should theoretically improve the occupant's survivability in a crash. We thus have a conundrum.

However, more recent studies (ref 45) have shown that the conventional wisdom is *wrong*, and based on faulty logic in clinical studies. These clinical studies compared rates of recovery for drunks versus sober people, without regard to how severe the original accident had been. When the latter facts are included, it is found that drunks are *more* likely to be hurt than are sober people for the same severity of actual impact. These new facts are in agreement with the notion, and theoretical prediction, that bracing for an impact allows the strong muscular parts of the human body to protect itself. Similar studies have also shown that small babies also suffer injuries more readily than adults, again due to an inability to brace themselves.

Occupant Motions

Newton's first law states that, during an accident, vehicle occupants will continue following their original paths unless some external force acts upon them. This external force is usually initially provided by either the seat, the seatbelt, or an airbag, or secondarily can be provided by contact with other parts of the vehicle. Thus, during a rearender, the occupant moves because the seat pushes them forward. During a frontal crash, the occupant only stops with the vehicle because the seatbelt and/or the airbag held them back. In the absence of either seatbelt or airbag, the occupant would simply keep moving as they were just before the crash, and thus would hit an interior part of the vehicle.

Which part of the vehicle interior is hit depends on the behavior of the vehicle. For a simple deceleration in a straight line, the driver would first hit the steering wheel, whereas the passenger would hit the dash. If either occupant also pivots about their feet, then both can subsequently rise upward and forward and hit the windshield. More complicated motions occur when significant vehicle rotation is induced.

If the vehicle rapidly rotates counterclockwise (as seen from above), the left front of the car (driver's side) will move to the driver's left, making it appear as if the driver and passenger had moved to the right, in addition to their forward motion. The reverse happens for a clockwise car motion. *How far* the occupant appears to move to the left or right depends on the relative speeds of the forward motion and the rotation. Thus the solution depends on solving the vectors for velocity, and the apparent differential velocity and direction of occupants versus car is given by the vector difference in these motions. Thus, if the driver moves forward at 30 mph (initial car speed) while the windshield moves to the left at 10 mph, the apparent driver motion is given by the hypotenuse of vectors which is $v_{net} = \sqrt{30^2 + 10^2} = 31.62$ mph, and the apparent angle to the right is given by $\tan\theta = 10/30$, or $\theta = 18.4$ degrees.

For severe forward pitching such as a vault over a boulder, the occupants will appear to fly forward and upward. Thus they either hit the roof or can go into or through the windshield. The rollover scenario is a frequently seen effect. Here, a sharp right-hand turn for the vehicle precipitating a roll to the left can result in the apparent driver motion being to the left door and upward to the driver's door window. In reality, the unbelted driver is simply moving along his original path, except for an additional drop due to gravity. If the window is open or is broken during the accident, the driver can exit the vehicle through the window. Unfortunately, the rolling vehicle then frequently proceeds to roll over the driver, since the driver is rarely thrown far enough to be out of the way to miss the rolling car.

Finally, for a severe vault which also has some form of other spin (yaw, etc.), and which involves a significant flight time (seconds), any unbelted occupants can be thrown about the vehicle with multiple bounces off the interior surfaces (roof, doors, windshield and seat). This can make identification of the driver difficult.

Seatbelts

If the seatbelts work properly and remain around the occupant, identity of the driver is obvious. However, this does not always happen. For example, for a frontal thrust on the driver which causes the latter to move to their right by more than about 30°, it is known that the torso can slip out of the shoulder harness (the same is true for the passenger, but for a move to the left). But, subsequently, the driver can also slip up and out of the lap belt, or perhaps the lap belt was not used (this often happens with "motorized" shoulder belts where the driver forgets, or ignores, the separate lap belt). This behavior can occur if the vehicle suffers multiple impacts. The reason is that a typical seatbelt only remains locked up for as long as a constant load is applied.

Many seatbelts are activated by a pendulum device that swings forward and upward when the vehicle suffers a strong deceleration along its major axis. This pendulum causes a pawl to engage teeth on a wheel attached to the axle that allows for belt spool-out. The wheel is suddenly stopped by the pawl, and the belt should no longer spool out. Provided the occupant now keeps a load on the belt, the pawl cannot disengage. Thus, normally the occupant is held back by the belt until the vehicle stops. However, suppose the vehicle's first impact does not completely stop the car, and/or the car is then hit a second time but in another direction, say from the rear. It then becomes possible for the occupant to be accelerated back away from the belt toward the seat. The load on the belt reduces, and the pawl can disengage. If the vehicle now comes to a violent stop due to yet a further frontal hit the pendulum may not activate again and the occupant may slip out of a loose belt. Regardless of how and why an occupant slips out of a seatbelt, if there are signs of belt friction and burns/bruises, or even broken ribs, the driver can still sometimes be identified. For the driver, the shoulder harness leaves friction burns/bruises from the left shoulder to the right hip, while for the passenger the burns/bruises are from the right shoulder to the left hip. Rib fractures follow the same pattern.

Frequently, the pendulum-activated belt latch system does not work for rearend collisions. The reason is twofold. Some designs simply don't work in reverse, and for those that do, the problem is that, as the pawl engages the toothed wheel, the occupant is moving slower than the seat, and thus apparently toward the seat. This removes the load from the belt. Consequently, by the time the occupant bounces out of the seat toward the belt, the pendulum and pawl system can sometimes disengage, and the belt may no longer lock. If it doesn't, for a sufficiently fast push speed on the target vehicle, the occupant can actually hit the steering wheel. This impact is less severe than one for an unbelted occupant in a frontal collision, but it can still stun the driver or cause some concussion.

The best modern seatbelts are those that employ inertia reels, web-grabbers and/or pyrotechnic-activated reel stoppers. Inertial systems react to sudden motion of the belt webbing itself, and rapidly lock the reel. They also frequently retract with the occupant as the latter sinks back into the seat. However, locking the reel still does not stop the problem of spool out. This is the situation where the belt still moves due to the self-tightening action on the spool; this latter problem can be solved by using a web-grabber that literally grabs the belt and stops motion. The pyrotechnic approach uses a signal from an impact switch or accelerometer to lock up the entire belt-reel system. However, these more sophisticated systems are usually only employed in expensive cars. As with an airbag, if the pyrotechnic device fires, it must be replaced. Of course, for a severe crash the entire belt system should be replaced anyway, assuming the vehicle is salvageable. Note that Audi use another method for tightening the seatbelts: they have a wire and pulley arrangement that connects the engine to the belts. Whenever the engine suddenly moves due to a crash, the belts tighten (ref 46).

Sadly, all these contrivances are technical fixes to a problem that did not exist earlier. Back in the days of "old" three-point seatbelts there was only one means of adjustment. This was a mid-buckle that allowed a belt to be adjusted to fit an individual, with the recommendation that only enough space exist between the belt and chest to allow insertion of a flat hand. Thereafter, once buckled, the belt was fixed. Such a belt did not allow for subsequent body motions. The belt only suffered from inherent stretch of the webbing, as do modern belts. The problems of film-spooling and reel-locking did not exist. These belts were effectively guaranteed to work, provided they were used, and not loaded so seriously that breakage occurred. Indeed, all modern race-car belts are of the fixed variety, as are most Air Force pilot belts, although both are also more complex, using a full harness going over both shoulders with a single quick-release buckle and additional leg straps.

Unfortunately, the US public could not be convinced to wear the fixed belts ("too uncomfortable"). It was to encourage the public to use belts that the movable belt, including the motorized shoulder harness, was introduced. Unfortunately, this didn't do much to increase use either. Even with many State laws subsequently making the non-use of belts an illegal act, the US still only has about a 65% compliance rate (compare this to places like the UK, where the compliance rate is about 95%). The net result of these technical fixes was to make seatbelts less effective (per crash event), not more. The balancing act is that, although the modern belts can be less effective than the old versions, more occupants are using them. Thus from an overall perspective things have improved, but individual crashes may actually be worse than they need be.

The old fixed belts stretched upon load; however, this stretch is typically only a few inches. Thus a driver should not be able to reach the steering wheel, unless they were sitting unusually close. Modern belts frequently *do* allow the occupant to reach the steering wheel or dash. In addition to the actual stretch, the film-spool effect can add another inch or two. Likewise, if the pendulum-activated pawl does not successfully engage on the first attempt, it may do so a tooth or two later (this is called tooth bounce). This again allows for a few more inches of movement. Last, because modern belts allow for occupant motion, it is possible for the occupant to be in the "wrong" position at the time of impact, including leaning forward to adjust the radio or reach the cigarette lighter, etc. Under these circumstances the occupant is already much closer to the steering wheel or dash than they should be.

It is precisely because seatbelts do not always work that airbags were introduced. The concept of airbags is quite old, but their introduction to cars is recent. This history is somewhat bemusing. The various "research" (engineering) departments of the motor manufacturers have studied safety issues for years, and are fully aware of the problems of bumpers, seat belts, airbags and limited car-side to occupant spacing. However, the "marketing" departments rapidly learned that safety was not a selling point. Too many consumers thought cars designed for safety were "ugly" (consider the Pacer). Thus engineering was subjugated to marketing. However, even the Government (NHTSA) has vacillated over safety, with many important improvements (such as treating the seat/headrest as a single unit) being first suggested and then scratched. Government rules like CAFE have forced the makers into designing smaller cars which, by virtue of physics, are less crashworthy than large cars unless built with very expensive materials and techniques. The result has been a history of "fighting" between the makers, the government, and environmentalists concerning safety features. Then the automobile manufacturers suddenly discovered that "safety" was a sellable concept. Now, every manufacturer falls over himself extolling the virtues of airbags and uses their incorporation as a selling feature! Note carefully: racing car drivers and AF pilots do not use them! (We wonder why not?). In the same vein, most manufacturers are again providing 5 mph bumpers as a safety feature. Yet it was the manufacturers who convinced the government to allow a reduction from the old standard of 5 mph down to 2.5 mph, back in 1983, mostly to allow compliance with CAFE.

Government regulations require that seatbelts lock for a deceleration of the vehicle of more than 0.7 g (strong braking), and with a web motion of less than one inch. This implies that the belt should lock in less than about 86 msec. Fast lockup is necessary to limit the occupant motion relative to the vehicle. Since a crash involves a pseudo-sinusoidal motion of the vehicle, the differential motion of the occupant versus the vehicle is given by $s = vt - (v/\omega)\sin(\omega t)$, where ω is the angular frequency. It was previously shown (chapter 4) that this has a typical value of about 20 radians/s. Consider a velocity change of 30 mph (44 ft/s) and a lockup time of 0.086 s. Then s = 3.78 ft – 2.18 ft = 1.6 ft = 19.3 inches. This is comparable to (or greater than) the usual separation between the driver's chest and the steering wheel, and ignores any belt stretch. To be useful, the belt must

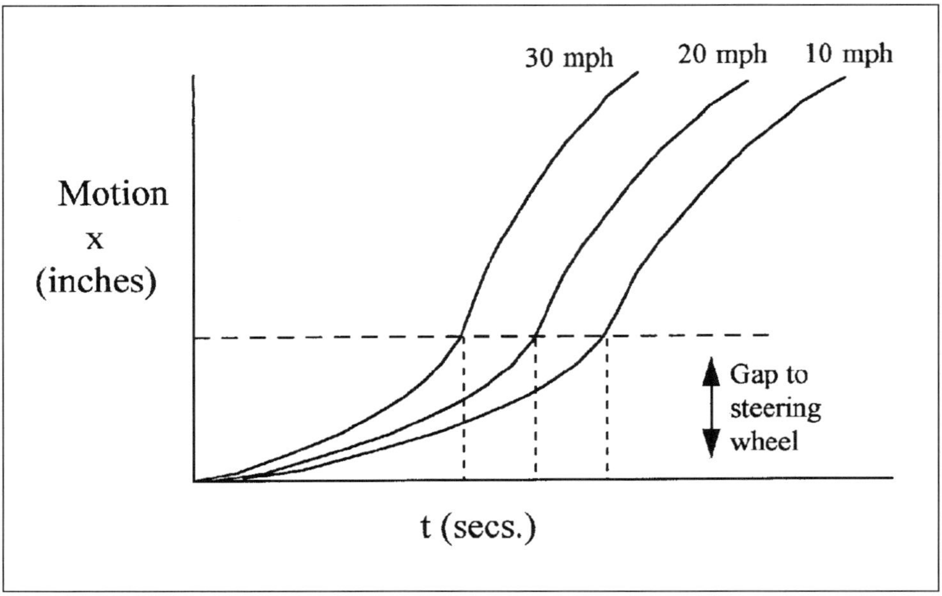

Figure 44 *Differential Motion – Occupant vs. Vehicle.*

lock faster than the above time. If the lockup time is only 0.05 s, the motion becomes 0.35 ft = 4.2 inches. This is a dramatic decrease (only 22% of the motion for 58% of the time), and explains why an early lockup is critical. These motions are proportional to the speed change, and are only one-third the above quotes for a 10 mph crash. See figure 44.

Two potential problems exist with motorized shoulder belts. The motor unit acts as the D-ring; however, since it is typically attached to the door frame rather than the B pillar, it is farther forward than the standard position. This causes two problems, particularly for a passenger in a seat which is moved back, as for a tall occupant. First, the restraining force of the belt on the occupant is a function of the angle of the belt versus the body of the occupant. If the belt is flat across the chest, meaning it does not wrap around the chest, then even a large force in the belt only represents a small force on the chest. This force is proportional to the sine of the wrap angle. This forces the occupant's motion to become larger in order to load the belt. Although the passenger has the greater space in front of them (no steering wheel) this still causes the passenger to jump away from the seat for a frontal collision, and it also prevents any chest loadings for a rearend impact where the motion is into the seat. It thus exacerbates the seat bounce effect.

The second problem has been experienced by the authors. The motor unit can be alongside the head. In the event of a side collision the motor unit can be

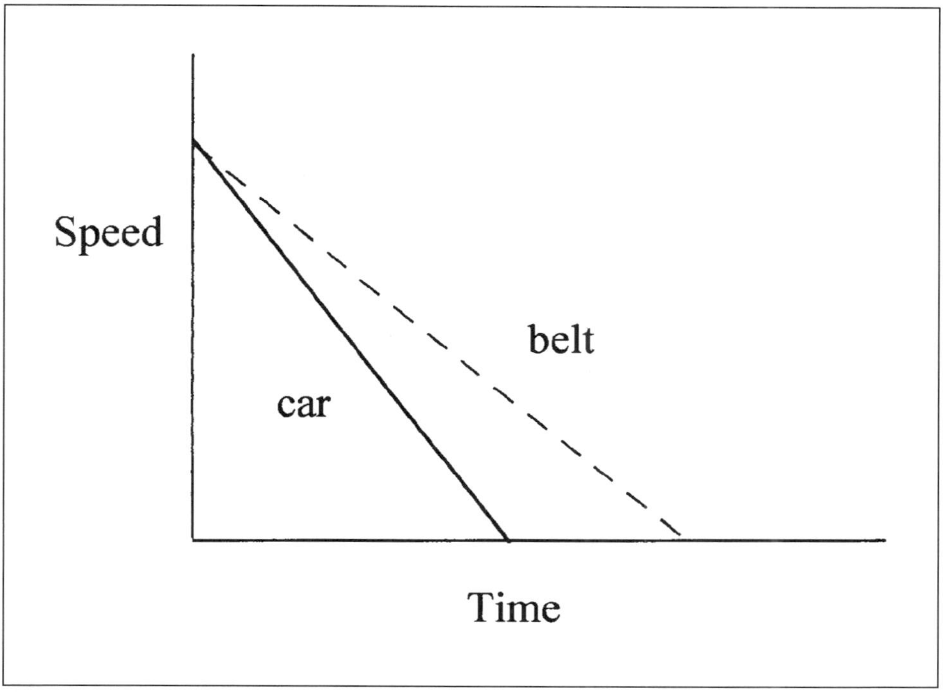

Figure 45 *"Ride-Down" with Seatbelt Stretching.*

driven into the head of the occupant. Being a small hard item this causes localized loading on the head which is worse than hitting the window, or even the B pillar.

It is frequently stated that the belt stretch is useful because it allows for a softer "ride-down" of the occupant. However, this logic is only applicable if the belt locks up *instantly*. This will happen if the belts are of the fixed variety, such as used by racing drivers, and employ negligible initial slack. However, a late lockup with the "comfort" belts can make the belt stretch a liability. The usual logic of the stretch is shown in figure 45. This is a plot of velocity versus time. The solid line indicates the car deceleration, and the area under the triangle is the stopping distance. The dashed line indicates the deceleration of the occupant. With a greater allowed stopping distance the deceleration is less. For example, for a 30 mph crash into a rigid barrier, the typical car stopping distance (the crush) is about 2 feet. The typical gap between the driver's chest and the steering wheel is about 1 foot. Thus to just reach the steering wheel with negligible speed, the driver's stopping distance can be increased to 3 feet. Since deceleration is inversely proportional to stopping distance for a fixed initial speed, this implies that the driver experiences a deceleration only 2/3 that of the car. However,

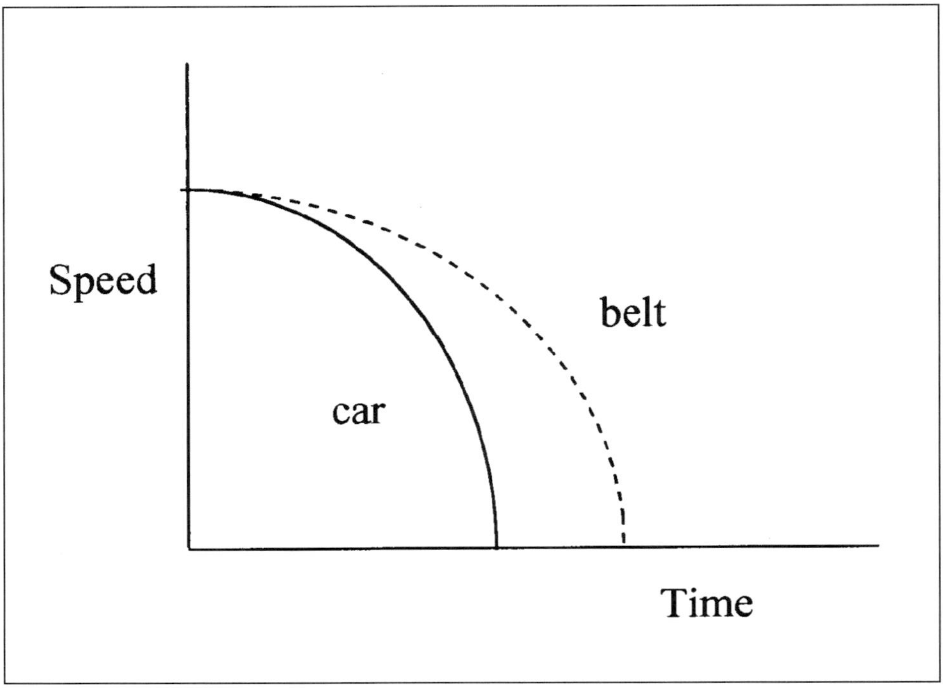

Figure 46 *Realistic "Ride-Down" Behavior.*

figure 45 is unrealistic, and should be replaced by figure 46. This is because neither the car nor the occupant experience constant deceleration. Instead, the car stops in a sinusoidal fashion, due to the stiffening behavior which makes the response similar to that of a spring. Likewise, the stretching seatbelt does the same thing. However, since peak deceleration is still inversely proportional to net stopping distance, then we still have the benefit of the extra belt stretch. For a sinusoidal deceleration, the peak deceleration is twice that for constant deceleration, for the same speed and stopping distance (deceleration = speed^2/distance versus speed^2/twice distance).

The problem with belt stretch occurs because of the delay in belt lockup. Figure 47 illustrates a more realistic behavior for an inertially-locked system. We see that with any delay in lockup, the occupant moves toward the steering wheel prior to the belt-induced deceleration. Now the belt stretch becomes a liability, since it may allow the occupant to reach the steering wheel. To prevent this, we would need a belt with less stretch. However, as seen in figure 47, this merely increases the final peak deceleration necessary on the occupant. We have the problem of needing to trade the belt stretch versus the delayed belt spool-out, and last-minute lockup implies very high occupant decelerations in order to avoid

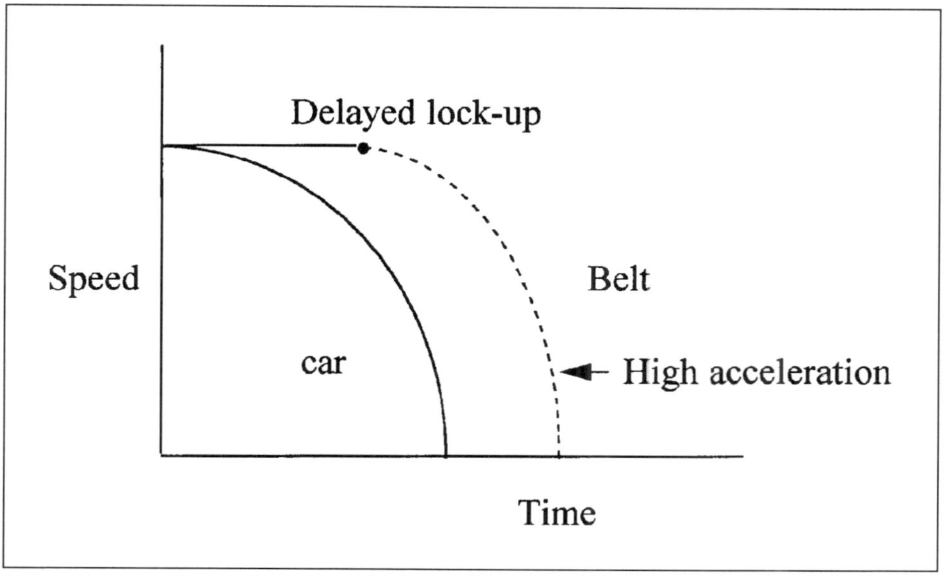

Figure 47 *True Case with Delayed Belt Lock-up.*

steering wheel impacts. This can result in peak deceleration *greater* than that of the car. These problems vanish for the fixed belts which are tight and less compliant, such as the racing driver belt, since now the worst that happens is that the peak deceleration becomes equal to that of the vehicle. Of course, these problems are less important for lower speeds. The lockup gap is less and the belt stretch is less, but also useful. It is because of these problems at the higher speeds that airbags were introduced.

Airbags and ABS

Airbags are usually designed to activate for frontal (or near-frontal) collisions above about 12 mph. This limit is chosen to avoid false firings (*i.e., unnecessary* firings at low speed). They inflate very fast, less than 35 msec, so as to catch the driver before the driver moves much. The rapid deployment of an airbag is again necessary to limit the differential occupant motion versus the vehicle. This is the same argument given before for seatbelt lockup. For a speed change of 30 mph, a deployment time of 0.035 s gives a motion of only 0.12 ft = 1.5 inches. Thus, the bag is designed to be fully deployed before any significant occupant motion, such that the occupant runs into the bag after it has stopped opening.

However, to prevent a strong bounce back from the bag the bag is designed to quickly deflate again, usually over a period of a few tenths of a second. This is fine for a single collision. However, problems occur if the vehicle suffers more than one hit, such as careening off a vehicle and then running into a tree. If the first impact was the more minor then the airbag is unable to do a useful job; indeed, deployment after the first hit can sometimes simply prevent the driver controlling the car for the second impact. For such cases the mere fact that the airbag deployed does not uniquely indicate all the circumstances.

Airbags do not deploy for side impacts, rear impacts, or side rollovers. Thus their usefulness is limited only to frontal collisions. While the latter are indeed usually the most serious, the fact remains that many crashes involve these other directions. Only a seatbelt can keep an occupant firmly attached to the seat. Hence the admonition that airbags are a supplemental restraint system (SRS), and should always be used *with* seatbelts. Unfortunately, many drivers seem to think the existence of an airbag eliminates the need to use the seatbelts! Also, an occupant who is out of position (leaning forward and/or sideways) can receive a strong impact from the bag, which can itself cause damage. The bag is designed to be fully deployed and *then* be hit by the moving occupant. It is not supposed to impact the occupant while still deploying.

Lastly, there is a problem with the use of child seats and air bags. If the child seat is mounted in the front passenger seat, it is known that the bag can hit the child seat sufficiently hard to endanger the child. Tests with child dummies have shown that the child can be thrown into the rear seat. The solution is twofold. Either put the child seat only in the rear seat, or if that is not possible, as with a front-seat only pickup, disengage the passenger side air bag. Government regulations are presently allowing the use of switches to deactivate air bags for the latter situation. Of course, this will require the driver to remember to reactivate it again if an adult passenger occupies the seat!

ABS brakes have two *potential* advantages. First, by preventing wheel lockup, they allow for some measure of steering in a panic stop. Second, by limiting the tire/road slip they can employ the peak in the tire/road friction. However, in reality these two advantages do not always exist. Some ABS systems actually *increase* stopping distances on normal dry surfaces, although they improve things for slippery surfaces. Further, although straight-line lockup can be avoided, the issue of the friction circle still exists. Hence, the ABS system doesn't always improve things for a car that is simultaneously trying to steer around a corner while panic braking. Of course, from an accident reconstructionist's point of view, ABS systems leave little in the way of skidmarks (either faint marks, none, or small "hops" along the road), although they have little effect on yaw marks.

There are other problems with ABS. Many drivers were taught to pump the brakes in order to avoid lockup. However, this should *not* be done with ABS, since the latter does the pumping itself, usually at about 15 cycles per second.

Instead, with ABS the brakes should be left on with firm foot pressure. When drivers pump ABS brakes, they merely confuse the system and can prevent proper action. However, the inbuilt pumping action can also sometimes cause a noticeable throbbing on the brake pedal, depending on design, causing some drivers to think something is wrong and release the brakes.

ABS logic has its own problems. With increasing brake pedal force application the frictional force between tire and road is known to first reach a peak. This is stiction, or static friction. After the frictional force peak is passed, the force decreases as full skidding takes place and stiction is replaced by normal, or dynamic, friction. For example, the stiction may reach a value of 0.8, while the friction may drop to about 0.7. If the ABS can sense when the stiction limit is reached, it can effectively allow for a higher average force. This shortens the braking distance for straight-line motion. However, it leaves no "headroom" for steering. Thus, the ABS does not improve steering capability. To allow for steering, the brakes must be released earlier, giving the necessary headroom. The problem is that the straight-line braking distance can now increase. Once again, ABS is a technical fix with its own problems.

It is of interest to note that the HLDI (Highway Loss Data Institute, part of the Insurance industry) has so far found that the existence of ABS has almost *no* effect on the average accident! The only significantly meaningful statistical results have been a decrease in vehicle-pedestrian accidents, but an *increase* in single-vehicle rollovers! The reasons for this are still not clear, yet, perversely, many insurance companies still offer a discount for owning a vehicle with ABS.

Newton's Cradle

A Newton's Cradle is an "executive toy" that can be found in many gift stores. It consists of a frame from which are hung five steel balls, all the same size and weight, and each hung on two nylon wires. The balls are arranged to just be touching when hanging undisturbed under gravity. The wires allow for pendulum motions along the axis of the frame. This contraption has its name because it demonstrates some of Newton's laws.

If a single ball is lifted at one end and then dropped, it will be observed that a pulse travels through the other four balls, and the other end ball bounces away exactly the same as the original incoming ball. If N balls (where N = 2, 3 or 4) are dropped simultaneously, it will be seen that N balls bounce out the other end! Thus, "what goes in is what comes out." This system is demonstrating conservation of linear momentum and energy for a system of identical elastic bodies!

Suppose 3 balls are picked up and moved out of the way, leaving only 2 neighboring balls. Dropping one ball will now give the following result. Upon impact, the first ball will "instantly" stop and the other ball will "instantly" take its place and bounce up as though it were a continuation of motion of the first ball. This is simple billiard ball behavior. Because the balls are identical and very elastic, the result is forced by conservation of momentum and energy, since no energy is lost and the balls merely exchange momentum and energy. However, if some damping material, such as modeling clay, is placed between the balls, the result is different. This time the two balls stick to each other and then swing as a pair. However, to conserve momentum the speed of the pair is only one-half that of the single original ball. Likewise, some energy has been absorbed. This has gone into plastic compression of the clay. Thus these two-ball cases illustrate the difference between an elastic two-car crash, approximately applicable at low speeds, and a plastic two-car crash, occurring at higher speed and with significant damage.

When more than two balls are involved the process is as follows. Upon dropping an end ball we first have a two-ball impact. However, as the second ball starts to move it rapidly runs into ball number 3. This simply repeats the two-ball impact and moves ball number 3 and number 4, etc. Thus the process repeats down the line until the end ball comes out. In principle the system would work for 100 balls. In practice it won't, because each collision is not truly perfectly elastic (the balls rub slightly on each other as they swing), so for a large number of balls the system would damp down before the end ball was reached. This damping is also why the five-ball case gradually converts itself into a case where all five balls simply swing together and gradually stop.

The Newton's Cradle applies to real life multi-car inline accidents, such as occurs during rush hour with stop-and-go traffic. As with the balls, if the various vehicles are reasonably similar in weight, and the damage is small (mostly bumper bounce), and a similar "pulse" can run down a line of cars. Thus an impact at one end of a line of (say) three cars can result in the last car bouncing out! This assumes close spacing of the cars and negligible braking for any car, of course, otherwise rapid damping occurs.

Improvements in Documentation

There is room for improvements in the standard documentation of accidents (such as the Uniform Accident Report, or UAR, as used by police). For example, while it is standard to note the use of seatbelts, it is not standard to note the positioning of headrests. For police investigations the major emphasis is usually on the more serious high speed cases, such as those involving fatalities. However, much civil litigation can involve the low speed cases including whiplash. Frequently, a reconstructionist must rely on the statements of the plaintiff or defendant in order to know where the headrest was. An independent note on the police report would be very helpful. Likewise, while great emphasis is often placed on the measurements of skid marks, little is noted concerning the final gap between the vehicles, especially for low speed accidents. Again, this can greatly aid in reconstruction. One modification of great help is the photographing of vehicles from above. Such photos can greatly improve interpretation, yet few police forces seem to do it on a regular basis.

The Use of Animations

Animations come in two basic forms: those that merely roughly indicate a sequence of events, and those that indicate real behavior based on the physics analysis of the situation. The latter are really a large number of still frames put together in the same manner as individual snapshots are drawn by reconstructionists. These snapshots are drawn to scale and represent the reconstructionist's interpretation of the physical evidence (distance moved versus time based on skid marks, etc.). The snapshots indicate the vehicle positions at "t-1, t-2, t- seconds," where zero time is the impact time. The animation uses the laws of physics to provide for many more frames.

The first type of animation, not based on physics, is really a form of cartoon, and while it can be helpful in providing understanding of a complex sequence, it cannot correctly illustrate why one interpretation is the correct one. The advantage of a physics-based computer animation is that it shows the sequence in a realistic smooth manner, and can illustrate several vehicle (or pedestrian/occupant) motions simultaneously. This can be very useful for a complex accident. Lastly, physics-based animations allow for the study of alternative scenarios, helping to explain why (hopefully!) *only one* scenario best fits all the data, and the other options do not.

Side Impact Protection

Recently, attention has been given to side impact problems. The real issue here is the very small distance between the side door and the occupant. Unlike the case of a relatively long hood, a side impact has to control the impact within a distance of only a few inches. Simple physics states that with such a small distance the ability to prevent serious side-impact injury is difficult.

An example of the problem is given by the issue of whether the doors should be stiff. If the door is very stiff, with little or no deformation, then the sudden side acceleration of the car will either induce large accelerations of the occupant (if firmly belted in place) or a sudden high speed impact on the driver (if the driver merely slides on the seat due to friction and is then hit by the moving door). The first action causes the driver's head and torso to undergo a sideways whiplash such that impact occurs on the door or the A or B frames. The second action leaves the driver mostly upright, but then he receives a blow to the left shoulder/arm and pelvis. Conversely, with a soft door (easily deformable), the door can be thrust directly into the occupant with limited initial motion of the latter. The correct solution is far from simple, although recent government regulations require door reinforcements.

Some recent solutions include the use of side airbags and/or side padding. The airbags can be mounted on the doors or on the side of the seats. Likewise, the padding can be part of the door or part of the seat design. To understand the problem consider the following. To maximize energy absorption, any form of padding should rapidly reach a maximum steady force, and then apply this force over the remaining displacement. This implies the use of a material that behaves perfectly plastically, with crush occurring at a fixed level of force (no strain-hardening). The plastic yield strength should be reached very quickly (very high elastic modulus), after which the force should stay constant (very small plastic modulus). However, while this approach maximizes energy absorption for a given amplitude of displacement, it still has problems. For example, the fixed plastic force level must itself be lower than that which can cause damage. Put bluntly, for real materials this imposes a tall order.

Injuries due to side impact include side head impact, shoulder/arm impact, thoracic impacts and pelvic impacts. Only a brief summary is given here. A common feature of most side impact injuries is that the body components usually display significant elastoviscous behavior. This applies for the thorax, abdomen, and pelvis areas. Thus much of the data involves discussion of impulse levels, meaning the integral of the thrust and time of application, and the shorter the time the higher the tolerated load. For this reason, many of the studies concentrate on the peak loads or accelerations that occur over a "3 ms clip." Further, side impact studies clearly indicate a tolerance which is dependent on both gender and age. For example, women are usually weaker than men for pelvic injuries. However, the strength of men rapidly drops with age above about 40, becoming similar to women at age about 75. Also, tolerance levels need to be adjusted according to the individual's weight and body proportions.

The tolerance level adjustment is done using the "Livi index." This index is given by Li = 10 $(\text{weight})^{1/3}$ /height, with weight in kg (1.0 kg = 2.2 lbs) and height in m (1.0 m = 39.4 inches). This index allows for a "corpulence rating." For Li less than 22 the person is very thin; for Li between 22 and 23 the person is thin; for Li between 23 and 24 the person is normal; for Li between 24 and 25 the person is stout; and for Li above 25 the person is considered obese. These factors can then be used to provide a "corrected" weight for an individual by using $w_c = w_a$ 23.5/Li, where w_c is the corrected weight and w_a is the actual weight. This is necessary because the experimental data best fit the corrected weights. To illustrate, consider a person who is 5 feet 8 inches tall (1.726 m) and weighs 165 lbs (75 kg). For this person the index is Li = 24.44 (stout) and the corrected weight is 72.13 kg = 159 lbs.

Experimental studies indicate that for side impacts, women can tolerate forces into the pelvis of about 1350 lbs regardless of age or pulse duration, although lower values of about 800 lbs have been observed, especially for the small (fifth percentile) woman. Women are more inclined to suffer from osteoporosis, and have a thinner pelvis than do men, to allow for birth. Men, however, can tolerate larger forces of up to 3000 lbs, especially the ninety-fifth percentile man. The average for men is about 2200 lbs, similar to the FMVSS allowed level of 2250 lbs. The typical pelvis represents about 0.134 of the total body weight (ref 10). Thus, for a 160 lb weight, a pelvis is about 21.4 lbs. A force of 2200 lbs then implies an acceleration of about 103 g is required if the force is acting only on the pelvis. For a 3 ms period, this implies a motion of about 0.18 inches and an induced speed change of about 9.95 ft/s or 6.8 mph. A least-squares fit for the pelvic tolerance is given by Force (lbs) = 19.8 w_c (lbs) - 1059. Thus, for a 165 lb man the force is 2208 lbs.

This very small amplitude of motion is partly the justification for ignoring the rest of the body weight, since the pelvis "talks" very little to the rest of the body, and the joints move only slightly. This is the logic involved when dealing with articulated portions of the body that do not have either time or motion to interact.

The limits for thoracic impacts are similar to those for frontal loadings. If an arm becomes trapped between the door and the thorax, the levels do not change significantly.

CTS and TMJ Injuries

These two types of injury have been left to the end, because they are still poorly understood with regard to mechanical causation in vehicle accidents. Carpal Tunnel Syndrome (CTS) is usually considered a repetitive stress syndrome (RSS). This problem is associated with entrapment of the medial nerve in the wrist. The result is weakness in the wrist. This can include pain and the inability to properly hold objects. Usually, the problem is diagnosed as a case in which the carpal tunnel ligament is pressing on the nerve, thus causing impairment. The most usual cause of this problem is repetitive motions, such as those associated with typing and use of computer keyboards (it thus most frequently occurs in people who tend to have jobs that require this behavior, and women tend to have such jobs more frequently than do men; hence CTS is more common among women than men). Overuse of the wrist in this maneuver can cause long-term pain. This pain can arise during sleep and can be difficult to deal with. Frequently, the solution is to relieve the pressure by cutting the ligament that covers the wrist. Based on anatomy, and medicine, there appears to be no good reason for the need for this ligament (rather like why no good reason seems to exist for the need of the appendix).

However, the problem is not associated only with repetitive actions; it can also occur due to sudden forceful loads. Consider a car occupant who suffers a sudden stop from speed. How can a sudden large load be applied to the wrist that might cause problems? There are two basic mechanisms. One is the "terror grip," in which the driver grips the steering wheel very tightly during a crash. Then, as the body moves forward, the wrist can be subjected to high loads. However, if the wrists bend and the elbows and shoulders bend, this effect is only able to apply high loads at high speeds. This is because such bend activity implies large stopping motions for the body. Thus, if the chest moves forward enough to reach the steering wheel the potential force on the wrist(s) is kept low. Only by very strongly gripping the wheel can high forces be applied at the wrist. Most people cannot do this since there is a natural tendency for the wrist to slip around the wheel as the arms bend. Further, this torso motion implies the seatbelts were either not being worn or failed to lock.

To illustrate this, suppose a driver's torso moves toward the steering wheel at 10 mph. For an average upper body weight of 70 lbs, this implies a kinetic energy of about 234 ft-lbs. If the arms flex so as to allow the chest to travel about one foot to the wheel, the necessary force to just stop the torso with both arms is about 234 lbs, or about 117 lbs each. If applied directly to the wrists this is a high load, particularly if the wrists lock on the wheel and do not slide around, such that the wrists simultaneously suffer a strong bend (extension). Indeed, if the driver tries to stop the torso motion mostly in the last few inches of motion the wrist forces are even higher. However, in most cases the driver does not actually stop his torso prior to hitting the wheel. In this case the wrist forces are much lower, and now the remaining necessary force to stop the torso is provided by the impact on the chest. If the resulting wheel impact speed for the torso is reduced from 10 mph to 5 mph then the arms only absorbed an energy of about 175 ft-lbs, and the combined arm force is now 176 lbs (88 lbs per arm).

The second mechanism is the "straight-arm impact." Here an occupant, usually the passenger, puts out an arm to stop themselves. If the arm is in the locked straight position with the elbows locked, the wrist can sometimes impact the dash. Since a straight arm has little compliance (the distance to stop the arm is the small degree of compression within the wrist, the elbow and the shoulder), this can sometimes give a large thrust onto the wrist.

An illustration of the latter case is an occupant who stops their upper body motion with one straight arm only. For an impact speed of only 3 mph, the total upper body kinetic energy is about 21 ft-lbs. If this motion is stopped by the one arm, and the effective stopping distance is only about 0.3 inches (a rigid dash is assumed here), the required force will be about 842 lbs. This is a very large wrist force. However, such a force can only exist if the alignment of arm and torso is such as to prevent rotation of the torso at the shoulder, such that the entire upper body is stopped within the small wrist-arm-shoulder compliance. While this could happen, it is far more likely that for a right arm stop the person's torso would rotate in a clockwise motion (as seen from above) about the shoulder, and the right collar bone (clavicle) and shoulder blade (scapula) would also move back relative to the spine/thorax. Also, the average car dash will itself have some compliance, perhaps one inch. Merely increasing the stopping distance from 0.3 inches to 1.3 inches drops the force to about 194 lbs. If torso/shoulder blade rotation allows for an effective further motion of 4 inches, the force drops to about 48 lbs. Taking only the weight of the arm (about 5.1% total body weight) of say 7.15 lbs and only the through-arm compliance of 0.3 inches, an impact speed of 3 mph implies a force of about 86 lbs.

Wrist loads below 100 lbs are unlikely to cause serious injury, unless the person is already at the incipient threshold for CTS problems. However, as the above examples illustrated, the exact force on the wrist will depend strongly on the exact motions. Consequently, a detailed analysis is necessary to evaluate the situation for a specific crash, assuming enough data exists to allow this.

Temporomandibular joint (TMJ) problems are also sometimes claimed for car crashes. The jaw bone weighs about 1.5 lbs, while the jaw muscles can exert forces of up to about 200 lbs at the molars. TMJ occurs when the facet joints suffer injury. Motion of the jaw causes "clicks" and abnormal motion and pain. How can TMJ be caused in a vehicle accident?

One obvious damage mechanism is a direct thrust on the joint region or on the jaw bone (the mandible). This can occur if the occupant strikes the steering wheel with their chin, thereby suddenly forcing the jawbone back relative to the rest of the head. Another option could be a direct impact of the joint region on the side of the headrest or door, etc.

Although the jaw can handle strong pseudo-vertical loads, as in biting, it is not designed for strong lateral loads (front to back or sideways). Suppose the head hits a steering wheel at 5 mph with direct thrust backward on the chin. For a typical head weight of about 10 lbs, this gives a kinetic energy of about 8.4 ft-lbs, with about 1.25 ft-lbs in the jawbone itself. Allow the jaw joint to move backward about 0.5 inches before serious joint damage. Then the necessary force to stop the head and jaw is about (8.4 - 1.25) ft-lbs / (0.5/12) ft = 170 lbs. While reliable quotes for joint damage loads are not available, this load is clearly close to the "natural" strength, but is not the "natural" motion. Hence it is probable that such a load could start to cause problems, particularly if the load was unbalanced, giving a larger thrust to one side of the jaw than the other.

Note that boxers wear mouthguards to prevent mouth problems. These guards not only protect the teeth but also act to lock the jaw. This forces the lower and upper jaw to behave as a single unit, preventing relative motion. Thus boxers can receive significant blows to the jaw without suffering from TMJ.

The muscles controlling vertical motions of the jaw are the masseter (zygomatic bone to the ramus of the mandible) and the temporalis (coronoid process of the mandible to the temporal bone of the skull). Those that control forward/backward and side motions are the medial pterygoid (inner surface of the ramus of the mandible and the maxilla bone) and the lateral pterygoid (condyle of the mandible and the sphenoid bone). While the vertical motion muscles are quite strong, those that control the lateral motions are weaker.

An alternative mechanism, whiplash, has been postulated. Here, it is assumed that a sudden rearward motion of the head can leave a loose jaw stationary if the jaw muscles are lax. This will give a motion equivalent to suddenly forcing the jaws open. The problem with this mechanism is that the jawbone does not weigh very much. Hence, to apply large inertial loads the required acceleration is high. For instance, suppose the load needs to be comparable with biting loads, about 100 lbs. Then, with a weight of only 1.5 lbs the acceleration needs to be about 67 g. This will be the rearward acceleration of the remainder of the head away from the jawbone. However, such large accelerations are considerably in excess of those causing neck problems, such as with the neck whiplash, where neck ligamentous damage can start at about 19 g rotational acceleration. It is thus difficult to accept this type of damage mechanism, and there is little in the way of direct experimental evidence to support it other than such interpretations by some dentists.

Standards and Regulations

We will not attempt to quote here all the various regulations and standards that apply to automobiles. Such quotes can be obtained in detail from the references by SAE (ref 1) and also by Limpert (ref 2). However, with regard to the ubiquitous slow speed rearender whiplash problem, it is of interest to note the regulations concerning headrests. These are extremely minimal: First, the headrest must exist. Second, it must not break off the seat for an applied rearward load (centered on the headrest) of less than 200 lbs. For a 10 lb head this is only a 20 g acceleration, which is close to the neck injury tolerance. There are no regulations defining how well a headrest should actually work, such as specifying adjustability with regard to height and rearward position relative to the occupant's head! No wonder IIHS discovered few existing headrests to be of much help. There appears to be an ingrained attitude that somehow rearenders do not cause injury.

Part III

Expert Witness Testimony and the Use of Demonstrative Evidence to Prove Causation in Low Speed Automobile Accident Trials

Chapter 11

Witness Testimony in Automobile Accident Trials

A witness's testimonial evidence is oral testimony offered by a witness, under oath or affirmation, from the witness stand in court or by way of a formal deposition. It differs from demonstrative evidence (i.e. a model of an automobile or a human body) in that the trier of fact must determine for each witness heard whether the witness correctly perceived the event described, whether the memory is accurate, whether the veracity is credible, and whether the proper words have been chosen to accurately describe the information. Normally, in compliance with the hearsay rule, only those who actually perceived the events in question may testify.

Rules of evidence are designed to reduce the dangers inherent in permitting witnesses to verbally describe events they claim to have witnessed, while allowing trials to proceed without unreasonable expense, time, or difficulty. The various rules of evidence represent a policy resolution to the process of balancing legitimate competing interests. As an example, consider that all witnesses unconsciously and naturally make inferences from events seen or heard, and recall such events colored by their own biases. Consider then that cross-examination is the method available under the rules of evidence to bring such biases to light and therefore place the entire testimony in perspective for the trier of fact.

Competency Requirements

Historically, the term "competency" meant simply compliance with the rules of evidence. In modern use, the term generally refers to whether the court finds a particular witness reliable enough to allow the trier of fact to hear the testimony. The modern trend is that any person may testify as a witness, subject primarily to reasonable rules regarding minimal physical and/or mental qualifications. (This differs, of course, from the weight given a particular witness's testimony once heard.) The Federal Rules of Evidence take this approach, and abolish old common law disqualification rules. They provide that: "Every person is competent to be a witness except as otherwise provided in these rules." Fed. R. Evid. 601. However, where the case turns on state law (e.g., in diversity jurisdiction cases) then the competency of a witness must be determined in accordance with the applicable state law. Super Valu Stores v. First National Bank, 463 F.Supp 1183 (M.D.Ga. 1979); Barton v. American Red Cross, 829 F.Supp 1290 (M.D.Ala. 1993).

General State Requirements

The question of a person's competency to be a witness is initially determined by the court. The standards for determining mental or physical capacity vary among jurisdictions, but generally encompass the ability to communicate, the understanding of the duty to tell the truth, and the requirement of personal knowledge.

The witness must be capable of expressing him or herself so as to be understood by the jury, either directly or through an interpreter. Where a witness testifies through an interpreter, it must be shown that the interpreter is qualified in the foreign language in question and is under oath to make a true and accurate translation. This last element is also a requirement of the Federal Rules of Evidence. Fed. R. Evid. 604.

The witness must also be capable of understanding the solemn duty and obligation to tell the truth, under the required oath or affirmation.

Finally, the witness must have personal knowledge of the matter described. Person knowledge is defined as a present recollection of an impression derived through the witness's own senses. An exception to this rule is, of course, available to those qualified to testify as expert witnesses.

Federal Requirements

Under the Federal Rules of Evidence, personal knowledge is the only requirement of competency for other than expert witnesses. Fed. R. Evid. 602. The witness's ability to communicate, and understanding of the duty to tell the truth affect only the weight and credibility of the testimony, not its admissibility for competency.

Opinion Testimony

An opinion is an inference or a conclusion drawn from facts that have been observed. In our courts, a nonexpert witness called to give direct evidence is normally not allowed to state opinions or conclusions drawn from those observations. The rationale is that a jury of lay persons should draw its own conclusions rather than rely upon a nonexpert's conclusions. Expert witnesses may be called to testify specifically to give opinion testimony in their area of expertise, however.

All Witnesses

The testimony of witnesses which is merely their opinion or conclusion is normally not admissible. Practitioners must remember that it is the content, and not always its form, which determines whether a statement is opinion. A response such as "I think" or "I believe" is not necessarily objectionable as opinion testimony. It is the basis of a witness's statement which determines its character as opinion or otherwise.

However, there are certain situations in which opinion testimony by either lay or expert witnesses is admissible because it may be helpful to the trier of fact. If because of the nature of the case no better evidence can be obtained, opinions by lay witnesses are permitted "...Which are (a) rationally based on the perception of the witness and (b) helpful to a clear understanding of the witness' testimony or the determination of a fact in issue." Fed. R. Evid. 701.

Some descriptive areas of permissible lay opinions maybe in order at this point. Physical description opinions will generally be admissible if the opinion is on a matter upon which normal persons consistently form reasonably reliable opinions. Examples may include taste, smell, appearance, weight, size, distance, time, speed, or sound. Opinions of personal identity will generally be admissible if the witness has some basis to identify another's physical characteristics or marks. Opinions of another's physical or mental condition may be admissible when it is the most effective way to describe the complex perceptions of the witness. Examples include descriptions of someone being nervous, someone being intoxicated, or the sanity of a close acquaintance. The important point here is that the court has a wide range of discretion with regard to witnesses not testifying as experts.

Finally, there are many areas in which the opinions of laypersons are inadmissible. The most common examples of such matters are those involving legal conclusions rather than factual observations. Again, some descriptive areas of impermissible lay opinion may be helpful. Witnesses are ordinarily not allowed to express their opinions concerning legal standard of care, such as negligence or fault. Furthermore, lay witnesses may not express opinions regarding the cause of an accident where the occurrence is of a type such that specialized or expert knowledge is usually required to determine its cause. A caveat to this rule is that when the accident is of a sort about which laypersons commonly form accurate opinions, a lay witness may properly give an opinion as to causation, if based on observation of the event itself. Schmidt v. Chapman, 131 N.W.2d 689 (Wis. 1964).

Expert Witnesses

Qualifications

In order to have a witness testify as an expert, counsel must first satisfy the trial judge that the witness possesses some special knowledge, skill or experience that qualifies the witness to render the opinion as an expert on the subject to which the testimony relates. Fed. R. Evid. 702; Knight v. Otis Elevator Co., 596 F.2d 84 (3d Cir. 1979) The qualifications of a proposed expert witness must be established as a prerequisite for the actual testimony. Preliminary information as to the witness's qualifications is elicited by the examining counsel with what are referred to as "qualifying questions." The determination of whether the witness qualifies as an expert is made by the judge and is binding on the trier of fact. (Again, the trier of fact may consider the depth of the witness's qualifications in determining the weight to be given to the testimony.) Among the factors usually raised by the qualifying questions, and considered in deciding whether a witness is qualified, are: education and training, experience, familiarity with authoritative references in the field, and membership in professional associations. Note that certain technical expertise is not always essential, but that any special experience or capability may qualify a witness as an expert in that field.

For example, law enforcement officers with special experience and knowledge have been held qualified as experts on the mechanics of certain numbers games, Moore v. United States, 394 F.2nd 818 (5th Cir. 1968); on identification of cocaine by visual examination, United States v. Bermudez, 526 F.2d 89 (2nd Cir. 1975); and the effect of alcohol on a person's ability to safely operate a motor vehicle, Marr v. State, 741 P.2d 884 (Okla. 1987). Compare those findings, however, with the holding in Deaver v. Hickox, 224 N.E. 2d 468 (Ill. 1967), which found that a standard police officer is not qualified to express an opinion on vehicular speed on the basis of skid marks and vehicle damage, since this requires a special knowledge of physics and mechanics.

Subject Matter

Normally, an expert's opinion is limited to matters within the expert's special field of expertise, and about which people lacking the witness's special knowledge are uninformed. Historically, an expert would not be permitted to render an opinion on the ultimate issue of the case (e.g. whether the automobile was properly constructed) as this would have invaded the province of the finder of fact. The modern trend is otherwise, however, and it repudiates the limitation as too ambiguous. The Federal Rule itself now states "Testimony in the form of an expert opinion is not objectionable because it embraces the ultimate issue or issues to be decided by the trier of fact." Fed. R. Evid. 704. The above rule notwithstanding, testimony on an ultimate issue may still be excluded if: it embraces a conclusion of law, Hermitage Industries v. Schwerman Trucking Co., 814 F.Supp 484 (D.S.C. 1993); it is not helpful to the trier of fact, Fed R. Evid. 702; or it is prejudicial, confusing, or a waste of time, Fed. R. Evid. 403.

Whenever some technical training or special knowledge is required to render an opinion on a matter, expert testimony is proper to aid the trier of fact in reaching their verdict. Generally, expert testimony regarding causation of an accident or occurrence is proper and admissible. Layton v. Yankee Caithness Joint Ventures, L.P., 774 F.Supp 576 (D.Nev. 1991).

Expert testimony is generally considered unnecessary and improper when the trier of fact is considered competent to draw its own conclusions on the issue at hand. Therefore, expert opinion is not allowed on the issues of fault or negligence, because these are conclusions that the trier of fact is competent to draw from the facts presented in evidence. For example, in Wilkerson v. City of El Monte, 17 Cal.App.2d 615 (1936), opinion testimony that a "dip in the highway" was a dangerous condition, or that the plaintiff was driving "too fast for highway conditions" were held improper, as these were inferences the trier of fact could readily draw from facts in evidence.

Admissibility Conditions

A witness may offer testimony as an expert only if several conditions are satisfied. First, as described above, the witness must be qualified as an expert by reason of some special knowledge, skill, experience, or training in the pertinent field. Fed. R. Evid. 702. Second, the opinions or inferences offered by the expert must actually depend on such special knowledge, skill, experience or training not within the ordinary experience of lay jurors, so that the witness's testimony will be of assistance to the trier of fact to understand the evidence or to determine a fact in issue. United States v. Fosher, 590 F.2d 381 (1st Cir. 1979). Third, the witness's opinion must be based on matters upon which other experts in the pertinent field reasonably rely in forming opinions regarding the subject in issue. Fed. R. Evid. 703; United States v. Watson, 587 F.2d 365 (7th Cir. 1978). Note that an expert will not be allowed to offer opinions based on that witness's personal assessment of another witness's testimony. United States v. Scop, 846 F.2d 135 (2d Cir. 1988).

Fourth, in many jurisdictions it must be established that the expert witness possesses "a reasonable degree of certainty (probability)" regarding the opinion or inference. State v. Mitchell, 390 A.2d 495 (Me. 1978).

Expert Witness's Source of Data

As suggested in the above discussion, the opinion of an expert witness may be drawn from one of four sources: opinions based on facts personally observed, opinions bases on evidence adduced during trial, opinions based on hypothetical questions, and opinions based on data conveyed by counsel, or others, outside of the courtroom.

The expert witness may, or course, express an opinion or conclusion based on facts personally observed (e.g. an attending physician may render a diagnosis on the basis of neck injuries clinically observed). Similarly, an expert may also take into account facts communicated by others (e.g. an attending physician may also render a diagnosis based in part upon the report of a radiologist). Furthermore, if the data on which the expert bases the opinion is of a type reasonably relied upon by experts in forming opinions on the particular subject, the data itself need not be independently admissible into evidence. Fed. R. Evid. 702 - 703; State v. Rupp, 586 P.2d 1302 (Ariz. 1978). In fact, the modern trend is to hold that such data does not itself constitute affirmative evidence, but is received solely to show the basis of the expert testimony. Paddock v. Dave Christensen, Inc., 745 F.2d 1254 (9th Cir. 1984).

An expert witness who has been present in the courtroom may also properly base an opinion on the evidence adduced during trial, unless that evidence is in conflict or dispute between the parties to the case. Kale v. Douthitt, 274 F.2d 476 (4th Cir. 1960).

Additionally, an expert witness may properly base an opinion on data conveyed to him or her by means of a hypothetical question. The general requirement here is that there must be some admissible evidence supporting the existence of the facts of the hypothetical question. Fed. R. Evid. 705.

Finally, under Federal Rule 703, the expert may also base the opinion on data presented by counsel, or others, outside the courtroom. Again, the data presented need not be independently admissible into evidence if it is "of a type reasonably relied upon by experts in the particular field in forming opinions or inferences upon the subject." Fed. R. Evid. 703. Therefore, any expert witness may base an opinion, at least in part, on information gleaned from texts, learned treatises, or consultations with other experts. United States v. Golden, 532 F.2d 1244 (9th Cir. 1976). Under Federal Rule of Evidence 803(18), when an expert witness has relied upon statements in learned treatises during direct examination, or they have been raised during cross-examination, those statements can be read into evidence by either party. Again, there must also be a demonstration in some fashion acceptable to the court that the treatise is recognized as authoritative. The statements are then usable as substantive evidence, and not merely for impeachment purposes. It is important to note, however, that several state jurisdictions still hold that an expert's testimony must declare that data relied upon would be admissible if appropriate foundation witnesses were produced. Department of Youth Services v. A Juvenile, 499 N.E.2d 812 (Mass. 1986). Most courts will permit an expert witness to ground an opinion in part upon the opinion of other experts in the same field, regardless of whether those opinions are themselves in evidence. It must be customary within a witness's discipline, however, to rely upon the opinion of others in forming an expert conclusion. Jenkins v. United States, 307 F.2d 637 (D.C. Cir. 1962). Interestingly, a handwriting expert can even base an opinion on writing exemplars which, due to prejudicial content, are themselves inadmissible. United States v. Shields, 573 F.2d 18 (10th Cir. 1978).

Disclosure of Expert Opinion Basis

Unless the expert witness personally observed the pertinent facts of the issue testified to, most state courts require the expert to disclose the data relied upon in forming the opinion prior to stating the opinion. State court procedure where the basis for the expert testimony was heard in court is that counsel merely asks the expert if he or she was in the courtroom and heard the facts described in previous testimony. Assuming an affirmative reply, the expert is then simply asked whether the opinion is based on the data described in that testimony.

State court procedures for a hypothetical question, that is, one the witness is asked to assume is true, vary. Some state courts require that the hypothetical question include every material fact, and not just those which support the conclusion that the expert will express. Ames & Webb, Inc. v. Commercial Laundry Co., 133 S.E.2d 547 (Va. 1963). The modern trend, however, is to eliminate this requirement as unnecessarily cumbersome, time consuming, and confusing. Facts that support a contrary conclusion can be brought out on cross-examination. Vermont Food Industries, Inc. v. Ralston Purina Co., 514 F.2d 456 (2nd Cir. 1975). The facts assumed in the hypothetical question must be in the trial record when the question is posed, or else examining counsel must indicate to the court that evidence of those facts will be presented in the course of the trial. Some states would require an offer of proof at this point. Takoma Park Bank v. Abbott, 19 A.2d 169 (Md. 1941).

Federal court procedures have attempted to simplify matters somewhat in recognition of the difficulties hypothetical questions have caused in the various state courts. Federal Rule of Evidence 705 permits examining counsel to ask an expert for an opinion and then immediately allows opposing counsel to cross-examine, without any disclosure of the data underlying the opinion. Vermont Food Industries, Inc. v. Ralston Purina Co., (supra). Unless there has been exhaustive pretrial discovery, this procedure may itself be problematic, since the cross-examiner may not readily be able to get the facts behind the opinion. Although Federal Rule of Evidence 705 allows them to do so, for practical reasons trial counsel are not likely to abandon the use of hypothetical questioning, if only because the method allows counsel to capsulize the evidence prior to presenting closing arguments. Note however, that this Federal Rule probably forecloses successful assignments of error based on a claim that opposing counsel's hypothetical question lacked sufficient foundation, by placing the burden of eliciting any missing data upon the cross-examiner.

Permissible Means of Cross-Examining Expert Witnesses

An expert witness may be cross-examined to the same extent as any other witness. Cross-examining of experts for purposes of impeachment usually involves attacking the expert's qualifications or presenting contrary views of other experts or treatises, especially if relied upon by the witness. Another possible technique is to alter the facts of a hypothetical used on direct-examination to demonstrate how the opinion would change as well. In addition, cross-examination about an expert's compensation is typically permitted.

The counsel conducting cross-examination may wish to show, either by cross-examination or independent evidence, that the expert witness lacks the qualifications claimed on direct, or that those qualifications do not make the witness an actual expert in the field in which expertise is claimed. Several states will permit opposing counsel to engage in a limited cross-examination immediately following the proponent's qualifying questions for the purpose of testing the witness's qualifications as an expert.

Through the process of cross-examination, counsel may reveal to the trier of fact that the expert previously expressed a different or inconsistent opinion in the present case. Most courts, however, refuse to allow impeachment on differing conclusions reached in other prior cases, regardless of similarities in the facts.

The facts of any hypothetical question posed to the expert on direct-examination may be altered or withdrawn on cross-examination, and counsel may then inquire whether, in light of the changes, the expert's opinion would change. It is also permissible to add facts to the hypothetical question if the record of trial reflects them or counsel represents that they will be elicited.

Because it may be of interest to the trier of fact in examining potential bias, most courts permit counsel to cross-examine the expert witness regarding the compensation, fees, or expenses the expert is receiving in connection with his or her reports and testimony. A typical statutory provision on this topic is found in the California Evidence Code, Section 722.

A very common and proper method of counsel cross-examining an expert is attempted rebuttal testimony offered by other experts. Similarly, it is permissible to show on cross-examination that pertinent texts, treatises, or articles in learned journals do not support the opinions expressed by the witness, at least if the witness stated that they were relied upon in arriving at the original opinion. Some states do not allow cross-examining counsel to use other texts, based on the fear that some cross-examiners might attempt to use certain hearsay opinions of less than reputable authors who cannot themselves be cross-examined.

Federal Rule of Evidence 803(18), and indeed, many states, allow cross-examination of an expert witness concerning views expressed in any recognized scientific text or treatise, regardless of whether the expert witness claims to have relied upon them. To restrict the cross-examining counsel in this regard would have permitted experts to always avoid a damaging cross-examination merely by denying any reliance upon texts contrary to their opinions. The principal safeguard under the Federal Rule 803(18) is that the text or treatise must first be shown to be authoritative and reliable. If the expert denies the reliability or authority of the author(s), independent evidence may be presented by other experts, or the trial judge may take judicial notice of its authoritative standing. In most courts, the text is admissible solely for impeachment purposes, and not as substantive evidence of the contrary views expressed therein.

Ruth v. Fenchel, 121 A.2d 373 (N.J. 1956).

Chapter 12

Uses of Demonstrative Evidence in Automobile Accident Trials

Demonstrative evidence is often distinguished from "real evidence." Real evidence is evidence that itself is alleged to have some direct or even circumstantial connection with the facts at issue in the case. Demonstrative evidence is not the real item; i.e., it is not the defective part of the automobile, etc. It is any tangible item apart from testimony that is used for exemplification or explanation purposes. It is a visual aid such as an anatomical model, a diagram, a chart, an animation, a map, a film or a photograph. The item may, however, be used both as illustrative and as real evidence, depending on how it is used. When an item is used to make a factual determination, as in a photograph of injuries, it is considered real evidence. However, when an item is used only to help the trier of fact to better understand testimony given, as in a chart or model, it is considered demonstrative evidence. If the item is demonstrative only, the item need not be offered into evidence, and need not be taken into the jury room. It may always be used as a summary of witness testimony during closing arguments, etc.

Categories of Physical Evidence

Original Evidence

This form of evidence is in existence independent of the trial. It most likely has some connection with the transaction or event in question at trial. Examples of this type of evidence are handwriting exemplars, etc.

Prepared Evidence

This form of evidence is made specifically for the trial, and had no prior relation to the events in question at trial. It is also described as prepared demonstrative evidence. Examples include models, animations, or sketches made to show the trier of fact.

Conditions for Admissibility of Evidence

The use of demonstrative evidence always presents some degree of danger of distortion in perspective or fabricated representation. Courts routinely seek to minimize this danger by seeking some testimonial assurances of the item's accuracy and relevance, whether or not the item is offered for admission.

Relevancy

As with all evidence, demonstrative evidence must be relevant to be admissible. If an item of evidence tends to prove or to disprove any proposition, it is relevant to that proposition. If the item of evidence is directed toward a fact within the range of allowable controversy, it is material to that controversy. In Federal Rule of Evidence 401, relevant evidence is defined as "Evidence having any tendency to make the existence of any fact that is of consequence to the determination of the action more probable or less probable than it would be without the evidence."

Thus, the modern trend is to regard relevancy as including both the element of materiality and the element of probativeness within the determination of relevancy.

Authentication

A second condition of admissibility of demonstrative evidence is that it be authenticated. Authentication requires that counsel show that the evidence is what it purports to be, or more specifically, that it is what its proponent states that it is. Authentication is necessary to protect against two dangers. The first is to prevent the introduction of an item different from the one testified about. The second is to ensure that the item itself has not undergone significant changes. The testimony of the qualified witness with personal knowledge of the item is typically sufficient to establish its authenticity.

Court's Discretionary Powers

Even if the evidentiary item is properly authenticated and is clearly relevant, the trial judge has a wide range of discretion to entirely exclude such items where, in the opinion of the court, its probative value will be outweighed by its prejudicial effect upon the trier of fact. The Federal Rule of Evidence 403 states that evidence will be excluded where "...its probative value is substantially outweighed by the danger of unfair prejudice, confusion of the issues, or misleading the jury, or by considerations of undue delay, waste of time, or needless presentation of cumulative evidence." Examples of such determinations include denying the exhibition of a gruesome wound in a personal injury case, denying the use of an out-of-scale chart in an automobile accident case, or mere repetitions of evidence previously presented. Even the expert testimony of a law enforcement officer is subject to this "probative vs. prejudicial—balancing test," as held by the court in U.S. v. Gutierrez, 995 F.2d 169 (9th Cir. 1993).

Note that the trial judge's discretion is not totally absolute. Some appellate courts have reversed the trial judge's decision allowing unduly prejudicial material into evidence. Commonwealth v. Dankel, 301 A.2d 365 (Pa. 1973).

Specific Modes of Presentation of Physical Evidence in Automobile Accident Trials

It is often said that the complexity of modern litigation severely impairs juror comprehension, and, therefore, the ability of the jury to render a fair verdict. In order to handle such complex cases effectively, counsel must recognize that such significant levels of complexity diminish the usefulness of conventional trial presentations. Trial practitioners should not resist available presentation technologies, therefore. A jury is typically quite capable of comprehending complex issues and advanced technologies if counsel are offering the jury the clearest presentation devices available. Additionally, practitioners should not overlook the advantages of using these powerful presentation technologies for purposes of settlement discussions, mediations, or arbitrations. Finally, expert witness testimony is invariably made more helpful when accompanied by appropriate demonstrative aids. The following modes of presentation are offered as key examples.

Photographs & Motion Pictures

Since both photographs and motion pictures are merely reproductions, they require authentication by specific testimony showing that they are faithful reproductions of the object or person depicted. Most courts hold that it is sufficient if the witness who identifies the photograph or film is both familiar with the object or scene represented, and also states that the photograph or film accurately represents the object or scene at issue. United States v. McNair, 439 F.Supp 103 (E.D.Pa. 1977). There are a few courts that require more, however. These courts seek testimony by the person who actually operated the camera, describing the angles used, speed, lighting, development process used, and care of the negatives to avoid any tampering. (See 9 A.L.R.2d 899).

Remember that authentication and relevancy are ever present requirements. In an automobile products liability action based on the allegedly defective design of the roof structure, it was not held as an abuse of discretion to exclude the manufacturer's film demonstrating the movement of occupants in a rollover accident when the filmed accident portrayed vehicles and circumstances different from the accident at issue in the case. Shipp v. General Motors Corp., 750 F.2d 418 (5th Cir. 1985). Conversely, in another products liability personal injury trial, motion pictures depicting plaintiff's work activities since the accident were held relevant, in that they refuted his claim of disability. Shushereba v. R.B. Industries, Inc., D.C.Pa. 1985, 104 F.R.D. 524.

Finally, remember that cumulative evidence is generally excluded by the court. For example, where defense counsel had previously presented the testimony of a firearms expert to describe the capabilities of a certain weapon used to threaten his client, counsel's subsequent attempt to introduce a videotape of the weapon's firepower was held to be unnecessarily cumulative. U.S. v. Falcon, 766 F.2d 1469 (10th Cir. 1985).

Charts & Models

Charts and models are typically utilized by counsel to illustrate testimony. Since they are mere reproductions or representations, they must be authenticated by some testimonial evidence showing that they are faithful representations of the information or object depicted. Failing to do so will most certainly lead to exclusion of the item. For example, an expert's use of a rubber doll in a demonstration of the amount of force necessary to cause injury to an infant was held to be not sufficiently similar to the events in question so as to be presentable to the trier of fact. United States v. Gaskell, 985 F.2d 1056 (11th Cir. 1993).

Views of the Actual Scene of the Accident

In situations where certain relevant evidence regarding the context of the events in question cannot be brought into court, the trial judge may authorize the jury to go to the scene of the events in question to view it for themselves. A typical example might be a jury's examination of the exact scene of an automobile collision to determine the rise of a hill or intersection visibility. Yeary v. Holbrook, 198 S.E. 441 (Va. 1938). Generally, the trial judge will require that an approved guide accompany the jurors to the scene to avoid confusion or misinformation. The decision whether to allow the jury to view the scene is squarely within the discretion of the trial judge. In many instances, the trial judge will refuse to permit a view of the scene because it may bring inadmissible evidence to the attention of the jury.

A few courts have held that the view of the scene is not evidence itself, but simply a device to aid the trier of fact in understanding the testimonial evidence. The majority view is otherwise, however, in that the view of the scene is considered independent evidence. This seems to be the better position, inasmuch as the court may allow a finding based upon the scene itself, apart from associated testimonial evidence. Otey v. Carmel Sanitary District, 26 P.2d 308 (Cal. 1933).

Physics & Engineering Animations

Although there remain a number of trial judges who are extremely reluctant to allow any form of computer generated animations whatsoever, the better view is one of case by case evaluation of the presentations. In People v. McHugh, 476 NYS2d 721, 722 (Sup. Ct. Bronx Co. 1984), the court stated: "Whether a diagram is hand drawn or mechanically drawn by means of a computer is of no importance."

Very little case law is available to guide the trial practitioner in the area of computer generated animations. Therefore, the standard rules of evidence should be the practitioner's starting point in such a process. The preparation for use of computer generated animations is essentially a three step process. First, counsel must lay an adequate foundation for the evidence by establishing its authenticity, also described as its accuracy and reliability. Second, counsel must establish the relevance of the computer generated animation. Third, counsel must satisfy the trial judge that the probative value of the computer generated animation is not outweighed by any prejudicial effects upon the trier of fact.

Authentication

The first step is to comply with the standard authentication requirements of the applicable evidentiary rule, such as Federal Rule of Evidence 901(a). A proper foundation is established when it is shown that every element of the computer generated animated is what it is purported to be. In the absence of published court decisions setting forth authentication guidelines for computer generated animations, the practitioner must generally rely upon guidelines established for other computer generated evidence. In a case in which the foundation required for admission of computer generated business records was at issue, the court held that; "If a machine is to testify against an accused, the courts must, at the very least, be satisfied with all reasonable certainty that both the machine and those who supply its information have performed their functions with utmost accuracy." United States v. De Georgia, 420 F.2d 889,895 (9th Cir, 1969). Based on this early case and those which followed it, it is established that proposing counsel must be able to show the accuracy and reliability of the entire production process. This is itself a three step process. First, show that the underlying data are accurate. Second, that the process by which the data was entered into the computer provides reasonable assurances that error was avoided. Third, show that some form of test is used to maintain the accuracy and reliability of the hardware and software employed in the procedure. Compliance with this authentication process can usually be accomplished by producing the people who collected the data, operated the computer system, and created the animation testify as to the above requirements. If possible, the same people should be involved in the process from data collection to the conclusion and production of the final product. Computer generated animations used for accident reconstruction are closely analogous to animated scientific reenactments in their reliance upon expert witnesses and scientific applications. Federal Rules of Evidence 702 and 703 influence the authentication process for such evidence, therefore.

The admission test of rule 702 is applied generally to expert opinion testimony about certain scientific experiments and associated supporting demonstrative evidence. In the Tenth Circuit, the Court of Appeals has held: "Admissions of evidence of experiments must be established by showing background proof that the experiments were conducted under conditions that were at least similar to those which existed at the time of the accident. Demonstrations of experiments used to merely illustrate the principles in forming an expert opinion do not require a strict adherence to the facts." Brandt v. French, 638 F.2d 209,212 (10th Cir. 1981).

Under Rule 702, if "scientific, technical, or other specialized knowledge will assist the trier of fact to understand the evidence or to determine a fact in issue," then "a witness qualified by knowledge, skill, experience, training, or education" may testify "in the form of an opinion or otherwise." The recent decision in Daubert v. Merrell Dow Pharmaceuticals, Inc., 113 S.Ct. 2786, 2796 (1993), set forth specific factors to be evaluated when making a Rule 702 evaluation: "Faced with a proffer of expert scientific testimony… the trial judge must…[perform]…a preliminary assessment of whether the reasoning or methodology underlying the testimony is scientifically valid, and whether that reasoning or methodology properly can be applied to the acts in issue.… The inquiry envisioned by rule 702 is, we emphasize, a flexible one. Its overarching subject is the scientific validity—and thus the evidentiary relevance and reliability—of the principles that underlie a proposed submission. The focus, of course, must be solely on principles and methodology, not on the conclusions that they generate." This position was further confirmed in the more recent civil case of Robinson v. Missouri Pacific Railroad Co., 16 F.3d 1088, 1088 (10th Cir. 1994).

Rule 702 will generally be used as part of the authority relied upon to make such admissions decisions in federal court because of the presence of one or more expert witnesses. Similarly, Rule 703 will apply in a way that will frequently assist counsel seeking the admission of computer generated animations.

Under Rule 703, experts witnesses need not base testimony solely upon first-hand knowledge or upon evidence previously admitted. Experts may actually base the opinion testimony upon any reasonable inferences that are common to that particular area of expertise. The court stated in Werth v. Makita Electric Works, Ltd., 950 F.2d 643,648 (10th Cir. 1991), that "[Federal Rule 703] lists three bases for expert testimony: 1) the expert may gather information by first-hand observation; 2) the expert may base his or her testimony on facts presented at trial by hypothetical questions of counsel, or facts from evidence before the court; and 3) the expert may rely on facts outside the record and not personally observed, but of a kind that experts in his or her field reasonably rely on in forming opinions."

Relevance

Assuming that counsel was able to adequately authenticate the computer generated animation, he or she must now satisfy the relevancy requirements of the applicable rules of evidence, such as Federal Rules 401 and 402. Federal Rule 401 requires a showing that the computer generated animation tends to make the existence of one or more material facts more or less probable. An example would be an automobile collision reenactment showing the defendant's position passing through a stop sign. Federal Rule 402 mandates that relevance is essential to the admission of evidence. When a computer generated animation accurately demonstrates some part of a material event in the case, proposing counsel should have no difficulty satisfying this requirement of relevance. The danger arises when the presentation is on a different matter than the exact events at issue in the case. For example, in Brawn v. Fuji Heavy Industries, Ltd., 817 F.Supp 187 (D.Me. 1993), the automobile product liability plaintiffs were not entitled to have admitted a videotape of an inverted drop test performed on a vehicle similar to the one in which the plaintiff was a passenger when the vehicle struck an object, because it was not intended to simulate the crash in issue, but simply to show the inherent danger of the product.

Probative Value vs. Prejudicial Effects

The third step in the process of admission of computer generated animations is the "balancing test" standard imposed by Federal Rule of Evidence 403. The rule allows that relevant evidence "may be excluded if its probative value is substantially outweighed by the danger of unfair prejudice, confusion of the issues, or misleading the jury, or by considerations of undue delay, waste of time, or needless presentation of cumulative evidence." In determining whether the probative value of evidence is substantially outweighed by the danger of unfair prejudice, it is a sound rule that the balance should be struck in favor of admission when the evidence demonstrates a close relationship with events at issue, according to the court in U.S. v. Clarke, 24 F.3d 257 (D.C.Cir. 1994).

Again, the practitioner must rely upon cases dealing with similar forms of evidence for guidance here, such as motion pictures or demonstrations, since there is virtually no case law established on computer generated animations. For example, the standard to be used in determining the admissibility of allegedly gruesome pictures is whether the probative value of the display outweighs the prejudicial effect on the jury, in that the evidentiary value must be balanced with the tendency to overwhelm reason and to associate the defendant with the acts and events without sufficient evidence. State v. Thom, La.App. 5 Cir.1993, 615 So.2d 355. Finally, while some presentations have the effect of clearly inflaming the senses of the jury, they may yet be admissible, as in Weathers v. American Family Mutual Insurance Co., 793 F.Supp 1002 (D.Kan. 1992), where the fire insurer's rights were not prejudiced by the admission of a videotape prepared by the insured's expert regarding foam rubber cushion burn tests, where the presentation on the burn test was helpful to the jury.

Part IV

Specific Examples and Animated Examples

Chapter 13

Specific Examples

General Background

This section is based on specific problems we have been asked to solve. Several of these are not "standard fare" and are not, to our knowledge, taught elsewhere. This section consists of a mixture of generic problem descriptions, depersonalized reports and analysis, and any animations that were produced to help support these cases. We believe that the examples discussed were correctly analyzed. However, that does *not* mean that we always won the argument. Sometimes we do, and sometimes we do not. Reality demonstrates that an expert witness analysis is merely an aid to a lawyer and his arguments. A lot depends on how well the case is argued and how good the opposing lawyer is. Likewise, results depend on the sentiments of the jury, particularly in view of the recent tort reform controversy. Lastly, no "brilliant analysis" is of much use if the expert himself is unable to explain his analysis and opinions in a clear, understandable and credible manner to the trier of fact.

Because we use depersonalized reports for examples, there is some degree of repetition in the wording. This is unfortunate but necessary to make each case readable and coherent. We recommend careful reading, however, since there are various subtleties and points made in the text.

The "Three Car Accident"

General Discussion

The following is a frequent event, particularly in rush-hour traffic on urban freeways. We have three vehicles all in the same lane, with #1 in front followed by #2 and #3. Vehicle 1 stops and is rearended by vehicle 2. The driver of 2 claims that he was pushed by vehicle 3 prior to hitting 1. Can the truth be determined? Is it possible for a small nudge given to vehicle 2 by vehicle 3 to result in a larger final impact between 2 and 1? The answer to both questions is frequently "yes."

The latter point may not be obvious. Consider the following example. When vehicle 1 stops the driver of 2 immediately applies his brakes. Suppose that *without* the nudge from vehicle 3, vehicle 2 can just stop behind vehicle 1. Assume the drag factor is near skidding with a value of 0.7. Let the speed of 2 at the instant of braking be v_1. Let the nudge raise this speed to v_2. At v_1 the stopping distance (s) is given by $v_1^2 = 2fgs_1$, whereas, after the nudge we have an increased distance given by $v_2^2 = 2fgs_2$. What was a "zero hit" is converted into a collision with impact speed

$$v_{collision}^2 = v_2^2 - 2fgs_1 = v_2^2 - v_1^2 = (v_2 + v_1)(v_2 - v_1).$$

The second bracket is the sudden nudge increase in speed of vehicle 2. This equation can also be rewritten in the form

$$v_{collision}^2 = (2v_1 + \Delta v)(\Delta v), \text{ where } \Delta v \text{ is the nudge.}$$

This can give surprising results.

Suppose the nudge is only 5 mph. If the initial speed, v_1, when vehicle 2 first starts braking is 5 mph, the result is $v_{collision} = ((10 + 5)(5))^{1/2} = 75^{1/2} = 8.66$ mph. If the initial speed is 15 mph, the result is $v_{collsion} = ((30 + 5)(5))^{1/2} = 175^{1/2} = 13.2$ mph, while if the initial speed was 30 mph, the result is $v_{collision} = ((60 + 5)(5))^{1/2} = 325^{1/2} = 18.0$ mph. Note that for *all* these cases the final impact speed of vehicle 2 into vehicle 1 is *greater* than the "small nudge!" Indeed, the *only* case where this collision can have the *same* value as the nudge is for a *stationary* vehicle 2, assuming similar braking in all cases, and assuming that vehicle 2 would have stopped with a negligible gap behind vehicle 1 without the nudge.

The small nudge of 5 mph is unlikely to produce damage to either vehicle 3 or vehicle 2. Conversely, the resulting impact between vehicle 2 and 1 can easily cause damage if the collision speed is above 10 mph. This produces problems. All too often an "intuitive" (usually wrong) answer is given: namely that the distribution of damage somehow "proves" that vehicle 2 must have hit vehicle 1 first!

Suppose vehicle 2 would have stopped with a gap between it and vehicle 1 of k feet, without the nudge. Now the solution is modified to give

$$v_2^2 = 2fgs_1 + 2fgk + v_{collision}^2.$$

We can rewrite to obtain: $v_{collision}^2 = v_2^2 - v_1^2 - 2fgk.$

Assuming k = 5 ft and f = 0.7, this becomes

$$v_{collision}^2 = (2v_1 + Dv)Dv - 225.4 \text{ where the speeds are now in ft/s.}$$

If the nudge is still 5 mph = 7.335 ft/s, and the initial speed of vehicle 1 is 30 mph = 44 ft/s, the result is $V_{collision}^2 = 473.9\ (ft/s)^2$. Thus, the collision speed of vehicle 2 into 1 becomes 21.77 ft/s = 14.8 mph. While this answer is less than the previous value (zero gap) of 18.0 mph, it is still much greater than the nudge of 5 mph.

Note that the initial speed of vehicle 2 was 30 mph for this example. Ordinarily this speed would not be considered "low," but remember our previous discussion, where we stated that the *difference* in speeds is what defines "low" and "high" speeds. Yet, the collision between vehicle 3 and 2 *is* a low speed impact, and that between vehicle 2 and 1 is *also* a low speed impact. Thus although vehicles 2 and 3 are initially moving at fairly "high" speeds, the ensuing impacts both constitute low speed cases.

So how can we prove the order of impacts? One clue can be descriptions of the final spacings between the three vehicles. For example, suppose drivers 1 and 2 both note that vehicle 3 "simply drove away" after all three stopped, *without needing to reverse first.* This immediately implies that the final gap between vehicle 3 and 2 was sufficiently large to allow vehicle 3 to steer around vehicle 2 and drive away. If vehicle 3 nudges vehicle 2 while "on the fly" this will increase the speed of vehicle 2 but also decrease the speed of vehicle 3, to less than vehicle 2. With similar drag factors, this immediately allows for a significant final gap between vehicles 3 and 2. Thus, a significant final gap implies vehicle 2 *could have been* nudged by vehicle 3.

The other option is that vehicle 2 hits vehicle 1 first, causing the frontal damage to 2 and the rearend damage to 1. Now, since there is no permanent damage to either the rear of 2 or the front of 3, we infer either no impact between 3 and 2 or a minor "late" impact after the impact of vehicles 2 and 1. For the latter, the final gap between vehicle 3 and 2 will be very small. Thus, vehicle 3 will need to reverse in order to drive away. Also such a late impact will usually reduce the gap between vehicles 2 and 1, giving an answer which is inconsistent with the energetics of the observed damage. Sometimes, a late impact can actually result in *two* impacts between vehicles 2 and 1.

This scenario, of a "hit on the fly," is all too common. While drivers 2 and 1 are worrying about their vehicle damages and possible personal injury, driver 3 just drives away knowing there is no damage to *his* vehicle. This results in driver 1 (and maybe 2) being forced into claiming a "phantom" vehicle, and thus creating a case of hit and run and an insurance claim of "uninsured motorist." Too often the police turn up after driver 3 has fled. The officer smiles politely when given the story, but sees no evidence and so disbelieves the story. Likewise, the insurance company disbelieves it also! It should be noted that "Reconstruction Schools" like NUTI do not describe or solve this type of accident. Since these schools train the majority of police and insurance company recontructionists, it's understandable that this type of accident is rarely correctly solved, and the wrong person gets the blame! Yet the elementary physics given above show how possible the scenario can be.

To be more specific let the vehicle weights be w_1 = 2500 lbs, w_2 = 3000 lbs and w_3 = 3500 lbs. Let vehicles 2 and 3 have 5.0 mph (7.335 ft/s) bumpers, while vehicle 1 has 2.5 mph (3.668 ft/s) ones. Let R_{01} = 0.6, R_{02} = 0.565, and R_{03} = 0.536. These values are in accordance with the $1/w^{1/3}$ rule). Let the initial speed of vehicle 2 (when nudged) be 30 mph (44 ft/s), and let the final gap between vehicles 2 and 1 *without* the nudge be 8 feet. Also, let the nudge be 5.0 mph with a coefficient of restitution between vehicle 3 and 2 of -0.7. What happened?

First, we note that the nudge of 5 mph implies that closing speed between vehicle 3 and vehicle 2 was (using equation 14)

$$v_{close} = [((w_2 + w_3)/w_3)/(1 - e)]v_{nudge} = 5.46 \text{ mph}.$$

Since vehicle 2 was moving at 30 mph when nudged, this says that vehicle 3 was traveling at 35.46 mph when it hit vehicle 2. After the nudge, vehicle 2 is moving at 35 mph (51.35 ft/s). The new speed of vehicle 3 is (using equation 15)

$$v_3' = [(w_3 - 0.7\, w_2)/(w_2 + w_3)]\, v_{close} = 1.09 \text{ mph},$$

relative to the initial speed of vehicle 2.

Thus, after the impact vehicle 3 is moving at 30 mph + 1.09 mph = 31.09 mph (45.6 ft/s). Assume vehicle 3 and 2 decelerate at 0.7 g. Then 3 stops in 46.15 ft. Vehicle 2 would need to stop in a distance of 58.49 ft. However, without the nudge, vehicle 2 would have stopped in a distance of 42.95 ft. With the nudge, the stopping distance becomes 58.49 ft. Thus, vehicle 2 needs an extra 15.54 ft. With the "original" gap of 8 ft (no nudge) this implies that vehicle 2 overshoots by 7.64 ft, and the collision of 2 into 1 occurs at a speed of 12.56 mph (18.43 ft/s).

The "critical closing speed" (no vehicle damage) for the collision between 2 and 3 is about

$$v_{crit}^2 = [(3500 + 3000)/3500][1 + (3000/3500)(0.565/0.536)^2(7.335/7.335)^2]5^2(\text{mph})^2$$

from equation 25. This gives the value 9.52 mph (13.97 ft/s). Thus, for an actual closing impact speed of 5.46 mph, there is no damage to either vehicle 2 or 3. However, the critical closing speed for vehicle 2 and 1 is

$$v_{crit}^2 = [(3000 + 2500)/3000][1 + (2500/3000)(0.6/0.565)^2(7.335/3.668)^2]2.5^2(\text{mph})^2$$

which is about 7.385 mph (10.83 ft/s). Since the actual closing speed is 12.56 mph there is damage, and the effective coefficient of restitution is about e = - 7.385/12.56 = -0.588, and including the "download factor" of 0.7 this gives about e = - 0.411. The resulting post-impact speeds are 9.67 mph for vehicle 1 and 4.50 mph for vehicle 2. If both vehicles stop at 0.7 g, the braking distances are 4.46 ft and 0.97 ft, respectively, giving a final gap of about 3.5 ft. The total distance moved by vehicle 2 is about 52 ft ("original" pre-hit braking distance + "original" 8 ft gap behind vehicle 1 + 1 ft post-impact stopping). But vehicle 3 stopped in 46.15 ft. Thus, the final gap between vehicle 3 and 2 is about 5.8 ft. Thus, this gap is larger than the one between #2 and #1.

The driver of vehicle 1 sees a sudden speed change (increase) of +9.67 mph. If the seat-bounce factor of restitution of -0.3 is included, his torso increases speed by about (1 - e) x 9.67 mph = 12.6 mph. Thus, if driver 1 is not expecting the rearend impact and has a poorly positioned headrest, he is above the threshold for extension neck damage (about 7.5 mph). Driver 2, however, suffers a sudden reduction in forward speed of only -(12.56 - 4.50) mph = -8.06 mph. This is too low to induce flexion neck damage. Neither driver 2 nor 3 suffer injury in the original impact between vehicles 3 and 2.

Using equation 12 the total absorbed energy (E_D) for the impact of 2 into 1 is

$$E_D = [(3000 \times 2500)/(3000 + 2500)](1 - e^2)(v_{close}{}^2/2g)$$

and for e = -0.411, and v_{close} = 12.56 mph, this gives E_D = 8403 ft-lbs. This is a significant energy loss. For example, if all this energy were due to crushing of only vehicle 1, and also vehicle 1 did not strain harden, then $E_D = 12R_{01}w_1x_1$, where x_1 (ft) is the crush. Substituting, x_1 = 0.47 ft = 5.6 inches. In reality, the crush is less due to (a) strain hardening and (b) vehicle 2 will also suffer some limited crush.

Actual Case

The following is an actual analysis similar to the one just described. The only difference is that vehicle 1 was itself moving slowly when impacted by 2. To depersonalize we use generic words such as Time, Place, Road, Plaintiff and Defendant.

Plaintiff versus Uninsured Motorist

Introduction

We have assessed the accident of Date which involved three vehicles: namely, the Chevrolet S-10 truck of Plaintiff (car #1), the Buick LeSabre of Defendant (car #2) and the "minivan" of an unknown driver (car #3). Although the "minivan" was not uniquely identified, the term usually means a Dodge or Plymouth minivan, or similar. Therefore, we used the vehicle properties of a typical Dodge minivan for the following analyses. For this analysis, we relied on the depositions of Defendant and Plaintiff, the answers to interrogatories of Defendant and Plaintiff, the police accident report, the vehicle photographs taken by Opposing Expert, Plaintiff's medical records, and private conversations with Plaintiff.

Description of Accident

The accident occurred during the morning rush hour at about Time. It had been drizzling such that the roads were wet. No skid marks were reported. Southbound traffic was merging from Road with southbound traffic on Road. Due to the scissors-crossing required for traffic heading for downtown Town using the Road and Road off-ramps, vehicles on the Place overpass were slowing. The accident occurred on southbound Road in the left-hand lane crossing the Place, where the vehicles were on the overpass above Place. Plaintiff slowed and, while still moving, was rearended by Defendant. Defendant stated that he, in turn, was slowing and had been previously rearended by a "minivan." Plaintiff states that he glanced in his mirror while braking and saw Defendant approaching with his car in the "nose-down" position, implying fairly strong braking. He realized he would hit him and he braced himself against the steering wheel prior to the impact.

The vehicle 2/1 collision was sufficient to cause damage to both the front of the LeSabre and to the rear of the S-10 truck, whereas the collision between the front of the minivan and the rear of the LeSabre did not cause any permanent vehicle damage. Damage to the rear of the S-10 included the rear bumper, the tailgate, the rearend of the truck bed and some small additional damage to the rear of the cab (caused by the bed moving forward into it). Damage to the front of the LeSabre included some to the front bumper, but mostly to the softer upper body work including grill and side fenders. The only obvious sign of a rearend impact to the LeSabre was from compression scrapes on the rear bumper isolators (as shown in photographs provided by the opposition).

Post-impact, Plaintiff and Defendant stopped and inspected the damage to their vehicles. In particular, Defendant tried lowering the truck tailgate to see if it still functioned (it did). Both persons observed a minivan also stopped behind Defendant. The unknown driver of this vehicle got out, inspected the front of his vehicle, climbed back in and drove off, swinging around Defendant's car to do so. Defendant states that this driver yelled "I didn't hit you" at him. Later, after the minivan driver drove away, they both moved their vehicles out of traffic and went to call the police.

The Issue

The issue in this case is the order of impacts. Did Defendant impact Plaintiff *first*, and was *then* impacted by the minivan, or did the minivan impact Defendant *first* and cause him to impact Plaintiff?

Analysis

The analysis requires the use of energy considerations to establish the *severity* of each impact, and then requires the use of time and motion considerations in order to establish the *order* of events. Finally, the sudden increase in speed of the S-10 will determine any possibility of personal injury to Plaintiff.

Energy Analysis

The two collisions are assumed to be essentially collinear. They can be solved by knowing: (a) the weights of each vehicle (including occupants), (b) the bumper capabilities, (c) the amount of permanent crush damage (if any), and (d) the crush strength of each vehicle. The collision speed required to just cause permanent damage is defined as the "critical speed." If damage exists (*e.g.,* car #2 into car #1), this critical speed is exceeded and the actual closing speed is determined from knowledge of the total crush in both vehicles. If no permanent damage occurs (*e.g.,* car #3 into car #2), the critical speed defines the *maximum* possible closing speed. The closing speed is the *difference* in speed between any two vehicles entering a crash.

During a collision the two vehicles first reach a common speed (target speeds up, bullet slows down) and then suffer a bounce, resulting in the struck vehicle (target) moving faster than the striking vehicle (bullet). The degree of bounce is highest for low closing speeds (where the impact is quite elastic) and lowers for higher closing speeds (where permanent damage absorbs energy and reduces the elastic component). From a knowledge of weights, determination of initial closing speed, and degree of bounce (bumper response and crush energy), the *output* speeds for the target and bullet can be determined.

For these two collisions we determine that for the minivan/LeSabre impact the closing speed was about 5 mph, whereas, for the LeSabre/S-10 impact the initial closing speed was about 10 mph. Thus, the LeSabre/S-10 impact was clearly the more violent collision.

For the minivan/LeSabre impact, the LeSabre suffers a sudden *increase* in speed of about 4.5 mph, while the minivan drops to a speed of almost the same as the *original* speed of the LeSabre. For the other impact, we determine that the S-10 suffers a sudden *increase* in speed of about 9.5 mph, while the LeSabre suffers a sudden reduction in speed to about 3.1 mph faster than the *original* S-10 speed when struck. Note that these numbers all refer to *changes* in speeds, and do *not* indicate the *original speed* of the target vehicles at time of impact. The actual true speeds must be determined independently from a time and motion study.

If the two collisions both involved impacts into stationary targets then, since the LeSabre/S-10 impact was the more violent one, it must have been the *first* collision. This logic is based on the fact that the output "push" on the LeSabre (4.5 mph) from the minivan impact is *smaller* than the required closing speed (10 mph) to account for the LeSabre/S-10 collision damage. However, this logic is *only* valid if the two collisions involve *stationary targets.* Since *no one* claimed they were stopped at the time of either collision then, with initial motion, the *order* of impacts can change and can only be determined from a time and motion study.

Time and Motion Analysis

The S-10 and LeSabre both stopped without leaving skid marks. Plaintiff states that he saw Defendant coming in a "nose-down" attitude, and that he was able to turn back forward and prepare to be hit. From the victims' statements, the final gap between them was about 4 to 6 feet, sufficient for Plaintiff and Defendant to go between the vehicles, inspect the damage and lower the truck tailgate. The final gap depends on the speeds of the vehicles immediately *after* the impact, and the drag factor (friction) associated with braking. For a rapid stop without skidding on a wet road, a drag factor of about 0.6 is appropriate. Plaintiff and Defendant both state that they were slowing to stop due to traffic slowing and stopping in front of them. While there is no direct information on the distance between Plaintiff and the vehicle in front of him, studies performed and reported by Opposing Expert have shown that drivers normally stop and leave gaps of between 6 and 10 feet (about 1/2 to 2/3 of a car length) between cars. If Plaintiff was traveling significantly faster than 5 mph when impacted by Defendant, then his consequential braking distance would have become very long (multiple car lengths). This could cause Plaintiff to impact the vehicles which were slowing and stopping in front of him.

Plaintiff states that he was hit forward by about 5 to 10 feet by Defendant's impact. This also implies a slow initial speed, since for any significant speed his natural braking distance would be so large that he would be unable to estimate the change due to the impact. Therefore, his "hit forward" distance must be comparable to his consequential braking distance. For example, if Plaintiff was moving at 5 mph, he would normally stop in about 1.5 feet. After being impacted by Defendant, Plaintiff would be hit forward to about 14.6 mph, from which he would stop in about 11.8 feet. This gives a change in Plaintiff's stopping distance of about 10 feet. Since stopping distances increase with the square of the velocity, significantly higher speeds for Plaintiff would cause his perception of the "hit forward" distance to become lost within his natural braking distance. In addition, these larger stopping distances would not be comparable to Plaintiff's consequential braking distance.

Plaintiff was unsure of his true speed just prior to impact time, but was sure he was still moving. Plaintiff stated that he may have been going 30 to 35 mph, but he had been slowing for some time. It should be noted that, from 30 mph, it only takes 2.3 seconds to come to a complete stop. Therefore, if Plaintiff has been slowing, it is not unreasonable that he would be traveling at approximately 5 mph at the time he is impacted. From the above logic, we deduce that Plaintiff was originally moving at about 5 mph and Defendant was moving at about 15 mph when he impacted Plaintiff.

There are two options for the order of impacts: (1) Defendant hit Plaintiff and then was himself hit by the minivan, or (2) Defendant was hit by the minivan and then hit Plaintiff. In order to determine the correct order of impacts, analysis is essential.

Option (1):

Plaintiff states that the minivan pulled up some distance behind Defendant's LeSabre. In particular, the minivan driver *did not* need to reverse away from the LeSabre in order to drive away. The minivan merely pulled around the car. To account for the minimum turning radius and vehicle width of a typical minivan, this means that the final gap between the minivan and the car was greater than about 6.5 feet. If the minivan impacted a *stationary* car at about 5 mph, the gap between it and the car would be much too small (about 1.1 feet) to allow this. Thus, Option (1) cannot occur with Defendant stopped. Therefore, Defendant must have been moving when struck by the minivan.

For Option (1) to be valid and account for a final gap of at least 6 feet due to a 5 mph impact of minivan/LeSabre, then the minivan speed at the time of the impact must have been at least 15.5 mph. However, following the minivan impact, Defendant's LeSabre is pushed forward so that the final gap between Defendant's and Plaintiff's vehicles is too small to allow Plaintiff's tailgate to be opened. In order to meet both conditions (*i.e.*, at least 6 feet gap between the minivan and LeSabre, and at least 4 feet gap Defendant and Plaintiff), the minivan speed at the time of impact must be at least 18 mph. However, to allow for the amount of damage done to the Defendant and Plaintiff vehicles, Plaintiff must have been traveling at least 10 mph when impacted by Defendant. This would have hit Plaintiff's vehicle to about 19.6 mph, from which he would have stopped in about 21 feet. Again this long stopping distance could cause Plaintiff to impact the vehicles which were slowing and stopping in front of him.

This analysis is based on the assumption that the minivan/LeSabre impact must have happened instantly after Defendant hit Plaintiff. If there was any time between the Defendant/Plaintiff impact and the minivan/Defendant impact, then this scenario would worsen as Defendant would slow toward stopping before being impacted. Therefore, Option (1) is plausible only if both the minivan hit Defendant at the same instant that Defendant hit Plaintiff and Plaintiff was planning to stop behind the other vehicles at a much greater distance than opposing expert has shown to be the normal.

Option (2):

In order for Plaintiff to be able to see the LeSabre in the "nose-down" attitude, the gap between the car and the rear of the truck must have been at least 24 feet at the instant of seeing him coming. This fact was established by having Plaintiff sit in his vehicle and telling us when he could just see low enough to observe the bumper-height of the car behind, since he states that he could see down to the bumper of the LeSabre. Since Plaintiff did not see the minivan impact Defendant, or see his sudden acceleration due to the impact, the minivan/LeSabre impact must have occurred before Plaintiff saw Defendant.

Since all vehicles are slowing, at the point in time when Plaintiff sees Defendant at least 24 feet behind him, Plaintiff is going about 26.5 mph and Defendant is traveling about 36.5 mph. However, if Defendant was impacted by the minivan just at this 24-foot distance, prior to the minivan impact Defendant would have been going about 32 mph. From 26.5 mph, Plaintiff requires about 39 feet to stop. In order to stop safely, Defendant must be able to stop within about 63 feet of being seen (*i.e.*, Plaintiff's 39 feet stopping distance plus Defendant's 24 feet following distance). From his original speed of 32 mph, Defendant requires about 57 feet to stop. Thus, slowing from this original speed, Defendant would not have hit the slowing Plaintiff and there would have been a final gap between Defendant and Plaintiff of about 6 feet. It should be noted that at the time Plaintiff saw Defendant, his speed is in the range of 30 mph as he has stated. Also, Defendant's original safe stopping gap behind Plaintiff is in the normal range previously mentioned.

However, since Defendant was hit by the minivan to 36.5 mph, he now requires about 74 feet to stop safely. Since this exceeds the 63 feet of safe stopping distance available, Defendant will impact Plaintiff. We see that the relatively "small nudge" (4.5 mph) given to the LeSabre by the minivan impact can easily convert a perfectly good braking maneuver by Defendant (*i.e.,* allowing him to stop behind Plaintiff *without* impacting him) into an *impossible* braking maneuver causing an impact, *because* Defendant is moving at the time he is impacted by the minivan. The reason is simple: since braking distance increases with the square of the speed, a sudden increase in speed dramatically increases the needed distance. Thus, for a fixed following distance, a collision with the truck suddenly becomes inevitable. Also, since the cars are slowing, then if the minivan/LeSabre collision occurs significantly further back than the 24 feet following distance, the vehicle speeds are all higher and the magnitude of the resulting LeSabre/truck collision becomes worse.

From his 36.5 mph speed induced by the minivan/LeSabre collision, Defendant will be traveling at about 15 mph when he impacts Plaintiff (who is traveling at about 5 mph). It should be noted that Plaintiff's speed is consistent with his being able to report a "hit forward" distance. At these speeds, it will be about 1.6 seconds from the time Plaintiff sees Defendant until the time he is hit by him. Following the collisions, as all vehicles stop, there will be a resulting gap between Defendant's and Plaintiff's vehicles of about 8 feet. There will also be a gap between the minivan and Defendant's vehicle of about 9.5 feet, sufficient to allow the minivan to drive directly away without the need to reverse. Using the above approach, for the cases where Plaintiff is doing less than 5 mph at the time he is hit by Defendant, the gap between his truck and the LeSabre is always larger than 4.5 feet, and the gap between the LeSabre and the minivan is always larger than 9.5 feet. Therefore, Option (2) is the only option that can explain both the crash severity (as measured by the vehicles' damages) and the statements of the witnesses (in terms of final distances between vehicles, "hit forward" distance, and reported speeds pre-collision).

Personal injury

Plaintiff's S-10 was suddenly accelerated forward by about 9.5 mph due to the impact by the LeSabre (note: this jump is due to the severity of impact and is independent of his absolute initial speed). Allowing for the "seat bounce," which can increase this speed by a further factor of 0.3, his torso could have accelerated by up to about 12.4 mph. Plaintiff knew the impact was coming and had time to tense up his muscles (particularly gripping the steering wheel). However, unless Plaintiff has *very* tensed neck muscles this speed jump is sufficient to induce soft tissue injury. Certainly, this speed-jump accounts for his head hitting the rear window behind him since his truck does *not* have headrests.

Conclusions

Based on these analyses, we conclude:

(1) The LeSabre/S-10 impact was more severe than the minivan/LeSabre impact.

(2) The former impact is sufficient to cause soft tissue damage to Plaintiff.

(3) The final gap between the LeSabre and the S-10 indicates that Plaintiff was moving at about 5 mph when impacted, and that the LeSabre was moving at about 15 mph entering the impact.

(4) Defendant was at least 24 feet behind Plaintiff when he saw him coming.

(5) Since Defendant was moving when impacted by the minivan, the resulting sudden increase in his speed converted a "safe" braking maneuver into a "non-safe" one, causing him to be unable to avoid Plaintiff.

(6) The suggestion that the Defendant/Plaintiff impact occurred first, followed by the minivan/Defendant impact, *only* accords with the impact damage *if* Defendant was practically stationary at the time of the minivan hit. Further, this order of events *cannot* account for the final gaps between all three vehicles.

(7) The minivan hit Defendant *first.* This is demonstrated by the fact that the minivan pulled up behind Defendant with at least a 6.5 foot gap, thereby avoiding the necessity of the minivan to reverse in order to drive off. Had the impact been *after* the Defendant/Plaintiff impact, this gap would have been much too small to allow this action.

Animation

The first animation illustrates such a three-vehicle situation. We give the "nudge on the fly" scenario at various replay speeds. Note the small final gap between vehicles 2 and 1, and the larger gap between vehicles 3 and 2. For the "late nudge" scenario, there would be a very small gap between vehicles 3 and 2.

The "Whiplash" Response

General Discussion

The overall logic of the rearend whiplash was given in chapter 7.

Plaintiff versus Defendant: Whiplash

Introduction

We have been tasked to analyze the above referenced case. We have reviewed the police report, the depositions of the two parties and of Dr. Medic, the photographs of the two vehicles, the estimate for repair of Mr. Plaintiff's vehicle (the only one sufficiently damaged to warrant a repair claim), and the medical reports.

Description of Accident

The accident occurred on westbound Road in Town on Date, at about Time. Mr. Plaintiff was driving a 1989 Buick Century, Mr. Defendant was driving a 1982 Mercury Cougar. The traffic was start-stop-start rush hour, and both vehicles were in the leftmost lane. Mr. Plaintiff braked as traffic ahead slowed or stopped. Mr. Defendant who was behind him also braked but was unable to stop in time and impacted the rear end of the Buick. There was apparently no serious damage to the front of the Mercury. Damage to the rear end of the Buick consisted of the bumper being pushed forward with consequential damage to rear fender panels and vehicle frame (repair estimate). The bumper was pushed in by about 1.5 inches on the left and about 0.5 inches on the right, for an average of about 1.0 inch across the vehicle. The estimates are based on observation of the photographs.

The impact caused Mr. Plaintiff's head to undergo the classic rearward rotation (hyperextension) relative to his body. The headrest was apparently in the "full down" position. A photo of Mr. Plaintiff sitting in his vehicle indicates that this position was too low to aid in stopping his head rotation, and instead his head would try to rotate over the headrest since the latter would merely act as a fulcrum. Mr. Plaintiff states that he saw a blinding flash and realized he had been hurt.

After the impact both cars pulled over to the side, Mr. Plaintiff called the police, and both drivers waited for the police to arrive and take details. Later that day Mr. Plaintiff sought medical help.

Analysis

(1) Vehicle Motions

We have performed an energy-of-crush analysis for the impact. The rear of the Buick suffered damage because it is weaker than the front of the Mercury for small amounts of damage. Our analysis indicates that the Mercury was moving at about 13 mph *faster* than the Buick at the time of impact. The result of the impact was to slow the Mercury by about 11 mph, and to increase the speed of the Buick also by about 11 mph. Note that both vehicle damage and body neck/head motion are dependent on the *differential* speeds involved, rather than the absolute speeds. These differential speeds are referred to as delta-V.

Mr. Plaintiff estimated that the final gap between the two vehicles, when both were stopped, was about 5 ft, but admitted this was a rough estimate. Based on typical decelerations for both vehicles of about 0.6 g (insufficient to cause skid marks, and none were noted), a gap of 5 to 10 ft implies that Mr. Plaintiff's *initial* speed at the instant of impact was very low, between about zero and 3 mph, and certainly not above his own estimate of about 5 mph. His speed after the impact is initial plus 11 mph. The absolute distance moved by Mr. Plaintiff's Buick immediately after the impact would be from 6.8 ft for a speed of 11 mph (i.e., his initial speed was zero) to about 12.5 ft if his speed became 15 mph (i.e., his initial speed was about 4 mph). Thus it was unlikely that the Buick would suffer a second collision with a vehicle in front of his, and no such collision was reported.

Mr. Defendant estimated that he was about one car length (about 15 ft) behind the Buick when the latter started braking, although he admitted his judgement of distance was not good. He also thought that both he and Mr. Plaintiff were doing about 30 mph before either of them started braking, with a similar quote being given by Mr. Plaintiff.

Because Mr. Defendant needs to exercise his perception/reaction (P/R) time before he can apply his brakes after seeing Mr. Plaintiff start to brake, it is possible for his vehicle to impact the Buick, depending on the initial vehicle speeds and the car-to-car gap. Typical P/R time for a young alert person is about 1 sec. If both vehicles decelerate in a similar manner, but with the P/R time delay, the consequential *differential* impact speed is simply delta-V = f g (P/R). Thus for f = 0.6 we have delta-V = 0.6 x 32.2 x 1.0 = 19.3 ft/s = 13.2 mph. This is thus consistent with the *differential* speed obtained from the crush energy analysis.

The critical speed to avoid a collision is V_{crit} = G/(P/R) where G is the initial gap in feet. Thus for a 15-ft gap the critical speed is 15 ft/s or 10.2 mph. This assumes both vehicles are initially at the same speed and both decelerate at the same rate. For a gap of 30 ft (two car lengths) the critical speed is 20.4 mph. Since the impact had a differential speed of about 13 mph, Mr. Defendant was clearly moving at at least this speed.

The time between Mr. Plaintiff first applying his brakes and the impact is given by

$$t_{col} = G/(f\ g\ (P/R)) + 0.5\ (P/R).$$

For f = 0.6, P/R = 1 sec and G (gap) = 15 ft, we get t_{col} = 1.28 sec, while for G = 30 ft we get t_{col} = 2.05 sec. The initial speed of Mr. Plaintiff before application of brakes is then either

$$V_{init} = f\ g\ t_{col} = 24.7 \text{ ft/s} = 16.8 \text{ mph, or } = 39.6 \text{ ft/s} = 27 \text{ mph}$$

for an initial gap of 15 or 30 ft, respectively. This assumes his speed at impact is zero, so allowance for the inferred small positive speed increases these estimates by a few mph. Thus we conclude that the vehicles were either only doing about 17 to 20 mph before Mr. Plaintiff braked for a one car length gap, or were doing

27 to 30 mph for a two car-length gap, with the latter answer being the more likely based on both drivers' estimate of initial speed(s).

(2) Mr. Plaintiff's Head Motion

When a vehicle is suddenly accelerated forward, the body moves forward with the vehicle and the seat. However, the unsupported head moves forward slower since forces must be applied via the neck. Thus, although *everything* (car, seat, torso and head) are moving *forward*, the *differential* motion between the torso and the head implies a *reverse* (i.e., backward) rotation of the head. For typical head/neck geometry, the center-of-mass (CM) of the head moves at only about 0.56 times the speed of the torso/shoulders. Thus the head apparently moves backward at about 0.44 times the speed of the torso/shoulders.

For a delta-V of the torso of 11 mph, the head moves forward at only 6.16 mph, and thus rotates backward at 4.84 mph (7.1 ft/s). The typical length from the pivot on the neck to the CM of the head is about 7 inches (0.58 ft). This implies a rotational rate of about 7.1/0.58 = 12.2 radians per sec. One radian is 57.3 degrees of rotation, thus we have 701 degrees per second. A normal head can only rotate about 60 degrees before "bottoming" at its natural limit. Thus it only takes about 60/701 = 0.086 sec to reach the limit. This is too fast for the muscles to be innervated.

In the absence of a well-positioned headrest, the only mechanism for stopping the head rotation is the application of forces within the neck itself. When the neck reaches its maximum extension, it "stiffens up" rapidly, such that further angular motion requires a rapid increase in force. For a sufficiently large force damage can occur (e.g., to ligaments, muscles, disks etc.). Because the head starts moving slower than the torso, but must eventually catch up with it (absent decapitation!), the force must be capable of applying the increase in kinetic energy over a small rotation angle. Because the initial speed of the head is only about 0.56 times that of the torso, this gives an energy increase of

$$\text{delta -E} = (w/2g)V_p^2\,(1 - 0.56^2)\ \text{ft-lbs}$$

where w is the head weight (typically about 9 to 10 lbs), V_p is the "push speed" on the car/seat/torso (equal to the delta-V of 11 mph, given above in the vehicle motion analysis), and g is the acceleration due to gravity (32.2 ft/s/s). Thus delta-E = 27.8 ft-lbs, for w = 10 lbs.

The head moves over an *additional* angle of no more than about 15 degrees at/near its limit. With a torque arm length (neck to head) of 0.58 ft, this gives a stopping distance of about

$$\text{delta-X} = 0.58 \times 15/57.3\ \text{ft} = 0.152\ \text{ft} = 1.82\ \text{inches.}$$

The average force is given by F = (delta-E)/(delta-X) = 27.8/0.152 = 183 lbs force. This is a torque force, acting perpendicular to the neck's local axis.

Ref 1 states that the "safe envelope" for the typical neck implies that the torque force should not be allowed to exceed about 190 lb force. However, this data is based on either healthy live males or male cadavers, with no preexisting neck damage. Thus the computed force is in the neighborhood of the allowed (or danger) level. This analysis also ignores any seat bounce which may increase this load by the factor 1.3 (to about 238 lbs).

After the head reaches its maximum extension, it will rebound in a more gentle manner. Provided the seat belt correctly locks up when the driver reaches their initial position in the seat, there will be a subsequent forward bounce out of the seat (moving the driver *faster* than the car), but insufficient for the driver to reach the steering wheel. Mr. Plaintiff's belt appears to have correctly locked.

Conclusions

Based on our analysis, we conclude:

(1) Mr. Plaintiff was moving at between zero and 5 mph when impacted in the rear,

(2) Mr. Defendant was moving at 13 mph faster than Mr. Plaintiff at the time of impact,

(3) Mr. Plaintiff suffered an increase in speed (delta-V) of about 11 mph due to the impact,

(4) The initial pre-impact calculated conditions are consistent with both vehicles moving at about 30 mph with an initial gap of about two car lengths, with both drivers decelerating at about 0.6 g (no skidding), and with a perception/reaction time for Mr. Defendant of about 1 sec.,

(5) The post-impact calculations imply a probable maximum motion of Mr. Plaintiff's vehicle of less than 12.5 ft (consistent with not hitting a vehicle in front) and a final gap between the vehicles of about 5 to 10 ft, consistent with Mr. Plaintiff's estimate,

(6) Mr. Plaintiff's head/neck very rapidly rotated to its natural fullest extent, and was stopped by its own natural strength by a torque force of about at least 183 lb. This is close to published recommendations of upper allowed torque force of about 190 lbs for males (ref 1).

(7) Other published data (ref 2) states that for a 10 mph jump the probability of damage is about 0.7, while for a 15 mph jump the probability is close to unity,

(8) Based on (6) and (7) there is a reasonable degree of scientific probability that Mr. Plaintiff suffered some form of neck damage.

Animation

The second animation shows the whiplash suffered by a driver who is subjected to a sudden increase of car speed of about 11 mph. A seat bounce factor of about 0.3 was assumed, and the seat compression was about 3 inches. A poorly-positioned, low, headrest was assumed. The calculations move the driver's hips with the car while allowing rigid body motion of the torso. This induces a forward motion together with a rearward rotation about the hips. As the torso "sinks" into the seat so it is accelerated up to the car speed and then rebounds and overshoots. The motion of the shoulders provides for the "driving force" seen by the head/neck. The neck is allowed "free" rotation (lax muscles) over an angle of about 60 degrees, beyond which the neck rapidly stiffens so as to stop and rebound. Again, the head/neck is modeled as a rigid body hinged at the lower neck. It is seen (especially clear on the final close-up, frame-by-frame version) that initially there is almost no net head motion. Then, the head begins to rotate in a backward direction, but also sees a forward motion, following the shoulders. The sum of these initial motions gives basically a downward motion only, at early time. As time continues, the head still rotates backward but now starts to obviously move forward. The torso is seen to bounce out of the seat and start moving faster than the vehicle. This merely forces the head to rotate even faster until the peak angular rotation is reached. Beyond this time the head also rebounds, and starts to overtake the torso.

The animation is as for a camera outside the vehicle showing the motion of the car. Importantly, it is seen that everything actually moves forward in the same direction of the car. Nothing actually moves backward. Note how rapid the entire sequence is, and how, for a poorly positioned headrest, large neck/head motions occur. Note how the head ultimately "comes down onto" the low headrest. The latter is clearly performing no useful function.

Since the computations used "rigid body" dynamics they are clearly something of a simplification. However, they show a remarkable resemblance to real life. For example, at the 39th Annual Stapp Car Crash Conference (November 1995, San Diego) high-speed cine film was shown of volunteers subjecting themselves to rearend impacts (ref 28). Although these volunteer experiments were at lower speed (up to about 6.5 mph) the movies showed very similar overall volunteer head/neck motions. Remember that the total angular motion of the head/neck is dominated by the natural physiological range (typically about 60 degrees) while only the excess angle is related to hyperextension.

Similar behavior is shown in the high-speed cine film available from IIHS. This film shows two dummies suffering rearend impacts. One is in a Ford Taurus ("poor" headrest), the other is in a Volvo ("good" headrest). Both impacts are at

10 mph, using a "concrete" car with weight 4057 lbs. The two cars each weigh about 3000 lbs. Thus, the imparted speed to the cars is about 8 mph. For the Volvo car the dummy's head only extends by a small amount before engaging the high, fixed headrest, and the seat only deflects and rotates by a small amount. For the Taurus the dummy's head extends back through a large angle and actually hits down the headrest, causing the "up" headrest to collapse into the "down" position on the seat. The dummy is also clearly seen to "ramp" up the seat, raising its head even more versus the headrest. The seat also rotates more than for the Volvo. Lastly, in both cases the movie clearly shows that the seatbelt is loose as the dummy moves back into the seat, and only starts to tighten when the dummy moves a significant distance towards the steering wheel. "Still" frames from these movies are also given in the September/October 1995, edition of the Accident Reconstruction Journal (page 53). The IIHS movie can be obtained from them by calling either Brian O'Neill or Adrian Lund at 703/247-1500.

This case is one where injury was not predicted.

Plaintiff versus Defendant: No Predicted Injury

Introduction

We have been asked to analyze the above referenced accident case. To do this we have studied the deposition of Mr. Plaintiff, the police accident report, and photographs of the damage to the rear of Mr. Plaintiff's car and the front of Mr. Defendant' pickup truck (PU), and the repair estimate for Mr. Plaintiff's bumper assembly. We have performed calculations to estimate the crash severity, the resulting push experienced by Mr. Plaintiff, and the consequential body forces experienced by him. We have compared these computations with published experimental data concerning damage levels to individuals who suffer rearend collisions.

Description of Accident

The accident occurred on Date at about Time. The weather was clear and dry. The impact occurred on Road near the intersection with Road, in Town. Mr. Plaintiff was driving a 1990 Toyota Corolla (weight about 2406 lbs, for a total of about 2524 lbs including driver), while Mr. Defendant was driving a 1987 Nissan pickup (weight about 2750 lbs, or about 3075 lbs including driver and passenger). Mr. Plaintiff states he was stopped due to traffic. Mr. Defendant states (police report) he was behind him and looking sideways to see if he could go around him but failed and impacted the rear of the Corolla. Mr. Plaintiff states he was wearing his lap/shoulder harness and that it worked properly and held him in place. He did not impact any internal portion of his vehicle, except perhaps the headrest. His stated injuries include his neck, back and right hip.

Vehicle Damage

The photographs indicate negligible damage to the rear of the Corolla, with only a small imprint near the center of the bumper. A photograph of the front of the Nissan PU also indicates some damage to the bumper area; however, this is stated as being prior damage existing before this accident. The Corolla bumper is a "plastic" one (polyurethane style on a steel back plate). The rated limit for this bumper is about 2.5 mph (maximum speed into a massive rigid barrier before frame/body/lights damage is induced), as per US government requirements at the date of manufacture. Such bumpers are capable of full compression and recovery *without* giving any obvious indication of compression. The exception is when there is strong localized loading (*e.g.*, from a license plate holder, or corner of another bumper) when an imprint can occur. Thus the imprint on the Corolla bumper is probably due to either the license plate of the Nissan PU or due to "partial offset" impact involving the corner of the PU front bumper (Note: the photographic evidence is too weak to allow precise determination, and a direct inspection is needed to identify the exact cause of this imprint). There was no other damage to the Corolla, indicating the bumper capability was not exceeded. The bumper of the PU is a steel item rigidly attached to the vehicle frame, with a speed limit of about 2.5 mph. The prior damage would have little effect on its subsequent performance in this accident.

Analysis

(1) *Vehicle Motions*

Whenever two vehicles collide there are two "critical speeds" associated with causing permanent frame/body/lights damage, assuming a bumper-to-bumper impact, as assumed for this accident. Below the first critical speed *neither* vehicle suffers permanent damage, and the worst that happens is some small scrapes and/or imprints on the bumpers. Above the second critical speed *both* vehicles suffer permanent damage. Within the "window" between these critical speeds, one vehicle (the *weaker* one) will suffer permanent damage while the other does not. For this accident the Corolla is the weaker vehicle (it is lighter) and will therefore suffer permanent damage *before* the PU does. Since the Corolla suffered from only an "imprint" type of damage, we conclude two things: (a) the impact was below the first critical speed, and (b) the PU did not suffer any permanent damage either. The latter conclusion is in accordance with the statement that the damage to the bumper area on the PU was due to a prior event.

The first critical speed is a function of the two vehicle weights (w_1 and w_2), the two bumper limits (v_{L1} and v_{L2}) and the two rigidities of the vehicles (R_1 and R_2, which are strengths per unit weight).

$$v_{critical}^2 = ((w_1 + w_2)/w_1)\ v_{L2}^2\ [1 + (w_2/w_1)(R_2/R_1)^2(v_{L1}/v_{L2})^2]$$

where "1" refers to the PU and "2" refers to the Corolla.

Using the vehicle weights, R values of about 0.6 (typical for these vehicles) and v_L values of 2.5 mph, the value of $v_{critical}$ is about 4.55 mph. This is the *maximum* closing speed of the PU into the Corolla. Since the Corolla was stopped, this is also the true upper impact speed.

Since no permanent damage occurred to either vehicle, there will be a reasonable bounce between them after impact. The *highest* possible value for the coefficient of restitution (e, degree of bounce) is -1.0. It can now be shown that the resulting speeds after the impact are given by

$$v_{Corolla} = (w_1 /(w_1+w_2))\ (1\text{-}e)\ v_{critical}$$

and

$$v_{PU} = (w_1 + ew_2)/(w_1+w_2)\ v_{critical}$$

For the value e = -1.0 this gives $v_{Corolla}$ = 5.0 mph, and v_{PU} = 0.45 mph. For any lower value of e (*e.g.*, due to any damping mechanism in the bumpers) the Corolla speed will *decrease* while the PU speed will *increase*, post impact. The above assumes a full bumper-to-bumper impact across the bumper widths. If the collision was offset, the speeds can only decrease since an offset impact causes concentration of energy on part of the vehicle(s) allowing permanent damage to occur even more readily. Thus the Corolla push speed of 5.0 mph is the maximum possible, and any lower speed is also possible, consistent with the observed evidence. Note also, the two vehicles first reach a *common* speed of about 2.5 mph before any vehicle bounce occurs.

Since no skid marks were reported, we assume maximum drag factors of 0.6. For a push speed of 5.0 mph of the Corolla, the braking distance is about 1.4 feet = 17 inches. Since the braking distance is proportional to the square of the speed, any lower speed (*e.g.*, 3.0 mph) will give even smaller distances (*e.g.*, 0.5 feet = 6 inches). The PU will stop even faster. Thus 0.45 mph = 0.01 feet = 0.14 inches, assuming the driver applies the brakes very quickly during/after the impact.

Mr. Plaintiff stated that he did not think his car "moved" due to the impact. While this is an impossibility (except for a *very low* push speed where tire "stiction" can prevent vehicle motion), a very small induced motion can easily be confused with the "suspension rocking" that a car undergoes when hit (the car oscillates back and forth on its suspension, in addition to being pushed). Thus his statement again suggests that the 5.0 mph push on the Corolla is an *upper* value.

(2) Occupant Response

Whenever a vehicle is rearended, *everything moves forward.* This includes the vehicle, the seat, the occupant's torso and the occupant's head. However, there is differential motion. The car and seat move fastest, the torso initially moves more slowly, and the head moves slowest of all. Consequently, the occupant suffers the sensation of "sinking back" into the seat, while their head suffers a rearward rotation (this is the origin of the so-called "whiplash" mechanism). As the torso sinks back into the seat (but actually moving forward) the latter compresses like a spring. Ultimately, this compression stops and the torso reaches the same speed as the car. Thereafter, the seat "unloads" and acts as a damped spring, resulting in the torso moving forward *faster* than the car. This excess push can be up to about 1.3 times the car push speed. Thus if the car is pushed at 5.0 mph, the torso can end up moving at up to 6.5 mph.

Whether the occupant actually sees this increase in speed depends on the lockup behavior of the seat belts (especially the shoulder harness). If the belt rapidly retracts with the torso while sinking into the seat and then immediately locks, the torso does *not* suffer this extra seat bounce: instead the person is strongly locked in their seat (the belt prevents the unloading behavior). If the belt "stays put" during seat compression, and locks only after the seat bounce then the extra seat push *does* occur. Mr. Plaintiff did not state his belt locked him tightly in his seat. Therefore, we assume the bounce *did* occur. Thus his *maximum* torso speed could have been up to about 6.5 mph.

(a) Head/Neck Motion

Because the head initially moves slower than the torso, it will rotate backward (in medical parlance it suffers *neck extension*). This rotation can be stopped by (a) early contact with the headrest, or (b) by ultimately stretching the anterior longitudinal ligament, or (c) by neck muscle action (in particular the sternocleidomastoid muscles). Calculations can be done knowing the typical head weight, and length of the neck, to predict the rate of rotation, and the maximum possible ligament loading, all as functions of the initial induced torso speed (including any seat bounce). Included is the effect of initial muscle pretensing. These calculations treat the head as a rigid mass on the end of a flexible shaft with a hinge (*e.g.*, the neck with a hinge at the C6-C7 level).

The *worst* condition occurs for the case in which the headrest is either missing or set wrongly (too far back and/or too far down), the occupant has very lax neck muscles (not expecting the hit), and has the head turned sideways (this "takes up" some of the available neck motion). Under these worst conditions, calculations show that ligamentous damage can initiate for a torso push speed of greater than about 7.5 mph. However, with any pretensioning of neck muscles this threshold increases. Further, if the headrest is correctly positioned, these large neck forces *do not exist*, since after a small rotation the headrest provides the necessary push to the head, and thus relieves the neck. The photographs of Mr. Plaintiff's Corolla show the headrest to be in the correct "up" position. Further Mr. Plaintiff is about 5 feet 5 inches tall, which implies he is not unduly tall relative to the headrest. Consequently, for this particular accident, the induced torso speed is too low to induce serious neck problems, and the headrest should have rapidly stopped his rearward head motion, thereby preventing any significant neck loadings.

These various points are illustrated in figure 33. Shown is the maximum torque force which can be applied to the neck ligaments as a function of sudden push speed of the shoulders. The straight line (lower left to upper right) is the calculational result for a person with very lax muscles (*i.e.*, not expecting a push, and merely balancing their head such that the neck acts rather like a frictionless pivot). The experimental threshold for ligament damage is shown as a horizontal line at a force of about 190 lbs. This value comes from experiments on cadavers as quoted in reference 1. It can be seen that the "lax muscle" line intersects the damage threshold for a push speed of about 7.5 mph. The curved lines to the right of the straight line indicate the results for increasing values of neck muscle pretension. The plots show that as muscle pretensioning increases so the necessary push speed to induce ligament damage also increases. For very strong individuals who have their muscles activated prior to a torso push the limiting speed can increase up to about 17 mph (this would apply to a professional football player expecting an impact from another player). Lastly, the concave upward rising curve simply indicates the condition where the maximum induced ligament force becomes equal to any initial pretensioning of the neck muscles.

The reason for "pretensioning" of muscles is due to the fact that above a low torso push speed of about 2 mph, the head extends backward too fast for the muscles to be activated (innervated) sufficiently to help fight the motion. Neck muscle innervation typically takes up to about 0.12 - 0.14 seconds to fully develop. Thus the muscle status cannot be changed *during* the rapid motion, and the muscles are either already tensed or not. Conversely, for a slow "jostle" (a bump in the shopping mall) the motions are sufficiently slow that the muscles can be used to control the head/neck motion.

Experimental data on volunteers are summarized in the attached Table 1. These data come from references 11, 12, and 28. It is seen that the experimental data is very consistent with the calculated expectations. Even persons with some mild form of predisposition have survived 5.0 mph torso pushes without any problems other than very transient muscle aches and/or spasms, provided the car headrests were correctly positioned.

(b) *Back/Spine Motion*

When his Corolla is impacted from behind, Mr. Plaintiff's seat will first compress and bend until he reaches the same speed as the Corolla, at which point the seat will rebound, pushing Mr. Plaintiff to a speed higher than that of the Corolla, after which he will be caught by the shoulder harness and slowed back down to the Corolla's speed. Properly including the springlike seat response, the typical seat amplitude for the maximum car push speed of about 5.0 mph (*common speed* of 2.5 mph) will be no more than about 2.5 inches and Mr. Plaintiff's torso would experience an acceleration of about 2.0 g for a truly linear elastic seat response, and only up to about 4.0 g even including typical seat "stiffening" for large compression amplitude.

Because a typical car seat does not load the spine uniformly, the spine is subjected to a rapid straightening effect. The spine's natural curvature (kyphotic at the thorax region and lordotic at the lumbar region) causes localized high force loadings at the pelvis and thorax regions. These thrusts cause the spine to straighten, which in turn causes rapid vertical motions of both the spine and the neck.

Typically, approximately one-half of a person's body mass is located in the torso. For Mr. Plaintiff, a 4.0 g acceleration on his torso (the largest value calculated) would indicate a force of about 236 lbs acting on his torso's center of mass. At his lower back (approximately 5 inches below the torso center of mass), this would induce a torque of approximately 98 ft-lb. For a person of Mr. Plaintiff's size, this would be the equivalent of lifting a 48 to 95 lb weight using only his back. Note that this is less than Mr. Plaintiff's weight. Such a load is below that required to cause permanent damage such as bone fracture, ligament damage or intervertebral disc herniation. However, such loads can sometimes induce transient muscle spasms which normally resolve within a time period of from hours to at most a few months.

Thus, we conclude that Mr. Plaintiff was impacted at less than 5 mph, and experienced a torso acceleration of less than 4.0 g. This would have caused a moderate torque of about 98 ft-lbs on his lower back. Again references 2 to 6 give similar experimentally determined torso accelerations for such torso push speeds.

There are no logical explanations for Mr. Plaintiff's complaints of right hip injury, since there was no impact on his hip with interior portions of his vehicle, and the torso accelerations are insufficient to cause high enough inertial loadings (*e.g.*, due to pelvis/leg weight) to induce injury.

Medical Evidence

Apparently, shortly after the accident Mr. Plaintiff did not have any clinical diagnostic tests done, such as plane X-rays, CT scans or MRI. However, he was tested ultrasonically for Thoracic Outlet Syndrome (a.k.a. Cervical Rib Syndrome or Brachial Plexus Syndrome) and apparently had a neurological test done when investigated by the IME. He also had some previous range of motion (ROM) measurements made (results unknown). He primarily was treated via chiropractic manipulations, physical therapy and trigger-point injections. No direct objective clinical findings were positive.

Previous History

Mr. Plaintiff states he was involved in a previous rearender in Date. He was sitting on a side-facing rear seat in a truck, facing left. He states he injured the right side of his neck and a leg (possibly the left one). These complaints are consistent with his seating position for that accident.

Conclusions

Based on these analyses we conclude:

(1) The *maximum* closing speed of Mr. Defendant's pickup into Mr. Plaintiff's Corolla was about 4.55 mph.

(2) The corresponding *maximum* push speed of the Corolla was about 5.0 mph.

(3) Mr. Plaintiff's own statement of negligible induced car motion further supports the calculation that the Corolla push speed was *less* than 5.0 mph.

(4) Even including a possible "seat bounce," the *maximum* push speed of Mr. Plaintiff's torso was about 6.5 mph. This is *below* the level necessary to induce permanent neck damage even *without* a properly positioned headrest.

(5) The headrest in the Corolla appears to have been correctly positioned, and would have rapidly stopped Mr. Plaintiff's neck extension: hence the probability of permanent neck injury is remote.

(6) Even allowing for "spine straightening" and seat-back compression the induced torso accelerations on Mr. Plaintiff (less than 4.0 g) are such that only transient muscle pains are expected to be induced.

Such problems resolve within a time frame of hours to weeks to (at most) a few months.

(7) The only rationale for any significant injury to Mr. Plaintiff would be that he was suffering from some form of *pre-existing* problems, such as continuing problems arising from the previous rearender in which he stated he suffered injury to his neck and left leg. His history indicates that he was continuously receiving some form of treatment from the date of the previous rearender (Date) up to almost the date of this accident. There is no logical explanation for his complaint of injury to his right hip associated with this accident.

This is a rearender involving possible CTS

Plaintiff Accident on Date: Possible CTS Problem

Background

We have been tasked to evaluate the accident in which Mr. Plaintiff (front right passenger) was rearended and injured his left wrist causing Carpal Tunnel Syndrome (CTS). To do this we have reviewed the description of the accident given by Mr. Plaintiff's brother, Mr. Brother, (the driver of the Plaintiff vehicle), and various photographs showing: the car, Mr. Plaintiff's sitting position in the car, and showing the approximate manner in which his arm hit the dash. We have also reviewed the medical records. To date, there are no depositions and no police report.

Description of Accident

The accident occurred in Town on Date, at about Time. The weather was clear and the road was dry and paved. The Plaintiff vehicle (a 1991 Mercury Tracer) was stopped behind a flatbed trailer, at the bottom of the hill on Road at the intersection with Road. Both vehicles were stopped due to red traffic lights. Mr. Brother estimates the gap between the Tracer and the trailer was about 8 - 12 feet. A large full-size car described as an early 1980's Cadillac, or similar, rearended the Tracer. There were no skid marks. Damage to either vehicle was negligible, with only a small imprint mark on the rear bumper of the Tracer. The impact appears to have been a simple full-bumper to bumper one, with some evidence that the thrust was slightly greater on the left side of the Tracer.

Mr. Brother estimated that the Tracer was pushed forward about 6 - 10 feet (insufficient to reach the trailer ahead), and that the gap between the colliding vehicles post-impact was about 8 - 12 feet. Mr. Brother also stated that he had his foot lightly on the brake at the time of impact.

Consequent to the impact, Mr. Plaintiff moved back into his seat. The seatbelt retracted with this motion and locked such that his body was held tightly in the seat. Mr. Brother had to undo the clip of the motorized shoulder harness at the passenger window in order to free Plaintiff. Mr. Plaintiff was holding a cigarette in his right hand, and so he used his left hand to brace himself. His left wrist impacted on the dash structure. The photos approximate his arm position at impact time, illustrating his statement that his arm was "straight" at impact time.

Analysis of Car Motions

Because neither car exceeded its bumper limit (5 mph for each) it is possible to estimate an upper speed of impact, and then estimate the upper push speed given to the Tracer and the decelerated speed of the other larger vehicle. Because the exact identity of the larger car is not known, we perform a sensitivity analysis to cover the options. The Tracer curb weight is about 2356 lbs, and with two occupants (Mr. Brother 175 lbs, Mr. Plaintiff 151 lbs) total weight is about 2682 lbs. The larger car (with 150 lb driver) could weigh between about 4200 lbs (1980 Cadillac Coupe de Ville) to about 4800 (1978 Cadillac Fleetwood). Based on these weights, the maximum collision speed to avoid bumper damage (to either car) is between about 8.9 mph and 8.6 mph. Thus the answer is not very sensitive to exact weight of the large car. The corresponding push speed for the Tracer is between about 10.9 mph and 11.0 mph. The post-impact speed of the larger car is between about 1.96 mph and 2.43 mph. Again, the results are not very sensitive to exact weights.

For a light brake pedal application, we assume a drag factor for the Tracer of about 0.4 - 0.5. For an initial push speed of 11 mph, this gives a stopping distance of between about 8.1 feet and 10.1 feet. These values are in close agreement with Mr. Brother's estimates. The larger car would apply higher braking effort (sudden "panic" stop), so we assume a drag factor of about 0.6 (insufficient for a skid). The stopping distance is between about 0.21 feet (2.6 inches) and 0.33 feet (3.9 inches), assuming the driver applies his brakes immediately after impact, or has them on prior to impact. Thus the larger car effectively "stops dead" after the impact, and the gap between cars post-impact is about 7.8 feet to 9.9 feet. These values are again close to Mr. Brother's estimates.

Analysis of Body Motions

In a rearend collision *everything moves forward.* This includes the car, the seat, the occupant's torso and the head. However, differential motions occur such that the torso initially moves forward slower than the car and seat, and the head moves even slower. Thus the torso *apparently* moves backward into the seat and likewise the head apparently rotates backward relative to the shoulders. In reality, the seat *overtakes* the torso, and the shoulders overtake the head.

The purpose of this analysis is to consider the CTS problem, rather than other effects such as head/neck whiplash. However, it should be mentioned that both Mr. Brother and Mr. Plaintiff did display classic symptoms of neck acceleration/deceleration trauma. This is consistent with the estimated push speed for the Tracer, since neither occupant was expecting the impact, and Mr. Brother stated that both the headrests were mounted low directly on the seats.

As Mr. Plaintiff's torso moved back into the seat so the latter acted as a damped spring and accelerated his torso up to the same speed as the car when the seat finally "bottomed." Thereafter, the seat would accelerate his torso to a speed *greater* than the car. For a typical car seat this bounce gives a final speed about 1.3 - 1.4 times that of the car, of about 14.3 - 15.4 mph. Thus the torso tries to move at about 3.3 - 4.4 mph faster than the car. If the seatbelt does not quickly lock up, the body can be thrown toward the steering wheel. If the belt locks up in the original occupant's position, the occupant is then rapidly decelerated back to the car speed (and oscillates between belt and seat).

However, for *this* accident the belt retracted with Mr. Plaintiff's torso as he moved back into the seat, and then locked. Consequently, with the seat attempting to push his body back he became "trapped" by the belt tightly in the seat. Had the shoulder harness been a full-body one his entire torso would remain tight in the seat, his maximum torso speed would be equal to the maximum car speed, and only his arms could flail about. However, as the front passenger he has a shoulder harness which goes from his left hip to his right shoulder. This belt stops motion of the right half of his upper body but the left half can continue to move forward by rotating about a vertical axis through the chest. Thus Mr. Plaintiff's left arm can continue toward the dash at the higher bounce speed.

Since his left arm was straight, the effective moving weight was that of the entire left arm (about 7.7 lbs) and some of his upper torso (about 16 lbs, being one half of his thorax), for a total of about 24 lbs. The average speed relative to the dash is about 3.9 mph (see above) which is 5.7 ft/s. Thus the kinetic energy is about 12.2 ft-lbs. For a "straight arm" impact into the dash the stopping distance is small. The actual "give" in the arm (wrist, elbow and shoulder) is only about 0.5 inches, while the give in the dash is probably also only 0.5 inches at most. Thus the average stopping force is given by the change in energy divided by the total stopping distance, which is about 146 lbs. For a springlike response of the arm and dash (the force increases with compression) the peak force could be almost twice this value, of about 292 lbs.

For an impact occurring directly on the wrist (palmar side), this level of force is high and would be concentrated around the Carpal Tunnel area. This could cause direct impact on the cartilage over the tunnel, or a severe jostling of the bones in that vicinity, causing restriction of the tunnel region and impingement of the median nerve. Note that if the impact was more toward the palm the hand would extend back and put the wrist into strong extension. This motion increases the net stopping distance, thereby reducing the peak force. However, this effect is counterbalanced by the "leverage" effect, since such wrist extension will produce high localized forces in the neighborhood of the Carpal Tunnel (*i.e.*, a force centered on the palm is much farther from the rotation point at the wrist then are the ligaments and muscles which try to control the extension). Thus high forces are expected for either option.

Other Considerations

CTS is known to mostly occur in women, but is also less often seen in men, and also to mostly be associated with "overuse." Thus many people who type or use computer keyboards can suffer. However, the problem usually mostly afflicts the dominant hand. Mr. Plaintiff is right-handed, thus the expectation is that for a job-related repetitive motion cause of CTS, it would be his right wrist which should be most affected. This is contrary to his complaint, which is of CTS in the left wrist. Although overuse is a common excuse for CTS, this is more of a correlation than an explanation, since no corresponding mechanical effect has been proposed to account for it. Further, although much rarer, CTS has been observed for cases of strong sudden loads on/near the wrist, again without precise explanation.

Mr. Plaintiff's medical records indicate that he was diagnosed as suffering from CTS, and had an operation to cut the cartilage and thus relieve pressure on the median nerve (a common procedure). However, it appears his pain symptoms have not completely resolved.

Conclusions

Based on the above analyses and available facts we conclude that there is a reasonable degree of scientific probability that Mr. Plaintiff did suffer a strong sudden force on/near his left wrist, and that this induced his CTS problems.

This case involves a vehicle inspection where a claim was made of a faulty air bag that failed to activate.

Truck Inspection: Faulty Airbag?

Background

We have been tasked to inspect the 1995 Chevrolet Cheyenne C-1500 pickup truck which was involved in a collision with a tree in a drainage ditch just outside of Town on Date. The license plate is License, and the VIN is VIN. The accident occurred on Road. The driver, Mr. Plaintiff, was travelling east and claimed an oncoming vehicle caused him to swerve to his right off the narrow road and into a drainage ditch, hitting a tree. These facts are in the police report. The driver suffered injury to his head (apparently his mouth hit the steering wheel). He claimed that the driver's airbag did not deploy.

Vehicle Inspection

On Date, the vehicle was inspected in Town, at the yard of Company on Road. The vehicle was manufactured in Date and delivered in Date, and the odometer read 28,688.3 miles. The trip mileage was 937.2 miles, but this must be due to failure to reset since it exceeds the logged rental mileage for Mr. Plaintiff. The gas tank read 1/4 full. The steering wheel was 3/4 turned to the right, in agreement with the right-turned position of the front wheels. The steering assembly was working.

The driver's airbag (only one provided) did *not* deploy.

The driver's seat belt assembly worked correctly. There was no deformation of the tongue or of the buckle. However, the plastic covering over the wire ropes (buckle to floor anchorage passing through the seat) was torn away from the buckle unit. It is not clear whether this was due to this accident or merely "wear and tear" (the other buckles were beginning to show mild tear-away damage). The driver's shoulder harness (belt) did not show obvious signs of actual stretching. However, there was a clear imprint on the belt from the "D-ring" on the B pillar. The latter ring has a black plastic coating, and pieces of this coating were observed on the belt, and were beginning to fall off the belt. The marks were positioned on the belt consistent with *a* driver actually wearing the belt. However, it was not clear if this imprint was due to the sudden load caused in *this* accident, or was the accumulated effect of wear by other drivers.

The bench seat has a seat back which can fold down forward. No latching mechanism could be found (this appears to be by design), so the back would try to move forward with the driver.

The steering wheel had a missing "chunk" (about 3/4 inch diameter) on the windshield side of the rubberized coating. This is probably where Mr. Plaintiff' mouth impacted the wheel (he "ate" the wheel). This would explain the observed pattern of blood. Blood was found on the steering wheel, on the lower part of the inside of the driver's door, on the front side of the driver's seat, and on the floor pan near the door and A frame section. The pattern of blood was not consistent with an injury to either a hand or a leg, since no corresponding contact point could be identified.

Ignoring the impact damage, the vehicle appeared in good condition. The tires were in good condition with plenty of tread. They were Make, of size P235/ 75R15. The only tire damage was some mild sidewall scuff marks on the right hand rear tire (poor curb parking?) and a very strong sidewall scuff on the left front tire. The latter was obviously due to the left front bumper which was pushing in on the tire. The brake system was in good condition with no sign of oil leakage. None of the wheels were bent or indicated violent side impact.

The collision damage was mostly to the left front of the vehicle. The bumper had been pushed back by about 11 inches (crush). The impact region was about 12 inches wide (across the vehicle front from the corner of the bumper), which is about 1/6th (0.167) of the vehicle width. On the right side there was some minor induced damage in the form of fender bending near the A frame. The left front bumper was pushed back sufficiently for the left frame "horn" to be punched through the plastic cowling just under the bumper. The bumper itself had rotated relative to the front of the vehicle such that the right corner was sprung forward by about 2 inches away from the bodywork.

There was also some damage on the right-hand side, consisting of a crease and scrapes and a push-in of the lower side of the truck bed extending from just behind the cab back to the right rear wheel arch. Also, the left lower corner of the driver's door had damage indicating an inward push at some time.

Analysis

The airbag did not deploy: can this be explained? It should first be noted that typical airbag assemblies employ a sensor which uses a "threshold" logic. Only for sudden reductions in speed *above* this threshold will the bag deploy. This threshold is usually equivalent to a rigid barrier impact above about 10 to 12 mph. This threshold is designed to prevent unnecessary false firings at low speeds, while providing necessary protection at higher speeds.

The effective equivalent barrier speed (EBS) can be deduced from the frontal damage on the truck using the following equation

$$(EBS)^2 = f\,\{12Rg\,[x^2/a + 2x + v_L{}^2/12Rg]\}$$

where EBS is in ft/s, f is the fractional width of the truck front which was crushed, R is the rigidity of the frame (this factor is crush energy per inch of crush per lb weight of vehicle), g is the acceleration due to gravity, x is the observed crush depth, 'a' is the stiffening factor for the vehicle, and v_L is the bumper limit speed.

To compute, we use R = 0.8, g = 32.2 ft/s^2, x = (11 inches/12) = 0.917 ft, a = 9 inches = 0.75 ft, v_L = 2.5 mph = 3.668 ft/s, and f = 0.17. Note that the R and 'a' values are typical of such a large vehicle (weight about 3827 lbs), and are based on the CRASH3 program data base, specifically that for heavy trucks.

Substituting, we obtain EBS = 12.6 ft/s = 8.6 mph. This is *below* the normal airbag deployment threshold. Even if we allow for a wider damage zone, with f = 0.3 (twice the observed width) the EBS only increases to about 16.7 ft/s = 11.4 mph, which is still near the threshold. We thus conclude that the airbag did not deploy because the sudden stop was not sufficiently intense to fire the bag.

It is because the crush was localized to the left front foot of width that these low values apply. The visual inspection of the damage is initially deceiving. Note that had the same 11 inches of crush existed uniformly across the entire front of the truck (*i.e.,* f = 1.0) the speed becomes EBS = 30.4 ft/s = 20.8 mph. For comparison, note that a full-width uniform crush of 24 inches gives a value EBS = 53.8 ft/s = 36.7 mph, which is typical of the crush observed in the 35 mph government NCAP test crashes.

Note that the EBS is the equivalent sudden stopping speed, NOT the actual collision speed. The latter could have been higher, since it would take into account any energy involved in either bending the impacted tree and/or involved in any subsequent vehicle rotation after the impact. However, the EBS *is* the relevant value for airbag deployment.

The fact that the left front tire had a scuff mark all the way around the tire (due to rubbing on the depressed bumper) implies that the vehicle continued to move somewhat after the impact. For a sudden thrust on the left front corner, the vehicle was probably forced to rotate about the tree, with a counterclockwise rotation (seen from above) the most likely motion. This may explain the damage seen on the right-hand side of the truck assuming the vehicle then ran into a low object (*e.g.,* the ditch bank?). However, for a truck of length 16.3 ft and width 6.4 ft the maximum torque-arm can only be about 3 ft, and this implies that the maximum spin rate would only be about 24 degrees/s, which is quite low.

Occupant Motion

Regardless of the true impact speed, the inferred EBS is the initial speed with which the driver would move forward relative to the vehicle. With any induced vehicle rotation there would also be an apparent small side motion of the driver (to his right for a counterclockwise vehicle spin). The fact that the driver impacted the steering wheel implies either that the seatbelt was not being worn, or that the belt failed to lock up sufficiently fast. It should be noted that the bench seat was in a forward position, leaving only a gap of about 9 inches between the driver's chest and the center of the steering wheel, for an average sized person. A head impact on the steering wheel at a speed of 8.6 mph is too low to induce serious skull/brain injury, but can injure the mouth. For an unbelted driver, a head impact at greater than about 12 mph is usually needed to cause serious damage (HIC =1000, which is the government allowed limit for the head injury criterion). This limit explains why the airbag threshold is about 12 mph.

Summary

The driver's statement that he had to swerve to his right is consistent with the positioning of the front wheels and the steering wheel. The impact damage indicates that the vehicle hit a localized object (such as a tree) on the left front, and may have then gently spun before finally stopping. The level and extent of the crush implies a sudden stop from a speed of about 8.6 mph. This speed is too low to activate the airbag. *Thus, the airbag did not malfunction.* The evidence is ambiguous with regard to whether the seatbelt was being worn at the time. The ability to impact the steering wheel implies either non-use of the belts or late lockup. The close positioning of the seat to the steering wheel would exacerbate this problem. The implied impact speed on the steering wheel is too low to cause serious skull/brain damage, but could cause mouth problems.

This case involves a localized "soft structure" impact.

Two-Vehicle Impact: Is Everything What is Claimed?

Introduction

We have been tasked to investigate the rearender accident between Mr. Defendant (bullet vehicle) and Mr. Plaintiff and his wife (target vehicle). The accident occurred on Date at the intersection of Road and Road. Both vehicles had come down Road and were turning south to enter Road and were in the turn-right "yield" lane. The target vehicle moved forward and then stopped. The bullet also moved forward, but the driver (Defendant) looked to his left and failed to notice the car had stopped in front of him and so rearended the car. Both occupants of the rearended car state they suffered from some form of "whiplash" with neck and back problems.

The Vehicles

Both vehicles were inspected on Date.

The bullet vehicle is a Toyota pickup truck, license License. The vehicle was unloaded at the time of the accident. The truck is in very good condition. It is somewhat high off the ground with the front bumper between 24 and 29 inches above the road. Attached to this bumper is a chrome-plated "brush guard." This guard has two vertical sides of 3/8 inch metal with a "point" at about 29 inches above the road. This point protrudes about 5.5 to 6.0 inches in front of the bumper (slightly less on the right than on the left). The total guard extends from about 15 to 16 inches (bottom) up to about 40 inches (top) above the road. The top of the guard is at the height of the truck hood. The guard is about 23.75 inches wide, and has three 3.0 inch diameter rods or tubes running horizontally across the bottom, top, and at the "point" region. Although the guard is not 100% "square" to the bumper assembly this appears to be due to the manner of original attachment. The guard shows no sign of impact-induced motion relative to the bumper. Likewise, the bumper shows no sign of impact. Lastly, the frontal panel below the bumper also shows no sign of impact and is in good condition with no dents or paint removal or transfer. The driver (Defendant) admitted to impact, and thought the hit must have been on the right hand "point" region of his brush guard. This is credible. However, the guard showed no obvious sign of impact (probably because it is so rigid).

The target vehicle is a Ford Tempo, license License. Overall, the car is in good condition. However, there is rearend damage, consisting of (a) a broken left light glass, (b) a bumper pushed in on the right-hand side, and (c) a dent in the trunk lid. The bumper was offset being about 5 inches back from the rear panel on the left but only about 3.5 inches from the panel on the right. An inspection of the isolators revealed scrapes on the right-hand one at least 1.5 inches long. There is a rubberized "corrugated cover" at either end of the bumper, and the one on the right side was clearly partially squeezed in. The rear bumper is between about 14 to 19 inches above the road. The damaged trunk lid consisted of a localized dent just to the left of the keylock and a less localized inward bend extending over a width of about 36 inches. The localized dent was pushed in by about 1.5 inches and extended laterally by about 4 inches. The localized dent indicated that the push was due to a "sharp" object. The trunk lid was also bent upward away from the side bodywork giving a vertical gap of about 5/8 inch on the left and about 3/8 inch on the right (each about halfway along the lid toward the rear window). There was no obvious damage to either the side bodywork or the rear window.

At the inspection Mr. Plaintiff stated that *all* this rearend damage was due to this accident. He also said that both occupants were wearing their seatbelts and that the headrests were in the down position on the seats, as observed during the inspection.

Geometrical Analysis

Since both vehicles were turning on a rightward curve, Mr. Defendant's suggestion that the right "point" area of his brush guard impacted the rear of the Tempo is logical, and would account for the "sharp" localized indent in the trunk lid of the Tempo. The relative heights of the brush guard and the car trunk lid are compatible with this scenario. However, the front bumper of the Toyota truck is too high to impact the rear bumper of the car except for a severe "nose-dive" of over 5 inches which is most unlikely since the pickup has relatively stiff springing. No scrape marks were observed on the top of the car bumper or on the bottom of the truck bumper. Further, the extension of the brush guard to the front of the truck prevents the front truck bumper from reaching the rear panel area on the car for a depth of crush of only 1.5 inches in the trunk lid. Likewise, the rear bumper of the car cannot reach back under the front bumper of the truck sufficiently to reach the low frontal panel on the truck. The result is that there is *no part of the truck* which could have hit the rear bumper of the car. This explains the lack of any obvious damage to the front of the truck. However, it also implies that this accident is *not* the source of the rear bumper damage on the car.

The left-hand front of the truck would be skewed away from the car. Thus no direct impact could cause the broken left light glass, only an indirect thrust could cause it. However, the direct thrust on the rear lip of the car trunk would move the rear panel away (forward) from the glass (thereby decoupling it), and the trunk itself would also not provide thrust to the glass. Thus there is no clear mechanism for breaking the glass. The broken light must be due to another source. Thus *only* the trunk damage can be caused by this accident.

Impact Analysis

The impact can be analyzed by noting that all the damage energy is associated with the relatively small trunk lid crush. Assuming the car was stopped at the time of impact the speed of the truck is given by

$$V^2 = [(W_1 + W_2)/W_1][1 + (W_2/W_1)(R_2/R_1)^2(V_{L1}/V_{L2})^2]V_{L2}{}^2 + 2E_Dg(W_1 + W_2)/(W_1W_2)$$

where '1' is the heavier vehicle and '2' is the lighter one, W is the weight, V_L is a threshold velocity to cause damage (*e.g.*, a bumper limit) and E_D is the total absorbed energy for the crash. We have W_2 = 2438 lbs for the Tempo and W_1 = 3160 lbs for the Toyota. The thrust on the brush guard of the Toyota will be directed through the front bumper and into the vehicle frame. Thus we use the "frame" value for R_1 which is about 0.6, and assume a typical pickup 2.5 mph (3.668 ft/s) bumper limit for V_{L1}. However, for the Tempo the thrust is not through the bumper, but into the trunk lid. Such lids are considerably less rigid than a frame (you can bend them with hands, pliers, and hammers, etc.), so we assume $R_2 = 0.3$ as a maximum. Likewise, the "equivalent bumper threshold" is low, estimated at about 1.0 mph (1.5 ft/s) maximum (V_{L2}). Note that the meaning of this "equivalent threshold" is the maximum speed at which the car could be driven (backward) into a rigid wall that could only impact the trunk (not the bumper assembly) before damage to the latter occurs.

For the small (1.5 inch) depth of trunk crush the total absorbed energy (E_D) is about $E_D = f_2R_2W_2x_2$ in ft-lbs, where x_2 is the crush in inches and f_2 is the fractional width of the vehicle that is actually crushed. The width of the Tempo is about 68.3 inches. Thus for the severe part of the dent, only about 4 inches wide, this gives f_2 of about 4/68.3 = 0.06. The wider (36 inches) region of partial crush (average about 1/2 inch crush) gives $f_2 = 0.53$.

Hence we get:

$$E_D = 0.06 \text{ x } 0.3 \text{ x } 2438 \text{ x } 1.5 + 0.53 \text{ x } 0.3 \text{ x } 2438 \text{ x } 0.5 = 260 \text{ ft-lbs.}$$

Substituting, we get for the impact speed (closing speed)

$$\begin{aligned} V^2 &= [(3160 + 2438)/3160)][1 + (2438/3160)(0.3/0.6)^2(3.668/1.5)^2](1.5)^2 \\ &\quad + 2\text{x}32.2\text{x}260\text{x}(3160 + 2438)/(3160 \text{ x } 2438) \\ &= 20.75 \text{ (ft/s)}^2 \end{aligned}$$

Thus V = 4.56 ft/s = 3.10 mph. This is very low. The corresponding increase in speed of the Tempo is given by

$$V_{Tempo} = (3160/(3160 + 2438))(1 - e)3.1 \text{ mph} = 0.56(1\text{-}e)3.1 \text{ mph} = 1.75(1\text{-}e) \text{ mph,}$$

where 'e' is the coefficient of restitution, which describes the vehicle bounce. If this had been a bumper-to-bumper hit 'e' can be about -0.7 for these speeds. However, for the brush guard-to-trunk lid hit very little bounce is expected. Indeed, we may approximate the value of 'e' by e = (threshold speed)/(impact speed) = -1.5/4.56 = -0.33. Thus, the maximum sudden increase in speed of the Tempo is about V_{Tempo} = 1.75 x 1.33 = 2.33 mph.

The final speed of the Toyota from the impact is given by

$$V_{Toyota} = [(3160 - 0.33 \text{ x } 2438)/(3160 + 2438)]3.1 \text{ mph} = 0.42 \text{ x } 3.1 \text{ mph} = 1.3 \text{ mph.}$$

Note that the low speed change for the Tempo would barely exceed the limit for fighting the brake friction on the ground if the Tempo had its brakes on strongly. Thus, the previous quotes of speed change can only be reduced for the Tempo in the event the brakes were on significantly. This sudden speed change is considerably below the level at which normal people suffer from whiplash.

Experiments with volunteers indicate that the usual threshold is above 6.5 mph. Data collected by Swedish researchers indicate problems for impacts below 12 mph. Thus the threshold is usually in the range of 6.5 - 12 mph. Calculations based on physics and experimental ligamentous damage limits suggest 7.5 mph +, increasing with neck muscle tone at the time of the hit.

To appreciate why the *lack* of a bumper-to-bumper hit is important, consider the results if we instead assumed the rear bumper of the Tempo was pushed in. For this case we have $R_2 = 0.6$, $V_{L2} = 5.0$ mph = 7.335 ft/s (note, all Fords have 5 mph bumpers), and the mean crush of the bumper was about 0.75 inches, and $f_2 = 1.0$. Then $E_D = R_2W_2x_2 = 1097$ ft-lbs. Substituting, we now obtain the impact speed of V = 12.87 ft/s = 8.76 mph, and the sudden increase in the speed of the Tempo would be about 7.9 mph. *Now* we are approaching the level where injury can be expected. However, *this* crash was not bumper-to-bumper. This simple calculation itself implies that a *previous* rearend crash into the Tempo may be the cause of the reported injuries.

Conclusions

Based on the geometry of the rear of the Tempo and the front of the Toyota this was *not* a bumper-to-bumper impact. Instead, the front brush guard of the Toyota impacted the rear trunk lid of the Tempo. *This* accident did *not* cause the rear bumper damage to the Tempo, neither is it likely that it caused the left rear tail light damage. The small degree of trunk damage, which is a *very soft (weak)* portion of the Tempo (certainly relative to a through-bumper thrust into the main frame) implies a low overall energy absorption, which implies a low impact speed. The relatively small degree of subsequent bounce then implies a low overall sudden increase in speed for the Tempo. This speed is well below the threshold for whiplash neck and/or back problems for normal people. Only if either occupant of the Tempo had some form of predisposition or some pre-existing problems would one expect to see injuries.

This case involves a "side-frontal" impact.

A Classic Frontal-Sideswipe Collision

No report was requested for this case; therefore, we merely summarize the salient features. The accident involved a Camaro and an F150 Ford truck. The Camaro was traveling at about 35 mph and approaching a junction to its right. At the last moment the truck proceeded out from this side road turning left across the path of the car. At the time of impact the truck was still traveling quite slowly. The impact was between the right front corner of the truck and the right side of the car. As the car moved past the truck so damage was caused along the passenger door until the truck bumper caught the B pillar at the back of the Camaro door. At this point the thrust suddenly rapidly increased causing the B pillar to collapse backward and cause damage to the right rear wheel of the Camaro. The ultimate damage to the truck was limited to only the right front corner.

This is a classic case of the frontal sideswipe. The truck was rapidly spun in a clockwise direction but with little overall net motion of its CM. The car received a thrust directed backward and inward to the rear of its own CM. Hence the car also suffered a clockwise spin, but with only a small reduction in the CM speed. The car proceeded to spin and skid for a considerable distance, finally coming to rest on the shoulder on the opposite side of the road.

The total degree of crush damage was remarkably limited, particularly with regard to the total energy absorption. Hence this crash is classified as "low speed" because the net *change* in speed for each vehicle was quite low. No one in the truck (three occupants in the bench seat) was injured, while the occupants of the car were injured to some extent mostly due to the passenger banging the head on the door window. While the Camaro was wrecked, the F150 truck was still perfectly driveable.

Animation

An animation was requested. This shows the vehicles motions, indicating how the truck was mostly "punched" out of the way of the car via the process of rapid spinning.

This case involves a driver sandwiched between two larger vehicles.

The Sandwich Accident

No report was requested for this case. Therefore, we summarize the salient features. The accident involved a large boom truck (vehicle 1), a small stake-bed pickup (vehicle 2) and an older Cadillac Fleetwood (vehicle 3). Plaintiff was in the middle vehicle (2) and had stopped about 5 feet behind vehicle 3 which was also stopped due to rush-hour traffic snarl-up. The defendant in vehicle 1 was moving behind and trying to see if he could switch lanes. Unfortunately, while trying this he impacted the plaintiff's pickup. The front bumper of 1 interlocked with the rear of the stake bed of 2 (which had no actual rear bumper) such that the two vehicles became locked together. The combined pair then slowed across the 5 feet gap to the Cadillac and impacted the latter. Thus the plaintiff became sandwiched.

The boom truck weighed about 11,000 lbs and had a very large front bumper which protruded several inches forward, serving as a platform. A short ladder was welded to this bumper. Traffic warning cones were on the bumper, between the bumper front and the truck grill. Upon impact with the smaller pickup, the boom truck bumper stuck under the stake bed frame of the pickup. This caused a significant deformation of the pickup frame, and damage to the ladder region of the boom truck and its bumper. Also, the boom truck's grill was damaged, presumably due to a thrust through the traffic cones sitting on this bumper.

The small pickup weighed about 3000 lbs, and suffered frontal damage in addition to the rear frame damage. This consisted of the front bumper being pushed back by about 2 inches with some small induced buckling damage to the side fenders. The windshield suffered a small crack. Additionally, there was internal damage to the pickup. This consisted of a permanently bent bar which ran across the lower length of the bench seat. The bend was clearly caused by loading on the lower back of the plaintiff.

The Cadillac weighed about 4800 lbs, and suffered no permanent damage.

The only stated injuries were those of the plaintiff, who complained that his head had whipped back and impacted the vertical metal rail of the sliding window assembly at the back of his cab. There were no headrests in this cab. Plaintiff also complained of lower back pain and right knee pain. He further stated that after moving backwards he was then flung forward and hit the steering wheel with his chest, although without significant problems.

To solve this accident we worked backwards. We first calculated the critical speed for zero damage for the combined boom truck/pickup (14,000 lbs) into the Cadillac. Assuming a 5 mph bumper for the Cadillac and a 2.5 mph one for the front of the pickup, this gave the value of 5.9 mph closing speed. Adding the energy absorbed in causing 2 inches of crush to the front of the small pickup then gave the actual closing speed of about 8.1 mph. This then implies a coefficient of restitution of about $e = -5.9/8.1 = 0.73$. With the "down-load" factor of 0.7 to 0.5 this gives the real coefficient of about 0.51 to 0.36. Thus, the Cadillac was accelerated up to between about 8 mph and 10 mph, while the boom truck/pickup combo slowed to between 4.95 mph and 5.27 mph. The common speed when all three vehicles moved together was about 6 mph. All three vehicles then stopped with only a small gap between the pickup and the Cadillac.

We then assumed a deceleration for the boom truck/pickup combo to be about 0.5 g across the 5 feet initial gap between the pickup and the Cadillac (there were no skid marks). This gave a speed for the boom truck/pickup combo of about 11.8 mph immediately after the first crash. Since there was no bounce between the boom truck and the pickup, the weight ratio then gave the initial crash speed for the boom truck of about 15 mph, for a stationary pickup.

For the boom truck impact into the small pickup the critical speed for zero damage was computed assuming the boom truck had a 5 mph bumper and the pickup rear frame bed acted as a 5 mph one also. This gave a critical speed of about 7.2 mph. Adding the energy for crushes of about 2 inches on the rear of the pickup and also on the front of the boom truck gave an actual closing speed of about 14.5 mph. This value is similar to that derived "backwards" given above. Note that the boom truck driver stated that just before the first crash he thought he was moving at about 25 - 30 mph. Our analysis indicates he had either slowed significantly without realizing it, or was wildly wrong in his own estimate.

Should anyone be injured? Consider first the boom truck driver. In the first collision his speed reduced from about 15 mph to about 11.8 mph, giving a sudden drop of only 3.2 mph. In the second crash the speed suddenly dropped from about 8.1 mph to about 4.95 mph (minimum) giving a drop of only about 3.15 mph. Neither of these speed changes is sufficient to cause injury for a frontal impact, and none was reported.

The occupants of the Cadillac saw a sudden increase in speed of between about 8 mph and 10 mph. The lower value is close to the threshold for possible whiplash and the higher is above the threshold. Neither occupant claimed injury, so either the speed was the lower estimate or the headrests worked adequately.

However, the plaintiff saw a sudden increase in speed of 11.8 mph for the first crash, luckily without an added vehicle bounce. This is above the threshold for whiplash injury. Although the plaintiff stated he saw the boom truck coming he also had his head turned to the right, as he was looking in his rearview mirror. Thus, he is still a candidate for injury, especially since there were no headrests in the pickup and the rear window of the cab was at least 5 inches behind his head. The bent bar behind his seat implies a thrust of about 300 to 400 lbs load. While this load is insufficient to break any bones, it is large and localized (the bar was about 7/8 inch diameter), and probably accounts for his complaints of lower back pain.

The plaintiff states he was wearing his seatbelt (one-piece shoulder and lap), but also states he moved forward and hit his chest on the steering wheel. This implies his belt failed to lock sufficiently fast. This could be due to his relatively small differential velocity versus his vehicle, or due to the small deceleration of his vehicle when locked to the boom truck prior to hitting the Cadillac, or due to some initial slack in the belts. Was this wheel impact due to the seat bounce or due to the second impact with the Cadillac? To determine which, we calculated his torso and head motions in the same manner as for the previous case (10(b)). These calculations allowed his chest to reach the wheel due to the seat bounce, just before the second impact, assuming no retardation from the seatbelt.

However, the impact speed on the wheel was calculated to only be about 3.5 mph, insufficient to cause rib damage.

Lastly, the plaintiff stated he hit his right knee. Observations of him seated in his pickup showed that there was only a 4-inch gap between his right knee and the ignition block on the steering column. It was therefore concluded that his knee shot forward and hit this region when his pickup was suddenly slowed due to the second impact with the Cadillac. His impact speed would be about 8.1 mph - 4.95 mph = 3.15 mph at worst. While this speed is insufficient to cause major damage, it could possibly explain the clinical observations of a torn meniscus.

Animation

We were asked to animate this scenario. The animation shows the three vehicles and the motions of the plaintiff. Note that the entire process, from first impact to final stopping was only about 1.1 seconds. The initial crash would last about 0.08 seconds, the time to cross the 5 feet gap would be 0.34 seconds, the second crash would last about 0.14 seconds (to final disengagement) and the subsequent braking to stop would last about 0.5 seconds.

References

(1) "Vehicular Occupant Restraint Systems and Components Standards Manual," SAE HS-13, 1993.

(2) Limpert, R., "Motor Vehicle Accident Reconstruction and Cause Analysis," Third Edition, Michie Company, 1989.

(3) Hollings, E. F. and Bryan, R. H., "Highway Safety: Reliability and Validity of DOT Crash Tests," United States General Accounting Office, Report to Congressional Requesters, GAO/PEMD-95-5.

(4) NHTSA Memorandum 79-17-N01-709, "1994 NCAP Final Report."

(5) *Accident Reconstruction Journal*, Volume 7, No. 4, July/August,1995, Victor Craig ed.

(6) "Medical School for Lawyers (three videos): 'The Complete Orthopedic Examination,' 'Medical Evidence of Soft Tissue Injury' and 'The Complete Neurological Examination,'" SEAK, Inc., Legal and Medical Publishers, distributed exclusively by Lawyers & Judges Publishers Co., 1995.

(7) Fung, "Biomechanics: Mechanical Properties of Living Tissues," 2nd edition, Springer Verlag, 1993. [This describes much of the physical workings of the body, with emphasis on elasto-viscous behavior].

(8) Mertz & Patrick, "Strength and Response of the Human Neck," SAE 710855, 1971.

(9) Gurdjian, Lange, Patrick & Thomas, "Impact Injury and Crash Protection," Charles C. Thomas, publisher, Springfield, Illinois, 1970.

(10) Damask, A. C., Damask & Damask, "Injury Causation Analyses" (two volumes), the Michie Company, 1990 and 1993. (Note: these books quote much data from Yamada, "The Strength of Biological Materials," Williams & Wilkins, Baltimore, MD, 1970)

(11) McConnell, et al., "Analysis of Human Test Subject Kinematic Responses to Low Velocity Rear End Impacts," SAE 930889, 1993.

(12) West, et al., "Low Speed Rear-End Collision Testing Using Human Subjects," Accident Reconstruction Journal, May/June 1993.

(13) Siegmund, et al., "Speed Change (delta-V) of Amusement Park Bumper Cars," Proceedings of the Canadian Multidisciplinary Road Safety Conference VIII; Saskatoon, Saskatchewan, June 14 - 16, 1993.

(14) Ommaya and Hirsch, "Tolerances of Cerebral Concussion from Head Impact and Whiplash in Primates," Journal of Biomechanics, Vol 4, Pergamon Press, Inc, 1971.

(15) Siegmund, et al., "Characteristics of Specific Automobile Bumpers in Low-Velocity Impacts," SAE 940916, 1994.

(16) Woolley R. L., et al., "Rear Stiffness Coefficients Derived from Barrier Test Data," SAE 910120, in SAE SP-853, 1991.

(17) Bohan, T. L. and Damask, A. C., editors, "Forensic Accident Investigation: Motor Vehicles," Michie, 1995. (Wood, D. P., Chapter 7)

(18) Szabo, et al., "Human Occupant Kinetic Response to Low Speed Rear-End Impacts," SAE 940532, 1994.

(19) "Expert AutoStats™," a computer program from 4N6XPRT Systems™, Forensic Expert Software, La Mesa, CA, 1994.

(20) Noon, "Introduction to Forensic Engineering," CRC Press, 1992.

(21) Baker & Fricke, "The Traffic Accident Investigation Manual," Northwestern University Traffic Institute, 1986, and "Traffic Accident Reconstruction," Northwestern University Traffic Institute, 1990.

(22) Noga & Oppenheim, "CRASH3 User's Guide and Technical Manual," U.S. Department of Transportation, 1981.

(23) Harris, "The Shock and Vibration Handbook," (Chapter 44), Third Edition, McGraw-Hill, 1988.

(24) Lundstrom, "The Safety Factor in Automotive Design," SAE West Coast Meeting, August 1966.

(25) "Crush Stiffness Coefficients for Vehicle Model Years 1960 - 1994," Neptune Engineering, P.O. Box 1597, Clovis, CA.

(26) Hull and Newton, "Estimating Crush Stiffness when Reconstructing Vehicle Accidents," SAE 930898, 1993.

(27) Eubanks, J., "Pedestrian Accident Reconstruction" (with Videotape), Lawyers & Judges Publishing Co., 1995.

(28) "39th Stapp Car Crash Conference Proceedings," SAE P-299, 1995.

(29) Campbell, "Energy Basis for Collisional Severity," SAE 740565, 1974.

(30) Nystrom G. A., et al., "Stiffness Parameters for Vehicle Collision Analysis," SAE 910119, in SAE SP-853, 1991.

(31) Alexander, R. M., "Exploring Biomechanics: Animals in Motion," Scientific American Library, 1992.

(32) Carola, R., Harley J. P., Noback C. R., "Human Anatomy & Physiology," Second Edition, McGraw-Hill, Inc., 1992.

(33) Crowe, H., Medical Symposium, 1928 (unpublished). Also Davis, A. G., "Injuries of the Cervical Spine," JAMA, 127: 149-156, 1945.

(34) Kroemer, Kroemer and Kroemer-Elbert, "Ergonomics," Prentice-Hall, 1994.

(35) Weimer, "Handbook of Ergonomic and Human Factors Tables," PTR Prentice-Hall, 1993.

(36) Backaitis, S. H., editor, "Biomechanics of Impact Injury and Injury Tolerances of the Head-Neck Complex," SAE PT-43, 1993. Specifically: Foust D. R., *et al.*, "Cervical Range of Motion and Dynamic Response and Strength of Cervical Muscles," SAE 730975, 1973.

(37) "Shopping for a Safer Car," IIHS Report, 1995.

(38) Backaitis, S. H., editor, "Biomechanics of Impact Injury and Injury Tolerances of the Head-Neck Complex," SAE PT-43, 1993. Specifically: Mertz H. J., and Patrick L. M., "Investigation of the Kinematics and Kinetics of Whiplash," SAE 670919, 1967.

(39) Gray, "Gray's Anatomy," Running Press, 1974.

(40) Netter, "Atlas of Human Anatomy," Ciba-Geigy Corporation, 1993.

(41) Miller, C. E., "How Insurance Companies Settle Cases," James Publishing, 1995.

(42) Ruan J. S., Khalil T., King A. I., "Dynamic Response of the Human Head to Impact by Three-Dimensional Finite Element Analysis," Transactions of the ASME, Journal of Biomechanical Engineering, Feb 1994, Vol. 116.

(43) Backaitis, S. H., editor, "Biomechanics of Impact Injury and Injury Tolerances of the Thorax-Shoulder Complex," SAE PT-45, 1994.

Specifically: Lau I. V., and Viano D. C., "The Viscous Criterion-Bases and Applications of an Injury Severity Index for Soft Tissues," SAE 861882, 1986.

(44) Backaitis, S. H., editor, "Biomechanics of Impact Injury and Injury Tolerances of the Thorax-Shoulder Complex," SAE PT-45, 1994. Specifically: Patrick L. M., "Frontal Force Impact Tolerance of the Human Thorax," SAE P-67, 1967.

(45) Evans, L., "Traffic Safety and the Driver," Van Nostrand Reinhold, 1991.

(46) "Automotive Handbook," third edition, published by Robert Bosch GmbH, 1993.

(47) Griffith, "Complete Guide to Sports Injuries," The Body Press, 1986. [This indicates the correlations between many contact sports injuries and those which occur in auto accidents].

General Bibliography

Engineering/Mechanics/Reconstruction Texts:

(48) O'Donnell J., "Does CAFE Kill?," Autoweek, March 4, 1996.

(49) Backaitis, S. H., editor, "Accident Reconstruction Technologies: Pedestrians & Motorcyclists in Automotive Collisions," SAE PT-35, 1990.

(50) Orner, P. A., "A Physician-Engineer's View of Low Velocity Rearend Collisions," SAE 921574.

(51) Grimes, W. D. and Day, T. D., "Accident Reconstruction: Technology and Animation IV," SAE SP-1030, 1994.

(52) "Automobile Safety: Present and Future Technology," SAE SP-925, 1992.

(53) "Occupant Containment and Methods of Assessing Occupant Protection in the Crash Environment," SAE SP-1045, 1994.

(54) "Accident Reconstruction: Technology and Animation," SAE SP-853, 1991.

(55) "Seat Safety: Comfort and Safety," SAE SP-963, 1993.

(56) "Accident Reconstruction: Technology and Animation V," SAE SP-1083, 1995.

(57) "Reconstruction of Motor Vehicle Accidents: A Technical Compendium," edited by S. H. Backaitis, SAE PT-34, 1989.

(58) Johnson W., and Mamalis A. G., "Crashworthiness of Vehicles," Mechanical Engineering Publications (MEP), Ltd., London, 1978.

(59) Carvill J., "Mechanical Engineer's Data Handbook," CRC Press, 1993.

(60) Bolton W., "Engineering Materials Pocket Book," CRC Press, 1989.

(61) Barrett C. R., Nix W. D., and Tetelman A. S., "The Principles of Engineering Materials," Prentice-Hall, Inc., 1973.

Biomechanics/Medical/Injury Texts:

(62) Nahum, A. M., and Melvin, J. W., editors, "Accidental Injury: *Biomechanics and Prevention,*" Springer Verlag, 1993.

(63) Levine, Dr. R. S., editor, "Head and Neck Injury," SAE P-276, 1994.

(64) Rothenberg, M. A., "Anatomy and Physiology for Lawyers," John Wiley & Sons, 1994.

(65) Goodman, H. F., editor, "Orthopedic Disability and Expert Testimony," Fourth Edition, John Wiley & Sons, 1993.

(66) Backaitis, S. H., editor, "Biomechanics of Impact Injury and Injury Tolerances of the Abdomen, Spine and Pelvis," SAE PT-47, 1995.

(67) "Guides to the Evaluation of Permanent Impairment," Fourth Edition, American Medical Association, Doege T. C., and Houston T. P., editors.

(68) Pascarelli E., and Quilter D., "Repetitive Strain Injury," John Wiley & Sons, Inc., 1994.

(69) Roberts A. C., et al., "Litigating Head Trauma Cases," John Wiley & Sons, Inc., 1994.

(70) Carroll C., McAfee P.C., Riley L. H., "'Whiplash' Injuries and How to Treat Them," Journal of Musculoskeletal Medicine, June, 1992.

(71) Youdas J. W., et al., "Normal Range of Motion of the Cervical Spine: An Initial Goniometric Study," Physical Therapy, Vol.72, No. 11, November 1992.

(72) Clark C. R., "Common Neck Problems," Chapter 23, Orthopaedics: Essentials of Diagnosis and Treatment, pp 285-294, 1992.

(73) Evans R. W., "Some Observations on Whiplash Injuries," Neurological Clinics, Vol. 10, No. 4, pp 975-997, November 1992.

(74) Hirsch S. A., et al., "Whiplash Syndrome: Fact or Fiction?," Orthopedic Clinics of North America, Vol. 19, No. 4, pp 791-795, 1988.

(75) Maimaris C., Barnes M. R., and Allen M. J., "'Whiplash Injuries' of the Neck: a Retrospective Study," Injury: The British Journal of Accident Surgery (1988), Vol. 19, No. 5.

(76) MaCNab I., "Acceleration Injuries of the Cervical Spine," The Journal of Bone and Joint Surgery, Vol. 46-A, No. 8, December 1964.

(77) Aubrey J. B., Dobbs A. R., and Rule B. G., "Layperson's Knowledge about the Sequelae of Minor Head Injury and Whiplash," Journal of Neurology, Neurosurgery, and Psychiatry 1989; 52: 842-846.

(78) Radonov B. P., et al., "Role of Psychosocial Stress in Recovery from Common Whiplash," The Lancet, Vol. 338: September 1991.

(79) Norris S. H., Watt I., "The Prognosis of Neck Injuries Resulting from Rearend Vehicle Collisions," The Journal of Bone and Joint Surgery, Vol. 65-B, No. 5, November 1983.

Appendix

Accident Reconstruction Definitions and Other Notes

Units Conversions

This book is written mostly in the old English "customary" units of lbs, feet and seconds. We have done this because most accident reconstructionists appear to be still using these units. Further, most police, attorneys, insurance adjusters, medics and even jurors seem more familiar with these units. However, the engineering professions (such as SAE) are trying to ween people onto the SI system (the "metric" system). The latter is used by all scientists and most engineers throughout the world. Accordingly, we give below some of the more important conversions.

MASS: 1.0 kg = 2.2 lbm = 0.068 slugs, or 1.0 lbm = 0.454 kg = 0.031 slugs.

LENGTH: 1.0 meter = 100 cm = 1000 mm = 39.37 inches = 3.28 ft. or 1.0 ft = 0.305 m

SPEED: 1.0 km/hr = 28.78 cm/s = 10.94 inches/s= 0.91 ft/s = 0.62 mph or 1.0 mph = 1.61 km/hr

1.0 m/s = 39.37 inches/s = 3.28 ft/s = 2.236 mph or 1.0 mph = 0.447 m/s

ENERGY: 1.0 Joule = 1.0 Nm = 0.2247 lb x 3.28 ft = 0.737 lb-ft or 1.0 lb-ft = 1.36 Nm = 1.36 Joule

POWER: 1.0 kWatt = 1.34 hp or 1.0 hp = 0.746 kWatt

FORCE: 1.0 N = 0.2247 lb or 1.0 lb = 4.45 N

ACCELERATION: 1.0 g = 32.2 ft/s^2 = 9.81 m/s^2

Units and Dimensions

- *Mass* (m) is a measure of the quantity of matter, such as how many atoms, and is measured in *slugs* or *kg*.
- *Weight* (w) is a measure of the *force* acting on a mass due to *gravity*, and is measured in *lbsf* or *Newtons (N).*
- *Gravity* (g) is the *acceleration* given to a body in free fall, and is *roughly constant* everywhere on the Earth.

- $g = 32.2$ ft/s/s $= 32.2$ ft/s^2 , or $g = 9.81$ m/s^2 $= 981$ cm/s^2
  w = lbsf or N.
  1.0 lbf = 0.454 kg x 9.81 m/s^2 = 4.45 N, or 1.0 N = 0.225 lbf
  m = w/g = slugs or kg
  1.0 slug = 1.0 lb/g = 1.0 lb/ 32.2 ft/s^2 = 0.031 lb x s^2/ft
  1.0 kg weight = 2.2 lb weight
- One Newton is the force required to accelerate one kg at 1.0 m/s^2.
  One lbf is the force required to accelerate one slug at one g.
  One poundal is the force to accelerate one slug at 1.0 ft/s^2.
- *Speed* is a *rate*: distance moved per time taken.
  Average speed is a finite distance moved divided by the finite time interval.
  Instantaneous speed is the local slope (or differential) of distance-time plot, *i.e.,* the speed at a given point in time, or a given position.
- *Velocity* is speed with a defined *direction.*
  If the speed remains constant, but the direction changes, the velocity changes.
- *Acceleration* is a *rate*: velocity changed per period of time.
  Thus, any change in velocity implies an acceleration, even if the speed is constant.
  Thus, moving along a curved arc always involves an acceleration, whether due to a change in speed or simply a change in direction.
- Speed or velocity are measured in ft/s or m/s or mph, etc.
  Acceleration is measured in ft/s^2 or m/s^2 or mph/h, etc.
  Deceleration is *negative* acceleration (slowing down instead of speeding up).
- *Linear Momentum* is the product of *mass* times *velocity.*
- *Angular Momentum* is the product of *mass* times *velocity* times a *fixed distance* perpendicular to the motion.
- *Impulse* is a rapid change in momentum.
- *Linear acceleration* is a change in velocity along a straight line path.
- *Angular (rotational) acceleration* is a change in velocity along a curved path.
- *Centrifugal force* is the *apparent* force that "pulls" a body "outward" when traveling along a curved path.
- *Centripetal force* is the *actual* force necessary to "pull" a body "inward" when traveling along a curved path (*i.e.*, forcing the body to follow the path).

- *Kinetic energy* (KE) is the energy possessed by a body due to its motion.
  Linear KE is due to straight-line motion.
  Angular (rotational) KE is due to motion along a curved arc.
- *Potential energy* (PE) is energy *stored* by virtue of a body's position. This can be due to a change in height (falling off a cliff, running down a hill, etc.), or can be due to compression and/or tension (squeezing a spring, etc.). This type of energy can be *recovered* by *reversing* the process.
- *Absorbed energy* (AE) is energy which is *permanently* converted into another form, such as skidding on a road, crushing a vehicle, generating heat and/or sound and/or light.
- Units for linear momentum are lb-s or N-s
  Units for angular momentum are lb-s-ft or N-s-m
  Units for KE, PE and AE are ft-lb or N-m (or Joules)
- *Dimensional Analysis* is the process of verifying an equation by checking the "dimensions." These dimensions are: M (for mass), L (for length) and T (for time). Speed or velocity are thus L/T, Acceleration is L/T^2 , Force is ML/T^2, Energy (all forms) is $M(L/T)^2$, Linear Momentum is M(L/T), Angular Momentum is $M(L^2/T)$.
  If the equation is "correct" then the dimensions on the left of the "equals sign" will match those on the right hand side; *e.g.,* Energy = Force x distance. So $M(L/T)^2 = M(L/T^2)L$.

Newton's Three Laws

- *(1) Steady State (Law of Inertia)*: Any body remains as it was unless an external force acts on it. Thus a stationary body remains at rest unless you push or pull it, and a moving body continues moving at constant velocity unless you push or pull on it.
- (2) If a force is applied to a body then the body will accelerate in proportion to the magnitude of the force and inversely according to the mass of the body.
  Thus a = F/m, or F = m x a, where F is the force, m is the mass and a is the acceleration. The acceleration is along the direction of the force, and vice versa.
- (3) For every action (force) there is an equal and opposite reaction. Thus, in order to push on a body, the body must "push back."

These three laws explain many effects. For example, if a force acts on a body the latter may accelerate (or decelerate). This means its speed increases (or decreases) and thus its KE increases (or decreases). Thus, the force must have done *work* on the body and the body gained (or lost) energy. The work done is given by the force *in the direction of the distance* times the distance. Forces which are perpendicular to the motion do not provide work.

The force is also the *net* force acting. If two equal forces act on a body but in opposite directions (on opposite sides) then the body does not accelerate. Instead, the body compresses (two pushes) or extends (two pulls). If two unequal forces are acting then the balanced portions compress (or extend) the body, while the remaining unbalanced portion provides the net acceleration. For example, if the force on one side is a push of 1200 lbf, and on the other side is a push force of 900 lbf (acting in the opposite direction), then this can be considered as a compression of the body due to two 900 lbf actions and an acceleration of the body due to the "excess" 300 lbf on the first side.

The laws also explain why, when two bodies collide one must slow down while the other speeds up, until usually both bodies reach a common speed. If the impact involved the storage of some energy (as in compressing springs) then some of the energy is returned in the form of a bounce between the bodies. When this happens the "bullet" is slowed even more and the "target" is sped up even more. This happens because of the action/reaction (law 3). Since each body is in contact with the other for the *same* time, then the product of *Force x time* is equal and opposite for each. This product is the *impulse*, and numerically equal to the changes in momentum of each body. Thus momentum is conserved.

Conservation of Momentum and Energy

Linear Momentum

Whenever two bodies impact linear momentum must be conserved. This means that *along any straight line* (*e.g.* a defined axis) the momentum must remain constant. For an in-line (collinear) collision, only one axis is defined. For a collision at an angle (either incoming or outgoing, or both) two orthogonal axes (*i.e.*, axes at 90°) can be defined, and the momentum must remain constant along each axis independently. For the angled collision, the two momenta along the two orthogonal axes also define a *total* momentum for both vehicles (see vectors, later). This total momentum must also remain constant.

Momentum is mostly exchanged between the vehicles *during* the impact. However, some is also transferred to the ground during the impact, either due to braking or a side skid, or an impact with a rigid object attached to the ground.

The brake/skid ground effect is usually only important for low speeds *during* the impact, but can be very important *after* the impact.

Angular Momentum

During an impact the angular momentum must also be conserved. This simply means that if a reference point is chosen (this can be arbitrary, but is usually chosen to agree with a known center of rotation), then the product of momenta times the perpendicular distance to the reference point must remain constant.

Turning Torque

"Torque" is also known as "moment" or "couple." In all cases the torque is the product of a force times the perpendicular distance to a point of rotation. TO REMEMBER, try this old physics joke: "Every *couple* has its *moments*, but we won't *torque* about that!" The effect of applying a torque to a body is to produce an angular acceleration. The angular acceleration is proportional to the magnitude of the torque and inversely proportional to the *moment of inertia* of the body (discussed later). This is the analog to a force producing linear acceleration for a mass.

Energy

All forms of energy must be conserved. However, the different forms can be exchanged with each other. Thus PE can be converted into KE (car runs down hill and increases its speed). KE can be converted into PE (spring is compressed). KE can be converted into AE (car crush, tire skid). See figure 48.

Scalars and Vectors

A scalar quantity is one which has magnitude *only*, such as speed, mass, time and all forms of energy. A vector has both magnitude *and* direction, such as weight, force, velocity, torque, momentum and angular momentum.

Basic Equations of Motion

Linear acceleration

The fundamental equation relating force (F), mass (m) and accel (a) is

$$F = m \times a \text{ , or } F = (\tfrac{w}{g}) \times a, \text{ or } a = \tfrac{F}{m}, \text{ or } a = (\tfrac{g}{w}) \times F$$

Whenever linear acceleration is involved the following applies

$$s_2 - s_1 = v_0 \times (t_2 - t_1) + \tfrac{1}{2} \times a \times (t_2^2 - t_1^2)$$

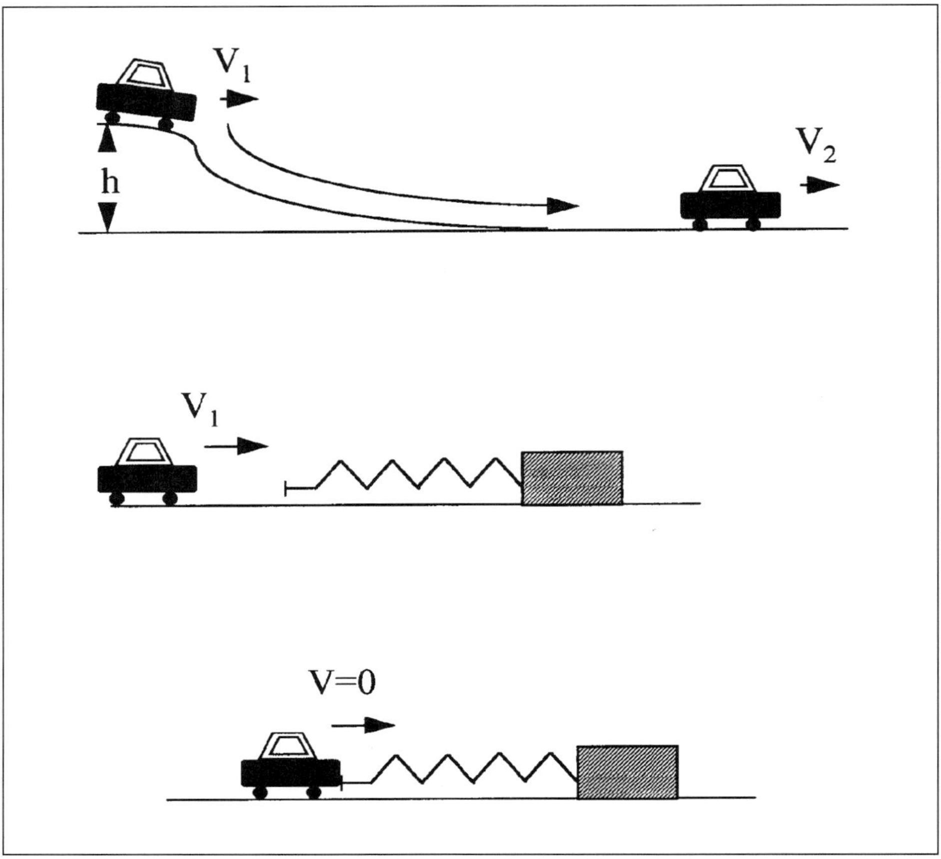

Figure 48 *Energy Conversions.*

where s_2 and s_1 are distances at times t_2 and t_1 , v_0 is the initial speed and a is the accel.

$$v_2 - v_1 = a \text{ x } (t_2 - t_1)$$

$$v_2^{\,2} - v_1^{\,2} = 2 \text{ x } a \text{ x } (s_2 - s_1)$$

where v_2 and v_1 are speeds corresponding to the distances and/or times. The value of a is (+) for increasing speed, and (-) for slowing down.

If the acceleration changes over either time ranges or distance ranges the equations are "ganged" to obtain the final result. Thus we may write

$$s_3 - s_1 = (s_3 - s_2) + (s_2 - s_1), \textit{ etc.}$$

$$v_3 - v_1 = (v_3 - v_2) + (v_2 + v_1) = a_{3\text{-}2} \text{ x } (t_3 - t_2) + a_{2\text{-}1} \text{ x } (t_2 - t_1), \textit{ etc.}$$

$$v_3^{\,2} - v_1^{\,2} = (v_3^{\,2} - v_2^{\,2}) + (v_2^{\,2} - v_1^{\,2}) = 2 \text{ x } a_{3\text{-}2} \text{ x } (s_3 - s_2) + 2 \text{ x } a_{2\text{-}1} \text{ x } (s_2 - s_1), \text{ etc.}$$

where $a_{3\text{-}2}$ is the value of accel for step 3-2, and $a_{2\text{-}1}$ is value for step 2-1.

Angular acceleration

The fundamental relationship for angular acceleration is

$$F \times r = I \times \ddot{\theta} \text{ or } \ddot{\theta} = F \times \frac{r}{I} = \dot{\omega}$$

where $\ddot{\theta}$ is the angular accel in radians/s^2 (one radian = 180°/π = 57.3°), r is the torque-arm, and I is the moment of inertia about the rotation point. The angular acceleration can also be defined as $\ddot{\theta} = \dot{\omega}$ where ω is the value of radians/s. Note that the use of ".." (two dots) over a symbol means " /s^2 " (per sec^2), while "." (one dot) means " /s" (per sec).

Mass-Spring response

For any system that behaves as a mass on a spring (occupant in the seat, bumper on a car), the equation for an *undamped* oscillation is

$$\omega^2 = \left(\frac{k}{m}\right) = \left(\frac{kg}{W}\right)$$

where ω is the angular oscillation rate (radians/s), k is the spring constant (change in force per unit distance of spring compression), m is the mass and W is the weight.

It is probably NOT obvious why the response is quoted in terms of ANGULAR motion. To help explain consider the following.

Imagine a mass rotating about a pivot at constant local speed with a fixed radial distance to the pivot. As seen "sideways" the body is simply moving in a circle. Now suppose you viewed the circular motion "edge-on" such that the circle collapses to a thin "line" (*i.e.*, you draw the circle on paper and then view the paper edge-on). The rotating body will now appear to move "up and down" along this line. However, since we now see the edge motion the speed appears fastest when the mass is near the middle of the line and slowest when near the two ends. This is *identical* to the observed motion of a mass on a spring.

Going further, suppose two identical masses were *counter-rotating* about a pivot (one clockwise and one counterclockwise), but at the same speed. Let the positioning (known as the *phasing)* be such that the two masses meet each other at the top of the circle and again at the bottom of the circle. Once again, if viewed "edge-on" the two masses would look like *one* mass oscillating "up and down."

The "edge view" is of the *components* of the motion, and involve sines and cosines of the true mass(es) positions. For example, when the masses are at the "top" or "bottom" of the circle, they are at either "end" of the straight-line.

At these points the radial lines are seen fully in profile and each "half line" has the length 'r' = $r_0$sin θ = r_0 , since θ = 90°. At the center of the "line," however, 'r' = $r_0$sin θ = 0, since θ = 0°.

Thus any *circular* motion can be broken down into equivalent *angular* motion.

The apparent motion of the rotating mass(es) will be of the form

$$r(t) = r_0 \text{ x } \sin(\omega \text{ x } t) = \sin\theta \text{ x } r_0$$

where r(t) means position from the center of the straight line as a function of time, t, r_0 is the constant true radial distance, ω is the corresponding angular rate (radians/s) and θ is the corresponding angle (radians) measured from the line pointing "at" the observer.

Now, since , ω = $2\pi f$ where f is the frequency (cycles/s or Hertz), we get

$$f = \left(\frac{1}{2\pi}\right)\sqrt{\frac{kg}{W}}$$

or since the period T = 1/f, we get

$$T = 2\pi\sqrt{\frac{W}{kg}}$$

where the period is in seconds, for a weight in lbs and a spring constant in lb/ft, and g in ft/s^2. Note that the period is for one complete cycle.

Thus, the period increases with the square-root of the weight and inversely with the square-root of the spring constant. So a rigid spring (high spring constant) and a small weight oscillate at a high frequency, and a soft spring and large weight oscillate at a low frequency. These effects are important for understanding how occupants can bounce in their seats. For example, with a rearender the person is driven forward with the vehicle *only* because the seat pushes on them. The result is to initially compress the seat. Eventually, the person "catches up" with the car, at which point the seat is at maximum compression. Then the seat continues to act like a spring and pushes the person forward *faster* than the car. If the seatbelt doesn't lock up quickly (and they frequently *don't* for rearend collisions) then the occupant can actually hit the steering wheel. The typical time period for these motions is a small fraction of a second.

Compressing a bumper also acts like a spring, and even the crushing response of a car is somewhat spring-like (the car gets stiffer as it crushes). The high stiffness of bumpers and frame relative to the weight of the vehicle cause high frequency response. Consequently, the contact time for many crashes is only about 0.1 - 0.2s. Because there is nearly always some relaxation of the bumper or frame, the two vehicles nearly always bounce to some extent, causing gaps between them after the collision. Note that unless there is some form of "sticking" between the vehicles, such as interlocked bumpers, or between the occupant and the seat (tight belt), these motions are really "half-cycle" oscillations, since the second half does not exist because the bodies "come apart" after the first half cycle.

Braking Effects

General Factors

If no wheels lock up a vehicle can be steered provided the lateral forces needed to cause the car to follow a path (curved or otherwise) do not exceed the maximum possible for the tire/road combination. However, once the frictional limit is exceeded then no steering is possible for that tire. This means that the tire in question wants to travel in the direction governed by the rest of the car's motion. If an axle locks up then the axle wants to travel in a direction which either depends on the motion of the rest of the car or on the initial motion of that axle. When all tires lock the entire vehicle travels with its center-of-mass (CM) moving according to any external forces. Thus, on a flat level road, the CM travels in a straight line, whereas, on a cambered surface the CM follows a path governed by gravity, which usually means the vehicle slides off to the side of the road.

Speed-from-skid analysis can be done based on considerations of the basic equations of motion, or based on energy arguments. Note that energy arguments are the more basic and fundamental.

The standard equation of motion approach is to use

$$v = \sqrt{2 \text{ x } f \text{ x } g \text{ x } s}$$

where s is the observed skid mark distance and f is the *net coefficient of friction* or, more properly, the *drag factor*. The drag factor is the overall effective friction between the vehicle and the road. Each individual tire may have a different coefficient of friction, μ, and each wheel may have a differing weight on it of w. Then the total drag on the vehicle is

$$(f \text{ x } W) = \Sigma(w \text{ x } \mu) = (w_1 \text{ x } \mu_1) + (w_2 \text{ x } \mu_2) + (w_3 \text{ x } \mu_3) + (w_4 \text{ x } \mu_4),$$

where

$$W = w_1 + w_2 + w_3 + w_4$$

The energy approach is to equate the lost KE with the frictional energy given to the road surface, *i.e.*, with the product of the drag force and the skid distance. Thus,

$$KE = \frac{W}{2g} \times v^2 = f \times W \times s$$

which can be rewritten as

$$v^2 = 2 \text{ x } f \text{ x } g \text{ x } s$$

which is the same as the equation above. The major advantage to the energy method is that it immediately allows for other energy terms to be included, such as that due to crush or due to change in elevation. For example, if a car firsts skids and then impacts a rigid barrier to lose crush energy E_c , then we write

$$KE = \frac{W}{2g} \times v^2 = (f \times W \times s) + E_c$$

$$v^2 = (2 \times f \times g \times s) + \frac{2g}{W} \times E_c$$

Thus, by knowing *both* the skid behavior and the crush energy, the initial speed can be obtained directly.

Number of Tire Tracks

When a car skids there may be anywhere from one to four skid marks (*i.e.*, up to one per wheel). What does this imply for the net drag factor? Assuming no definite proof of brake failure, or knowledge that an axle does not have brakes, the usual assumption is that those wheels not giving skids are providing at least as much friction as those wheels that are giving skid marks (but this should be checked).

The logic behind this is that tires will first climb to a maximum in friction, and will then drop in friction as the slip between tire and road increases. Those wheels with the lowest ratio of friction to vertical load will skid first. Thus the assumption is that the tires giving the skid marks have already passed the limit, whereas, the other tires are just about to reach their limit. This logic then suggests that the *longest* skid mark is the one to use to establish the pre-skid speed.

Differing surfaces

Of course, sometimes the various wheels may be on different surfaces known to give different friction. In this case the appropriate value of friction should be applied to each wheel in turn, using the fractional weight of the vehicle on each wheel. An example is when a car is half-off a road with two wheels running on dirt. Another example is when the car sequentially skids across several in-line surfaces. For this case, the energy loss per surface must be computed. Thus

$$KE = \frac{W}{2g} \times v^2 = f_1 \times W \times s_1 + f_2 \times W \times s_2 + f_3 \times W \times s_3, etc$$

$$v^2 = \frac{2g}{W} \times (f_1 \times W \times s_1 + f_2 \times W \times s_2 + f_3 \times W \times s_3) = 2g \times (f_1 \times s_1 + f_2 \times s_2 + f_3 \times s_3)$$

where the f values represent the mean drag factors over the various s distances.

Linear Skids and Yaw Marks

True skid marks are essentially straight and show striations parallel to the skid. They are caused by the non-rotating tire leaving rubber on the road according to the tread design, or scraping on the asphalt or dirt. When a tire slides sideways with a non-rotating wheel, a skid mark is also left, but the treads are usually less distinct (they can overlap). However, if the tire is rotating and sliding sideways the result is not a true skid but rather a yaw mark.

For a yaw, the mark will show "side lines" which run *across* the "skid." If the wheel is undergoing free rotation (no acceleration or deceleration) these marks are essentially perpendicular to the major longitudinal mark. For a wheel undergoing acceleration along its motion, the side-marks are observed to "lean backwards" relative to the major mark, whereas, for a wheel undergoing deceleration, the side marks "lean forward." The reason for these side marks is that the slipping/rotating tire is really "screwing" its way along the road, and thus the marks are those of a corkscrew. See figure 49.

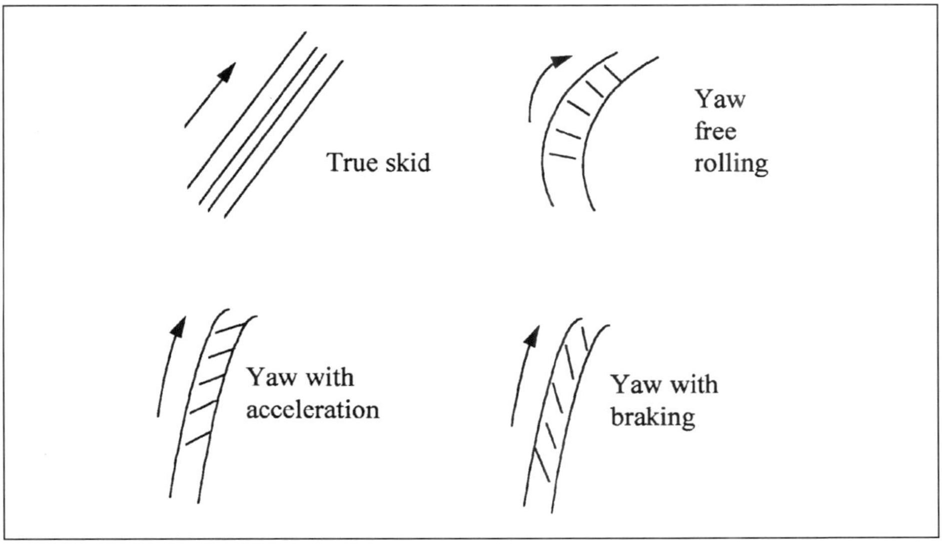

Figure 49 *Tire Marks.*

The Friction Circle

As a first approximation it can be assumed that the maximum friction possible between a tire and the road is the *same* regardless of the direction of motion of the tire versus the road (*i.e.*, along the rolling direction or perpendicular to it). This leads to the concept of the *friction circle*. This states that the *net* maximum friction can never exceed an upper limit for a given tire/surface combination, defined as a *radial vector* (see vectors, later). Thus, if the *vector sum* of the longitudinal and transverse frictional forces equal or exceed this radial value, no further increase in friction is possible, regardless of tire direction. This means that if the tire is almost at the longitudinal limit of skidding then any additional side slipping will immediately cause a true skid of the tire in the direction of motion of the vehicle. Likewise, if the side slip force is almost at its limit, then any additional braking effort will also cause a true skid to occur. This is the reason why it can be dangerous to try to sharply steer *and* brake hard at the same time. See figure 50.

Tracking the Arc

If a car both skids and rotates, the true definition of the skid mark length is that *along* the individual arcs, not merely that along the CM motion of the vehicle. This is because, for a true skid the energy consumed is due to forces which

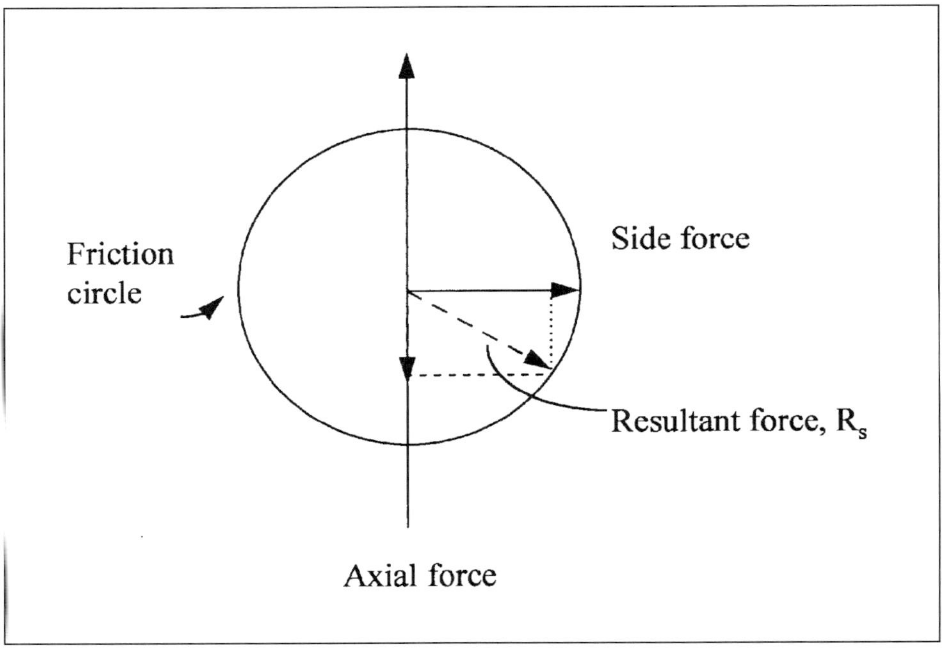

Figure 50 *Tire/Road Friction Circle.*

act along the local arc direction. However, frequently the degree of rotation is small relative to the CM distance, and can thus be ignored as a first approximation. If the rotation dominates the total motion, the true arc lengths must be used.

Road Grade and Camber

Usually, most roads have quite low grades such that the latter can be ignored for many cases of skidding. However, when significant the grade can be included by using

$$f_{net} = \frac{\mu+G}{\sqrt{1+G^2}}$$

where f_{net} is the net drag, μ is the true friction and G is the grade. If the vehicle is skidding uphill the value of G is (+), whereas, for skidding downhill G is (-). If the road additionally has a significant side camber the result for a skidding car is to produce a "gravitational trajectory" causing the vehicle to slowly slide sideways off the road, with a path which describes a parabolic section. This parabolic path is really the same as that for a body which falls at the same time as it moves horizontally (see flips and vaults, later), except that it occurs on a flatter surface rather than involving a truly vertical fall. This simply reduces the effective value of gravity (g) ($g' = g \sin \theta$, where θ is the slope off horizontal).

Critical Yaw Speeds

When a vehicle follows a curved path it does so only because there are side forces acting on the tires which force the vehicle to make the turn (the centripetal forces). These necessary forces will eventually exceed the local maximum value of friction, at which point sideslip yawing will occur. The corresponding maximum speed when this occurs is known as the *critical yaw speed*. Because a force is really a product of mass and acceleration, the critical speed can be understood by considering the lateral accelerations.

When turning a curve at speed v and radius R, it can be shown that the corresponding radial acceleration (centripetal) is given by

$$accel = \frac{v^2}{R} = R \times \omega^2$$

where ω is the corresponding angular rate of change (radians per sec). To cause the tire to follow this curved path, the corresponding side tire force is

$F = f \times W$ where W is the weight and f the friction. Then, equating accelerations

$$accel = \frac{v^2}{R} = \frac{F}{m} = \frac{g \times F}{W} = g \times f \text{ and thus}$$

$$v_{crit}^2 = g \times f \times R \text{ or } v_{crit} = \sqrt{g \times f \times R}$$

Thus the critical speed depends on the square-root of the product of the friction and the radius of the curve.

Perception/Reaction Time (PIEV)

There is always a time delay between a driver first seeing a possible problem and actually reacting to it. This time delay has several components, which are known as *Perception* (an event is noticed), *Interpretation* (the event is recognized as a threat), *Evaluation* (the appropriate response is decided) and *Volition* (the action is taken, such as applying the brakes). Hence: *PIEV*.

The actual components take differing times, depending on the individual and the circumstances of the situation. Typically, *Perception* lasts for about 0.1 - 0.2 s, whereas *Interpretation* takes about 0.2 - 0.4 s. *Evaluation* can last from 0.2 - 1.0 s, and depends strongly on the complexity of the situation (*e.g.*, how many options may exist for a solution). *Volition* is the actual act of motion (applying the brakes, or turning the steering wheel) and can take from 0.2 - 0.5 s. Thus, for a simple reaction (brake or no-brake) the total PIEV is from 0.7 - 2.1 s, with a frequently quoted average of about 1.0 s. All the above quotes assume a reasonably alert driver who is sober. Alcohol can increase these times up to 3 - 4 s. For road design purposes (AASHTO) a response time of 2.5 s is frequently used. However, this "long" time is intended to include even slow-witted or partially impaired drivers, and is NOT a true definition of "typical" response time. See figure 51.

Skid Marks at Low Speed

It is frequently assumed that for strongly applied brakes skid marks can always be created regardless of speed. However, this ignores the timing issues in PIEV. In reality, once the decision to brake is made the foot is removed from the throttle and then moved to the brake. As this happens the car begins to slow merely due to the fact that it is suffering engine drag. Further, even when the foot reaches the brake, there is still a finite time delay before maximum braking effort can be applied. During these times the car is decelerating. Consequentially, for a slow enough initial speed, it is possible for the car to effectively stop *before* skidding can be induced. To complicate the matter, tire/road friction is usually highest at low speeds. Hence, for slow speeds (below about 3 mph) it is possible to rapidly stop a vehicle *without* producing skid marks even for attempted very hard braking. Also, tire/asphalt marks require heating which is small at low speeds.

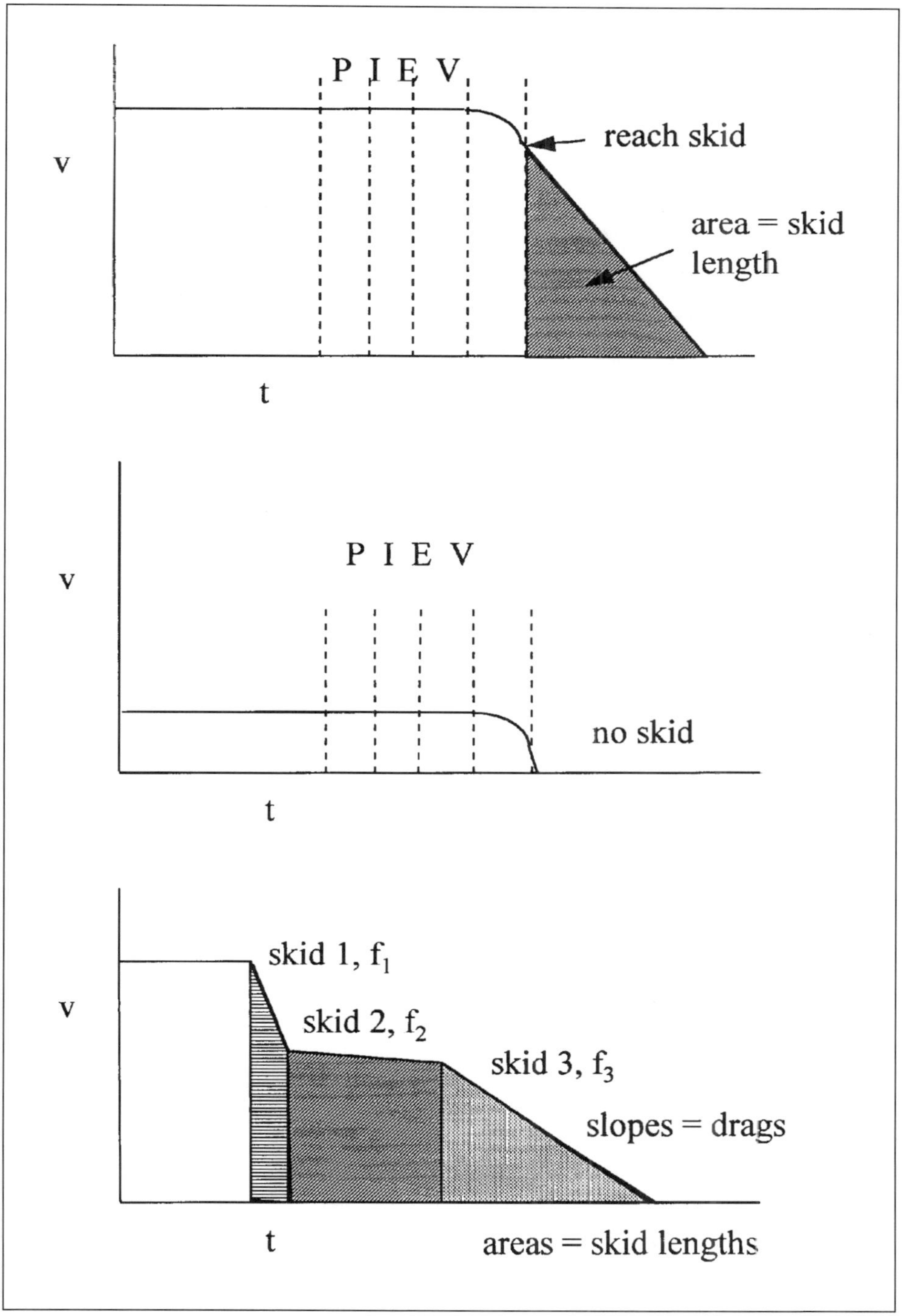

Figure 51 *Reaction Timing and Skidding.*

Final Point

It should always be remembered that braking can occur *without* leaving skid marks. This rather obvious fact is sometimes overlooked. The speed estimated from skid marks is always the *lowest* possible, since it is possible for the vehicle to have been applying the brakes prior to actual skidding without leaving clear evidence. For example, a driver perceives a need to brake and starts to do so with gentle force. However, the driver then realizes that he won't stop in time, and so then he slams the brakes on hard and causes skidding. Clearly, *none* of the pre-skid behavior will leave direct evidence.

Of course, it is also rare that the actual coefficient of friction for a given case is known. Attempts to replicate the situation don't always work either. The problem is that the vehicle used for tests should have the same type of tires, the road surface should be identical to that for the accident (at that time), and the temperature should be the same (since tire and road performance can change). Lastly, a trial test may wrongly account for reaction time. Frequently, the trial test yields *too high* an apparent friction versus that which effectively applied at the time of the accident, which in turn gives estimates for the crash speed which err on the high side.

The Concept of Vectors

Definition of a Vector

A vector is a quantity which has both magnitude and direction. Examples include velocity, momentum and force. A vector is drawn as an "arrow," with a "head" (tip) and a "tail." Its length represents the magnitude of the quantity, and its direction indicates the direction of the quantity. Any convenient "scale" can be used (example: one inch equal 5 lb-s for momentum), and any direction on the paper (or whiteboard, etc.) can represent the required initial wanted direction (rather like arbitrarily drawing North on a sketch).

Properties

Any vector can be redrawn as a pair of other vectors which are then called *components* of the original vector. The most common use for this is to draw these components as two vectors which are at 90° to each other (*i.e.*, orthogonal), and which have the two components along required orthogonal axes. The converse of this is that any two initial vectors can be drawn to give either the *sum* or the *difference* of the two vectors.

Vector Sum

Two vectors can be summed in the following way. First draw the two vectors with their "tails" joining. Now "complete the parallelogram" by drawing two "ghost" vectors from the "heads" of the first two vectors such that the two ghosts are parallel and equal to the initial two vectors. The result is to draw a parallelogram. The "diagonal" which joins the two mutual "tails" of the first two vectors and the new "head" of the parallelogram gives the *sum* of the two vectors.

Vector Difference

For the same parallelogram, the "diagonal" which extends between the two heads of the initial vectors gives the *difference* of the two vectors.

Uses of Vectors

Vectors are used whenever directional quantities need to be added or subtracted. Examples include adding forces to find the equivalent net force, adding momenta to establish the net momentum and subtracting velocities to find the effective closing velocity between two moving bodies. In all cases the new information gives both the magnitude and direction. Adding is simply finding the *sum*, whereas subtracting is finding the *difference*.

The most common use for vectors in accident reconstruction is to establish total momentum for a two body collision, and from this, establish the initial speeds and directions of each body before impact.

The Two-Car Crash Using Vectors

Whenever a two-car crash is to be solved there are generally *seven* (7) *momentum* vectors to be drawn. These are: the two *output momentum* vectors (one per car), the two *input momentum* vectors, the common *total momentum* vector, and the two *difference momentum* vectors. See figure 52.

The problem is solved in reverse. From a knowledge of the post-impact vehicle speeds (*e.g.*, based on skid marks, etc.), vehicle masses and initial directions *leaving* the crash (note NOT necessarily the same as the overall final directions) the two *output momentum* vectors can be drawn. From these two vectors the *total momentum* vector can be derived (completing the parallelogram).

This *total momentum* vector must remain the same as the one for the two *input momentum* vectors. Thus any choice for these input vectors *must* give the same final total momentum vector. Usually, at least one of the vehicle's pre-crash motions are known (speed and direction). Thus, for this vehicle an *input momentum* vector can be drawn. Then completing the parallelogram based on the total momentum vector allows deduction of the missing input momentum vector for

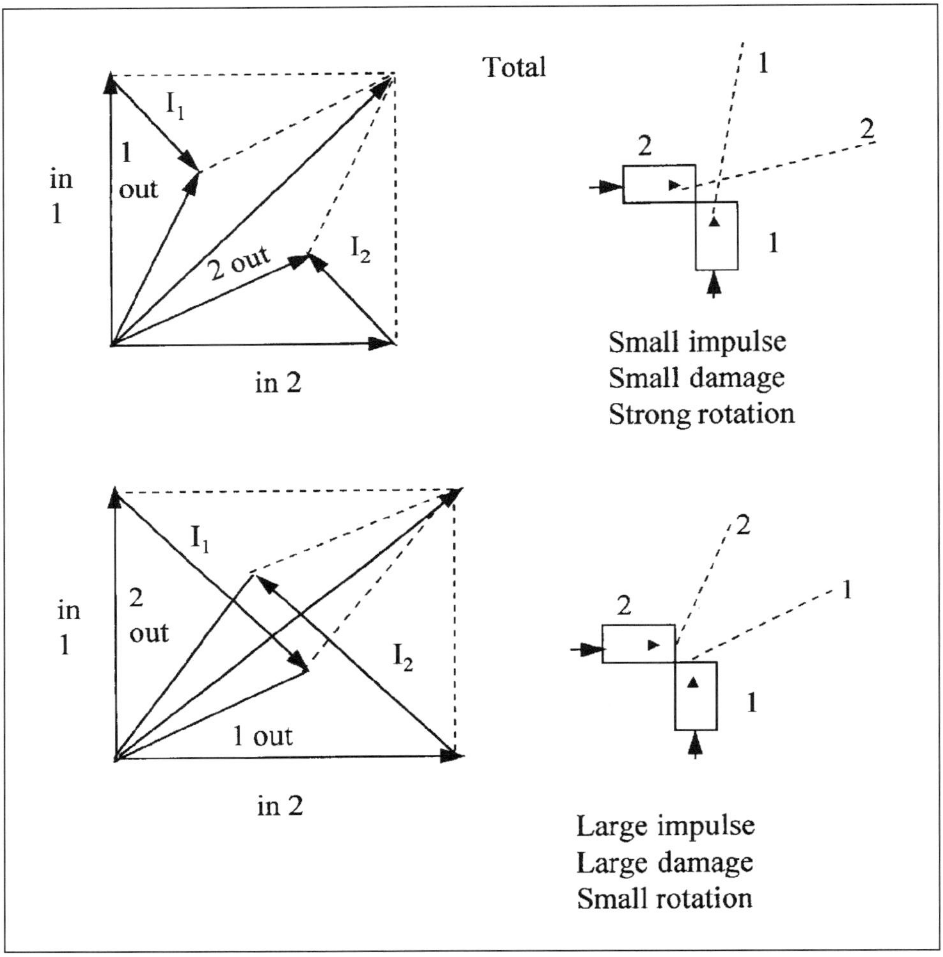

Figure 52 *Two-Vehicle Vector-Momentum Logic.*

the other vehicle. Since the vehicle mass is known, the speed and direction are known.

Once the input and output momentum vectors are known, then the *difference* vectors can be derived. These are the vectors that stretch between the "heads" of the "input" and "output" momentum vectors *for each vehicle independently.* If done properly, it will be found that these two difference vectors are *equal in magnitude and opposite in direction* (and parallel to each other but not usually collinear). These two difference momentum vectors describe the two *impulses* seen by each vehicle. The direction of these difference vectors defines the Principal Direction Of Force: PDOF.

Sometimes, the exact input vector is not known for either vehicle. In this case, an estimate of the PDOF gives details of the direction of the difference vectors. Thus knowing the PDOF can allow estimation of the input conditions since the overall reconstruction must give the difference vectors in accordance with the PDOF, while the total momentum vector also constrains the options.

Trips / Flips / Vaults and Roll-overs

Definitions

A trip is any general process whereby a vehicle is rapidly decelerated at the contact point between the wheels and ground, such that the vehicle proceeds to start a spin. If the resulting spin involves little lift off the ground then it is usually a form of rollover, especially for sideways rotation. If the result is to launch significantly into the air then for a side rotation it is called a flip, whereas, for an end-over-end rotation it is called a vault.

Side Rolls (Rollovers)

A vehicle can only roll over sideways (about its longitudinal axis) if the rotational turning torque is greater than the restoring gravitational torque. For a side-slip motion on a road the side force is that due to the tire friction and equal to F = f x W. This force acts as one through the CM together with a torque of F x h = f x W x h, where h is the height above the ground of the CM. The restoring gravitational torque is W x T/2, where T is the track width. Thus to cause rolling we need

$$f \times W \times h \geq W \times \tfrac{T}{2} \quad \text{or} \quad f \geq \tfrac{T}{2 \times h}$$

For *most* cars $T \geq 2 \times h$, and so the vehicle can *not* roll simply due to side friction, because f is almost always *less* than 1.0. However, some "sport utility" vehicles have unusually high CMs and small wheel tracks. For these vehicles a high value of side friction *can* initiate a roll. Once a roll starts the situation rapidly becomes uncontrollable. This is because, as the vehicle tips over (balancing on only one set of wheels on one side) the CM rises which increases the turning torque, while the effective track width decreases owing to the inclination of the vehicle. Thus, for a rotation about the side wheels we have

$$R^2 = h_0^2 + (\tfrac{T_0}{2})^2$$

where R is the diagonal between the side wheel/road and the CM. This defines an initial angle for this diagonal relative to the road surface. See figure 53.

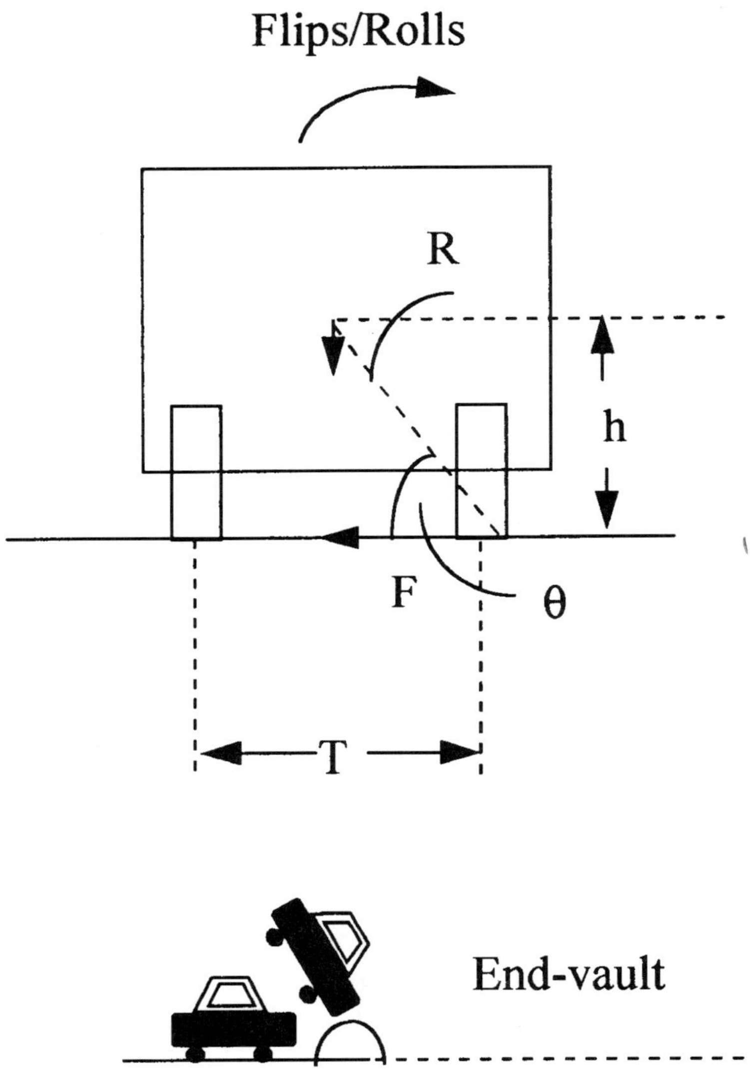

Figure 53 *Roll Logic.*

$$\sin\theta_0 = \frac{h_0}{R} \text{ or } h_0 = R \times \sin\theta_0 \text{ and } \frac{T_0}{2} = R \times \cos\theta_0$$

where h_0 and $T_0/2$ are the true initial values before rolling. As rolling progresses, the value of θ increases causing the local value of h to increase while the local value of T/2 decreases. Therefore, the situation becomes ever less stable, and can only be corrected by *very fast countermeasures*, such as a quick counter-steer.

However, if the vehicle impacts a *rigid low object* (*e.g.* a curb) then the effective value of f is much larger than simple friction. For this case a roll can easily be induced. The limit to cause a complete roll is given by the condition that the vehicle KE sideways be greater than the energy needed to lift the CM to a vertical position above the side wheels. This "lift" is simply $H = R - h_0$, and the corresponding change in PE is W x H. Thus the car can roll if

$$\frac{W}{2\times g} \times v_{CM}^2 \geq W \times H = W \times (R - h_0) = W \times [\sqrt{(h_0^2 + \frac{T_0^2}{4})} - h_0]$$

$$v_{CM}^2 \geq 2 \times g \times [\sqrt{(h_0^2 + \frac{T_0^2}{4})} - h_0]$$

If this condition is not reached the car will start to rise but will not complete the roll. The velocity is the one perpendicular to the "curb." Similar effects occur if the curb is replaced with a "rut," in short with anything which can suddenly stop the wheel side motion.

Ordinarily, merely steering a vehicle around a curve will not induce a roll because the maximum side force is still limited by tire friction. However, the situation can occur if the vehicle turns in an "uphill" direction when on a "sloped road." For example, let a vehicle be traveling North on a road which leans "down" toward the East. The vehicle makes a sharp left turn to the West. The vehicle will transfer weight to the right hand wheels. However, due to the initial lean the CM will be higher than normal with respect to these RH wheels, while the effective track width will also be shorter than normal. This is equivalent to altering the initial value of the angle θ. Thus a vehicle which is normally stable on a horizontal road may become unstable on a sloped road. This effect is quite common for "off-road" driving where a vehicle may try to go "sideways" up a dirt hill and then turn sharply in the "up" direction.

Vaults

A similar "forward flip" can occur if the front of the vehicle is suddenly stopped by a low rigid object (a high curb or large rock). This object must be sufficiently high to prevent the front wheels from simply riding up over the obstacle. For such a forward flip the half-wheel base is involved instead of the half-track width. Since the wheel base is usually significantly longer than the track width, the ability to flip is less than for a side flip.

For sufficiently high impact speed these flips may cause the vehicle to become airborne, in which case we have a *vault*. Except for very high speeds where air-drag must be included (usually above 50 mph) the trajectory is governed by gravity. The path followed by the vehicle is a *ballistic trajectory*. Let the motion involve an initial speed of v_0 at an angle θ to the horizontal. The velocity vector has two components, namely, a vertical velocity of $v_v = v_0 \times \sin\theta$ and a horizontal velocity of $v_h = v_0 \times \cos\theta$. The vertical velocity will be reduced to zero by gravity in the time $t = v_v/g$. During this time the vehicle CM will rise a distance given by the energy balance equation

$$\frac{W}{2\times g} \times (v_0 \times \sin\theta)^2 = W \times H \quad \text{or } H = \frac{v_0^2 \times \sin^2\theta}{2\times g}$$

while the horizontal distance moved is given by

$$D = v_0 \times \cos\theta \times \frac{v_0}{g} \times \sin\theta = \frac{v_0^2}{g} \times \sin\theta \times \cos\theta$$

For a flat horizontal ground this will describe the half-trajectory. Thus the time to return to the ground is the same as the rise time, and the total horizontal distance moved before re-impacting the ground is 2 x D. Thus the total distance is

$$D_{total} = \frac{2\times v_0^2}{g} \times \sin\theta \times \cos\theta$$

It is easily shown that the product sinθ x cosθ is a maximum when θ = 45°, with a value

$$\sqrt{\frac{1}{2}} \times \sqrt{\frac{1}{2}} = \frac{1}{2}$$

Thus

$$D_{total,Max} = \frac{v_0^2}{g}.$$

This equation then gives the *lowest* speed necessary to produce a given total horizontal motion. For any other launch angle the speed must increase. In the absence of a known launch angle the value of 45^0 is frequently assumed in order to obtain conservative speeds.

If the ground is not level, such that the launch point is above the fall point by an amount Δ, then the two half-trajectories must be calculated separately. For example, if the fall point is lower than the launch point the time taken to fall is

$$H + \Delta = \frac{g}{2} \times t_{fall}^2 \quad \text{or } t_{fall} = \sqrt{\frac{2\times(H+\Delta)}{g}}$$

and during this time the horizontal motion is v_0 x cosθ x t_{fall}, etc. If the fall point is higher than the launch point we simply use $H - \Delta$ instead.

All the above treats the motion of the vehicle CM (*i.e.* we treat the vehicle as if it were a "point-mass"). This works fine provided the vertical motions are large compared to the vehicle dimensions. If not, then we should include the effects of any vehicle rotation (especially forward pitching), since the impact point may be on the nose instead of the wheels. In this case the CM is higher off the ground at impact. Some form of forward pitching always occurs, whether due to impacting a low rigid obstacle before launch or simply because the front wheels leave the ground before the back wheels do. Once the front wheels leave the ground the vehicle is balanced only on its back axle. Hence gravity starts a forward pitch about the rear axle, and an angular acceleration (nose-down) occurs. This acceleration stops when the rear axle leaves the ground, at which point the vehicle has developed a steady angular rotation rate. The total angle seen by the vehicle before re-impacting the ground is simply the product of this rotation rate and the time taken to reach the ground. Thus

$$\ddot{\theta} = W \times \frac{L}{I}$$

where L is the torque-arm equal to the distance between the CM and the back axle, and I is the moment of inertia for a *pitch motion about the rear axle.* Then

$$\dot{\theta} = \ddot{\theta} \times t = W \times \frac{L}{I} \times \frac{WB}{v}$$

where WB is the wheel base and v is the road velocity, and t_{rot} is the time between the front axle leaving the ground and the rear axle doing so. To this we must also add the angle achieved during the acceleration, which is

$$\theta = \frac{W}{2} \times \frac{L}{I} \times \left(\frac{WB}{V}\right) \times \left(\frac{WB}{V}\right)$$

Finally,

$$\theta = \dot{\theta} \times t_{fall}$$

where t_{fall} is the total fall time, and is the total rotation.

Combined Flight and Skid

Sometimes a body suffers a flight *followed* by a skid. An example is when a pedestrian is hit forward by a car. The body first flies on an airborne trajectory and then finally comes to a halt by skidding. Let the drop height for the pedestrian's CM be H, and the friction on the ground be f, and the induced initial horizontal velocity be v. Then we first compute the fall time and then the horizontal motion during the fall. Upon hitting the ground the body still has the same horizontal velocity. We next compute the resulting skid. The flight plus skid then give the total horizontal motion from the point of impact (POI). Thus,

$$t_{fall} = \sqrt{\frac{2 \times H}{g}}, D_{Horiz} = v \times \sqrt{\frac{2 \times H}{g}}, D_{skid} = \frac{v^2}{2 \times g \times f}, D_{total} = D_{Horiz} + D_{skid}$$

Thus

$$\left(\frac{v^2}{2 \times g \times f}\right) + \left(\sqrt{\frac{2 \times H}{g}} \times v\right) - D_{total} = 0$$

Compare with

$$(A \text{ x } v^2) + (B \text{ x } v) + C = 0$$

This is a *quadratic* equation, with the solution

$$v = -\frac{B}{2 \times A} \pm \frac{\sqrt{B^2 - 4 \times A \times C}}{2 \times A}$$

where

where $A = \frac{1}{2 \times g \times f}$ **and** $B = \sqrt{\frac{2 \times H}{g}}$ **and** $C = -D_{total}$.

In reality, since we need a positive solution, the term is always +.

About the Author

Alan J. Watts, Ph.D., is the chief scientist at POD Associates, Inc. in Albuquerque, NM. He received his B.Sc. (1965) and Ph.D. (1969) in physics from Exeter University, England. His Ph.D. included studies of metals using ESR (electron spin resonance) and NMR (nuclear magnetic resonance – the forerunner of the medical MRI). He performed research for the British Government at the Atomic Weapons Research Establishment, where he studied the effects of dynamic impacts, the use of high explosives, and the effects of rapid, very strong energy deposition in materials, which automatically involved the studies of shock-wave behavior and material failure modes. His studies ranged from the design of low-impulse momentum gauges to the use of high-pressure stress gauges, and the synergistic effects of thermal-mechanical material responses.

Since 1979, he has since performed research on behalf of the US Government civilian and defense agencies. His studies have emphasized the effects of material responses to various stress-strain loadings, whether weapon related or impact related. This has included producing complex computer codes to evaluate the synergistic effects of thermomechanical responses, and the use of two-stage "gas guns" to evaluate the shock response and equation-of-state of various materials. He has previously made use of three-dimensional finite element codes (3-D FE) such as DYNA-3D (using a CRAY computer), which is now used by the car industry to assess car crush behavior. Recently, he formulated scaling laws for NASA allowing predictions of cratering and/or perforations for satellite structures due to hypervelocity impacts (space debris and/or micrometeoroids with impact speeds of several miles per *second*), with results comparing favorably to large hydrodynamics codes such as CTH from Sandia National Laboratory. Materials studied have ranged from metals through various plastics and composites to elastomers and glasses, with response modes ranging from simple elastoplastic through elastoviscous to phase change effects.

Dr. Watts has performed accident analyses on behalf of both plaintiffs and defendants, and has worked for both the US Attorney's and the Public Defender's offices. He is a member of the American Association for the Advancement of Science (AAAS), and a member of the National Association of Professional Accident Reconstruction Specialists (NAPARS). He has authored over one hundred refereed technical publications and presentations.

Dale Atkinson, B.S., is a senior scientist at POD Associates, Inc., in Albuquerque, NM. He has a BS in Aeronautical Engineering from the University of Arizona. He is a member of the Society of Automotive Engineers (SAE), the National Association of Professional Accident Reconstruction Specialists (NAPARS), the National Research Council International Committee on Micrometeoroids, the National Research Council International Committee on Debris, the American Institute for Aeronautics (AIAA), the Professional Aerospace Contractors Association (PACA), and a lifetime member of the Tau Beta Pi Engineering Honor Society. He has authored over fifty refereed technical publications and presentations.

Corey J. Hennessy, M.A., is a senior scientist at POD Associates, Inc., in Albuquerque, NM. He has a BS in Physics from the University of Wisconsin-Superior, did graduate work in Physics at Montana State University, and graduated *summa cum laude* with an MA in Organizational Management from the University of Phoenix. He is a lifetime member of Sigma Pi Sigma, the national physics honor society, and has authored over twenty-five refereed technical publications and presentations.

Randall Kehl, J.D., is Chairman of the Board at POD Associates, Inc. in Albuquerque, NM. He has a Juris Doctorate from Pepperdine University School of Law; a Master of Business Administration from the University of North Dakota; and a Bachelor of Science from the United States Air Force Academy. He also served as a White House Fellow for the Office of the President. He received a Certification in Commercial Litigation from the NCA, Stanford University; an Advanced Certification in Regulatory Studies, NARUC, from Michigan State University; and is admitted to practice before the United States Supreme Court. Mr. Kehl served as Staff Counsel and Vice Chairman for the White House Working Group on the Commercialization of Federal Laboratory Technology from 1990 to 1992. Previously, he served as Chief of the Energy Branch, Civil Litigation Division, Headquarters, USAF at the Pentagon; Legal Counsel for the USAF Space Technology Center at Kirtland AFB, NM; and Chief Prosecuting Attorney, and Special Assistant US Attorney at Elmendorf, AFB, Alaska.

Index

Train Accident Reconstruction and FELA & Railroad Litigation, Second Edition with Supplement #0969

by James R. Loumiet, BSME and William G. Jungbauer, Esq.

Train collisions usually result in serious injury or death to motorists and pedestrians, often resulting in litigation. Yet the railroad industry presents complexities not known to the average person, making it difficult for an attorney to prepare a successful case. Even experienced accident reconstructionists are usually unfamiliar with the operation of railroads and trains. Yet the ability to reconstruct train collisions is often vital to the successful conduct of railroad litigation.

This ground breaking reference text by Loumiet and Jungbauer is the first of its kind in the are of train accident reconstruction, FELA and Railroad litigation. It explains how the railroads operate, the design and operation of trains, how to calculate train speed and successfully conduct FELA and railroad litigation. This text is for both the novice and experienced litigator and reconstructionist. It contains information and formulas that can be found nowhere else. 6 1/8" x 9 1/4", 686 pages.

1996 Train Accident Reconstruction Supplement #0970

by William G. Jungbauer, Esq.

Includes new text on Checklists and Procedures, Railroad harassment of FELA Claiments and Witnesses, The FELA Negligence Claim, Railroad Safety Laws, Americans with Disabilities Act of 1990, Third Party Liability, Grade Crossing Cases, Discovery, FELA Compensation and Railroad Benefits, and FELA and Railroad Articles. 6" x 9", 160 pages.

Aircraft Accident Reconstruction and Litigation #5155

by Dr. Barnes W. McCormick, Ph.D., P.E. and Myron P. Papadakis, Esq. (1996)

This book teaches you how to investigate accidents and discover evidence. Your ability to reconstruct aircraft accidents can make the difference between successful and failed aviation litigation. Yet even experienced accident reconstructionists are often unfamiliar with the myriad complexities of aircraft. Now, whether you're a reconstruction expert or an experienced litigator, you can access a wealth of information in this ground-breaking text. In fact, much of the data, formulas, illustrations and investigative tools available to translate wreckage reconstruction data into credible and probative evidence suitable for introduction in the courtroom are available here exclusively, saving you hours of tedious calculations and research. It's the most comprehensive listing of aviation state law and cases ever published. Written in a hands-on format to give you the vital tools needed to investigate, reconstruct, and litigate in the technical and sophisticated arena of aircraft accident reconstruction. 6" x 9", hardbound, 720 pages, also includes 84 page Addendum List of Experts.

Bicycle Accident Reconstruction and Litigation #0918

by James M. Green, Paul F. Hill and Douglas Hayduk (1996)

Your ability to reconstruct bicycle accidents can make the difference between successful and failed litigation. Yet even experienced accident reconstructionists are often unfamiliar with the myriad complexities of bicycles. Now, whether you're a novice or an experienced litigator, you can access a wealth of information in this ground-breaking text. In fact, much of the case research data and formulas are available here exclusively, saving you hours of tedious calculations and research. This book is divided into three sections: engineering analysis; bicycle metallurgy; and legal analysis. You'll have informative diagrams and drawings, plus a complete index, appendix and citations. 6" x 9", hardbound, 784 pages.

Motorcycle Accident Reconstruction: Understanding Motorcycles #5031

by Kenneth Obenski, P.E. (1994)

Riding a motorcycle has been estimated as five times more complex as driving an automobile...and reconstructing an accident can be equally difficult. This text, written by a professional engineer who has investigated over 170 motorcycle accidents—and has safely ridden motorcycles for more than 35 years—gives you the detailed information you need to reconstruct and litigate accidents. In clear, jargon-free language the text sets out the basics of motorcycle operation, and the unique interactions between riders, passengers, machines, and other traffic. You'll understand why motorcycles frequently leave less evidence at the scene of an accident, and how a trained reconstructionist can observe and translate even scant evidence.

Of special significance is the section that explains what motorcycle operators can and cannot do, as well as what they should and should not do. Also included is training information published by the State of California, which is a basic source of motorcycle safe operating instruction. Your single source for motorcycle safety standards because its supplemental appendix contains the Department of Transportation (D.O.T.) Motorcycle Safety Standards as well as the preambles and superseded standards. With this detailed history you'll understand D.O.T.'s philosophy in arriving at each standard. 6⅛" x 9¼", hardbound, 296 pages.

Snowmobile Accident Reconstruction: A Technical and Legal Guide #5023

by Richard Hermance, ACTAR (1995)

The increased popularity of snowmobiling over the past few years has resulted in a rise in snowmobile-related accidents and injuries, and reconstruction of these types of accidents poses a unique challenge for you. This ground-breaking reference and law text is the first of its kind in the area of snowmobile accident reconstruction and litigation. You'll find detailed reference material covering the technical aspects of snowmobile safety, trail design and administration, maintenance, mapping, accident investigation and reconstruction, as well as snowmobile law.

The author is a nationally recognized and accredited accident reconstruction expert who has been involved in over 50 snowmobile accident investigations and reconstructions. An avid snowmobiler for the past 25 years, Hermance has ridden extensively in the northeastern and northwestern United States and Canada. He also designed and taught the New York State Snowmobile Accident Reconstruction course given to New York's State Troopers, Forest Park Police, Sheriff's Department, and local police. 6" x 9", hardbound, 700 pages.

Notes

Notes

Notes

Notes